THE BOYS

Christopher Fitz-Simon

The Boys

a double biography

NICK HERN BOOKS
London

A Nick Hern Book

The Boys first published in Great Britain in 1994
by Nick Hern Books, 14 Larden Road, London W3 7ST

This paperback edition published in 1994

Copyright © 1994 Christopher Fitz-Simon

A CIP catalogue record for this book is available from
the British Library

Typeset by Country Setting, Woodchurch, Kent TN26 3TB,
and printed in Great Britain by Mackays of Chatham PLC.

ISBN 1-85459-271-8

Christopher Fitz-Simon has asserted his right to be identified
as author of this work

Contents

	7	*Illustrations*
	9	*Acknowledgements*
Prologue	13	*The Freedom of the City*
Chapter 1	15	*A Meeting by the River*
Chapter 2	22	*Alfred and Bobby*
Chapter 3	38	*Wanderjahre*
Chapter 4	50	*Galway and Dublin*
Chapter 5	68	*Brilliant but Dangerous*
Chapter 6	84	*Flight into Egypt*
Chapter 7	103	*Agamemnon, Hecuba, and the Theatre of War*
Chapter 8	121	*In a State of Emergency*
Chapter 9	143	*Broadway at Last*
Chapter 10	155	*Tush! Never Tell Me*
Chapter 11	169	*Maura, My Girl*
Chapter 12	177	*The Old Vic, Elsinore, and Croke Park*
Chapter 13	191	*Contagious to the Nile*
Chapter 14	207	*The End of the Rainbow*
Chapter 15	226	*The Importance of Being Hilton and Micheál*
Chapter 16	247	*Roscius Hibernicus*
Chapter 17	267	*Wilde and Friel*
Chapter 18	285	*The Gate Renaissance*
Chapter 19	303	*The Gift of Theatre*
	310	*Select Bibliography*
	315	*Index*

Illustrations

1. Alfred Willmore (Micheál MacLíammóir) in *Joseph and His Brethren* (Mander and Mitchenson)
2. 151 Purves Road, Bethnal Green (Christopher Fitz-Simon)
3. Alfred Willmore as a child (Michael Travers)

4. Hilton Edwards as a child (Patrick McLarnon)
5. Hilton Edwards in *Love on the Dole* (Northwestern University Library)
6. Netherwood, East Finchley (Christopher Fitz-Simon)

7. Orson Welles in 1934 (National Library)
8. Anew McMaster as Coriolanus (Mary Rose McMaster)

9. Costume design *Diarmid agus Gráinne* (National Library)
10. Costume design for *Mogu* (Northwestern University Library)
11. Caricature of Coralie Carmichael, Micheál MacLíammóir and Hilton Edwards (National Library)
12. *The Old Lady Says 'No!'* by Denis Johnston (Dublin Gate Theatre)

13. The Gate Company in Cairo, 1937 (Liam Gaffney)
14. Micheál MacLíammóir (Dublin Gate Theatre)
15. Hilton Edwards (Dublin Gate Theatre)

16. Micheál MacLíammóir and Cyril Cusack in *The Importance of Being Earnest* (Northwestern University Library)
17. The Opera House, Valetta (University of Malta Library)
18. Poster for *Macbeth* in Belgrade (Northwestern University Library)

19. The Gate Theatre, Dublin (Bórd Fáilte Eireann)
20. Edward and Christine Longford (G.A. Duncan)

21. *Not for Children* by Elmer Rice (Northwestern University Library)
22. Denis Johnston (Dublin Gate Theatre)
23. *Marrowbone Lane* by Robert Collis (Northwestern University Library)

24. *The Clandestine Marriage* by Colman and Garrick
         (Bristol University Collection)
25. Sybil Thorndike (Northwestern University Library)
26. Shelah Richards (Irish Theatre Archive)

27. Micheál MacLíammóir and Orson Welles in the film *Othello*
         (Northwestern University Library)
28. Eithne Dunne as Ophelia (Dublin Gate Theatre)

29. Patrick Bedford (Dublin Gate Theatre)
30. Patrick McLarnon (Northwestern University Library)
31. Sally Travers (Northwestern University Library)
32. Maura Laverty (Barry Castle)

33. Micheál MacLíammóir and Peggy Ashcroft (Northwestern University
         Library)
34. Siobhán McKenna (G.A. Duncan)

35. The Don Juan scene from *Man and Superman* (Dublin Gate Theatre)
36. Brian Friel (Fergus Bourke)
37. Eamonn Morrissey and Fionnula Flanagan (Northwestern University
         Library)

38. Hilton Edwards (Northwestern University Library)
39. 4 Harcourt Terrace, Dublin (Keane Mahony Smith)
40. Micheál MacLíammóir (Bórd Fáilte Eireann)

41. Costume design for *The Taming of the Shrew* (Northwestern University
         Library)
42. Costume design for *An Ideal Husband* (Northwestern University Library)
43. *The True Story of the Horrid Popish Plot* by Desmond Forristal
         (Northwestern University Library)
44. Record sleeve for *The Importance of Being Oscar* by Micheál MacLíammóir

45. *The Signalman's Apprentice* by Brian Phelan (Dublin Gate Theatre)
46. Micheál MacLíammóir as Hitler (Northwestern University Library)
47. Hilton Edwards as Herod (Dublin Gate Theatre)

Cover
Hilton Edwards and Micheál MacLíammóir in the Jardin du Luxembourg,
Paris, in the early 1930s (Richard Pine)

Acknowledgements

SPECIAL THANKS

The author is grateful to Mr Michael Williams, executor of the estates of Hilton Edwards and Micheál MacLíammóir, for his help and encouragement.

He is particularly recognisant of the unfailing assistance and support of Mr R. Russell Maylone, Curator of Special Collections at the Library of Northwestern University, Illinois, in whose enthusiastic care the Dublin Gate Theatre archive is preserved; also to his supremely helpful staff, and to Mrs Tina Howe who catalogued the collection with such understanding and sympathy for its contents.

Micheál MacLíammóir's niece, the actress Mary Rose McMaster, and his grand-nephew, the painter Michael Travers, have also been exceptionally helpful, as have many former members of the Dublin Gate Theatre company, especially Patrick Bedford, Helena Hughes, Roy Irving, Harry Fine, Patrick McLarnon and Patricia Turner.

The author also wishes to thank the following:

DIPLOMATIC AND CONSULAR

The Minister for Foreign Affairs, Mr Gerry Collins, T.D., Professor Brendan Kennelly, Chairman of the Cultural Relations Committee, and Mr Patrick Scullion of the Cultural Section; His Excellency Mr Patrick McCabe, Irish Ambassador to Moscow, and Mr Tom Russell, Charge d'Affaires; His Excellency Mr Joseph Small, Irish Ambassador to Vienna; Mr Patrick Sammon, First Secretary, Irish Embassy, Athens; and Mr Niall Burgess, Vice Consul, Chicago, for research beyond the call of duty.

AER LINGUS

Mr Cathal Mullan, Chief Executive.

THEATRE, CINEMA, AND BROADCASTING

Innumerable members of the profession shared their memories with unfailing generosity, among them John Aitkin, Gerry Alexander, Margaret Anketell, Dame Peggy Ashcroft, Patrick Brock, Brendan Burke, David Byrne, Simon Callow, Mary Cannon, Patrick Carey, Shiela Carden, Robert Carrickford, Daphne Carroll, Derek Chapman, Christopher and Kay Casson, Christopher Cazenove, Michael Colgan, Pan Collins, Joan Cross OBE, Dr Cyril Cusack, Sorcha Cusack, J. Alistair Davidson, Margaret D'Arcy, Treasa Davison (née Curley), Brian de Salvo, Dermot K.Doolan, Lelia Doolan, Conor Evans, Seamus Forde, Caroline Fitzgerald, Geraldine Fitzgerald, Fionnula Flanagan, Pauline Flanagan, Renée Flynn, Laurence Foster, Scott Fredericks, Liam Gaffney, Liam Gannon, Sir John Gielgud, Bill Golding,

Aiden Grennell, Máire Hastings, Hurd Hatfield, Denys Hawthorne, Hugh Hunt, Maureen Hurley, Micheal Johnston, Bil Keating, David Kelly, Eamon Kelly, Frank Kelly, Rachel Kempson (Lady Redgrave), Ann Kennelly, Eamonn Kenny, Mary Kerridge, John Keyes, Iris Lawler, Oscar Lewenstein, Leo Leyden, Molly MacEwen, Wesley Murphy, May and T.P. McKenna, Gerard McSorley, Anna Manahan, Ronald Mason, Noelle Middleton, Eamonn Morrissey, Laurie Morton, Claire Mullan, Ann Myler, Brendan Neilan, Máire ní Ghráinne, Colm O Bríain, Brendan O'Brien, Maurice O'Callaghan, Padraig O Cearbhaill, Colm O'Doherty, Micheál O hAodha, Liam O'Leary and the Liam O'Leary Film Archive, Máire O'Neill, Alpho O'Reilly, Finola O'Shannon, Milo O'Shea, Pam Pyer, Joan Reddin, Alan and Faith Richardson, Joyce Roche, Charles Roberts, Marie Rooney, Ann Rowan, Phyllis Ryan, Leslie Scott, Jeremy Swan, Carolyn Swift, Maureen Toal, Bill Twomey, Adrian and Angela Vale, and Eve Watkinson.

AUTHORS AND CRITICS

The following writers, many of whom were friends of Hilton Edwards and Micheál MacLíammóir, were most helpful: Mary Manning Adams, Bruce Arnold, Patrick F.Byrne, Eilís Dillon, John Finegan, Rev. Desmond Forristal, Dr Brian Friel, Ronald Harwood, Jennifer Johnston (for permission to quote from the unpublished memoirs of her mother, Shelah Richards), Brenna Katz Clarke, Eugene McCabe, Eoin Neeson, David Nowlan, Jerry O'Connell, Ulick O'Connor, Joe O'Donnell, Brian Phelan, Richard Pine, Val Mulkerns, Desmond Rushe, Mrs Betty Rainsford (Betty Lowry) and Terence de Vere White.

OTHERS

Many private individuals gave advice or helped in a number of valuable ways, among them Sylvia Makower, Catherine O'Brien, Barry Castle (née Laverty), Mrs J.Gant (née Trimble), R.T.West, Basil Rooke-Ley, Terence O'Brien, Cyril Donovan, Mrs Derrick Waldron Lynch (née Carney), Michael Purser, Joe Purser, Mrs Babin Phillips (née Jellett), the Rev. Christopher Jarman, Colonel Robert Jarman, Gabriel Manley, Ann and Charlo Quain, Seán O Críadáin, Peter Lamb, Dr Patrick Sheehan, Dr Gerald Tolkin, Iseult McGuinness (née MacDonagh), Kenneth Jamison, Dr Hazel Morris, Frank P. Lloyd, Blanaid Reddin, Marie Twomey, R.T. West, Eric A. Willats; and in the United States, Professor Robert Collins and Professor Kathleen Kaun, of Northwestern University; Professor and Mrs Robert Treacy of the University of California at Berkeley; Dr and Mrs Richard Crampton of Charlottesville, Virginia; Miss Ursula Corning and Dr and Mrs Jack Downey of New York.

INSTITUTIONS

Special thanks to Dr Patricia Donlon, Director, National Library, Dublin, and the staff of the library and manuscripts room; Dr Bernard Meehan, Keeper of Manuscripts, and Stuart O Seanóir and Felicity O'Mahony of the Manuscripts Department, Trinity College, Dublin; Dr John McCormick, Director of the Samuel Beckett Centre for Theatre and Drama Studies, Trinity College, Dublin; the Director General of Radio Telefís Eireann and Martin Ryan, Personnel Executive; Mary Clarke, Curator of the Irish Theatre Archive; Helen Davis of University College Library, Cork; Deirdre Rennison Kunz of Gill & Macmillan; Jean Spenser, Records Secretary, and Stephen Chaplin, Archivist, Slade School of Fine Art, London; Dr Harriet Harvey Wood, Dr Ken Churchill and Shibnath Roy of the British Council; Dr James Fowler, Chief Curator, and Claire Hudson, Head of Library Services,

Theatre Museum, London; Neil Somerville and John Jordan of the BBC Written Archives Centre, Reading; Anna Stanford, National Film Archive, London; David Withey, Finsbury Reference Librarian; Chris Robinson of the Bristol University Theatre Collection; Bridget Keane and Timothy Evans of the Grange Museum of Community History, London Borough of Brent; F. Mary White of the Shakespeare Birthday Trust; Janet Lewis of the North Middlesex Family History Society; Wilmot Bennitt of the Islington Archaeology and History Society; Jonathan Smith, Manuscripts Cataloguer, Trinity College Library, Cambridge; Apollonia Lang Steele, Special Collections Librarian, University of Calgary; Magdalen O'Connell, Administrative Asistant, National University of Ireland; Richard Mangan, Director, Joe Mitchenson, co-Founder and Janet Trow, Research Assistant, Mander and Mitchenson Theatre Collection; Rev. Brother David Robinson and Terence O'Brien, St Aloysius' College, Highgate; James G. Rizzo, Head of the Ministry of Tourism, Malta; Dr Paul Xuereb, Librarian, University of Malta, John Sultana, Head of the Malta Public Libraries Department; Iain G.M. Bamber, Superintending Queen's Messenger; Steward Gillies, Local History Librarian, Barnet Libraries; the Gilbert Collection Librarian, Dublin Corporation Public Libraries; Jane Rosier, Publicity Assistant, Birmingham Repertory Theatre; Lorna Ferguson, Press Officer, Glasgow Citizens Theatre; Elizabeth Margaret Watson, Glasgow University Library; Seamus Ryan of Cork County Council, and Anne Kelleher of The Southern Star, Skibbereen.

QUOTATIONS

The author is grateful to the following authors and publishers for permission to quote:

Mr Michael Williams, executor of the estate of Micheál MacLíammóir, for *All for Hecuba* by Micheál MacLíammóir, Methuen, 1946;

Eyre Methuen Ltd, for *Put Money in thy Purse* by Micheál MacLíammóir, first published by Methuen & Co. Ltd, 1952, republished by Eyre Methuen Ltd, 1976;

Thames & Hudson Ltd, for *Enter a Goldfish* by Micheál MacLíammóir, 1977;

The O'Brien Press Ltd, for *No Profit But the Name* by John Cowell, 1988;

Colin Smythe Ltd, for *The Old Lady Says 'No!'* by Denis Johnston, 1992 edition;

George Weidenfeld & Nicholson Ltd, for *Orson Welles* by Barbara Leaming, 1985; and for *Odd Man Out*, a biography of James Mason by Sheridan Morley, 1989;

An t-Uas. Micheál O hAodha, for a letter in his book *The Importance of Being Micheál*, Brandon 1990;

Reed Book Services, for *To Be a Pilgrim* by Robert Collis, Secker & Warburg, 1975.

International Thompson Publishing Services Ltd, for *Each Actor on His Ass* by Micheál MacLíammóir, Routledge and Kegan Paul, 1961.

The author is grateful to the Written Archives Officer of the BBC Written Archives Centre at Reading, England, for permission to quote from a broadcast talk given by Micheál MacLíammóir in 1954 on the subject of *Hamlet*; and for some other short quotations from BBC programme material.

To Anne

Prologue
The Freedom of the City

'Micheál MacLíammóir and Hilton Edwards are two men who rightly deserve
the highest honour the City of Dublin can bestow on any of its citizens,'
declared the Lord Mayor, the Right Honourable Alderman Frank Cluskey, at
7.30 p.m. on Friday 22 June 1973, in the Oak Room of the Mansion House,
before a large gathering of Government Ministers, members of the Judiciary,
Civic and Church dignitaries, leading academics, writers, artists and actors.

Ireland, being a true democracy, does not accord national honours. Irish
universities award honorary degrees and Irish municipal bodies confer the
freedom of their cities – though on very rare occasions and only to the truly
exalted and distinguished; before 1973 no member of the theatrical profession
had been made a Freeman of Dublin. In extending official recognition to the
two men who had founded the Dublin Gate Theatre, the Corporation was
making an unprecedented gesture. Micheál MacLíammóir and Hilton Edwards
had inaugurated their company in 1928, bringing to Dublin, and to Ireland, a
kaleidoscopic cross-section of modern European and American drama, at a time
when Ireland floated in cultural isolation in mid-Atlantic; and in turn they
brought back to Europe, America, Africa and Australia, to Broadway and the
West End, some of the richest, and many of the more bizarre, components of the
Irish stage.

The Corporation of Dublin had, many times, bestowed the Seal of the
Freedom of the City on visiting Heads of State and other prominent foreigners,
but neither Micheál MacLíammóir nor Hilton Edwards were of such elevated
provenance; nor was either of them a Dubliner, and only one of them was Irish
– indeed, it was darkly rumoured that neither of them was Irish; it was even
hinted that one of them was Jewish. They were, in the flippant terminology of
their day, 'gypsies', members of an almost rootless, highly volatile yet curiously
cohesive and, within its own terms, closely-knit itinerant community. They were
strolling players who had found themselves – due to chance and harsh
economics and, quite literally, the fortunes of war – in a country where the
English language was spoken and respected far more deeply than it was in
England, and where ordinary folk still liked a good story well told as much as a
jig or a tale of bawdry; and where, in spite of an unusually censorious political

regime allied to a pharisaical church, there was a widespread and natural tolerance, often amounting to admiration, for those brave enough not conform to the normal social conventions of place and time.

Dublin Corporation, and its theatre-going Lord Mayor, were demonstrating the genuine gratitude of the city for, in Alderman Cluskey's words, 'the vision and initiative of these two men'. 'Our lives,' he declared, 'have been brighter for your being among us.' He was also demonstrating his Corporation's sophisticated attitude to the world of dissimulation, of make-believe, of masks, of painted faces and wigs and powdered hair, of illusion, and of fleeting images; of nature's mirror, and of the abstracts and brief chronicles of the time; and he was articulating the Corporation's view that a city without the capacity to encompass such elements in its very fabric was a city which could not claim to be civilised.

Micheál MacLíammóir and Hilton Edwards, 'having expressed their app-reciation of the great honour accorded to them,' as the minutes of the meeting duly recorded, 'and having affixed their signatures to the Roll of Honorary Burgesses of Dublin, were each presented by the Chairman with a Certificate of Freedom under Seal.'

This freedom lasted for less than a decade. Within five years, Micheál MacLíammóir, the elder, was dead; within nine Hilton Edwards had died too – from loneliness, it was said. Forty-six years before the ceremony in the Mansion House, they had met as members of Anew McMaster's Intimate Theatre Company among the tall blue-slated grey-stuccoed houses of Enniscorthy, where the road from Dublin to Wexford crosses the River Slaney over an old six-arched stone bridge; they were touring artistes, rogues or vagabonds perhaps, and with youthful zest they decided to found a theatre in Dublin and startle the public with their certainly novel, if possible outlandish, but definitely professional, ideas. They did so; and they passed through many purgatories on their long, eventful, showy and dangerous journey.

Chapter 1

A Meeting by the River

Anew McMaster's Intimate Theatre Company was billed to open its Irish tour in mid-June 1927 at the Enniscorthy Athenaeum, an echoing all-purpose hall half way up the hill between the river and the top of the town. McMaster, tall, commanding and still winsomely handsome at thirty-six, had formed his own company two years before. He had been playing with Gladys Cooper in her own production of Pinero's *Iris* at the Adelphi Theatre in London, and, well into its long run, was puzzled to note Ivor Novello frequently seated in a box. One Saturday night he found the dresser packing his clothes, and on enquiring the reason learned that Mr Novello, the darling of the West End, would be taking over his part the following Monday – hadn't he known? Miss Cooper, whom McMaster later described as 'possessing the outstanding characteristic of cold efficiency', had not troubled to tell him; he was handed a week's pay *in lieu* of notice, and Miss Cooper's latest choice of juvenile lead moved in.

McMaster vowed never to play in the West End again. (It was a short-lived decision.) The fact was, however, that he loved touring, and had by that time performed in most of the Number One dates of the British Isles, and also on a tour of Australia with Oscar Asche's company which was extended from one to three years, when he gained most of his experience in Shakespearian rôles. He had toured Ireland many times with the James O'Brien and Harry Ireland combination, when the fare was equally divided between Shakespeare and melodrama; McMaster relished the latter in a gleefully schoolboyish way, and introduced Du Maurier's *Trilby*, Lewis's *The Bells* and Parker's *The Cardinal* to the repertoire of his own company, considering these to be his 'nights off' from Othello, Shylock or Macbeth. By 1927 he was starting to leave the English towns off his itinerary, concentrating on what he called 'the Irish smalls', where he found a readier public for his simple style of production, where the text was pre-eminent, the costumes – usually designed by his wife, Marjorie – historically accurate, and the settings fairly rudimentary. As long as the painted backdrop depicted the blasted heath in a way which would also serve pleasingly as the forest of Arden, and as long as the hall in the castle of Elsinore could double economically with the Venetian senate-chamber, he was perfectly satisfied.

Among the players whom he engaged for the spring and summer of 1927 were Esmé Biddle from the Shakespeare Memorial Theatre for the more mature female leads, the *petite* Ann Clark and the tall and graceful Coralie Carmichael for the younger parts; there was David Basil Gill, a versatile leading man, Raymond Percy (who came from County Down and whose real name was Raymond Russell Wood), George Hagan, and Micheál MacLíammóir. Micheál was the brother of Marjorie McMaster. He had been a child actor in London, moved on to art-school, became a painter and illustrator, and now at twenty-eight was hoping to regain a foothold on the stage. McMaster allowed him to play Lorenzo, Laertes, Puck, and that cemetery for aspiring actors, the County Paris.

Micheál MacLíammóir's *curriculum vitae* informed the press that he had been born in the city of Cork. Anew McMaster claimed for himself the town of Monaghan as his birthplace, and Warrenpoint, County Down, as the scene of his earliest memories. MacLíammóir was an ardent advocate for the revival of the Irish language, and, while living in London, had gone to the laudible extreme of learning it at evening classes at the Ludgate Circus branch of *Connradh na Gaeilge*, the Gaelic League. He was an admirer of the Celtic Twilight school of poets; in his drawing he was heavily influenced by Aubrey Beardsley, Arthur Rackham and Charles Ricketts. His other passion was for the ballet designs of Léon Bakst. All this placed him firmly in the previous generation, and he admitted throughout his life that he should have been born thirty years earlier: he was a late arrival at the feast of J.K. Huysmans, Max Beerbohm and Oscar Wilde. He should have submitted his work to the *Yellow Book*.

A crisis developed during the early weeks of the tour in the south of England. To McMaster's horror and disgust, David Basil Gill was drinking before arriving in the theatre. When Gill was removed by the police from a licenced premises in Tunbridge Wells for 'disturbance of the peace', McMaster sacked him. So, while the company was travelling to Ireland on the Great Western steampacket via Fishguard and Rosslare, McMaster had to go to London to find a quick replacement.

The replacement travelled with Anew and Marjorie on the evening of 16 June, arriving in Enniscorthy early the next morning. Members of the company, knowing that there would be frantic rehearsals to insert a new Iago, Claudius, Macduff and Antonio, not to speak of Taffy in *Trilby*, into their respective plays, were very anxious to know what kind of actor they were getting. Was he a quick study? Was he middle-aged as most of the parts demanded? May Barry, the wardrobe mistress, who had met and breakfasted with the new arrivals, reported that he dressed in very good tweeds, had acted in all of Shakespeare's plays but two, was very young, had a big nose, and had recently been in the London production of Solomon Anski's *The Dybbuk*. When McMaster introduced Hilton Edwards to the company in the Athenaeum, they found that he was polite and punctilious, had the English public school way of addressing men by their surnames, a passion and enthusiasm for hard work, and was prepared to continue late into the night if someone would stay up to hear his lines. MacLíammóir agreed to be this someone.

THOUGHTS BOTH WILD AND MAD

In the country districts of Ireland bonfires are lighted on the Feast of Bealtaine, or St John's Eve, the midsummer solstice; the rites are connected with fertility and purification and the demi-god Balor of the Evil Eye, but in the course of time have been reduced to carnival festivities. In one of the intervals between rehearsals and line-learning, Micheál and Hilton climbed to the top of Vinegar Hill about a mile outside Enniscorthy, and helped the local boys pile tarred branches on the flames. Hilton's good tweed overcoat was ruined; but it became a useful item in the theatrical wardrobe for any number of disreputable characters; in the course of time it assumed the dignity of a memento, recalling the easygoing start of their ultimately tempestuous friendship. Edwards celebrated the occasion in a poem which appeared in his collection *Elephant in Flight* in 1967:

> . . . So many things conspired to brand upon
> my mind the happenings of that summer night . . .
> A coat that I was wearing bore the stain
> of molten pitch for ever afterwards
> and there were thoughts both wild and mad abroad
> that left their mark upon me to this day.
> > . . . And it was then
> you told me of the chain you helped to forge
> that binds you fast, even though she is dead,
> to that doomed girl whose needle wit and strength
> of soul have now become a part of you . . .

The 'doomed girl' was Mary O'Keefe, romanticised by Micheál as *Máire ní Chaoimh* in his desire that everything possible be translated into its Gaelic equivalent. He had met her at an art college in London, and had lived with her and her mother, he told Hilton, in Ireland, Switzerland and the south of France, where she had died the previous year – her death being one of the reasons why he had precipitated himself back into the theatre.

THE IRISH SMALLS

The tour proceeded to other small towns of Munster – Cappoquin, Dungarvan and Cóbh. Edwards was constantly talking of a new kind of theatre, where one did not have to rely on painted scenery for a sense of location, where effects of sound and music and massed movement would have as much importance as words, where electric lighting would come into its own. Coralie Carmichael often formed a third in their discussions in the back parlours of country-town pubs, on little trains rattling their way alongside the great rivers of the south, or on the strands where the whole company would go swimming when there were no matinées. Micheál MacLíammóir said that if they were to start a new theatre it would have to be in Dublin as far as he was concerned, and Hilton Edwards declared that he didn't mind where he lived so long as there was an audience.

It was the kind of talk which goes on in a hundred dressing-rooms and which is quickly forgotten at the end of the run of the play or the conclusion of the tour. All this might have been similarly consigned had it not been for the fact that in Cóbh Hilton felt unwell, and by the Sunday night was unable to go on stage. On Monday Micheál MacLíammóir and George Hagan took him to a nursing-home; Micheál, who had watched Mary O'Keefe die of pulmonary disease, was alarmed when pneumonia was diagnosed. The troupe then left for Midleton, and between them all the members made cuts in the texts and doubled the parts, and the plays continued without Hilton.

Midleton is only ten miles from Cobh, but nobody owned a car, and a taxi would have used up a whole week's wages; a complicated rail journey with a change at a wayside station called Dunkettle could be managed only if there was no rehearsal or matinée, but MacLíammóir successfully negotiated the trip on the Wednesday and found the patient improving. When the tour ended eleven days later in Ennis, and the other members of the company, including the McMasters, departed for London, MacLíammóir found himself taking three trains to get himself back to Cobh. He telegraphed to Mary O'Keefe's mother, whom he called Aunt Craven, and she sent him £10, which covered the medical bills. Hilton was better, but not well enough to travel to London, let alone take part in a broadcast song recital at the BBC next day. Almost penniless, they decided to make for Cork together – it was only half an hour away by train – and see what work they might find until the next McMaster tour in the autumn.

They had only known each other for seven weeks. Yet in travelling back to Cobh, Micheál, whether he understood it or not, was surely making more than a kindly gesture to a colleague in difficulties; and in deciding to go to Cork, and from there a few weeks later to Dublin, Hilton was surely acknowledging something stronger than a passing professional relationship. There was little reason for him, a Londoner with connections at the Old Vic and the Vic-Wells Opera, to go to Dublin: what good might he find there?

They were completely different in temperament and outlook, these two fugitives from the Shakespeare fit-ups. MacLíammóir was tall and dark, and seemed to be perpetually studying ways of remaining handsome. Edwards was short and chubby, with small, dark, twinkling eyes. MacLíammóir was the most Celtic person imaginable, and he took pains to resemble such a being – or at least one of the mythological figures in the early plays of Yeats which he admired so much. Edwards was interested in the latest theories of the director Meyerhold as they filtered through from Moscow, and the revolutionary ideas of staging and lighting formulated by the Swiss designer Adolphe Appia; he also loved cars and was never happier than when leafing through the Autocar

Magazine. MacLíammóir overdid everything which would flaunt his Irishness; Edwards was a naturally well-brought-up Englishman, and the idea of flaunting anything was foreign to his nature – one could sense cricket-bats and midnight feasts in the dorm, and tea with muffins at the vicarage, in his every gesture and in every nuance of his speech.

They, like MacLíammóir's brother-in-law Anew MacMaster, had chosen the theatre as their profession, and in the theatre things are not always what they seem. The theatre meant magic and mystery; actors then, as now, presented themselves to the press and public as they wished to be seen, rather than as they were. What the public was not told was that the histories of MacLíammóir and Edwards – and of McMaster too – were more than a little different from the information supplied to journalists or printed on the back of playbills. The Celtophile MacLíammóir's forebears had no connection with Ireland whatsoever – the name does not exist in the lexicon of Irish clans and families – and his only true claim to early familiarity with his 'native' city of Cork was as a child actor in a post-London touring production of *Peter Pan*. Hilton Edwards did not attend a great English public school, or even a minor one; nor did he ever go up to Cambridge – let alone come down. For reasons professional, private, or what can only be described as 'peculiar' in both senses of the term, they either invented interesting and extensive backgrounds for themselves, or excised certain elements from all utterance. Many of the myths which MacLíammóir created about himself were not revealed to be such until after his death. Edwards, when asked about his past, often remarked that it was 'so boring it is not worth talking about' – when in fact it was quite unusual, and at times bizarre.

ANEW

Anew McMaster was the only person whose opinion Micheál MacLíammóir and Hilton Edwards accepted on professional matters throughout their careers, although he was only a few years older. He remained, for them, a kind of oracle, even though the theatre which they created became a part of the *avant-garde*, at a time when that term had a meaning, while his remained firmly rooted in the nineteenth century. He was probably the last of the actor-managers in the English tradition; his Coriolanus at Stratford-upon-Avon in 1933 was described as the greatest of his generation; his James Tyrone in *Long Day's Journey into Night* on the national tour of the United States towards the end of his career was said to be 'the definitive interpetation'. In Ireland, he became the undisputed monarch of the Shakespearian repertoire. 'Mac', as he was universally known, was a kind of uncle-figure to Hilton and Micheál, appearing in some of their productions at the Dublin Gate Theatre whenever a part requiring immense presence came up; he also performed for them on one of their Mediterranean tours.

Andrew McMaster – 'Anew' was a childish mispronunciation which remained to distinguish him from his father, who bore the same name – was not born in 1895 as stated in his entry in *Who's Who in the Theatre*, nor was he born in Monaghan, but at 2 Palm Hill, Claughton, a suburb of Birkenhead, on Christmas Eve 1891. His parents were of Ulster Presbyterian extraction, and he certainly visited Warrenpoint as a child. In later life he referred to his family as having been 'in shipping', and this was true to the extent that his father was a stevedore. After the death of Anew's mother, Andrew McMaster senior married a Miss Zoë Papayanni, a daughter of one of the partners in the Ellerman & Papayanni shipping line of Liverpool. Andrew then rapidly climbed the mercantile ladder, planning a career in banking for his elder son. Anew, however, was 'hopeless at figures'; he was inextricably attracted to the theatre, and found the Sabbatarian atmosphere of the Merseyside home oppressive. He took the train to London to seek employment with the only West End company he had heard of, that of the illustrious Fred and Julia Neilson Terry at the New Theatre. 'The name Terry,' as he recalled in a broadcast talk in 1961, 'hung like a banner over the theatrical world of those days.' As luck would have it, the stage-manager, John Turnbull, was engaging tall, handsome young men for the crowd in *The Scarlet Pimpernel*. McMaster was taken on at £1 per week, with half-a-crown extra for matinées other than those on Saturdays. He also recalled on radio that he was seventeen at the time, but he must have been nearly twenty, for *The Scarlet Pimpernel* opened in June 1911.

Andrew senior refused to provide any financial support. When he died in 1940, he had never seen his son on the stage, not even when he was engaged in Liverpool for a season, or when he played Hamlet at Stratford-upon-Avon. Anew stayed with the Terrys for over two years. Sometimes he appeared in 'special matinées' – the current euphemism for (usually unpaid) showcase productions of 'interesting' plays at the Court, the Playhouse and the Aldwych, where unknown authors and young actors were given a chance to develop their work. He always acknowledged his indebtedness to Fred and Julia Neilson Terry – they were his theatre school, where he paid no fees, but was paid to learn; yet the great influence on his acting style was Beerbohm Tree, with whom he never worked, but whose performances he used to watch at His Majesty's Theatre.

When Anew McMaster went to see Tree as Fagin in *Oliver Twist* in 1912 there was a little boy cast as Oliver – up to that time the part had always been taken by an actress, and not always a very little one. This particular little boy had received much warmhearted praise from the critics; he was billed as Master Alfred Willmore, he was twelve, and McMaster had already seen him as Michael in *Peter Pan*. They met at Appendrodt's, a German *konditorei* in Piccadilly Circus, frequented by members of the theatre profession between matinée and evening performances, and by what would now be described as the gay community. Anew used to go there with his actor friend Bobbie Andrews – with whom he had played in a 'special matinée' of *The Golden Land of Fairy Tales* and who was still known (to his annoyance) as Master Bobbie even though he was seventeen and had long given up playing child parts. One evening, as Anew later wrote in The Irish Times, 'three youngsters entered the restaurant – members of the *Peter Pan* company, and Bobbie Andrews introduced them to me – there was a leggy boy with an alert amusing face, a boy with curly hair and big brown eyes, and his sister, a tiny girl with two long plaits of hair with big black bows'. The leggy boy was Master Noël Coward; the curly-haired boy was Master Alfred Willmore; the tiny girl, who was in fact some years older, was his sister – his chaperone, or minder, in accordance with the strict bye-laws of the London County Council in regard to juvenile performers, and her name was Marjorie.

It is certainly true that McMaster attached himself to this trio, and it is likely that he fell in love with both Alfred and Marjorie. He became the mentor and confidant of Alfred while the latter went through the lengthy (as it turned out) transformation from child to adult actor and from English Willmore to Irish MacLíammóir. Fourteen years later Anew McMaster married Marjorie Willmore.

Young Alfred Willmore, who had not yet read Yeats or discovered the Irish language classes where he clumsily translated his name into MacLíammóir, recalled his introduction to Anew McMaster slightly differently, though the tone is the same, and so is the location. In 1977, a year before he died, MacLíammóir published a *roman-à-clef* entitled *Enter a Goldfish* in which an account of his first meeting with McMaster at Appendrodt's is probably nearer to what actually happened, for McMaster's recollections of the details of the past are generally inaccurate. MacLíammóir described the fictionalised McMaster as a 'tall, golden-haired, absurdly good-looking young man in a pale grey suit' at a party at Appendrodt's given by a certain 'Geoffrey Leigh-Craig', who had also befriended the *Peter Pan* children, and who appears in the book as a highly cultivated man-about-town. In real life his name was Wilfred Rooke-Ley.

Actual names vie with stage names which are further confused by fictionalised names. Alfred Willmore took the stage name of Micheál MacLíammóir, (Liam: William), but he describes himself as 'Martin Weldon' in *Enter a Goldfish*. Anew McMaster's stage name for a time was Martin Doran – he toured Ireland under this name for at least ten years; in the book he is clearly 'Alexander McMullen'. Hilton Edwards, who at the time of Peter Pan and the cream teas in Appendrodt's was only nine years old, was of far too downright a disposition ever to assume a stage name, but MacLíammóir could not forbear to fictionalise him as 'Linden Evans'. His family, however, called him Bobby; and Bobby he remained until his early twenties.

Chapter 2
Alfred and Bobby

Alfred Willmore was born far from the banks of the Lee, the river which, in the words of the poet Spenser, 'encloseth Corke with his divided flood'. When Alfred made the conscious decision to become an Irishman, in the interests of providing himself with some kind of topographical foothold, he chose Black-rock, as his birthplace. It is an old-established suburb of pretty houses with long gardens reaching down to the river; colleagues have conjectured that the idea for Cork came to him because his mother's maiden name was Lee – an attractive notion. The reality was No. 150, Purves Road, Kensal Green, London N.W.10, a small rust-coloured brick house resembling all its two hundred or so neighbours in the same street. Purves Road extends for over half a mile from Kensal Rise railway station to Willesden Junction; the uniformity of the two-storied dwellings creates a drab prospect in a part of London never noted for its charm – yet the dullness is alleviated somewhat by the bow-fronted room of each house which lends a measure of articulation to what is otherwise an unassailably dreary late-Victorian street. In the 1890s Purves Road would have been deemed highly respectable, the domicile of clerks and schoolteachers and people in business in a small way – definitely not working class; middle-class, rather, though of the lowest dispensation of middle-class. It would have been deemed 'convenient', for there was quick and efficient transport to central London and the West End.

Alfred Willmore senior, who was the leaseholder of No. 150 from 1891 until 1913, was a forage-buyer. It was his duty to maintain contact with suppliers of hay, straw and grain, and make arrangements for the purchase of large quantities of these commodities for the firm which employed him, Whitney's of Bayswater, who sold to private owners of horses in the more affluent parts of the city where everyone had a carriage, and to the large firms which ran drays for deliveries. (Whitney's, which still exists though now in other lines of commerce, was disguised as 'Whiteley's' in *Enter a Goldfish*.)

*

Little Alfred was born into a family of four sisters, all of them older than himself. His mother, Mary, was called 'Sophie', and that is about all that is known about her. There is no true picture of her except as an ever-cheerful, hard-working housewife and a supportive parent with an instinctive understanding of the unspoken needs of her children. Unfortunately the image of an emigré Irish family which the son who called himself MacLíammóir tried to create is filled with rural sentimentality. In fact, his mother was a Londoner from the Peckham Road, and had originally come from Islington. Her husband was living in Finsbury at the time of their marriage, and it is assumed he came from a similar *milieu*. Purves Road, Kensal Green, would have been a small step up the social ladder.

Alfred's sisters were Dorothy, the eldest, who subsequently married a man who died after two years; she founded a small private school in Sussex which she ran until her retirement. When visiting her 'Irish' brother in Dublin, she always struck those who met her as being 'a nice English Protestant lady', causing some wonderment as to how she had become *so* English if she was born in Cork: only the very shrewd, like the stage-designer Kay Casson, understood that her Englishness was genuine, while her brother was acting the part of an Irishman. Alfred's second sister, Christine, used to read scenes from Shakespeare to him, and this encouraged him to improvise plays for himself in the privacy of his room. Christine married the stained-glass artist, Martin Travers; they had two children, Nicholas and Sally; Sally joined the Dublin Gate Theatre in 1938 on her mother's death, and became very much a part of the Edwards-MacLíammóir extended family circle; later she married Alan Sharpe, the author of *A Green Tree in Gedde*. Her brother Nicholas joined the Royal navy, and his son, the artist Michael Travers, settled in Ireland in 1974 and came to know his great-uncle Alfred/Micheál, by then the *doyen* of the Irish stage.

Alfred's third sister was Marjorie, sometimes know as Mana – and also, later, as 'Mrs Mac' by three generations of actors in the McMaster company. Anew and Marjorie McMaster had two children, Christopher (born in 1925) and Mary Rose (1926), both of whom went on the stage, Christopher later becoming a distinguished television director; one of his early assignments was the popular series *Coronation Street*. Alfred's youngest sister, Peggy, was sometimes known as 'scatty Peg'; she married W. Hugh Higginbotham, the author of *Frightfulness in Modern Art*; they had two children, Deirdre and Moira.

None of the descendants of Alfred and Mary Willmore have inherited word-of-mouth memories of their great-grandparents in Purves Road. Micheál MacLíammóir's affectionate if lavishly fictionalised accounts of his parents and of their impecunious yet cosy little home are all that remain. The factual residue is that they were all well-read, that education meant a great deal to them – as it so often does in families attempting to 'better themselves' – that they were members of the Church of England, though not ardent church-goers, and that they attended the theatre, especially pantomimes, of which there were many at Christmas both in the West End and in the suburban theatres of Kilburn and Finchley. It is curious that such a large proportion of the children and grandchildren of

Alfred and Mary became connected in one way or another with literature and the arts, but there are no easy explanations, save perhaps in their voracious reading.

Two of the girls took part-time jobs while in their early teens, which was not at all usual at the time, even among the lower-middle-classes. When Alfred Willmore senior introduced his son to an aquaintance on the accounting staff at His Majesty's Theatre, wondering if young Alfred's addiction to performing scenes in front of his mirror might mean that he had latent talent, and if he should arrange for his son to audition for Sir Herbert Beerbohm Tree, there is more than a whiff of a feeling that the father was thinking perhaps the young chap could be earning some money like his sisters.

Alfred Willmore junior went to a Board School, possibly the one in Kingsgate Road near Kilburn railway station, where, in the best traditions of the burgeoning artist, he was perfectly miserable. There were four hundred other boys, in none of whom did he find a kindred spirit, and he used to look through the iron railings of his prison at the girls' playground and wish that he could join in their much more sensible pastimes. Whether or not his parents decided that school was too much for his sensitive nature and withdrew him, is open to question; the inspector would certainly have found out, and there is no record of his having been allowed to stay at home on medical grounds, for he was healthy if not robust. Certainly his education was given into the hands of his sister Marjorie and other women when he started to work in the theatre, for stage children were obliged to spend a number of hours each day taking lessons from a suitably designated person, and this rule was especially rigid when touring; but as he was eleven when he was first introduced to the professional theatre, it is probable that he had to endure the indignities of the Board School up to that age.

Alfred's earliest stage appearance was in the double rôle of Reggie and King Goldfish in *The Goldfish* written and produced by Miss Lila Field, with music composed by a gentleman whose name was printed on the programme as Mr Eyre O'Naut. Miss Field, who was born in Peru and educated in a convent in the United States, ran a children's theatre company which was described as 'artistic' (in the strictly non-pejorative meaning of the word in that era) and was of an extraordinarily affected kind. She had plenty of little girls in her troupe, but used to resort to placing notices in the local papers to find boys, Mr Willmore and a Mrs Coward answering her advertisement. By this means she was introduced to Master Alfred Willmore and Master Noël Coward, who auditioned for her and were immediately engaged. She called Alfred 'Bubbles' after Sir Edward Millais' painting of the child with curly hair, which had been commissioned by the Pears' Soap Company. Master Coward believed himself to be far too grown-up to be addressed in such a way, and impressed Alfred no end, for he referred to rehearsals as 'work' and the production as an 'engagement' – but they were both accepted.

They performed Miss Field's delightful and morally improving drama before crowds of other children and their parents (generally their mothers) on nine afternoons at the Little Theatre in January 1911, and subsequently for two weeks at the Scala and two more weeks at the Court. The reviewer from The Morning Post wrote that 'Master Alfred Willmore, the pretty little boy who played Reggie with the utmost sangfroid . . . was not in the least put out by the annoying behaviour of his socks and curls.' The Daily Express disclosed that Miss Field referred to Master Willmore as 'my little Herbert Tree' – she was clearly adept at thinking up cringe-making nicknames for her young Thespians – and continued: 'He will surely be heard of again' – a notice which must have interested the Willmore parents, who may have been wondering if all this public exposure was good for Alfred, for Miss Field had remarked that he was 'highly strung – dear little chap!' To a person of her temperament to be highly strung was probably something in one's favour. Other parents might have taken fright and sent their child out at once to play football, but as Alfred was paid £2 a week for his endeavours, Alfred senior may have decided there was no harm in it.

To be told by the press that you will surely be heard of again would have a strongly encouraging effect on a performer of twenty, not to speak of one of eleven. Alfred was indeed heard of again as early as June of the same year, also with Miss Field, in *Fly-Away Land*, enticingly described as 'a phantasy'. At about the same time Alfred senior's acquaintance at His Majesty's arranged for little Alfred to meet Tree, who was casting *Macbeth* to open in August. Tutored by Marjorie, he rehearsed a dialogue involving both Katherine and Petruchio in *The Taming of the Shrew*, and Tree's only comment was to ask him if he did not know the scene was meant to be funny? Tree then enquired if he would like to play a drunken Porter, to which Alfred replied that he'd rather play Macbeth; there was a lot of laughter from those present, which annoyed him, because he thought they were laughing at his performance; but soon a letter arrived in the post offering him the part of Macduff's son at £2.10.0d a week, and later, when rehearsals were going well, the stage manager, Cecil King, asked him if he would also like to be the apparition of the bleeding child, and he graciously accepted, though there was no additional fee. Sir Herbert, who was known as 'the Chief', played Macbeth, and Violet Vanbrugh was Lady Macbeth. David Basil Gill (destined to be dismissed for unseemly behaviour by Anew McMaster sixteen years later in Tunbridge Wells) was Malcolm.

Sir Herbert Beerbohm Tree had inherited the sumptuous illustrative style of Shakespearian production from the tradition of Sir Henry Irving at the Lyceum. He delighted in grandiose effects, and excelled in the romantic, eccentric or grotesque rôles in which his imagination had freest play. (He was probably better suited to Fagin than Macbeth.) He took a genuine interest in passing on his experience to the young, and part of his production process was the 'teaching' of new performers; he was a co-founder of the Royal Academy of Dramatic Art. He transcribed his thoughts on the subject in 1905 in a monograph succinctly entitled *How to Act* – the generation of actors which included Anew McMaster fell upon this publication with intense excitement. Tree felt that 'too refined and genteel an education is by no means the best for the stage', for the natural tendency of education was 'towards the suppression of the representation, if not the perception, of emotion'; he thought that too much reading was 'destructive', but a knowledge of music 'an advantage'. 'To my mind, however, the greatest of all the technical requirements of the actor is instinct. It is greater than learning. It is inherited knowledge.' He had a hundred 'tricks of the trade', which he used to impart to those working closely with him – such as 'to let the appropriate gesture slightly precede the speech'. He spent what the young Alfred Willmore thought were hours – it was probably only minutes – helping him with his few lines as Macduff's son, Tree calling him 'Boy Blue' because of the woollen pullover which his mother had knitted for him so that he would look as if he came from a grand home.

Alfred seems to have enjoyed rising up through a trap door into a huge cauldron surrounded by grey and crimson draperies as the Second Apparition, more than the straight acting required for the young Macduff. It was his appearance in the latter part which led to his being engaged by Dion Boucicault (on the recommendation of Miss Viva Birkett, who played Lady Macduff) as Michael Darling in *Peter Pan* in December. Boucicault was the son of the Irish actor, manager and playwright of the same name; he was lessee of the Duke of York's Theatre where in 1904 he produced *Peter Pan* – and where he had produced almost all of J.M. Barrie's plays – originally with his sister Nina Boucicault in the title rôle. Master Alfred was now introduced to the world of Kirby's Flying Ballet, of fairies and pirates and Captain Hook and the crocodile and the Lost Boys, but more especially to the 'boy who wouldn't grow up', played with infinite charm in this season, and in many more, by Miss Pauline Chase.

The play, with its mixture of boyish adventure, fantastic visual effects, and a pessimistic view of the approach of adulthood, has proved to be a gold-mine for Freudians delving into the tunnels of the personality of the most successful dramatist of the day. Barrie yearned for children of his own and practically adopted the family of one of his friends. Bernard Shaw thought it 'an artificial freak which missed its mark entirely, and was foisted on children by grown-ups'. (He might have said the same, and with considerably more emphasis, of Miss Field's *Fly-Away Land*.) Boucicault was hardly concerned with anything more than presenting the tale for all its sentimental action-filled worth. Master Alfred, accompanied by the faithful Marjorie – how can she and the other chaperones have occupied themselves, when their little charges were disporting themselves on the stage? – with Master Noël (for he, too, had joined the world of the Never-Never Land) played 'six weeks of two hysterical performances a day', pelted at the close of each with violets and thimbles which, in that emotionally inhibited world, represented kisses; and then they went on the road for two months, starting in Kennington in south London – from where he and Marjorie could travel home to Purves Road at night – and after that to distant cities, not returning to London until mid-April.

Alfred Willmore was engaged in *Peter Pan* for four to five months each year from December 1911 until March 1914. He and his sister (who was given the part of the Second Twin after the first tour) had an unquenchable thirst for sightseeing; they would visit every public monument or exhibition on their winter itinerary. While in Bradford, they decided they must walk to Haworth, for of course they had read *Wuthering Heights* and *Jane Eyre*, and they set out in the morning not realising that the distance was far too great, taking fright in time to hurry back for the evening performance. What they may have seen in Dublin is anyone's guess. In later life MacLíammóir spoke of attending plays at the Abbey Theatre, but how he could have done so when *Peter Pan* was playing afternoons and nights at the Theatre Royal is something of a conundrum. The Abbey had an irregular schedule, it is true, and he could have seen a Monday matinée of Lady Gregory's *The Rising of the Moon* with John Guinan's *The Cuckoo's Nest* on 24 March 1913, for example – but Mondays are 'get in' days in the touring companies and the cast is usually on call for technical rehearsal. He certainly could have seen an exhibition of stage designs by Gordon Craig at the Central Hall in Westmoreland Street the same week; and, even at the age of thirteen, might have been interested to read that the Gaelic Athletic Association had announced a rule that 'no member of a team shall, while playing a match, speak any language but Irish'. The leisurely pace of life in Dublin must have seemed very different from the bustle of the industrial cities of England which were the staple of the tours; and Cork must have been like a drowsy village. It was a different country: not the province it was regarded as by English people who had never been there.

For the 1912-13 tour Alfred was promoted from Michael Darling to his elder brother John, which meant that he did not have to make a precarious entrance on the back of the big dog Nana, and he could take part in the jolly Pillow Fight Dance with Master Noël, who was playing Slightly, one of the Lost Boys – a curiously significant appellation. Master Noël did not enjoy the part, for he had to make himself appear to be stupid, and (as MacLíammóir recalled more than half a century later in *Enter a Goldfish*) complained, 'It really is unbelievably difficult to act like a moron when one isn't a moron. And I have very little sympathy, darling, with morons. Rather like you, darling, in your absent moments.' If the reportage is accurate, which it quite likely is, here were two very young actors, not yet fourteen, already using the adult backstage jargon which would set them apart from what is generally regarded as normality, for the rest of their lives.

Alfred Willmore's first Irish press notice appeared in The Freeman's Journal in March 1913, when the reviewer stated that he and another young player impersonated John and Michael Darling 'gracefully'. After three seasons of

Peter Pan he retired equally gracefully from the cast, for he did not turn up at the Duke of York's in early December of 1914 to see if he would be re-engaged. His voice had broken, and he must have known that the interview would be an embarrassment. Pauline Chase, in a memoir called *Peter Pan's Postbag*, wrote that 'Every December a terrifying ceremony takes place before *Peter Pan* is produced, and this is the measuring of the children who take part in it. They are measured to see if they have grown too tall. Measuring Day is one of the tragedies of *Peter Pan*.' It is a remarkable metaphor for the ending of childhood, set against the faintly morbid atmosphere which pervades Barrie's conception of the Never-Never Land. The retention of a semblance of youth was to become one of Micheál MacLíammóir's most powerful private preoccupations once he passed the age of thirty; the dye-brush, the hair-piece, the pan-stick, all made their appearance long before they were really necessary – and most of his acquaintance did not believe they were necessary at all.

PLEASE SIR, I WANT SOME MORE

Alfred was sent for by Tree shortly after he returned from his first *Peter Pan* tour, and offered the star part of Oliver Twist. In rehearsal Tree had difficulty in convincing him that he should be 'natural'. 'Be yourself, and believe in what you are saying, and what Mr Dickens has given you to say.' He admonished him not to pose in beautiful attitudes, and told him he had been watching too much of 'that damned Russian Ballet!' He had indeed been going with Marjorie to see as much of the Diaghilev season as they could afford. Diaghilev had been coming to London with his Imperial Russian Ballet for four years; that summer London saw *The Firebird* for the first time; Pavlova was no longer in the company, but appeared in her own seasons with her partner Novikoff, whom Alfred admired more than the famous Nijinsky; Novikoff was, even to his young eyes, a more virile dancer. It is clear that MacLíammóir-to-be already had a *penchant* for men who were definitely men.

He was able to watch Novikoff at much closer quarters on 14 May at the Royal Opera House, Covent Garden, when a 'Dramatic and Operatic Matinée', in which Alfred had a tiny part, was given in aid of the *Titanic* disaster fund, in the presence of His Majesty King George V and Queen Mary. Three committees – Executive, General and Programme – representing the highest in the land of the theatrical and musical establishment, arranged a concert with eighty performers (not counting the orchestra). George Grossmith and the Gaiety Theatre company gave an excerpt from *The Sunshine Girl*, Mrs Patrick Campbell appeared as Paula Tanqueray, Madame Edvina and Signor Samperini performed Act II of *Tosca* with other singers from the Royal Opera, Madame Clara Butt sang an Elgar aria, the Imperial Russian Ballet gave four *divertissements*, and there was a scene from *The Count of Luxembourg*. It must have been an extraordinary spectacle; one is left wondering irreverently where did they all dress? and for how long did the entertainment continue? Tree was the organising secretary, and he decided to present the tournament scene from *Richard II*, with a cast drawn from his own and other reputable companies. Tree was the King, Phyllis Neilson-Terry the Queen; Gerald du Maurier, David Basil Gill and Godfrey Tearle had speaking parts, and the walk-ons were sustained by a legion of leading players, among them Lilian Braithwaite, Marie Lohr, Lillah McCarthy, Nigel Playfair, Marie Tempest and Irene Vanbrugh. Master Bobbie Andrews was Aumerle's page, and Master Alfred Willmore was page to the Queen.

In later life, Micheál MacLíammóir remembered how the Queen's horse – for Miss Neilson-Terry entered the stage on a real charger, caparisoned with tapestry drapes and jangling trappings – 'while accustomed, of course, to an entourage of stars, was overwhelmed by the presence of genuine royalty, and at the distinguished sight of the unmistakable faces in the royal box was moved to commit one of those nuisances for which horses, more than any other animals, seem to have such a surprising capacity.' (Who cleaned up the mess? How did Pavlova accomplish *Le Cygne* on the same spot?) His undying memory of the event, however, was of being presented to Sarah Bernhardt, to whom Tree had generously allocated the final item on the programme, when she recited her famous monody on the cathedrals of France. He kissed her hand, as he had been taught by Tree, 'and I remember nothing more, except that I knew, even at that age, that I was in the room with the incarnation of the theatre, with one who had an indescribable brilliance and seductiveness about every movement she made; her voice was a live creature that caressed the mind and tore at the heart . . . ' He noticed that the frills of brown lace which fringed Madame Bernhardt's hand were uncannily still, and when describing this to Anew McMaster afterwards, McMaster explained, 'Gummed to her hands, dear.' The theatricality of the device impressed them both.

After *Oliver Twist* opened on 15 June 1912, Alfred and Marjorie, often joined now by Anew McMaster and Wilfred Rooke-Ley, attended whatever Russian Ballet matinées could be fitted in. Alfred was captivated by the décor of Bakst, seeming to understand that it was not necessary to paint every leaf on every tree as was done by the scenic artists for the productions in which he had appeared, but possible to provide an appropriate atmosphere with imaginative arrangements of shapes and colours. The names of McCleery and Harker, who provided scenery for Tree and other London managements, were later taken as examples of what MacLíammóir wished *not* to emulate. Curiously, no credit for design appears on the programme for *Oliver Twist* though there are six alternating scenes. Pictures of the production were issued to the press, and, a novelty at the time, postcard-sized photographs of the principal performers were made available to the public. Two of Alfred Willmore were published, one showing Oliver in rags, in an alert, frightened pose, and the other as a neatly dressed and thoroughly respectable boy with shiny buckled shoes, carrying three portentous books under his arm; the former is much the more interesting, and the expressive face suggests much more than an attractive young lad dressed down for a character part.

The reviews were more than encouraging. While there is a proliferation of phrases such as 'sad and sweet' and 'appealing', some of the critics recognised an unusual talent. Reynold's News noticed 'the Oliver of Master Alfred Willmore, a very clever and natural boy actor'. The Stage said that the rôle was 'most satisfactorily entrusted to a charmingly natural boy actor, Master Alfred Willmore, who made a very pitiful, pathetic and winsome figure in the part. The casting of a boy certainly makes for *vraisemblance*, and Master Willmore endowed the child with old-world grace and almost dignity.' The Lady's Pictorial said 'The Oliver Twist of Mr' – this must have pleased him – 'Alfred Willmore is new, and realises to the full the terror, the simplicity and the childish timidity . . . ' The word which recurs is 'natural'; this would have been as a result of Tree's coaching.

It was obvious that this 'appealing' boy should be cast as Benjamin in the next play at His Majesty's, a new production of the ubiquitous *Joseph and his Brethren* by Louis N. Parker, with Tree as Jacob, Maxine Elliott as Zuleika and George Relph as Joseph. The printed programme states that 'the music has been selected and arranged by Adolf Schmid from ancient Egyptian and Hebrew melodies'; eleven sumptuous scenes were painted by the despised Joseph Harker. Sacred choruses were sung in the orchestra pit before each scene, as if to remind the audience that the plot was taken from Holy Writ. The critic of The Times commented unkindly, 'if only the choruses could have drowned Mr Parker's writ!' It was melodramatic spectacle, and the words were no more than the vehicle for linking one magnificently choreographed incident to the next. In adulthood, and hiding behind the mask of prose fiction, Micheál MacLíammóir wrote of the final reconciliation and brotherly embrace of Joseph, who had 'more than once during the scene declared "his bowels yearned"' for Benjamin; he wondered what on earth this could mean, but thought better than to enquire.

*

Alfred Willmore appeared in at least four films during his juvenile career. In 1911 he was a page in Tree's *Henry VIII*; the play had been produced at His Majesty's before Alfred joined the company, but was reproduced for the screen with some changes in cast, 'to enable me to hand down to posterity a faithful, silent and permanent record' of the stage production,' Tree wrote, evidently unaware of the risibility of a silent version of Shakespeare with the actors mouthing all the speeches. It is probable that Alfred was also in the filmed record of *Macbeth*. In 1914, just before his fifteenth birthday, he was in *Enoch Arden*, a tale taken from Tennyson and set on the Cornish coast. It was directed by Percy Nash for the enterprising Neptune company with May (later Dame May) Whitty, and though Alfred's name does not appear in the list of leading players it is reasonable to assume that he was 'Enoch's boy companion' who is 'disposed of by a shark' (an addition which would have surprised Tennyson), as mentioned in The Bioscope for November of that year. A year later he was featured as Micah Dow, a young Gypsy, in another Neptune film, *The Little Minister*, a three-reel romance based on the play by J.M. Barrie. The director, Cecil Hepworth, one of the pioneers of the British film industry, cast him in *Comin' Through the Rye* in 1916, but by then he had passed out of the category of child actor.

While Micheál MacLíammóir refers to his early stage career in three of his books, he does not give any impression of how fine a young actor he must have been. There was a great deal of fun, he visited several interesting cities and stayed in as many grand hotels, and he had the opportunity of seeing other plays, as well as the ballet and the opera. He met a large number of amusing and intriguing people, some of whom remained friends for the rest of his life, he mixed with the great; he found a welcome escape from the tyranny of school and, probably, from the tyranny of the enclosed suburban family circle at Kensal Green. Yet, judging not only from his press notices, but more from the fact that he was repeatedly sought by two of the most eminent and influential producers of the era, Boucicault and Tree, he must have been very talented indeed. To command the audience in a large West End theatre in a title rôle, as he did night after night in *Oliver Twist*, requires immense resources of concentration and technique. He clearly had the temperament, the facility, and above all the presence, to captivate these audiences, and he seems to have done so with a disarming nonchalance. He probably never knew quite how good he was during those years.

Those years came to an end with the changing of the voice, and the realisation that he was too old for juvenile parts, too young for adult parts, and that parts for boys of the in-between years were scant. The career of the classical dancer often ends in the mid-twenties, which is considered to be very young; but that of the child actor ends at fourteen. He had stepped out of the Never-Never-Land, and it was hard to predict what new land would welcome him as its engaging citizen.

BOBBY

In the year when Master Alfred Willmore of Kensal Green had been taken out of school and was tasting the previously unimagined delights of appearing before an audience in a real theatre, an event occurred which had a sad and lasting effect on a much smaller boy in north London, for Bobby Edwards, aged eight, learned that his father had died. In later years he could not recall exactly how he heard the news, or just how the accident – which he supposed had something to do with a motor-cycle – had happened. He often said that he could remember long theatre parts with ease, but 'had a capacity for wiping other things out', and also that as a child he was 'of a very unenquiring mind' and never asked his parents, or other relatives, about the whys and wherefores of their lives. His may have been the classic case of the child who expunges unhappy things, or he may simply have *pretended* not to remember.

If he was of 'an unenquiring mind' in regard to family matters as a child, he continued in adult life in the same vein. He spoke of his father having been in the 'foreign office' (Thomas George Cecil Edwards was in the Indian civil service), but also that he was 'Governor of Hyderabad and Sind' (the position he held at his death was Collector and District Magistrate for the United Provinces of Agra and Oudh). The anecdotes which Hilton Edwards – or Bobby, as he was known at that time – passed on about his father can only relate to the period from April 1909 to January 1910, when Thomas was in England on leave, and Bobby was six. In fact, he can only have met his father in two short periods of their lives, for Thomas first saw his son when he was only a few months old during an earlier period of 'extraordinary leave' which was extended to 'furlough' and 'subsidiary leave' lasting until Bobby was two and a half, and Bobby was unlikely to have remembered any of this. Thus, Bobby can only have been in the company of his father for a total of two years and eleven months. In 1973 Hilton Edwards told the Dublin theatre critic Desmond Rushe that he was 'a neglected child in a way', and that he 'only started to live as a conscious human being' from the day he joined Charles Doran's theatre company in January 1921, when he was just coming up to his eighteenth birthday.

Hilton Edwards always affirmed that after the death of his mother in 1926 he was left with no living relatives. (One almost expects him to add that he had been placed in a handbag in the cloakroom at Victoria station.) He left no descendants either; these factors, and his own real or assumed lack of interest in his background and family history, makes the chart of his early years resemble those primitive maps in which the cartographers filled the blank spaces with neat curling calligraphy stating 'here be monsters' – the monsters of misinformation or malinformation. He was born on 2 February 1903 at, according to his birth certificate, No. 1 Bathurst Mansions, 460 Holloway Road, London N.7, though the Register of Electors states that a Thomas Edwards occupied No.2; the birth certificate is probably incorrect because No.1 was for a long period the residence of a Mr Vincent and a Mr Bishop who were the owners of Bishop's Pure Drug Company (Bishop's Dispensing Chemist in 1993) on the ground floor. The building is a massive five-storey corner house on the north-eastern side of the junction of Holloway Road and Seven Sisters Road; it is quite out of scale with its neighbours and looks as if the district had been due for redevelopment in late Victorian times but that the contractor had lost heart after erecting the first rather Teutonic-looking block. It has an ogival dome, pedimented dormers and *art-nouveau* lettering proclaiming 'Bathurst Mansions' – probably named in honour of Henry, third Earl of Bathurst, who had been secretary to the Board of Trade.

Hilton Edwards, who mentioned to several people, among them the actors Patrick Bedford and T.P. McKenna, that his earliest family home was a house called Netherwood in East Finchley, did not claim that he was born there; in fact shortly before his death he told the critic J.J. Finegan that 'the house wasn't ready, or I arrived too early, and I was born within a stone's throw of Highgate'. This would have been Bathurst Mansions, and Highgate is certainly not very far from Holloway, though the former has a more salubrious connotation. Two things are odd: the first that Thomas Edwards retained the apartment at Bathurst Mansions until 1906 – perhaps the only way he could obtain accommodation for the pregnant Mrs Edwards was by taking a four-year lease – and once they had moved to Netherwood there might have been a source of income from sub-letting. The second is that Thomas's profession is given on his son's birth certificate as 'Christmas card designer'. No such artist or tradesman is listed in the appropriate directories, but a number of old friends confirmed that Hilton spoke of his father's chief interest, or hobby, as being printing and graphic art, and that he even invented a typewriter which purported to print musical notation, and lost a considerable amount of money in trying to market it. No doubt Thomas intended to take up these interests at leisure during his first long period of leave from India, but as he was still there (according to the India Office records) at the time of his son's registration of birth (as Hilton Robert Hugh Edwards) it is strange that his wife would have written 'Christmas card designer' when in fact he was Joint Magistrate (Second Grade), Calcutta, at the time. Either she had a complete disregard for the social pretensions which the title of Joint Magistrate (even of Second Grade) conferred, or she had a commendable sense of humour, or else she had something to hide.

Mrs Edwards was the former Emily Murphy. Her son often mentioned that though his mother had an Irish name she had never been to Ireland, and that she had said she was christened at a Roman Catholic church in Soho. There is more than a faint feeling that she may not have belonged to the same social class as her husband, who had been educated at University College School and Trinity College, Cambridge, and whose family had been resident at Dulwich; the name 'Murphy' in that era would hardly have suggested international building contractors or financial brokers in the city. She was Thomas Edwards' second wife, and he was said to have had a son by his first marriage, who went to Chile, and that this son inherited his father's estate. Where this son lived, or who looked after him, prior to his emigration to so distant – and, one has to add, outlandish – a destination, is not known, but its very improbability gives a certain mythic substance.

Netherwood House was situated on the Great North Road in East Finchley, in comparatively open country, but only a hundred yards from the entrance to Church Lane, a heterodox collection of old-world cottages and newer villas leading over the Great Northern Railway bridge to East End Road. Netherwood was demolished in the 1950s to make way for a huge suburban spread, but it had gone out of the ownership of the Edwards family in 1915, according to the Borough of Barnet records. The Barnet library, however, has preserved a watercolour of the house, dated 1949 and thought to be one of a number painted by a local amateur artist depicting East Finchley 'as it was', when news of the impending housing development was announced. It is a pleasant, probably early nineteenth century building, with the traditional three windows on the upper floor, and a centre doorway, flanked by a window on either side; the glazing-bars certainly appear to be pre-Victorian. An extension to the right, with French windows to the garden, could have been part of the 'refurbishments' Hilton Edwards described as having been delayed at the time of his birth.

Though he was never taken to India, Edwards recalled that he almost felt he had been there, for all the conversation, when his parents were at home, was of that empire beyond the seas. He had an ayah, which would have strengthened the illusion. Presumably this ayah looked after him all the time, for Emily Edwards was certainly in Agra when her husband died in 1911. Edwards told the playwright Brian Friel that his parents entertained regularly, and that he used to creep out of his bedroom at the top of the stairs at Netherwood to watch the fine company arriving. This was his first theatre, and he was a member of the audience: he longed to be a part of the play. He told the actor Conor Evans that his father took him in a hansom cab to the West End one day and left him in a Lyons' Corner House, telling him that he could eat as many chocolate eclairs as he liked. His father went about his business and forgot him, and when he returned to Netherwood, Emily asked, 'Where's the boy?', and he had to go back to find him. The story is an amusing one, but it immediately suggests the oft-absent parent, unused to children, doing his duty to entertain his little son, but not really having him in his thoughts. ('I was a neglected child, in a way . . . ')

East Finchley Grammar School was situated on the Great North Road on the same side as Netherwood, between the intersections of Park Road and Chapel Street. It has long since vanished, and the Greater London Education Authority did not retain the record books of the schools which it caused to close, or took over. Hilton Edwards' entry in *Who's Who in the Theatre* states that he attended this school, and it was probably here that the incident occurred when he was beaten by a larger boy and was persuaded by his father to tell what had happened. In one version of the story (told to Conor Evans) he was taking part in a boxing tournament, and was unfairly matched against a much bigger boy; Thomas Edwards demanded to see the teacher who had organised the contest, punched him, and removed his son from the school. In another version, published by J.J. Finegan in the Evening Herald, he was 'trounced' by a bigger boy 'behind the sacristy of St Mary's, East Finchley' – and this was the reason for his 'outsize nose'. Certainly there must have been an affray of some kind; but a little boy of six would hardly have been taking part in a boxing competition, and if he was removed from the school, where did he go? – for he did not enter St Aloysius' College until he was eleven. The notion of the father taking revenge is touching and significant: was it a wish fulfilment dream, or did his father take appropriate action against the school authorities on some other, less violent, issue?

In January 1910, a month before his son's seventh birthday, Thomas Edwards returned to Agra to resume his duties. It is not clear whether Emily went with him or joined him later. It was quite common for service couples to leave their children 'at home' – it was more convenient, and it was believed that the Indian climate was unsuitable for children over the age of one year. The climate was responsible for Emily being absent from Agra on 4 July, for she was spending the hot season in the hills. According to a report in The Times of India on Wednesday 5 July: 'The death of Mr T.C. Edwards, late Collector and District Magistrate of Agra, is the result of a pig-sticking incident which occurred a couple of days ago. After a very restless night Mr Edwards began to sink gradually on Tuesday morning, and passed away at 12.45 p.m. Mrs Edwards, who was spending the summer at Naini Tal, came down on Monday. The greatest sympathy is felt for her and the people of Agra are mourning a zealous, kindhearted and courteous officer.' (There was no mention of a motor-cycle.) On 6 July the same paper reported that 'Mr T.C.Edwards was buried on Tuesday evening in St Paul's Cemetery, Civil Lines. The cortège was about a mile long, all classes of the community being represented.' A notice was printed in the deaths column of The Times on 7 July. Presumably Emily telegraphed the household at Netherwood, and presumably she returned from India shortly afterwards.

Three and a half years later, when he was almost twelve, Bobby entered St Aloysius' College, Highgate, two stops down the Northern Line from Netherwood, or a short omnibus ride from Seven Sisters Road, to which Emily had probably moved. The college had been founded by the Belgian order of the Brothers of Our Lady of Mercy on the invitation of Cardinal Manning to provide 'middle class secondary education for boys of the Roman Catholic persuasion'. The war memorial, dedicated to the memory of past pupils who died in two world wars, lists a remarkable number of Irish names; Hilton Edwards, on coming to Ireland just over a decade later, far from feeling like a foreigner, would have found the atmosphere and the iconography instantly recognisable. St Aloysius' was founded to provide something more than a secondary education for the sons of Roman Catholic families – it was also founded to give them a dignity; only their very wealthy co-religionists could afford the boarding-schools at Stoneyhurst or Downside, which were modelled on the Anglican public school system. It would be true, if unkind, to state that St Aloysius' in 1915 was the poor man's Ampleforth.

In his entry in *Who's Who*, Hilton Edwards gives St Aloysius' College as his seat of secondary education. College documents were lost during evacuation to Chingford in 1939-45, but some of the old ledgers were left in 'the vaults', and in one of these there is an entry stating that Edwards, H.R.H., was admitted on 14 January 1915, and discharged on 1 November of the same year. A scribbled marginal note baldly provides the information that he was 'Removed by his mother'. Her address is given as 170 Seven Sisters Road, Holloway. One has to assume, judging from the corroborative oral tradition, that she was in straitened circumstances, that she could no longer afford to pay the very modest fees, and that the proceeds of the sale of Netherwood had gone to her stepson. The terrace in Seven Sisters Road was destroyed in the Luftwaffe bombing of 1941, but it would have looked very much the same as the other mid-nineteenth century houses in the same street – mainly flats over small shops; Mrs Edwards is not listed as the householder, presumably having taken 'rooms' for herself and her fatherless boy. Patrick Bedford remembered Hilton Edwards saying that his mother had to go out to work, and was employed for a time in the de-coding office – for the First World War was in its second year; a 'Miss' E. Edwards is listed in the appropriate section of the Imperial Calendar for 1915: this may be a misprint, or it may be the usual title given in a period when it was not considered proper for married ladies to be in paid employment.

From the end of 1915 until some time in 1919 Hilton Edwards vanishes from view. He might as well have gone into a coma like the Sleeping Beauty. He told Desmond Rushe that he went up to Cambridge – but none of the twenty Cambridge colleges and halls which were in existence at the time has any record of a person of his name applying for entrance during the years 1918 to 1925, nor has the university registry office. He said to Desmond Rushe: 'I went up to Cambridge, but I had to make a sudden choice; whether I should stay up, maybe very much to the detriment of my mother's position, or whether I should come down and get a job. And so I left rather ignominiously in a hurry, without completing my education or getting a degree. This was a period I almost consciously blot out from my mind. It was a traumatic experience for me.' Was Cambridge wishful thinking or pure invention – or did he perhaps reconnoitre Cambridge, decide against it, and attend some less expensive third-level establishment in London for a time? He also told Desmond Rushe that he joined the army – 'the Machine Gun Corps. This was late in 1917, and I was a private, but I did attain the rank of acting unpaid Lance Corporal without privilege of stripe.'

A search among the Medal Rolls in the Public Records Office at Kew discloses nobody of that name in any of the forces in 1917: but the rolls do reveal 'Pte EDWARDS Robt 88332 MGC Class Z (AR) 9-7-19'. 'MGC' signifies Machine Gun Corps, and the date is that of demobilisation. Bobby Edwards must therefore have been accepted for service before the armistice of November 1918, for the rolls show that he was awarded the Victory Medal. 'Class Z (AR)' means that he was placed on the army reserve until March 1920, up to which date he could be liable for recall, if required. He was stationed at Alexandra Palace, not two miles from his place of birth, his late father's house, and his mother's more recent place of residence. A Captain Brownlow signed the document, verifying that the facts contained in it were correct.

Hilton Edwards was anything but a stage-struck young man. He attributed his initiation to the professional theatre to a suggestion made by a relative, Elizabeth Arkell, who was or had been an actress, and was married to Reginald Arkell whom Edwards described in 1943 to Sean Dorman, editor of Commentary, as 'a journalist'. Arkell was, in fact, the author of some dozens of stage revues, including *Savoy Follies*, *Chelsea Follies*, and the long-running musical version of *1066 and All That*. Elizabeth Arkell probably thought that this young man simply needed a job; and it may have been her husband who provided the necessary introduction, for he had collaborated on two shows with Russell Thorndike, a leading actor at the Old Vic. Bobby went along to the Old Vic, where he was interviewed by the producer, Robert Atkins – described many years later by Sir John Gielgud as 'a boozy old survivor of the days of Forbes Robertson'. Atkins told him something he might have thought of beforehand, which was that he did not have any experience and so could not be hired – but he passed on the information that Charles Doran was casting for a Shakespearian tour. Bobby went to see Doran, and was taken on as an assistant-stage manager, the duties of which would enable him to appear in crowd scenes and also to take some very minor rôles. Bobby then became Hilton; among those engaged on the same day were a young man called Donald Woolfitt (as he then spelled his name), another called Reginald Jarman and another called Raymond Percy – the latter to be a link with McMaster's future company and the Gate in Dublin. All four were destined to work together over the years as the whirligig of time and theatre business decreed.

Charles Doran was born in Cork in 1877. He started his career with Sir Frank Benson's Shakespearian Company, acted with Tree, and appeared in the West End, the United States and South Africa. After army service in the First World War he formed his own company, with the solemnly declared intention of 'satisfying an inherent ambition as an artiste, and at the same time to do some public educational work'. He seems to have had rather the same aims as McMaster, but lacked McMaster's breadth of personality and prodigious sense of fun. The plays were *The Merchant of Venice*, *As You Like It*, *The Taming of the Shrew*, *Hamlet*, *The Tempest*, and *Macbeth*. Hilton was given speaking parts sooner than he expected – the First Player in *Hamlet* for his stage speaking début at the Theatre Royal, Windsor, on Thursday 27 January 1921, and Alonzo in *The Tempest* the next evening – having walked on in the crowd on the earlier nights of the week. His eighteenth birthday was spent at the West Pier Theatre in Brighton. The company remained on the road for twenty-two weeks, from Windsor to Westcliffe-on-Sea. It was a highly conventional theatrical beginning in the context of the times.

Chapter 3

Wanderjahre

While Hilton Edwards 'did his bit for England', in the popular phrase of the day, even if he never saw active service, Micheál MacLíammóir (or Alfred Willmore, as he still was) had no such patriotic ambitions. When conscription was introduced he thought of joining Anew McMaster, who had changed his name to Martin Doran and retreated to Ireland to work with the James O'Brien and Harry Ireland company – much to the disapprobation of Marjorie Willmore, who believed that England needed 'all the men she could get' at the front. After his final performance in *Peter Pan* in Manchester on 28 March 1914 he and Marjorie returned to London, and it is supposed that his father, wondering what on earth this bright young fellow could be set to do, proposed a visit to Spain to stay with relatives for a year. It was long before the fashion for teenage boys to be sent abroad to learn a foreign language became prevalent, though well-to-do girls often went to European countries, strictly chaperoned, to 'finish' their education. It is not at all clear why the trip was arranged at a time when the Great Powers were doing more than rattle sabres; it would also have cost more money than a buyer for Whitney's could afford. Micheál MacLíammóir often claimed that his paternal grandmother was Spanish, and in *Enter a Goldfish* 'Martin's' father travels with him to Seville, so as he will not be bewildered, and so as he too can have a pleasant little outing among his Andalucian relatives, before leaving young Martin/Alfred in their care.

The Spanish visit may have been a complete fabrication, created to give piquancy, not to say a certain mildly erotic *frisson*, to the autobiographical novel *Enter a Goldfish*, incidents from which have been taken by the unwary as actuality in colourful attire. In the book, the young hero accepts the sexual advances of an attractive (male) Spanish cousin; the scene has the circumjacence of an initiation, and has been taken as representing such. It is much more likely that the author was crystallising a number of experiences – which may have occurred in far less exotic surroundings than the Calle San Fernando, such as Brondesbury or Leeds; after all, backstage society was notoriously latitudinarian, and Master Alfred was patently quite a charmer. The signs for caution, as far as the truth or otherwise of the Spanish summer is concerned, are that there is no proof that the Willmores inherited Spanish blood, and great-grandchildren of Alfred and Emily are sceptical of any Spanish connections whatsoever. There is another, unverifiable, story, and it is that young Alfred did go to Spain that year, where he was the victim of the sexual advances of an older person. This, if it happened, would have made less than pleasant reading in a book which is plainly intended for the general market.

'Spain, to me, means *doom!*', MacLíammóir was to write to the Gate Theatre secretary, Patricia Turner, half a century later; he may have been thinking of something nasty, not one of those harmless little affairs like the well-known relationship of Master Noël and Master Bobbie Andrews. When he returned – if he had indeed been away – it was to an England preparing for war, and to the decision, whether or not imposed on him by his parents, to attend an art school, for he had made dozens of little sketches of scenes in the theatre, and, with Marjorie, was an intrepid visitor to art galleries. The Middlesex Educational Committee had opened a Polytechnic in Priory Park Road, Kilburn, towards the end of the nineteenth century, to which was added in 1904 a splendid new building in Glengall Road on the site of the house once occupied by the bookseller W.H. Smith, containing among other departments, studios for the teaching of drawing of all kinds. A Mr T.R. Mumford was Head of the School of Art, and the fee charged was ten shillings a term. According to pictures in the booklet produced to celebrate the opening of this extension, the life classes made use of heavily draped models, but there was also 'drawing from the antique', for which plaster casts of classical statuary must have been considered quite seemly enough to place before female, as well as male students, without embarrassment to either.

It was here that Alfred Willmore met Mary O'Keefe, whose mother, a former nurse, had married an Irishman, found him intemperate and unreliable, and left him – or so the story went. Alfred and Mary became inseparable friends; their relationship was uncannily like that of Noël Coward and Esmé Wynne. They invented a legendary Irish past for themselves; she, whose paternal forebears came from County Tipperary; he, who could claim visits to Ireland, and who was deeply engrossed in W.B. Yeats' *Ideas of Good and Evil*, which had been given to him by an admirer, the 'Geoffrey Leigh-Craig' of *Enter a Goldfish*. He submitted drawings to Punch, one of which was accepted and received attention in the press when a reporter for The Star devoted a column to his achievement – which evidently surprised Mr Mumford, who probably would have preferred to have been consulted before a student offered work for payment. The same reporter referred to young Willmore's theatrical career, and Alfred again mentioned his enthusiasm for the Abbey Theatre, and his interest in the plays of Yeats.

While it is easy to dismiss his visits to the Abbey on the grounds of dates and timetables, there is an obvious explanation much nearer to hand: the Abbey Players frequently performed in London, so that during his juvenile-professional years from 1911 to 1914 Alfred could have seen Synge's *The Playboy of the Western World* and *In the Shadow of the Glen*, Lady Gregory's *The Workhouse Ward* and *The Bogie Men*, Lennox Robinson's *Patriots*, T.C. Murray's *Maurice*

Harte and *Thomas Muskerry*, and Yeats' *The Countess Cathleen*, as well as plays by Rutherford Mayne, Joanna Redmond and Lord Dunsany produced by other Irish companies. The Abbey Players usually performed at the Court Theatre, which would have been just as accessible, and certainly less expensive, than the Russian Ballet at Covent Garden; and the work of those Irish writers would, at that time, have seemed highly experimental, not to say *avant-garde*, revealing, like the Russians, a world quite different from that of His Majesty's Theatre on the one hand, and Kensal Green on the other: the world of escape.

A year after entering the Polytechnic in Glengall Road, Alfred Willmore applied, and was accepted, for a place in the Faculty of Arts at London University, better known as the Slade School, named in honour of the art collector Felix Slade, who endowed the professorship of Fine Art. It was the most prestigious art academy in the United Kingdom. A body of opinion existed in Dublin many years later to the effect that attendance at the Slade was 'just another of Micheál's inventions' – but it was no such thing. His entry-form of 20 September 1915 shows that he took the two-year course in drawing, and attended classes in this subject on three days a week. There was a composition fee of £1, and a tuition fee of £5.5.0d per term in a three-term year. He was not on a scholarship; how could he, or his father, have afforded such a high premium – one which effectively excluded all but the sons and daughters of those who lived at far classier addresses than theirs? The answer is given in the section devoted to Parent or Guardian. The name of Alfred Willmore senior is not entered, but that of Wilfred Rooke-Ley, of Richard Reynolds House, Old Isleworth, Middlesex, who, in the small print, 'undertakes to be responsible for the payment of College dues'. It is not difficult to translate this name from that of the man-about-the-theatre 'Geoffrey Leigh-Craig', who had first introduced Master Alfred to Anew McMaster at Appendrodt's, who had been a constant matinée-going companion, and who had given him the copy of Yeats' essays. It was he who arranged Alfred Willmore's ascent of the social staircase which raised him out of the front-parlours of north London. Only in the cloudy half-world of pseudonyms and false trails in *Enter a Goldfish* is it mentioned that Alfred Willmore possessed, and was indebted to, a patron of so well-born and well-to-do a complexion.

The house in which Rooke-Ley lived is situated on a picturesque reach of the Thames near Richmond Bridge. An estate-agent could truthfully describe it as 'a Georgian dwelling of unique charm, with an elegant Adamesque doorcase, original plasterwork, fine marble chimneypieces, and a delightfully secluded garden'. When they met, Wilfred Rooke-Ley would have been in his forties. For a time he ran a private residential tutorial school at Oxford for Roman Catholic students wishing to enter the university (one of his unsuccessful pupils was the Duke of Norfolk). He became a free-lance broadcaster, and a writer for the Radio Times. Harman Grisewood, Controller of the BBC Third Programme, remembered him as 'a dilettante, ninetyish figure'; he was not only 'a man of taste, but a man of robust and humble piety'. The actor Robert Speaight, when reviewing Grisewood's autobiography *One Thing at a Time*, recalled Rooke-Ley as 'a man with a gift for the younger generation'. Such was Alfred Willmore's patron; and it is easy to comprehend how the house at Isleworth, and the kind of people whom Alfred met there, would have given him an insight into a relaxed world totally different from the hectic activity of the theatre, which is ruled by the terrifying and inevitable nightly rise of the curtain, and the penny-pinching, warm, but ultimately claustrophobic family circle. It is quite possible that the devout Rooke-Ley also introduced Alfred to Roman Catholicism.

Alfred Willmore's Slade record shows that he was now living at 71 Calcott Road, Brondesbury. The Willmores had left Purves Road in 1913, but the local directories do not give the name of the householder in Calcott Road. They may have rented the house – which is a large one in a three-storied Victorian terrace – or it may have been student lodgings rented for Alfred by the generous Rooke-Ley. Alfred was now attending Irish language classes. His interest in Irish literature has been seen as extraordinary, but it was no more so than that of any bright young person discovering and exploring the complexities of a little-known foreign language. In 1916 he started using the old Irish lettering when signing his name on the daily attendance roll at the Slade. A middle-name creeps in: Michael, thought by colleagues in the theatre to derive from his first part in *Peter Pan*. Early in 1917 he was cast in a supporting rôle – evidently small enough for him to rehearse and still keep his Slade term – in a comedy at the Haymarket, *Felix Gets a Month*, directed by E. Lyall Swete – another member of the Rooke-Ley circle. The programme for this play contains a note in bold type stating that 'All male members of the cast are exempt from Military Service.' By this date, too, there were only six male students left on the roll at the Slade. There is no reason to doubt that as Alfred's seventeenth birthday approached he would have been dreading the arrival of his call-up papers. (Noël Coward was conscripted into an outfit called the Artists' Rifles, but took ill after a while and was discharged.)

Why, precisely, Alfred decided not to finish his two year course at the Slade, removing himself from the probability of a good diploma, and travelled from Holyhead to Kingstown on 26 March, a full seven months before he was old enough to be called up, can only be explained by the possibility that he was seizing an opportunity presented by the O'Keefes. Mrs O'Keefe, whom he now called 'Aunt Craven' because of something she had once said about craving a nephew (perhaps what she really craved was a son), was scared by the Zeppelins. The threat of German bombing was a very real and frightening one. As there was no reason why she should live in London, for she had a small private income, she decided to remove to Dublin. There was also mention of sea air for her bronchitis. Mary had no reason to remain in London either, for she had finished her course at the Polytechnic, and no doubt both she and Alfred encouraged Mrs O'Keefe in her scheme. The facts are that they arrived in

Kingstown on 27 March, rented accommodation in Sandymount, and later moved to the first of two cottages on Howth Head, in the second of which Aunt Craven lived for most of the remainder of her life, only leaving for trips to the continent and to enter a nursing home shortly before her death in 1954.

Alfred had introductions from the actress Una O'Connor, who was performing in London prior to the start of her Hollywood career, to Mrs Theresa Reddin and Mr Joseph Holloway. Theresa Reddin, a member of a large and influential legal and business family, held an agreeably crowded At Home once a month at 45, Fitzwilliam Square, Dublin. Her son, Norman, was to become a director of the Gate Theatre a decade later, and her nephew, Tony, the manager of the Capitol Theatre and the representative in Ireland of Paramount Pictures. Among Theresa's eccentricities was her habit, said by milliners to be technically impossible, of smoking cigarettes through a net veil. Joseph Holloway was an architect and patron of the arts; he had remodelled the old Abbey Street Theatre for the National Theatre Society, and was famous for attending opening nights at all the Dublin playhouses; he kept a prodigious, gossipy and opinionated journal, sections of which were later published, recording his thoughts on these occasions. Una O'Connor had done right by suggesting Alfred should call on this good-natured and eccentric man, for he immediately bought three of his drawings, and, what was just as valuable, introduced him to the greenroom society of the Abbey Theatre.

If Micheál MacLíammóir – into whom Alfred Willmore was gradually transformed – expected to find acting work at the Abbey or any of the Dublin theatres, he must have been disappointed. The larger houses were mainly little more than 'dates' on the English touring circuits, and the Abbey had been founded specifically to produce Irish work. Though it is evident that he assumed a kind of rural *blas* or accent, he would not yet have been credible as a character in the plays of most of the Irish writers of the day. It was not until six months after his arrival that he was cast as the crippled son of a Dublin tenement family in *Blight* by Oliver St John Gogarty and Joseph O'Connor, but it was a part with very few lines. In the cast were Maureen Delany and Arthur Shields, who were to become firm friends, Maureen Delany playing many parts at the Gate, including the housekeeper in MacLíammóir's earliest comedy, *Where Stars Walk*, in 1940. He was also cast as a policeman in the film of Charles Kickham's novel, *Knocknagow*, but, as he told the cinema archivist, Liam O'Leary, he was seventeen (actually he was eighteen) but looked fourteen on the screen, and so his policeman finished on the cutting-room floor. (He said he was much more impressed by the films that he saw than the films he was in.) He did meet the child actor, Cyril Cusack, on the location; they would also work together many times.

MacLíammóir earned what must have been a meagre living, chiefly as a freelance graphic artist. Although photography had made its impact on the newspapers, they still employed designers to decorate articles and stories. He illustrated some books for the Talbot Press – the most significant was the cover for an edition of Daniel Corkery's *A Munster Twilight*. MacLíammóir's drawings are 'Celtic' in the accepted manner of the time, and it is clear that he had been much influenced by Jack B.Yeats. In 1922 his own book of illustrated children's stories, *Oidhcheanna Sidhe (Faerie Nights)*, was published by the Talbot Press. The line drawings are careful in technique and attractively composed – there is an especially fine one of children playing around a bonfire on St John's Eve – but the colour frontispiece is garish and entirely derivative of the worst excesses of Arthur Rackham: a coy little girl peers through the foliage at four foolish-looking elves seated on unusually phallic toadstools; the predominant colours are mauve, purple and crimson. In spite of the children being called Gráinne and Ciarán, and in spite of their places of domicile being Dublin and Connemara, the tone is irrefutably that of Hampstead Garden Suburb.

*

The woodcuts for *The Woman at the Window* by Pádraic O Conaire, published a decade later, show a much surer style and comprehension of the cultural background – but by this time MacLíammóir had become an important figure in the world of stage design. It may be understandable that he found it difficult to obtain regular acting work in Dublin in his early years, but at first glance it is strange that his design talent was not recognised in the theatre. Yet upon examination it becomes obvious that the Abbey Theatre had no real professional interest in what what were generally referred to as 'backgrounds'; photographs of contemporary productions show ill-lit flimsy-looking interiors, and murkily-painted exteriors. There was much talk of Gordon Craig's screens, but they made few appearances. A designer of MacLíammóir's talent and training could have changed all this – for even the dullest-sounding kitchens and living-rooms can be given a visual impetus which promotes the meaning of the text – but the Abbey was not ready for such an *outré* notion. He designed the setting for a play by Edward Martyn at Hardwicke Street – a draughty hall on the theatrical fringe – which was scornfully dismissed by the critics; he also appeared in a small part in a Galsworthy play at the same venue.

There is an oral tradition that at this period Micheál MacLíammóir was 'taken up' by the army Chief of Staff. The story cannot be substantiated, but is too ubiquitous to be summarily dismissed. Had there been a public scandal, documentary evidence would be available; fortunately for both parties such did not take place.

Mary O'Keefe was not as active an artist as her friend. She seems to have preferred going for long walks on the hill of Howth near her mother's cottage. She and Micheál joined a Sinn Féin club in Harcourt Street, but their interest in politics was nothing more than that of the engaged foreigner indulging in romantic notions of the new Ireland, and they soon stopped attending meetings. This brief association with the republican movement may have been the reason for the raid by the Black-and-Tans – a British armed force identified by its mixture of constabulary and military uniforms – on Mary's mother's cottage, which left all three extremely shocked.

In 1918 Micheál's mother suddenly died. The news was conveyed in a letter from Marjorie, who often came from London to visit the cottage on Howth. Close aquaintances, many years later, said he was greatly upset, but even more so when his father married again. A further blow came when a Dublin doctor diagnosed that Mary's persistent 'influenza' throughout the winter of 1919-20 was in fact tuberculosis. The mountain air of Switzerland was prescribed; and after, presumably, much discussion about arrangements, Micheál decided to accompany mother and daughter to Davos Dorf, where he could continue to support himself as an artist, and help to care for the invalid – who was quite determined not to behave like one.

The war was over. Anew McMaster had returned to London and was playing at the Savoy in the long-running comedy *Paddy the Next Best Thing* with Ion Swinley, Lawrence Blake and Una O'Connor. Marjorie seems to have been keeping herself in a variety of undemanding jobs. Christine Willmore, now Travers, had a little daughter, Sally. Hilton Edwards had not yet entered this scene. A period of travel – or wandering – was in store for MacLíammóir. The early 1920s might be fancifully describable as 'lost' years – were it not for that fact that MacLíammóir enjoyed being on the move and savoured the very things which made countries, peoples and languages differ from one another. Economically speaking it was a struggle, but there were extraordinary and brilliant compensations.

TOTENTANZ

The few snapshots which survive from Howth and Davos show Mary O'Keefe as a tall rather intellectual-looking young woman, with an oval face usually surmounted by a cloche hat, or a patterned woollen skull-cap in snow scenes – there are pictures of groups on sledges, or in fancy costume on balconies overlooking pine-shrouded peaks and valleys; one imagines that some of the well-dressed people attending these outdoor parties were enjoying themselves for the last time. It was a dance of death on the slopes of the magic mountain. Mary has the face of the kind of woman whom one would rather expect to meet at an evening recital of poetry in Bloomsbury – but the Bloomsbury crowd were hardly likely to be seen on bobsleighs, or bedizened for the evening in the garb of cowboy and gunman's moll. There are fringed lampshades and basketwork chairs, and windows with wooden shutters carved with fretwork hearts and flowers – the place and the period might well have been created fifty years later by a nostalgic set-dresser for a film. Mrs O'Keefe never looks anything but the sensible English lady which she no doubt was. Micheál is very slim, and occasionally glimpsed in *lederhosen* with prominent braces, as if he had decided to take the *cliché* image of the Engadine seriously.

Mary was not obliged to enter a sanitorium; nor did the trio stay in one of the many hotels, for they could not afford them. They rented a series of small apartments with south-facing verandahs, and in these they modestly entertained whatever residents they happened to fall in with. Micheál held a successful exhibition of watercolours and drawings in a Davos art shop called Herntz & Roussel. In the summer they returned to Howth, via London, and this became a pattern. In 1923 MacLíammóir had a joint exhibition with a painter called Susan Perrin at the Leigh Gallery in South Kensington; and during the summer of 1924 he took part in a film, shot mainly in the surroundings of Bantry Bay – *Land of her Fathers*, with Phyllis Wakeley in the lead; she does not appear to have made many films, and MacLíammóir described her to Liam O'Leary as 'a very charming Protestant girl from Ailesbury Road – the Meriel Moore of her day, but not as good'. Maureen Delany, Barry Fitzgerald and F.J. McCormick were also in the cast, and a young actor whose devout Catholicism intrigued MacLíammóir, for he said his prayers aloud, at great length, and very reverently, before undressing and getting into the bed which they shared.

Mary's health improved. They did not always return to Davos for the winter, but also chose Vevey and Roquebrune, and finally Menton. Micheál made many friendships, lasting and otherwise. He went on a trip through France with an American professor called Robert Hamlet, and travelled to Naples to meet Anew McMaster off the liner from Sydney, following a protracted tour in which Mac had played several Shakespearian rôles, as well as Baldasarre in *The Maid of the Mountains*. They stayed for a few blissful days on Capri and then went on to Rome, where Mac was entranced by a melodrama, *Il Cardinale*, which turned out to have been written by the author of *Joseph and his Brethren*. When he returned to London he acquired the English-language rights, and often played it in later years with his own company.

MacLíammóir had a number of passing *affaires* with older men, if the revelations of *Enter a Goldfish* are to believed, one of which apparently inspired a journey to Sicily. In Davos he met a young Irish lawyer who was recovering from a respiratory complaint; it was one of those cases of both parties immediately seeming to know and understand everything about the other. His name was Jack Dunne; after his first visit to the apartment in the Villa Berna, where he made a good impression on the observant Mary, she said to Micheál, 'At last you have found a friend who's really worth your while. And don't, my darling, go falling in love with him if you can help it. Because I somehow think he won't respond, I don't feel he's the type who would. And I don't want you to be hurt.' These words were recalled and transcribed many years later, when Jack Dunne's legal practice in Kildare had acted on behalf of the Edwards-MacLíammóir company in some if its bitterest financial negotiations. He remained one of Micheál MacLíammóir's closest friends and was directly responsible for organising the first private performance of *The Importance of Being Oscar*, which brought MacLíammóir international recognition in 1960.

Arriving in London in the summer of 1924 to stay with relatives of the O'Keefe's, Micheál found a postcard from his sister Marjorie casually announcing that she and Mac had just been married. He hurried round to congratulate them at the address in Portman Square, and found a party in progress, attended by Constance Collier, who had played Nancy in *Oliver Twist*, and Ivor Novello and Bobbie Andrews: the London he knew had not changed. Two years later, meeting Novello by chance at the ballet in Monte Carlo when Micheál, Mary and Aunt Craven were staying in Menton, Novello remarked of Mac and Marjorie, 'They've two children now, a boy and a girl. I think it's so *clever* of them!'; and this may have been the occasion of the apocryphal story of Mac exclaiming to Micheál, 'You know, duckie, ladies like it too!'

During the winter of 1926-27, a fourth joined the little group in Menton – Hubert Duncombe, a young Anglo-American whom they had met by chance at Roquebrune the previous year, and who visited them at Loughoreen cottage on Howth the following summer. Hubert seems to have added an element of stability to the curious family unit, and also to have taken charge of the practicalities of living; and Aunt Craven evidently enjoyed having another 'nephew'. Round about Christmas both Mary and Craven succumbed to influenza. Hubert became worried about Mary, and insisted on sending for a doctor. She had pneumonia. For a person with a history of tuberculosis, this was grave news; it was before the discovery of antibiotics, and virtually useless remedies were prescribed, like egg-flips, and hot-water-bottles and fresh air. Mary improved, but only to sustain a relapse. On the morning of 7 January 1927 she died, in the presence of a nurse, her mother, and her two friends, having kept up a cheerful flow of conversation until the last day.

*

Micheál arranged for a cremation in Marseille. After a dismal short holiday in Ventimiglia, where he, Craven and Hubert tried to keep each other's spirits up, knowing that Mary would have scorned a period of mourning, they went their separate, but not very separate ways. Micheál wrote to Anew McMaster and asked to be considered as an actor for his forthcoming tour. Hubert continued his wanderings through Europe, joining the new Gate Theatre company in Dublin for its season in 1930. After a few months in England, Aunt Craven returned to Howth.

During the McMaster rehearsals in London, Micheál took a day and a night off to travel to Dublin and back, for he had promised that in the event of her death, he would scatter Mary's ashes to the winds on May Eve, on the mountain-top of Beann Eadair, the highest point of Howth Head. They had walked there every day when living in Craven's cottage, looking out across the bay towards Dublin, talking of their work and their plans, and of the play which Micheál was always intending to write on the story of Diarmuid and Gráinne, part of whose story was connected with that place. The conductor of the Howth tramcar, from which Micheál alighted near the summit, was suspicious of this young man carrying a silver trophy under his coat, and on the vehicle's return to

Howth informed the Civic Guards. Micheál was unaware of these proceedings, but he was unable to open the casket, and in a frenzy of despair left it by a boulder. Some time later a letter was forwarded to him from the superintendent, who must have set a detective to work, for Mary's remains were found and brought to the barracks, where on May Eve a year later, when in Dublin making plans for the new Gate Theatre Studio, Micheál MacLíammóir finally committed the ashes of Mary O'Keefe to the four winds of Howth.

A CLOWN OF ANTIC CAPERS

After his first season with Charles Doran in 1921, Hilton Edwards was re-engaged in slightly larger parts, including Amiens in *As You Like It*, in which he was favourably noticed by the critic of the Cork Examiner. Before the end of 1921 he also appeared at the Grand Opera House in Belfast, the Opera House in Derry and the Gaiety Theatre in Dublin. In Cork he asked Doran if he might remain with the company in the new year, if possible at a higher salary than the £3 he was earning; Doran agreed, and offered him half-a-crown extra. During the Christmas break in London he auditioned for Robert Atkins at the Old Vic, now being able to claim that he had some experience. Atkins, who did not approve of drama schools and disliked even more the highly educated young actors from Oxford and Cambridge who presented themselves to him, was happy to be able to offer Hilton Edwards £3.10.0d. for very much the same work as he had been doing for Doran – assisting backstage, crowd parts, and occasional speaking parts; so Hilton gave Doran notice. There was tremendous prestige in being attached to the Old Vic and for Hilton there was the added advantage of being allowed to attend singing classes with the Vic-Wells Opera.

The official records of the Royal Victoria Hall, the governing body of the Old Vic, were destroyed by German bombs in 1940, but it is possible to piece together the chronology of Hilton's career there from other sources. Between January and June 1922 he was in nine Shakespeare productions, one Molière and the morality play *Everyman* – a Lenten offering: addresses of a devotional nature were given each evening as a prologue by distinguished church and lay figures, among the latter the Irish playwright, St John Ervine. His largest part in his first season was Marcellus in *Hamlet* and there was an 'end of term' show called *Vic Vicissitudes*, devised by Russell Thorndike, in which he appeared as Caliban. He was re-engaged in September, the parts growing bigger; and in that season he appeared in eleven Shakespeare plays, in Massinger's *A New Way to Pay Old Debts* (as Watchall), a nativity play at Christmas, and a pageant drama called *Arthur* by Laurence Binyon with music by Elgar, conducted by Charles Corri, the resident director of music. Edwards played Sir Agravaine in this rambling work, for which Elgar was hastily called upon after the dress rehearsal to write some extra, and very loud, fanfares, to cover the noise of the scene changes. The New Statesman remarked that the play had 'little finish, and nothing memorable in any individual performances.' On 23 April 1923, at the annual Shakespeare birthday concert, Hilton Edwards impressed in Arne's 'O Mistress Mine' and a setting of 'Full Fathom Five', for which no composer is listed. He finished the eight-month season as Starveling in *A Midsummer Night's Dream*.

He then became greatly taken up with his singing, and was said to have irritated the play producer (presumably Atkins) by frequent requests for time off for vocal practice. He sang Melot in *Tristan and Isolde* on the night of 11 October 1923; in 1992 Joan Cross, who was a close friend with whom he used to take coffee at the Appendrodt branch in the Strand, said that he 'never came in right' – but he must have persisted, for he is believed by several people to have sung Wolfram in *Tannhäuser* and Escamillo in *Carmen*; his name is not given in the programme for any Vic-Wells productions of these operas, so he was probably called upon as understudy. During the 1923-24 theatre season he appeared as Fezziwig in *A Christmas Carol*, and in twelve Shakespeare plays, culminating as Feste in *Twelfth Night*, his first leading part. A reviewer in an unidentified paper wrote, 'I admired the Feste of Hilton Edwards extremely. Here we have a clown of antic capers and excellent singing voice, able to "draw three souls out of one weaver".'

When the theatre reopened after extensive refurbishment, he was cast as Montano in *Othello*; and by February of 1925 he could boast that the only Shakespeare plays in which he had not appeared were *King John* and *Measure for Measure* – and he never did have an opportunity of completing the canon.

At this time Hilton Edwards is believed to have been living with his mother in Gray's Inn Road – midway between their earlier homes in East Finchley and Holloway, and the Old Vic in Waterloo Road. The Gate Theatre designer, Molly MacEwen, understood him to have told her that following his three years at the Old Vic he joined 'a *pierrot* show in somewhere like Brighton'. This would have been during the Old Vic's summer recess of 1925; the company was Ronald Frankau's Cabaret Kittens, and the show a breezy musical revue. Ronald Frankau, who would have been thirty at the time, was an Old Etonian, had attended the Guildhall School of Music, and then moved into the unlikely world of music-hall and variety. Thrice married, intensely sociable and amusing, he was also a strong disciplinarian and only engaged artistes of the highest calibre. It is interesting, therefore, that he should have picked an actor from the classical theatre: but the worlds are far from being mutually exclusive. Edwards' musical experience would have appealed, and if, during his talent-spotting, Frankau had seen Edwards in one of his comic Shakespearian rôles, where the timing of the often highly obscure lines is the only way of getting the laugh, he would have been impressed. There is no way of knowing why Hilton Edwards did not return to the Old Vic at the end of the summer: he may not have been invited, he may have tired of an almost endless routine of Shakespeare, or he may simply have been enjoying himself. As Frankau was planning a tour of South Africa and

Rhodesia there was the attraction of foreign travel. Be that as it may, Hilton stayed on with the Cabaret Kittens.

The only memories of the South African trip which survive are a remark made to Patrick Bedford that Hilton believed himself responsible for planting numerous peach groves in that country, for he was constantly throwing peach-stones out of the windows of trains onto the *veldt*; and a statement published in the magazine Commentary in 1943, where he said that cabaret 'brought home to me the tremendous power of direct contact with the audience, which became less in the theatre, with its remoteness; and I felt that the technique of the variety stage would help to bridge this gap. I consider the variety stage to be the only legitimate theatre. I have been greatly influenced by this experience. But when I returned to London, I found . . . that the people from the Old Vic with whom I associated were more concerned in plays of historical interest than those likely to prove long in run. The last two plays which I did before I came to Ireland were Lawrence's *David* and, under my old producer Atkins, with Jean Forbes-Robertson, a Jewish play called *The Dybbuk* at the Royalty Theatre.'

Then came the McMaster tour, his meeting with Micheál MacLíammóir in Enniscorthy, his illness, and the visit to Cork. Here they sought the director of the Cork Broadcasting Station, Seán Neeson, who, with his wife Geraldine, introduced Hilton to Ernest Wates of the Pavilion ciné-variety theatre where he was given a week's singing engagement and Micheál to Sydney Gilbert who quickly arranged for an exhibition in the gallery of the family department store in Patrick Street. The takings amounted to almost £30, and this helped them through most of the summer of 1927. Hilton left Cork for Dublin wearing a shirt loaned by Seán Neeson; in later years the Neeson home became the social centre for Dublin Gate Theatre seasons at the Cork Opera House.

In Dublin Hilton sang for Tony Reddin at the Capitol; in 1992 the soprano, Renée Flynn, remembered him in a gypsy scene wearing a coloured headband, with curtain-rings dangling from his ears, rendering the spirited baritone number 'In My Caravan'. He also sang at the Corinthian on Aston's Quay, where there was a very shallow stage and singers appearing before the front-cloth had only two feet in which to manoeuvre. He had a week's engagement at the Opera House in Derry; and all the time he and Micheál were talking of the German expressionists, of Copeau and the Pitoëffs, of O'Neill and the new American drama, which seemed to be so greatly influenced by J.M. Synge and T.C. Murray, of the play which MacLíammóir was now completing in Irish called *Diarmuid agus Gráinne*, and of their own new theatre.

Chapter 4

Galway and Dublin

Geraldine Neeson, official piano accompanist at the Cork Broadcasting Station where her husband, Seán, was director, described 'the lads', as they came to know them, as arriving at their house 'like a whirlwind'. In an article in the Cork Examiner she said that Micheál was 'as beautiful as a young god' and that Hilton was endowed 'with exuberant spirit and all-embracing gestures' – diplomatically implying that perhaps he was somewhat less prepossessing. Her son, the writer, Eoin Neeson, recalling much later visits, remarked that the house would be 'bubbling with excitement' even after they had left. They certainly must have cut a dash, as the saying went, but for the time being this had to be in the small towns of the west, whence Anew McMaster's autumn and winter tour took them, except for a brief fortnight's respite on the stage of the Abbey Theatre in December.

While playing in Galway they met Líam O Bríain, the dynamic young professor of romance languages at the university. He was a member of a committee which aimed to form an entirely Irish-speaking theatre in the city; funds were – astonishingly – available for the purpose. There were two difficulties: no Irish-speaking actors, and no indigenous plays. O Bríain, like everyone else, believed that MacLíammóir was a native Irish speaker; had he known that he was not, it would hardly have mattered, for enthusiasm was the order of the day. The proposition was that MacLíammóir should select players from Irish-speaking amateur groups and produce the plays, as well as supervise the equipping of the building which had been purchased in Middle Street, and which would be called the Taibhdheardhc – the 'place of magic', 'illusion' or 'wonder'. O Bríain and his colleagues would translate mainly European plays, until Irish writers emerged.

It was an offer as full of imponderables as it was unexpected. On a sudden impulse, Professor O Bríain asked if Hilton Edwards would also join in the project . . . ? By the time the McMaster tour ended in June 1928 they had both decided to accept – but Hilton nevertheless went to London to talk to his friend Peter Godfrey about the intricacies of raising funds and planning a programme for the new company which he and Micheál were forming in Dublin, on the lines of the one which Godfrey was successfully running in London, and which they were resolved to name, by way of homage to Godfrey's initiative, the Gate.

In Galway, the committee took the imaginative decision to open their new theatre with a new play, and Micheál MacLíammóir's *Diarmuid agus Gráinne* was accepted with acclamation. He cast himself in the leading part, and designed the settings and costumes. Several of the young people whom he selected for the company later proceeded to professional careers in the theatre or into the artistic life of the six-year-old state. Proinnsias MacDiarmada, who succeeded him as producer at the Taibhdheardhc, in due course became one of the longest-serving directors at the Abbey; he was a member of the army's Irish-speaking batallion and an enthusiastic amateur actor at the time he was cast as Oisín in *Diarmuid agus Gráinne*. The Gráinne was Máire ni Scolaidhe, a well-known *sean nós* ('old-style') singer. Mairtín O Direáin, who became one of the foremost exemplars of the modern school of Irish poetry, had a minor rôle; and Líam O Bríain, not to be excluded by any means, was cast as Fionn MacCumhail. A large company of supporting players was selected.

There was tremendous excitement at the opening performance on 27 August 1928: a new theatre, the first and only theatre dedicated to the presentation of plays in Irish, and a brand new play in the same language; it looked as if the oft-ridiculed language-revival movement, and the clause in the constitution of the new state which enshrined Irish as its first language, were being justified in a highly significant way. The Governor-General and Mrs McNeill were present to add distinction to the occasion. It is possible that any play, in which the actors remembered the words and the scenery did not actually collapse, would have been well received in that euphoric atmosphere. It is equally probable that most of those present did not appreciate that *Diarmuid agus Gráinne* was very much a play of the modern European movement, indeed highly derivative of a number of strands of that movement, although its story was taken from Celtic mythology; and that the settings and costumes, while certainly 'Celtic', interpreted Celticism in a contemporary way – very much in the manner whereby the old Russian legends had been given a new visual charge in the work of Bakst, Benois, Golovin and others. What remained to be seen was whether the impetus subscribed to the new institution by the work of two highly innovative young professionals would be sustained; Hilton Edwards had doubts about the ability of amateurs, no matter how dedicated, to continue in the way they had begun.

While masterminding the stage arrangements before rehearsals began, Hilton was travelling to and from Galway, speaking at rotary clubs and seeking subscriptions from anyone who would listen to his pleas for support for the outlandish theatre which he was planning in Dublin. There were no state or municipal financing agencies upon which he could draw for this highly experimental kind of project. Micheál – while designing the décors for *Diarmuid agus Gráinne*, and studying his own very large part in it – was also making designs for *Peer Gynt*, with which they hoped to inaugurate their Dublin company. They decided to take the Peacock, the small and under-used theatre attached to the Abbey; Madam Daisy Bannard Cogley, an active member of the labour movement, who ran a theatre club at 29 Harcourt Street, and Gearóid O Lochlainn, a drama enthusiast in the Department of Education, agreed to become what was grandiosely referred to as their 'patrons'.

For three years after the opening of the Dublin Gate Theatre Studio at the Peacock Theatre, Micheál MacLíammóir continued to work for the Taibhdheardhc – he needed the salary for one thing – and he had to travel to Galway as often as three times a week, remaining there for concentrated periods when opening nights were approaching or when he was taking part in one of the productions. He appeared as Pierrot in his own translation of Granville Barker's *Prunella*, with Máire ní Scolaidhe in the title rôle and Proinnsias MacDiarmada as the Statue of Love. The Connacht Tribune described MacDiarmada as 'a national army soldier who stuck to his post with a perfection of posture which must have taxed his resources to the utmost'; it was an ironical piece of casting, for MacLíammóir was said, in the graphic jargon of the day, to have a 'crush' on this amateur actor on loan from the barracks, and with whom he later had a bitter falling-out.

MacLíammóir also directed and designed Douglas Hyde's *An Pósadh* with two other one-act plays, and he wrote a short comedy called *Lúlu* 'representing the tribulations of a Galway household containing two unmarried daughters and a gouty father . . . A short, easily staged, play', according to the Irish Statesman. He directed and took the leading rôle of a gallant airman in *Bean an Ghaisgidhig*, adapted from the Spanish of Martinez Sierra. A year after the inauguration of the Taibhdheardhc, he told the editor of the Tribune that his great difficulty was in finding new plays in Irish. Of the dozens read, only one (*Cór in Aghaidh an Chaim* by Micheál Breathnach) had been judged as suitable for stage presentation. He said that the only faults in the theatre administration were the advertising and booking system, 'which should be completely reorganised'. He added, 'I see no reason why it should ever look back now that it has been extablished.'

His last production at the Taibhdheardhc (until he returned for its twenty-fifth anniversary) was *Arms and the Man*. Shaw wrote to him authorising the translation – *Gaisce agus Gaisgidneacht* – in which Micheál was a flamboyant Sergius; but by now even a part-time advisory relationship with the Galway theatre had become impossible. He continued his involvement with Irish-language drama with a Dublin group known as An Comhar Dramaíochta, which was given the hospitality of the Gate stage for over thirty productions.

A COAT OF PEACOCK COLOURS

The dream of Hilton Edwards and Micheál MacLíammóir came true on 14 October 1928. Hilton had collected the nucleus of a company, which consisted of himself and Micheál, Coralie Carmichael, who had bravely decided to forego the regular salary of the next McMaster tour, and May Carey, an English actress married to a senior civil servant, who magnanimously declared that her contribution to the Gate would be that she would perform without payment: seven years later she was ruefully admitting that she had been just a little too generous. Her son Denis, later a West End director, appeared as a child in the crowd of *Peer Gynt*, which also contained several other young people who would make their mark on the Dublin stage.

No Irish company had ever mounted a production of *Peer Gynt* before, probably because it required an enormous cast and several stage settings. It was either an extraordinarily enterprising choice or a foolhardy one, whichever way one chose to look at it, and most people took the latter view. Hilton Edwards already had a close understanding of the text, for he had appeared in two tiny parts in Robert Atkins' production at the Old Vic when he was nineteen; he also had the feeling that Atkins' production was 'all wrong', and that such a play of its nature did not require a series of heavily naturalistic scenes: he believed everything should be suggested through movement and lighting, against MacLíammóir's 'angular black steps' which at some little stretch of the imagination in this context could be taken for the mountains of Norway, or indeed anywhere.

Hilton also played the part of Peer. Micheál was unable to appear, due to commitments in Galway, but he was at the opening night. He wrote in *All for Hecuba* that 'the applause was spontaneous and frantic. At least it was as frantic as one hundred and one pairs of hands could make it' – and he wondered if the ensuing acclamation was just people 'being charming about it all?' Evidently it was not. C.P. Curran, the most influential critic of the day, referred to Hilton Edwards' 'great skill' as a director – probably unaware that he had never directed a play on his own before. Many of the reviewers wrote in admiration of the lighting, noting in particular 'the silhouette effects' which were to become a feature – and in the course of time something of a cliché – in Gate productions. An Londubh ('The Blackbird') wrote in The Irishman that he had 'seldom seen as perfect a piece of stagecraft where acting, light and music combined'. The first Gate venture was an undoubted success – but the company was already in rehearsal for its second, the British Isles première of O'Neill's *The Hairy Ape*, and there was no time to pause and bask in the warmth of surprised adulation.

MacLíammóir took care to be available for the part of Diarmuid in his English translation of his own play, though it meant rehearsing concurrently with *Prunella* in Galway. The fourth play of the Gate's first season was Wilde's *Salomé*, which had never been professionally performed in the United Kingdom, due to the Lord Chamberlain's ban – ostensibly because of its representation of biblical characters.

Most of the critics, and in particular C.P. Curran, 'An Londubh', and Samuel Beckett's friend, A.J. Leventhal, saw at once that the Gate Theatre Studio productions at the Peacock were no mere effusion of high-minded artistic intentions unbraced by technical skill. These three critics remained consistently supportive of the 'movement', as they saw it, recognising that it was professional as well as provocative; at times, like all genuine well-wishers, they were quite stern in their condemnation of any lowering of standards or lapse in taste. There was a great deal to astonish. Firstly, the repertoire, which was carefully balanced, novel and eclectic. Secondly, there was a serious visual interpretation of the texts. Thirdly, 'production' clearly meant much more than simply telling the actors where to stand or sit, or how to move about without distracting attention from whatever else was going on.

Looking back on his early design work in an article in The Leader in 1938, MacLíammóir wrote, 'I started out and made a lot of coloured designs, pleasant enough, I hope, and showing certain qualities of pattern and colour and dramatic value, a certain inventiveness, and not a little economy, thank God, for we had hardly a penny.' He said that Hilton Edwards, 'who combined a practical sense with a rigidity of theory alarmingly purist in one so young' was greatly in favour of what was then called 'symbolic' scenery, such as the famous black steps. He went on to say that his painterly instinct often took over, and this was a mistake, because he was mixing the idea of significant shapes with that of something approaching pictorial realism – the very thing he had set out to avoid.

His conclusion, therefore, was that his *Peer Gynt* design was not a success. He then proceeded to enumerate the artistic and practical pitfalls of the conventional stage setting: 'A collapsing backcloth, a door that has got stuck, or a fireplace that totters to ruin at some touching moment in the third act, will often create more sensation than the most subtle design ever conceived, and will be used in the daily papers . . . to make cruel jokes about the audible bad language of the hero when the heavily barred door of his dungeon swings lightly open during his best speech on the miseries of incarceration. . . . ' The progenitors of revolutionary movements in the arts, or in any other branch of human endeavour, cannot often be credited with a strong sense of humour – often very much the same thing as a sense of proportion; one of the great strengths of both Edwards and MacLíammóir at the time of their youthful pioneering work in a Dublin notably scant in artistic innovation, was their willingness to perceive themselves as others saw them, and to laugh when the spirit took them, which was often. Serious in their objectives, they were never solemn.

The English version of *Diarmuid and Gráinne* was well received, though without the rapture of Galway ; C.P. Curran said, 'The play brims over with metaphors and magniloquence, but is buoyed up triumphantly with the surge of genuine emotion.' He added that there had been nothing like this for twenty years: if he was to be taken literally, he was saying that there had been nothing like this since *The Playboy of the Western World*. A questioning note enters Lady Gregory's diary at this date, for she went to see the play in the Peacock, which was part of the premises of her own theatre: 'It was *Diarmuid and Grania* [*sic*] by Michael [*sic*] MacLíammóir – beautifully staged and lighted; no plot, just the simple story of Finn and the lovers. Simple language, a straight story, very moving. It had been given in Irish in Galway and very successfully there. A new departure. I felt far more in sympathy with it than with the *Big House* [by Lennox Robinson] next door.' She well might have been wondering about this new wave of talent, for MacLíammóir had only been cast once, and in a very poor part, at the Abbey; and she had just rejected a new play by a young man called Denis Johnston, and Johnston had called at the theatre asking for the £50 which he said Yeats had promised to help stage it elsewhere – which would be the Gate at the Peacock; she thought the £50 'a bad precedent'.

Six months later, in May 1929, Lady Gregory took Yeats to see *The Unknown Warrior* by Paul Raynal – 'beautifully acted by MacLíammóir. I scribbled a note on the programme and sent it round, asking him to lunch as Yeats would like to meet him. He answered, accepting, and in reference to Yeats he says, "I must thank you for giving me an opportunity that I have desired for sixteen years". They got on very well at lunch, especially as to visions . . . ' MacLíammóir's version of the encounter, published in *All for Hecuba* in 1946, says 'I was a little late from rehearsal [for *Tristram and Iseult* by J.H. Pollock, known as 'An Philibín'] and when I was shown into the familiar room, he rose to his feet, tall and slow and stately, as grey as time, as vague and as vivid as a dream, and advancing with a curiously hesitating step, his right hand raised as if in benediction, he said, "You told Lady Gregory you had wanted to meet me for fourteen [*sic*] years: you are exactly fourteen minutes late." I said it had seemed like forty, to which I naturally expected he would ask, "years or minutes?", to which in turn I would have said, like Lady Bracknell, "Both, if necessary, I presume", but he wouldn't play up so early in the day and, sinking into his chair, he murmured: *"You are a magnificent actor"*.'

Nothing tangible came of this encounter, except perhaps that MacLíammóir was invited to create the part of Michael Love in Lennox Robinson's *Ever the Twain* at the Abbey the following October. Lady Gregory, who described the play as *We Twain*, and the actor as 'Diarmuid' MacLíammóir – presumably because of the character in his own play – wrote in her journal that he was 'the best, among all good'. His performance came to the attention of Dorothy Macardle, a young writer who was at that time a teacher of English at Alexandra College – she later published a standard reference work, *The Irish Republic* – who wrote in The Nation, 'We see Micheál MacLíammóir as Michael Love the Irish poet out to win dollars, roguishly playing the rôle he is paid to play . . . . A kind of intellectual merriment is provoked, and the whole thing is so entertaining, one listened without asking for action, climax or plot . . . Michael Love posing as Michael Love, and finding that the other pose is almost the reality, is in the true Pirandellan vein.' Miss Macardle, as well as being a perceptive critic, must have been blessed with the gift of prophecy, for MacLíammóir was to become much engrossed with Pirandellan themes in his own plays at a much later date.

As the Gate programme at the Peacock became more and more assured, and as the demands on energy required to keep the programme running each year from September until June became more pressing, MacLíammóir and Edwards – as well as Coralie Carmichael and May Carey, joined soon by Meriel Moore and Betty Chancellor – appeared less and less frequently with other managements. The first of an annual series of fund-raising balls was given at the Plaza on 27 November 1928. The Evening Mail reported that 'the leading lady of the Gate Theatre, Miss Coralie Carmichael, came in a frock of moonlight blue and black lace', and listed Sir Thomas and Lady Miles, Lady Hemphill, the Hon. Gordon and Mrs Campbell, Mr and Mrs Seán McEntee, Miss Nora McGuinness, Mrs Heron . . . ' as being present; observers of the Irish social scene would have been quick to notice the unusual mixture of *ancien* and *nouveau régime*, the Anglo-Irish nobility, the Protestant middle-class, the rising commercial sector, newly elected deputies of the Free State parliament, the Dublin arts circle (Mrs Heron, Samuel Beckett's aunt, fitted into three of these categories). If Denis Johnston had not already written his poetic satire *The Old Lady Says 'No!'* one would be tempted to believe that he had obtained much of his inspiration at this curious gathering. Only four months after the Gate's first production, the Daily Express Dublin correspondent reported that at their first nights 'cabinet ministers and Supreme Court judges rub shoulders with poets, artists and writers. Peers and labour leaders exchange criticisms in the lobby, where one hears half-a-dozen languages spoken in the interval . . . ' Hyperbole of course, but the Gate became a synonym for hyperbole.

The critics pounced on the poor speaking of many of the small-part players in *Salomé*, but the leading actors and the production were praised, and the bravery of the choice. An Londubh wrote of Coralie Carmichael, who played Salomé, 'I have seldom watched finer poise or heard better intonation. Hilton Edwards [Herod] managed to get an extremely unreal character across, giving us the Roman puppet . . . ' Ibsen, O'Neill, MacLíammóir and Wilde (as well as Nicolai Evreinov, whose short play *The Theatre of the Soul* was billed with *Salomé* and described by C.P. Curran as 'a feeble attempt at symbolic drama') formed the sequence up to Christmas, and plays by Leo Tolstoy, Elmer Rice, Karel Capek, Paul Raynal, 'An Philibín' (J.H. Pollock) and two newcomers, David Sears and 'E.W. Tocher' – whom all Dublin knew to be Denis Johnston – were announced for the spring and early summer of 1929. The first play of 1929, however, was a new American work, *Six Stokers Who Own the Bloomin' Earth* by Elmer Greensfelder, which C.P. Curran dismissed because 'it combines the well-known vices of (1) the allegorical play, (2) the thesis play, (3) the propaganda play. It might appeal to the less experienced infants in a foreign section of a New York ethical Sunday School.' He was gaily demolishing pretentiousness, that pervading weakness of the experimental theatre. (It is revealing to note that neither Edwards nor MacLíammóir cast themselves in *Six Stokers*.)

Hilton Edwards as Chris Christopherson in O'Neill's *Anna Christie*, and Coralie Carmichael as Anysia in Tolstoy's *The Power of Darkness* came out best in the reviews of plays performed during the spring of 1929; Micheál MacLíammóir designed all of them, but was still chiefly engaged in directing or acting in Galway. He was in the Gate's first original play (if *Diarmuid and Gráinne* is discounted), David Sears' *Juggernaut*, an early attempt to deal with the effect of the 'troubles' of 1922 on the middle-classes. It also provides the earliest example of the critics using the Gate as a stick with which to beat the Abbey – the National Theatre. This debate was re-opened in June, when Denis Johnston's *The Old Lady Says 'No!'* was first produced by the Gate company; it has continued in Irish literary and theatrical circles ever since, just as the rights and wrongs of the Abbey's initial decision not to produce Seán O'Casey's 'expressionist' play, *The Silver Tassie*, in the previous year is still a matter for heated argument.

Denis Johnston was a Dubliner of Ulster-Presbyterian ancestry, educated in Dublin, Edinburgh and Cambridge, and called to the bar in 1925. It was not customary for members of the legal profession to use their names for non-legal activities, so he took the pseudonym E.W. Tocher, borrowed, he said, from a poster advertising a mission given by a visiting preacher of that name. He submitted his first play to the Abbey Theatre. Its rejection led to its title, for Johnston found a note scribbled on the envelope saying, in reference to Lady Gregory, 'The old lady says "no"'. The actress Shelah Richards, who was Johnston's first wife, recalled the incident in an unpublished memoir: 'In recent years he has denied how his famous first play got its final name, but this is my own recollection of the matter. He had written a play which he called at one time *Symphony in Green* and at another time *Shadowdance*, and under one of those names he had submitted it to the Abbey. Its fate was to be decided at a directors' meeting one night, and I remember seeing Lennox Robinson coming down the stairs after the meeting.' (Shelah Richards was appearing as Cordelia in *King Lear*, Denis Johnston's earliest Abbey production.) 'I quickly went over and asked him, "Well, what about it? Are they going to do Denis's play?" And he shook his head sadly and said, 'The old lady says "no"'.

These stories were current in Dublin at the time of the first production, and they were a valuable peg on which to hang the Gate's promotional material. Irritated by the reference to the 'old lady', Robinson wrote to Johnston after the play's second production at the Gate, saying 'I habitually spoke of her as "Lady Gregory" though some people, Jack Yeats for instance, might speak of her as "Aunt Augusta" . . . The point is . . . she was in favour of the play being done, rather strongly if I remember rightly and it is hard lines that she should be saddled with the blame.' The fact is, Lady Gregory was *not* in favour of the play being done at the Abbey. The decision was a Board one; but in her journal (not published until 1987) she noted that she, Yeats and Robinson read only the first two acts – 'we were all satisfied it would not be worth producing. Just as well, for we should have been worried by criticism.'

Perhaps indeed, if the Abbey *had* produced the play, there would have been 'criticism' from the many sections of Irish society which were pilloried in it – but the Abbey had withstood criticism from political, religious and other quarters with a superb sense of artistic dignity in the past. This rejection should therefore have been attributed to an error of judgement, for there was no basis for the feeble excuse later put about that they did not have the right facilities for this kind of work: they could have obtained them. Be that as it may, the Abbey's difficulty was the Gate's opportunity. Hilton Edwards seized upon the script and found that, like most of the innovative Irish drama, it had its stylistic roots in Europe rather than in England – in this case the romantic expressionism of Germany; if Micheál MacLíammóir the playwright was close cousin to Maurice Maeterlinck, Denis Johnston was a near relation of Ernst Toller. He found in it opportunities for massed effects of movement, choral speaking and shadow play; he found a rhythm in the speech which he arranged for tympani; he devised a lighting plot which counterpointed the vocal and musical rhythms, and, without the aid of a computerised board, his electrician, who must have had four hands with ten fingers on each, followed it without error. (Years later in New York, with electronic aids and a full staff, the cues were invariably mistimed.)

The Old Lady Says 'No!' opens as a parody of a sentimental nineteenth century historical melodrama in which the patriot Robert Emmet comes to woo his beloved Sarah Curran; one of the actors playing a soldier clubs the Emmet actor too realistically, rendering him unconscious; the play cannot proceed, and a member of the cast calls for a doctor from the audience. (A member of the company has been planted – but many times real doctors helpfully made their way to the stage.) The rest of the play is a series of hallucinatory incidents, tracing the journey of the concussed actor/Emmet on his peregrination through the pages of Irish history and mythology, and the streets and salons of the post-revolutionary Dublin of the 1920s. In an article in The Bell in 1948 Edwards wrote that it was still the finest work written for the Irish theatre since his own arrival in Dublin in 1927; 'It is marred a little by obscurity. This is the hall-mark of the period. In the twenties we credited the audience with the kind of intelligence few of them claimed . . . But the play has genuine greatness, real power to move, and leaves a lasting impression; more, it has humour. How could it be otherwise in a man reared among the cave-boys and girls of Dublin's intelligentsia? Their motto is: "Don't look; smite with your laughter, and back to the cave unless you are trapped into admiration or respect" . . . ' In a much quoted phrase, Edwards also said that the play 'read like a railway guide and played like *Tristan and Isolde*'.

Micheál MacLíammóir was cast as the Speaker – the actor who plays Emmet; Coralie Carmichael was not considered suitable for the principal female figure, who has to be the romantic personification of Hibernia transformed into a harridan Cathleen ní Houlihan in the guise of a sharp-tongued Dublin flower-seller. Hilton Edwards had probably noticed Meriel Moore in a Sunday night Drama League performance of *The Cherry Orchard* on 29 February – it is unlikely that he would have missed what would then have been a rare opportunity of seeing Chekhov. Denis Johnston had worked with her, and arranged for Hilton and Micheál to meet her at his parents' home in Lansdowne Road. She was an extremely pretty brunette, came from a prosperous south Dublin family, had already toured in England, and was not at all the gifted amateur which so many of the Drama League players turned out to be. She liked (she said) country life, trees, mountains and dogs; she disliked towns, dress rehearsals and cats. She had been impressed by the Gate productions, and was eager to take part in one. She was quite capable of playing the two aspects of the leading rôle and, as matters turned out, she played with the company regularly for twenty years, with engagements now and again in the West End and Hollywood. The Sarah Curran/Flower seller in *The Old Lady Says 'No!'* was her first major rôle; and the rôle of the Speaker was the major rôle with which Micheál MacLíammóir was to be identified for thirty years.

The Old Lady Says 'No!' was the play the Gate had been looking for. Its opening night on 19 June 1929 caused a real sensation – much more so than the company's first production, *Peer Gynt*. Many more persons than the diminutive Peacock auditorium could possibly have held have since claimed to have been present. Rutherford Mayne, then the *doyen* of Irish playwrights, wrote to Denis Johnston to say, 'You have written one of the most original plays I have ever seen and used a new form of expression of stage techniques in a masterly way . . . I couldn't help going behind to congratulate Edwards and MacLíammóir on a most wonderful production. It is a delight to an old stager to see youth rising with all such brilliant talent to light up Irish drama . . . ' A.J. Leventhal, who was, if anything, a young stager among the *cognoscenti*, wrote to Johnston after the play had been running at the Peacock for four weeks – a long run for that time, even in a theatre of small capacity – to say that he had not read the reviews, and had come expecting 'a well-made play on the subject of Robert Emmet'. 'I fortified myself with a cocktail to put up with yet another interpretation of Ireland's whims and woes. What a shock I had! Instead of whimsicalities (which are in the tradition) I found witticisms, and instead of heroics I got dynamics . . . I do feel that you can do for English [*sic*] drama what Joyce has done for the novel . . . ' Certainly nothing of this kind had been produced in England by a native writer. It is revealing to compare Johnston the dramatist, with Mainie Jellett, the painter, who was exhibiting cubist work in Dublin long before English painters had adapted the style to their particular vision.

Whether Hilton Edwards and Micheál MacLíammóir fully understood the magnitude of their discovery is open to question, but, even if they did, they could hardly sit back and boast about it, for their work had to proceed. They had proved that Ireland was willing to see, as they expressed it in a memorandum to potential subscribers, 'the work of other writers and other countries, if only to further her understanding and appreciation of her own'. In order to do this they had to find premises: they had an office in an old house in South William Street, and the Peacock Theatre was not their own. With the help of Michael Scott, an architect with a talent for acting who had appeared in the crowd in *The Old Lady Says 'No!'*, they obtained a lease on the Rotunda Assembly Rooms, a handsome hall designed by Richard Johnston in 1785 as part of the complex of buildings in the grounds of the Rotunda Hospital, built to house the concerts, routs and *soirées* which were organised to keep the hospital in funds. Hilton Edwards had remarked on the fine seven-bay façade with its classical columns and pediment when they had stayed in the small hotel opposite on one of their visits to Dublin from the McMaster tours; it had the advantage of being centrally situated at the north end of O'Connell Street. Michael Scott built a raked floor in the auditorium, achieved an 'end-stage' effect rather than a proscenium arch, by removing a wall and placing the stage in what would have been the adjoining salon, and also providing a small forestage so that intimacy was created between actors and audience. There was a small, curtained side-stage for musicians. The superb eighteenth century plasterwork gave an air of opulence and occasion – for Hilton was quite sure he did not want their theatre to be one of those 'gloomy sheds or caverns', which tended to be associated with productions of contemporary drama.

Denis Johnston, in some unpublished notes for an article on the Dublin theatres, observed that in spite of the reconstruction of the building, the ceiling of the scene-dock was lower than the height of the standard stage flats, which therefore had to be slanted for painting or storage, and that it was impossible to get previously-constructed sets in from the street because of the narrow doorway and staircase. (He also drew attention to the fact that in the Peacock no entrance could be made from stage-left because there was a wall, and that in the Abbey no important action could take place stage right – so much for Dublin's magnificent tradition of theatre!) While the Rotunda Assembly Rooms were being converted, a pageant drama, *The Ford of the Hurdles*, was written by Micheál MacLíammóir and presented in the Round Room of the Mansion House for the committee of the Dublin Civic Week in September 1929; and this was followed by a revival of *Diarmuid and Gráinne* at the same venue. The whole autumn was spent in decorating and equipping the new theatre. On the way from their office in William Street to the Gate, Hilton and Micheál often called in backstage during Anew McMaster's rehearsals at the Abbey, which he had taken in order to present Mrs Patrick Campbell in *Macbeth* and *Ghosts*. 'Mrs Pat' was McMaster's greatest idol after the 'Divine Sarah' ('She's a fiend, dear, in what may have once been a human shape!'). She turned out to be far from word-perfect in either rôle ('You have to forgive a great actress if she . . . well, you just have to *overlook* these moments, that's all.') Mrs Pat believed that Mac starved the constitutionally thin Marjorie, and used to bring bananas to the theatre to feed her.

On 15 November Micheál, Hilton and Coralie travelled to Galway, where they gave a recital at the Taibhdheardhc in aid of their Dublin endeavours, ably assisted by Máire and Móna ní Scolaidhe who provided the local talent and, presumably, an accompanist, though none is mentioned in the Connacht Sentinel. Hilton sang arias from *Tannhäuser* and *Pagliacci*, three Shakespearian songs from his Old Vic repertoire, and several ballads. Micheál and Coralie did the closet scene from *Hamlet* (his first appearance in the part) and the wooing scene from *Diarmuid and Gráinne*, which the Galway public had not seen in English. There was an exhibition of step-dancing by the Misses Scolaidhe, and later in the programme they sang a selection of duets in Irish. Micheál performed the death of Romeo as a solo, and Hilton and Coralie appeared as the two Macbeths. It must have been a tiresome conglomeration, but the Sentinel dutifully deplored 'the lamentable fact that we do not get such treats so often'.

PROFESSIONALS AND MEDALLISTS

The Dublin Gate Theatre Company Ltd was incorporated on 24 December 1929, with Edwards, MacLíammóir, Daisy Bannard Cogley, Norman Reddin and the Hon. Gordon Campbell (later Lord Glenavy, husband of the painter, Beatrice, and father of the novelist Michael and the humorist, Patrick) as directors. The capital was quoted as £2,500 in £1 shares, and not all of these were taken up. The opening play, on 17 February 1930, was Goethe's *Faust*. Hilton Edwards had appeared as Frosch at the Old Vic in 1924: now he was Faust. MacLíammóir was Mephistopheles, with Coralie Carmichael as Margaret, Meriel Moore as the Mater Dolorosa and Betty Chancellor, another recruit from the Drama League, as Elizabeth. She was usually cast in comedy rôles – she had an apparently laconic, yet deftly sharp sense of timing; later she surprised everyone in dramatic parts, her great success being Jane Eyre. (In the parlour-game of Heavenly Parents, which appears to have been played repeatedly backstage, Betty's parents were nominated as Bo-Peep and Ivan the Terrible.) Like Meriel Moore she remained with the Gate for most of its productions over twenty years, with breaks in the other theatres and abroad. She was deaf, and had to be placed onstage where she could see the person who was to give her her next cue.

Hubert Duncombe, who appears to have been leading a fairly aimless existence wandering in Europe since the death of Mary O'Keefe in Menton, joined the company for the opening productions, and stayed, filling small parts until he went to the Cambridge Festival Theatre in 1931. The new auditorium was painted in bronze and black. A huge figure throwing open a symbolic gate was painted on the front curtain – this became the company's logogram. A quartet, consisting of Gretta Smith, Máirín O'Connor, Sidney Grief and Cathleen Rogers (the pianist) occupied the musicians' gallery. Music was selected by Hilton Edwards and arranged by Rhoda Coghill. The three hundred and fifty members of the first night audience, though very cold due to the failure of the heating system, were impressed by all these details, and by the signs on the lavatory doors done in a dozen different languages – *here* was cosmopolitanism if one was looking for it! C.P. Curran in the Irish Statesman was pleased that there was nothing in the *Faust* of Gounod, only of Goethe, and that the visual presentation dispensed with the accretions of naturalism: an arrangement of Gothic arches, in which the rapid succession of scenes was lucidly exposed.

The Irishman printed some 'helpful suggestions' – sixpence was too much for a cup of coffee, and threepence too much for the programme, no matter how beautifully printed. This provoked a letter from a reader who said that the critic could not have sat at the back of the stalls – 'if he had, he would certainly not have omitted from his list a complaint about the diabolical discomfort of the seats. They are hard, they are narrow, and they are exactly at the wrong angle to the floor. Whoever is responsible for them should be condemned to sit on them for three hours on end every night for a month.' (They remained until 1956.) No one seems to have complained about the price of these seats, which was 1/3d; the most expensive seats were 4/6d.

Now that the theatre was open, it behoved the directors to keep it open. A policy of presenting the British system of weekly repertory placed a great strain on the core of actors who played the leading parts – the minor parts were taken by students, mainly from the Dublin University Dramatic Society and the Elizabethan Society (the principal women's debating and dramatic group in Trinity College – women students were not allowed to join the 'DUDS') and the subsequent non-segregated Dublin University Players; and also from among the adherents of the Drama League (which the Irish Statesman of 30 March 1930 believed was becoming 'submerged' by the Gate). As well as these sources of unpaid talent, there were the 'Drumcondra medallists' – the originator of the epithet is unknown – who appear to have been members of a section of society which habitually entered for competitions in verse-speaking, ballad-singing and step-dancing, all of whom (it would seem) resided in the exceedingly dreary and genteel suburb of that name. These, and other enthusiasts, were certainly made good use of by Edwards and MacLíammóir. The students predominated, some of them becoming accepted as 'professionals', till at one time in the mid-1930s as many as six members of the company were recent Trinity graduates.

Twenty productions were given during the Gate Theatre's first year of operation, though four were of one-act plays, three were revivals of plays first given at the Peacock, and one was a Christmas revue. As early as April the Irish Independent was asking if this was too much for the company to sustain, also commenting that it was ' difficult to discover upon what principle the plays are chosen by the directors. It might appear that the only criterion is lighting effects.' This was a sharp blow to the midriff of Hilton Edwards. The same critic wrote of Kaiser's *Gas* in April, 'The simplification is overdone, and the curious thing is, while personalities are banished in favour of what the programme note calls "representative entities", these "representative entities" are much more voluble than human beings . . . ' This was a jab at Hilton Edwards' undoubtedly precious programme note. The writer was probably Mary Manning, though the articles are unsigned. When she became the Independent's principal critic she signed her reviews 'M.M.', infuriating Hilton Edwards with her comments on his programme-planning. One day he invited her to the theatre and told her he would 'like to take a whip and lash you across the shoulders!' Recalling this in 1993 she confessed to having been terrified; but they struck a bond of mutual accord – Hilton must have realised that she aspired to the highest standards in criticism and that her aim was to see such standards maintained in the institutions she admired – and the interview ended with an invitation to let him read the play which she said she was writing with the help of her friend Samuel Beckett. In due course Hilton produced the play, Mary became part-time editor of the Gate's house magazine, Motley, and a lifelong friendship with both Micheál and Hilton began – founded, no doubt, on mutual respect, and sharpened on the glinting edge of mockery – for all three were masters of the verbal thrust, especially when directed at others.

Mary Manning was not writing regularly at the time of the first production of *The Old Lady Says 'No!'* in the Peacock, but when the play was revived at the Gate two years later, she described it as 'the voice of Young Ireland. It is very loud, very disturbing, very insistent, but it must be heard . . . ' She said that Denis Johnston had 'shattered the Celtic Twilight at one blow'. This last remark may have sounded a disappointing note for MacLíammóir, who was raking the dying embers of the Celtic Twilight for himself with the sense of wonder of the Johnny-come-lately, but it did not deter him from continuing to write in that vein. In the year of *The Old Lady Says 'No!'* his collection of articles, reminiscences and short stories, *Lá agus Oíche* [*Day and Night*], was brought out by the Fallon publishing house, with assistance from Oifig an tSolathair, the government agency which encouraged literature in Irish. The uneven nature of the contents make it an unsatisfactory book, as if every short piece he had written, whether fact or fiction, had been thrown together to fill the space between the covers – but several of the items were to prove useful as source material for later work.

Mary Manning's anxiety about the resources of the company being overstretched were shared by its members; 'weekly rep' was soon replaced by 'fortnightly rep', and sighs of relief were breathed when a production was doing well enough to be retained for longer. This meant that dates of productions could not be announced very far in advance, but the public at that time seems to have been attuned to booking for the theatre rather on the spur of the moment.

The notion of the 'commercial' play was introduced in March of the first Gate season in its own premises, and with some trepidation on account of the company's self-drawn 'artistic' profile. Balderston and Squire's *Berkeley Square* was given on 3 March 1930 and might well have roused the indignation of the likes of Miss Manning and Mr Curran, but criticism was muted, for the performances and the production were seen to be more polished than what the Dublin public was accustomed to in similar plays on tour from the West End. The plot has a young man of the 20th century make a bodily visit to his ancestral home in the London of Reynolds and Garrick; it is well-constructed *kitsch,* and was revived in four seasons during the ensuing decade, as well as being received with rapture in such contrasting cities as Cork and Cairo.

The pleasures of Victorian melodrama were rediscovered a few weeks later with *Ten Nights in a Bar Room*; *Sweeney Todd* was produced in 1931, and *The Drunkard* in 1934. The approach was to provide a conscious transference of viewpoint, to 'cheer the hero and boo the villain' in the way the Victorian audience would have done – the idea being quite novel in 1930. The Irish Times rather meanly dismissed *Ten Nights* as 'typical of the Queen's or the Mechanics [Theatres] of the past', but Mary Manning in the Independent understood the intention and praised the show accordingly – especially 'Mr Edwards' striking ditty "Father's on the Engine", and Mr MacLíammóir's complacent simpers as he acknowledged every clap we gave him'. In 1931, in expectation of a handsome and much-needed box-office boost, *Ten Nights* was presented by the Gate in the very large Olympia Theatre; but Edwards and MacLíammóir were in for a shock, because what passed as sophisticated entertainment with their own *clientèle* was taken very seriously by quite a different kind of audience, who followed the story with close attention but failed to laugh at the sparkling *jeux d'esprit* of the presentation. It was the wrong theatre, and the wrong moment in theatrical history.

Ten years later, however, when they rather tentatively re-revived a much-revived Gate success, *The Drunkard,* at the sumptuous Gaiety Theatre, popular taste was found to have altered, and the big audience responded joyfully – especially when it discovered that Poppy La Vere, the heroine's mother, was played by a man: there was a gasp, and a voice from the gallery pronounced, 'Jaysus! It's Roy Irving!' Mr Irving, one of the ex-Trinity members of the company, then performed a can-can in a scarlet dress, while Hilton Edwards conducted the orchestra in *Oh! Listen to the Band!*, receiving a triple encore on the Saturday night, which Irving said nearly killed him – 'and then I had to appear in Heaven as Coralie's *late* mother, with wings!' In yet another revival at the Gate ten years later, it appeared that the joke was over; at one particularly dismal matinée, Hilton Edwards, irritated beyond endurance by the feeble reaction, announced, 'not a sinner among you is going home until you sing the chorus!' – and he threatened that Mr Coady, the front-of-house manager, would lock the doors of the theatre until they gave a better account of themselves. It was like a parody of Yeats telling the Abbey audience that it had disgraced itself again.

MONEY

The matter of state funding for artistic enterprise was debated in Dáil Eireann, the Irish parliament, on 29 May 1930. To date the only government money voted for the theatre had gone to the Abbey and the Taibhdheardhc – the latter under the heading of 'assistance to Irish language activities'. Mr Seán McEntee (Fíanna Fáil, South Dublin) stated, 'In regard to the Abbey Theatre, there is another theatre established in Dublin recently, and it is doing substantial work for the drama.' McEntee and his family were patrons of the Gate, and he felt that 'the grant should be divided between the two theatres.' The Minister for Finance, Mr Ernest Blythe, curtly replied: 'The Abbey has made it possible for the Gate to be established.' He surmised that if money were to be provided in future for the encouragement of the writing and production of plays, 'it ought to be for plays in Irish.'

Edwards and MacLíammóir were discovering just how problematic it was to run a theatre purely from the box-office. They had difficulties in paying for regular services such as electricity and advertising; and they did not have anyone whose complete attention could be given to budgeting and accounting. Fancy-dress balls, and a series of garden parties with music provided by Miss Bay Jellett – sister of the painter Mainie Jellett – and her trio in a marquee, did not bring in very much money.

The most elaborate production of 1930, and the most prodigal of resources, was *Back to Methuselah*, Bernard Shaw's 'metabiological pentateuch'. The theatre was closed for two weeks prior to its first night on 23 October, so that the whole cycle of three full evenings of drama could be adequately rehearsed. Season tickets were on offer, and vouchers for dinner in a nearby restaurant. No other theatre in Ireland, and few in the world, would have taken on such a challenging work. Contemporary witnesses spoke of 'staggering home' at the conclusion of the cycle. – 'Never know whether I'm rehearsing Confucius or the Snake!', MacLíammóir remarked to a reporter from the Daily Express. 'We rehearse all day and we act at night. When we go home we learn our lines for the next play. Besides rehearsing ourselves, Hilton is directing, and I am designing scenes and costumes, and haranguing scene-shifters.' What the reporter may not have appreciated was that what he was saying applied not only to the extraordinary *Back to Methuselah*, but to everything they did.

Their next play was *A Flutter of Wings* by T.C. Murray. Like *The Son of Learning* by Austin Clarke earlier in the year, it was an Abbey reject, and it is easy to see why; few of the National Theatre's rejections turned out to be of the quality of *The Old Lady Says 'No!'*. This was followed in December by a project as imaginative in concept as *Back to Methuselah – The Merchant of Venice* played on alternate nights with St John Ervine's *The Lady of Belmont*, a sullen comedy, which attempts to show what happened ten years after the famous trial with its innocently pastoral aftermath: roistering and marital infidelity, according to Ervine. The reviews were generally favourable, but the Irish Times noted that 'there was a lamentably small audience'. When the first Annual General Meeting was held before Christmas it was disclosed that £1,200 worth of shares were as yet unsold, and that there was a deficit on the running costs of £700 (approximately £23,000 at 1993 values) – it would have been much greater, if so many people had not given their services backstage and front-of-house as 'voluntary labour'. Hilton Edwards, as Chairman, was nominally responsible; Gordon Campbell, who was secretary to the Department of Industry and Commerce and the only member of the Board with financial training, was completely aware of the consequences, as was the solicitor, Norman Reddin. The Gate Theatre would have to close.

This, to Edwards, MacLíammóir and Madam Cogley, was not only unthinkable; it was heresy. It is probable that the meeting would have been adjourned for further consultation, had not one of the £1 shareholders, Edward Arthur Henry Pakenham, Sixth Earl of Longford, struggled to his feet – he was unusually portly, not to say gross, for a man of twenty-seven – and offered to buy all the remaining shares. (It is significant that he did not offer to clear the deficit.) What is usually described in legal dramas as 'sensation in court' must have followed. It was known who he was, that he was extremely rich, and that he was not the kind of person to make magniloquent pronouncements and deny them the next day. He was also known as one of the few Irish peers who had decided to support wholeheartedly the institutions of the new state. He had even gone to the trouble of learning the Irish language, and had withstood the scorn of those who declared that he spoke it with an Oxford accent; he was frequently to be seen in the counties adjacent to Pakenham Hall, his family seat, presenting prizes for agricultural endeavour and prowess in rural crafts, folk music and Gaelic games. He and Lady Longford, who could have been described as a 'bluestocking' and would have appreciated the term, had attended most of the Gate productions. In buying the outstanding shares, Lord Longford immediately became the major shareholder. He was elected chairman of the Board the following year.

The theatre, of its nature, is a place of tensions; but the morning's disagreement is usually forgotten at the rise of curtain; and the slights and jealousies of members of a closely integrated company, which has been formed by friends who continue as colleagues, are not often of great moment. It is when those in control of the administration of such a company become a prey to slights and jealousies, and these in turn develop into public expressions of increasingly divergent views, affecting corporate outlook and policy, that danger for the whole institution is signalled. The presence of the civilised, well-intentioned and industrious Longfords created the first real tensions in the life of the Gate – tensions which were to explode within five years, with lasting consequences for everybody. Yet, for the time being, the company could hardly have been happier, more zestful, more hardworking or more relieved at their rescue from the brink of liquidation.

Chapter 5
Brilliant but Dangerous

Christine and Edward Longford were contemporaries of Hilton Edwards and Micheál MacLíammóir, MacLíammóir being the eldest, Christine a year younger, Edward two and a half years younger than she, and Hilton a year younger than Edward. The Fifth Earl of Longford had been killed at Gallipoli, Edward inheriting the title at fourteen, while still at Eton. He had been brought up chiefly at North Aston Hall in Oxfordshire, and proceeded to Christ Church, Oxford, where he met the twenty-one-year-old Christine Trew, who was up at Somerville. Their biographer, John Cowell, says that Christine used to describe herself as being 'as old as the century – and I was born in Cheddar, where the cheese comes from.' She said that she was 'quite disconnected, like the Bennets in *Pride and Prejudice*, middle-class, though my mother would never admit it. Upper-middle, if you like, but certainly middle, with the claim to gentility that is so common in England.' She had a grandmother from County Cork – a real one, not an invention like MacLíammóir's Cork forebears; she told John Cowell that she was always 'passionately interested in Ireland'. While at Oxford she became a peripheral member of the Garsington circle – not a bit overawed by Lady Ottoline Morrell, and somewhat attached to Bertrand Russell; she met E.M. Forster, Lytton Strachey and W.B. Yeats there.

There is a curious resemblance in the early photographs of Christine Longford to Mary O'Keefe, though perhaps it is only because of what are, after all, period features – the bobbed hair, the cloche hat – but both certainly possess an intellectual look, and both seem rather careless about their attire: 'good tweeds' must have covered a multitude of boring decisions. Both, too, possess a faint air of mystery. Micheál MacLíammóir, in his notoriously inexact autobiography of 1946 – a work more noted for what is omitted than for what is printed – is nonetheless reliable on descriptions of persons. He refers to Christine's 'detachment' as striking a sympathetic chord with him – 'one felt a certain beautifully concealed impatience, the puzzled rather distant smile of the writer for the actor's brazen emotionalism and showmanship.' By the time he published his autobiography, Christine had written several successful novels, among them *Making Conversation*, *Country Places* and *Printed Cotton* – subtly ironic, full of understated observation of place and character – and half-a-dozen plays, less successful perhaps, though her dramatisations of Jane Austen and Maria Edgeworth were popular.

Edward's parents had not shown much interest in their Irish property, but Edward fell in love with Pakenham Hall – the estate, known as Tullynally, had been granted to an ancestor by a grateful Oliver Cromwell – and he determined to live there, occupying as many as possible of the 120 rooms which ran in layers beneath the towers, turrets, castellations and crenellations. Edward and Christine were married in 1925, and one gleans from the reminiscences of their contemporaries that they were restlessly searching for an occupation until they became involved in the affairs of the Gate Theatre at the end of 1930.

In the early years of the Longfords' friendship with Edwards and MacLíammóir, all four seem to have been almost inseparable. Hilton tended to resent Edward's interest (as chairman) in the casting of plays, for he believed – and never ceased to believe – that Longford was an amateur in such matters. The Longfords affectionately referred to Micheál and Hilton as 'the Boys'. They used to take them out to supper after the fall of curtain, usually to the restaurants of O'Connell Street which were almost invariably attached to cinemas – the Savoy, the Carlton and the Grand Central – but sometimes to Jammet's, the only restaurant of international reputation in Dublin. Edward always paid. Louis and Yvonne Jammet were patrons of the Gate, and Yvonne became one of Micheál's closest friends; she was one of the true *bel esprits* of Dublin, a connoisseur of modern painting and a talented designer of costumes, dressing Gate productions when invited, with imagination and *finesse*; yet she never seems to have been quite accepted by those who, at the time, made the running in society – members of the Royal Dublin Society, those who went to the races at Punchestown, or who belonged to the Royal Irish Yacht Club. Naturally neither Hilton nor Micheál aspired to membership of such institutions. They lived in bachelor disarray in an upstairs flat at 60 Harcourt Street. The Longfords bought Grosvenor Park, a Victorian mansion in the suburb of Rathmines, for their town residence, and filled it with Chinese, Balkan and inherited works of art. No two homes could have been more different. When dining out, Hilton and Micheál tended to talk animatedly and noisily, as much for the ears at other tables as for those of their hosts. Their association with the Longfords lent them a certain respectability, which they probably did not consider necessary; but the wider public, during that reactionary period of intensely inward-looking nationalism and puritanical Catholicism, may well have felt that the 'Bohemian' atmosphere of the Gate was out of line with proper moral thinking.

It was rather difficult for people of various shades of philistinism to attack the Gate with confidence. It could not be described as as 'anti-national' – a favourite label of discredit – for Micheál MacLíammóir was, after all, a Gaelic speaker, and he had translated poems by Pádraic Pearse, the executed leader of the 1916 Rising. Hilton Edwards, though English, was a Roman Catholic – as he had told several journalists, some of whom had supposed that his understanding of the Jewish playwrights which he directed so superbly was inherited. Edward Longford sprang from a planter family which had crudely displaced many local landowners and peasants – but that was a long time ago, and here he was, signing himself *Eamonn de Longphort*, and writing propaganda leaflets for the *Cumann na nGaedheal* (Free State) party.

There was also 'talk'. Talk that MacLíammóir was more friendly than appeared to be seemly with the army Chief of Staff: if this were not so, then why on certain nights after the fall of curtain was there an armoured car waiting, its engines throbbing expectantly, outside the theatre? There was talk that MacLíammóir's Mediterranean complexion, which endured the greyest of Irish winters, might not be quite natural – yet how could anyone tell? As for that Edwards fellow: was he quite – you know? He was living with MacLíammóir, but was supposed to have been engaged to the beautiful London actress, Adela Ferguson, until his friend Reginald Jarman had walked off with her – that was only rumour of course, though indeed his name was also linked with the actress Meriel Moore, who came from a very good family in Ballsbridge. (The world is full of surprises, and one knows what actresses are.) Gossip apart, Micheál O hAodha, in his tribute to MacLíammóir, *The Importance of Being Micheál* – the earliest work to give credence to the fact that its subject was not Irish at all – quotes the Roman Catholic Archbishop of Dublin, John Charles McQuaid, as warning his pupils, while he was a teacher at Blackrock College, that the Gate was 'brilliant – but dangerous'. It was a description which Micheál, Hilton, Edward and Christine would have relished.

A minor scandal broke out following the first performances of the Gate's Easter show for 1931, *The Dublin Revue*, scripted by Denis Johnston and others, foreshadowing incidents of like nature in the future. On the evening of 8 April a Mr Hugh P. Allen, a prominent member of the Catholic Truth Society, noisily walked out of the theatre, accompanied by a small group of supporters. The demonstration occurred at the end of a 'divertissement' billed as *Le Chèvre Indiscrète*, danced to music by Debussy (it was presumably a parody of *L'Après-midi d'une Faune*), and it alarmed some of the players. There had already been complaints about this item, including a letter in the Evening Herald signed 'Disgusted, Harold's Cross'. In the sketch, a mad goat found to be untamable by a farmer, his wife, a policeman and a shepherd, is declared to be possessed of an evil spirit and is duly exorcised by a priest, assisted by acolyte, bell, book and candle. Mr Allen later issued a statement saying 'the entire impropriety of this caricature of a sacred Catholic rite should be apparent. I make not the least apology for my protest. If the ladies of the ballet were annoyed, the blame must lie with those who put them publicly into an unenviable position.'

MacLíammóir countered that 'as an Irish Catholic' [*sic*!] he thought that 'political and religious protests which take the form of bullying and terrorism, especially against young women during a performance, are a disgrace to any religion.' Curiously, not one of the critics had objected to the item, making one wonder how the Catholic Truth Society had heard of it. Hilton Edwards later announced that there was nothing offensive to any religious feelings in the fantasy, but they decided to alter its ending 'in order not to give offence to even the most sensitive of our patrons'. (The 'offensive' portion was changed to a Mayor miming a reading of the Riot Act.) In spite of this undoubtedly weak-minded gesture from the management, Mr Allen remained unmollified, for he wrote to the papers again to state his reasons why the sketch should never have been produced. Further letters ensued – one of them, supporting the Gate Theatre's right to engage in satire, was signed 'J. Dunne, Kildare' – MacLíammóir's Davos friend. Mr Dunne enquired where Mr Allen had been when *Back to Methuselah* had been produced – for he certainly should have had his 'super-Catholicism' outraged by Shaw's treatment of Adam and Eve and the serpent, 'on which the whole edifice of Christianity is based'. The letter is subtly tongue-in-cheek, and calculated to give the *maximum* offence.

The other items in The Dublin Revue show that the Gate Theatre was quite prepared to make fun of itself and its personalities. One sketch has for its subject the provision of state aid to publishers who encouraged writing in the Irish language, irrespective of literary quality:

MAN. I have here a small work of mine. I thought the Government might publish it.
OFFICIAL. Is it in the National Language?
MAN. It is. And prepared from the best dictionary in the Swords Public Library.
OFFICIAL. Well, fill up that form, stating your name, address, birthplace in block capitals, and stating whether you belong to any organisation of a military nature.
MAN. I see. And where do I put the name of the book?
OFFICIAL. Never mind the name of the book. If everything is in order we'll print 3,000 copies.

Micheál MacLíammóir gave an impersonation of 'a famous English actress as Lady Macbeth in the recent McMaster season', and there was a Gilbert and Sullivan item to the tune of *Tit Willow* concerning the blowing up of a statue of William of Orange:

In a street in this city a statue once stood,
    King Billy, King Billy, King Billy.
As an effort in sculpture he wasn't much good,
    King Billy, King Billy, King Billy.
But he gladdened the heart of the Orangeman bold,
    And made him remember the brave days of old,

While the Papist adopted an attitude cold,
  Towards Billy, King Billy, King Billy . . .

The Longfords began to contribute plays to the repertoire only a few weeks after
Edward became chairman. His first was *The Melians*, taken from Thucydides'
The Peloponnesian War – the parallel is the First World War, the island city of
Melos is Ireland and the maritime empire of Athens is the British Empire.
Mithridates might be any German, and the magistrates of Melos any Irish
politicians of the period ten years prior to the production of the play. The Times
of London thought Lord Longford had made political discussion dramatic, but
found fault with his attempt to tailor history to suit his purpose; nonetheless, it
was 'refreshing to discover a new Irish playwright who is not afraid to dramatise
ideas, and who has the talent to do it well'. Six months later, on 15 March 1932,
Christine's comedy *Queens and Emperors* was produced. It appears to have
been one of those plays which receives neither good nor bad notices and which
vanishes from everybody's mind very quickly, leaving not a script behind.
Edward's adaptation of Joseph Sheridan LeFanu's Gothic novel, *Carmilla*,
which John Cowell says had been suggested to him by John Betjeman, appeared
two months later. It was immensely successful, and was evidently played for its
full horror's worth by Betty Chancellor as the young heroine, Coralie
Carmichael as the vampire of the title, and Hilton Edwards as 'a hunchback'.
The Irish Times said that only the production could excuse the play; the
language was 'stilted', and 'Hilton Edwards and Micheál MacLíammóir wisely
decided to treat the whole thing as a fantasy.'
    A year later, in February 1933, Edward Longford's version of the *Agamemnon*
was produced, with Lionel Dymoke as Agamemnon, Micheál MacLíammóir as
Orestes, Shelah Richards as Kassandra, and Cyril Cusack as Apollo; and a
month later Christine's *Mr Jiggins of Jigginstown*, a comedy on the eccentricities of country life among the Anglo-Irish (a term which she abhorred). If
she had allowed herself the licence to amuse her audience in the way she
allowed herself to amuse her dinner guests, it could have been an extremely
funny and perhaps even enduring comedy of manners, but there is a fatal
restraint which probably stemmed from her own gentle upbringing, and also
from the kindness which she concealed from most of the world; the play is only
of passing interest as a result. Edward's most substantial play, *Yahoo*, was
produced in September 1933 – much influenced by Denis Johnston in technique,
but without the same astringency or wit. The Manchester Guardian felt he was
'a little over-anxious to portray Swift as an Irish patriot'. Hilton Edwards made
a considerable impression as Swift – possibly more than he did when he gave a
much more intellectualised characterisation of the same figure in Denis
Johnston's *The Dreaming Dust*.
    Micheál MacLíammóir, with hindsight in his autobiography, *All for Hecuba*,
saw these productions as the visible sign of Edward Longford gradually 'taking

the reins'. Longford was 'a rich man new to the theatre, forcing the pace with plays that are just wrong, paying salaries to an increasing number of amateurs, lending us money when we get into a hole' – but he had the grace to admit that 'the Gate would be dead without him, probably'. Longford was inclined to be over-generous with young auditionees whom Edwards or MacLíammóir found unsuitable, cajoling one or other of the partners into allowing them to join the cast in minor parts, and agreeing to cover their salaries himself. This practice did not make for appropriateness of casting, businesslike administration, or healthy professional relationships.

A number of very talented young people did find their way into the Gate in the early and mid 'thirties, however, whether by luck, by audition or by virtue of experience elsewhere – among them Ria Mooney, Eve Watkinson, Geraldine Fitzgerald, Roy Irving, James Mason, Orson Welles and Cyril Cusack. Cusack had, in the time-honoured theatrical term, been 'brought up in a property basket'. He had acted at the Abbey as a very young man, but was attracted to the Gate by its 'theatricality', which put him in mind of his own touring in the fit-ups as a child actor; Micheál MacLíammóir reminded him of his step-father, the actor-manager, Breffni O'Rourke. His first Gate engagement was in *Cyrano de Bergerac* in 1932 – 'in a thankless part – but I had the pleasure of kissing Coralie Carmichael'; within nine months he was playing Jack in *The Importance of Being Earnest* opposite Micheál's Algy – and a quarter century later Micheál was playing Claudius to Cyril's Hamlet at the Gaiety Theatre. Probably because Cyril was a disinterested party, Micheál confided in him about his homosexuality. 'To my shame, when Micheál first mentioned it to me, in a pub not far from the Gate – it was not a matter which had crossed my mind about him – I said without thinking, "What a pity!" and he was hurt, and said in a childlike way, "Oh, Professor O Bríain never said that!"' MacLíammóir told Cyril that he found being in bed with a man was 'a great comfort' – he said it was something which had been with him 'from the beginning, at least from the age of five'.

ORSON

The young actor whom Edwards and MacLíammóir were to influence most, and who was to provide them with sporadically startling stage and film opportunities over the next forty years, joined the company in the autumn of 1931. This was Orson Welles. Cyril Cusack did not appear in the same plays as Welles , but he recalled in 1993 that even at the age of sixteen, Welles had 'a terrific stage presence'; at that time he was, surprisingly, 'quite slim and angular in his movements'. Cusack felt that Welles' 'personality overtook his acting'. If the young Cusack was impressed, it is no exaggeration to say that MacLíammóir was quite *bouleversé* by this ebullient young American, bursting with con-fidence and self-esteem, patently not short of a dollar or two, who turned up at the Gate one afternoon in early October without an appointment and demanded an audition. MacLíammóir saw him as 'a very tall young man with a chubby face, full powerful lips, and disconcerting Chinese eyes . . . The voice, with its brazen, transatlantic sonority, was already that of a preacher, a leader, a man of power; it boomed and boomed its way through the dusty scene-dock as if it would crush down the little Georgian walls and rip up the floor . . . ' Welles told the partners that he was eighteen, and had acted with the New York Theatre Guild; they did not believe him, but allowed him to imagine that they did. He was given the part of the Duke of Wurtemburg in Feuchtwanger's *Jew Süss*.

According to Geraldine Fitzgerald – who was too young to have worked with Welles at the Gate, but was a member of his Mercury Theatre in New York in 1938 – he had had a nervous breakdown following the suicide of his father, and was sent to Europe to recuperate. In later years Welles gave various accounts of his Irish visit, creating a widespread belief that he was exceedingly successful on the Gate stage – indeed, that he had caused something of a sensation. He also gave florid accounts of his relationship with Hilton and Micheál.

The reviews in the Dublin papers of the six plays in which he took part show that he certainly made an impression, though hardly a sensation. Socially, he *was* sensational – those who met him were invariably intrigued and charmed: not irritated, as one might have expected from one whose subsequent public image was nothing if not bumptious. Late in life, Orson told his biographer Barbara Leaming that Micheál was terrified that his man-to-man relationship with Hilton would result in the break-up of their now well-established partnership, and that there was evidence of little jealousies at every turn. Welles claimed that once he had proved himself in *Jew Süss*, Micheál did everything to denigrate him, and so his rôles grew smaller and smaller. In fact, there was no binding reason for the Gate to give him any further engagements, if his presence was causing disharmony – at this time there was no such thing as a long-term contract; but as he was subsequently cast as the ghost of Hamlet's father, a part which any actor, let alone one in his teens, should have been exceedingly grateful for, his memory on the matter of casting must have played him false.

Mary Manning in the Independent was critical of Hilton Edwards in giving Welles a rôle for which he was much too young, in David Sears' new play *The Dead Ride Fast*; the part was that of an American visitor, and Edwards probably cast him because of the authenticity of his accent. Mary Manning wrote that older parts kept Welles 'in a state of permanent semi-intoxication: we all want to see Mr Welles without a wig.' (The press photograph in a false moustache and beard makes him look grotesque.) Offstage, Mary Manning found Orson fascinating, but earnest; at a party in the house of the painter Hilda Roberts she told his fortune, and, knowing that he took his first professional engagement very seriously, she told him that the cards showed his future to be very successful – in stockbroking. He was enraged. She met him again in New York in 1940, before he had come to international prominence in *Citizen Kane*, and wrote to Denis Johnston that he was like an overgrown schoolboy. 'He's really a pain, Denis. A big gas-filled balloon which has just stayed up a while longer than than most balloons . . . Geraldine was on the air with him lately. They both sounded just as spirited as the Leeson Park Dramatic Society.' Eve Watkinson, who first saw him in *Jew Süss* and found his performance 'wonderfully filthy and lecherous', met him three months later when she was a lady-in-waiting in *Hamlet*; he was supposed to be 'dating' Betty Chancellor, who had 'stood him up' and he took Eve to see Laurel and Hardy at the Savoy Cinema, and to dinner afterwards. She found him 'odd-looking', and wondered if the rumour, currently circulating on acount of his chubbiness, that he was the illegitimate son of the Earl of Longford, could be correct!

Orson Welles appeared in most of the plays throughout the winter season of 1931-32. As well as *Jew Süss*, *The Dead Ride Fast* and *Hamlet*, he was in *The Archdupe*, *Mogu* and *Death Takes a Holiday*. The Independent – not Mary Manning on this occasion – annoyingly referred to him as Orsin Willis. He came in for better treatment in Padraic Colum's *Mogu*. Rejected by the Abbey, it was probably chosen because it gave a splendid opportunity to MacLíammóir to draw upon Islamic art for a series of richly patterned gauzes and cloths. Welles was praised by the Irish Times as the Persian King Chosroes for 'using his fine physique and great voice to advantage'. Not much of the physique could have been visible, however, if MacLíammóir's rich costume design is to be believed; in fact, it rather looks as if the designer wished to conceal the wearer's person. In *Death Takes a Holiday*, MacLíammóir, as Death, 'held the stage for the greater part of three acts . . . Mr Orson Welles, as Baron Lamberto, did much to satisfy those who have doubts of his possibilities.'

It is clear that Welles did not take Dublin entirely by storm in the way he chose to remember, but Dublin made a lasting impression on him – as any foreign city might on an exuberant lad of sixteen going on seventeen, encountering a receptive spirit of congeniality, when liberated for the first time from the constraints of home and school. Nor can he have felt so scornful of Micheál MacLíammóir in the way he later remembered, else he would hardly have invited both partners to be the principal guest artists at a summer school and repertory season which he organised at Woodstock, Illinois, in 1934 – their participation was promoted as a conspicuous *coup*, and his letters to them show much genuine affection. He would certainly not have invited MacLíammóir to play Iago opposite his own Othello in the 1950 motion picture, if he felt MacLíammóir's presence would have a deleterious effect on the work. What was probably on his mind, when he referred to MacLíammóir in a dismissive way, was a much later incident, when MacLíammóir seems almost to have deliberately caused a falling-out at the time of a production of *Chimes at Midnight* in Belfast and Dublin in 1960. MacLíammóir told Simon Callow that Orson was 'one of the three deep loves of my life', and it was unfortunate for him, if Welles as a very young man possessed the traits of tease or flirt.

'THE YOUNGEST HAMLET'

Micheál MacLíammóir made his début as Hamlet on 2 February 1932, with Hilton Edwards as Claudius, Coralie Carmichael as Gertrude, Meriel Moore as Ophelia and Betty Chancellor as the Player Queen – the Gate's core group, now very much an experienced ensemble. 'In this production,' The Standard reported, 'Hilton Edwards and Micheál MacLíammóir justly claim to have devised a method of presentation of the utmost severity and simplicity, with a minimum of scenery and properties, which yet gives sufficient stimulus to the imagination to assist the action and satisfy the demands of the most exacting audience.' Dorothy Macardle, in a contemplative column which she was developing in the Irish Press, said he was the youngest Hamlet she had ever seen – which suggests that the rest of them must have been middle-aged. She saw his characterisation as that of 'an enlightened spirit in a barbarous age'. When Micheál MacLíammóir was approached by the BBC producer, John Davenport, in 1954 to write and record a twenty-minute dissertation on his view of Hamlet – other contributors to the series were John Gielgud, Alec Guinness and Donald Wolfit, whose insights were much less eloquently expressed – he intrigued listeners by starting his talk with the information that 'there is in Ireland, and probably in many other countries where simplicity and isolation retain a little hold on the popular imagination, a belief that no man can look upon the face of a spirit and remain unchanged . . . ' This piece of calculated hokum had the instant effect of catching the ears of the BBC's enormous public.

MacLíammóir did not believe, as he thought many actors believed, that Hamlet was a born neurotic. The truth for him lay first, and significantly, in Hamlet's capacity for friendship; 'an unrequited friendship, as I see it, for the sturdy and faithful Horatio is inadequate to respond to the Prince's iridescent moods and perceptions'; it also lay in 'his turbulent and ever-stirring imagination, in his glowing sense of beauty, in his longing for the warmth of the fire of life, in his instinctive feeling for homely, hardy, cheerful people like soldiers, actors, court jesters and grave-diggers . . . ' It was a deliberately unscholarly analysis, and one in which he allowed himself several humorous flights of fancy – Hamlet's gift of eloquently expressed second sight was 'shared by his sentries', and he had no particular talents, 'except for dabbling in dramatic criticism and, we may suppose, fencing'; and, if he had had work to do, 'Hamlet as we know him, or rather seek to know him, would never have existed.'

This Hamlet was revived many times in Ireland, and was also taken to London, Cairo, Alexandria, several Balkan countries and the Shakespeare Festival at Elsinore. (MacLíammóir later said his worst performance was in London in 1935 and his best in Zagreb in 1939.) Meriel Moore played Ophelia in most of the productions. In 1941, when she had been with the company off and on for over ten years, she wrote to Shelah Richards to say 'I get tireder and tireder of that there Gate as the years go by, and Micheál gets more and more bloated and McMaster-like, and Hilton gets more and more muddled, and I'm so sick of saying I'm so sorry for poor Coralie, and Betty, poor child, is deafer and vaguer every day, and every skirt and stocking I have is torn to ribbons grovelling on the floor being Ophelia, and whenever I grovel I always seem to be masking Micheál, which is, of course, the Sin against the Holy Ghost.' Because of her ill-concealed affair with Hilton, she was not on easy terms with Micheál – even after she had married the actor Pat O'Moore. She met O'Moore while on a theatre tour of South Africa with another company. Mary Manning believed this tour to have been her sensible and diplomatic way of absenting herself for a few months from the Gate. 'Somebody squealed about Hilton,' said Mary Manning. 'Micheál was desperately upset and had dreadful rows in rehearsal with Hilton, and everybody knew what it was about. Micheál even threatened to leave the Gate, and though we all knew he wouldn't, we were very frightened. Meriel was no fool, so she had to adjust, if she was ever going to play leads at the Gate again.'

Naturally this incident is not mentioned in Micheál MacLíammóir's memoirs – he merely records that 'Meriel, feeling restless, and in a mood for experiment, had betaken herself to South Africa with a contract for a longish tour with Mr Alan Doone, who specialised in Irish drama of the old school.' The Gate, however, could hardly do without one of its triumverate of very fine and very different actresses, so presumably when she returned to Dublin nothing more was said.

This, and the season with Orson Welles, and the marriage of Jack Dunne, all came fairly closely together; and then there was the news of the suicide of Hubert Duncombe in Cambridge. Terence Gray, the director of the Festival Theatre, wrote 'We do not know why he died, but he was a fastidious man, and the manner of his death was fastidious. Many people go about declaring that they had rather not be alive, but this man said nothing and went his way.' Before he died, he sent a bracelet belonging to Mary O'Keefe, which he had as a keepsake, to Mrs O'Keefe in Howth. Members of the Gate company were greatly shocked by the tragedy, but it must have been an especially trying and sad time for Micheál. Perhaps, in a subliminal way, these emotional upheavals affected his performance, and may even have contributed to the profundity and resonance of his ghost-ridden Hamlet.

INVEST ME IN MY MOTLEY, AND GIVE ME LEAVE TO SPEAK MY MIND

When Mary Manning gave up her part-time reviewing job with the Independent at the end of 1931 and took up another part-time job as editor of the Gate's new house magazine, Motley, her first play, *Youth's the Season – ?*, was in production. The setting is the wealthy suburbia of Ballsbridge or Rathgar, the characters are bright young things, there are 'boy-friends' and 'girl-friends', the cocktail-shaker is very much in evidence, and the mixture of flippancy and bitter introspection suggests something of the world of Noël Coward's *The Vortex*.

'Oh,' groans the effeminate Desmond Millington, 'the imitation Chelsea! The imitation Bloomsbury! The *un*original sins!' The character Egosmith, a bartender who never speaks but listens to everyone, was suggested to Mary Manning by Samuel Beckett. The Irish Times thought the play was finely written, with many telling lines, and a light wit, but 'probably nowhere but in Dublin will its loving cruelty be fully appreciated.'

Meriel Moore wrote to Shelah Richards, who was on tour with the Abbey Players in the United States, to say that they had 'just embarked on Mary Manning's play, which I think is very good and justifies my support of poor Mary when Hilton was "going to hound her out of Dublin" for being flippant about his productions. Micheál's playing a Paddy Perrott [a Gate costume designer] part, and not nearly as good as he could be if he thought he was playing the Hope of the Gaels with a shield – I mean, give Micheál a green and silver cloak and a free rein with his curls, and he *is* Paddy Perott, but put him in a drawing-room and he is the Hope of the Gaels. Betty's going to be perfect as someone called 'Toots', and poor Hazel [Ellis] is playing her own sweet self – "Pearl, a blonde". Mary wants me to play a part called Connie, rather nice, but Coralie's playing that, and I'm playing a young woman who has a Grip on Herself and takes Senior Fresh [second-year arts examination in Trinity College, Dublin] in a collar and tie, but melts eventually upon the bosom of a Young Doctor, having lost the Grip ("which all sounds very Meriel", says that Shelah – so let me tell you here and now that our Producer explained the part as being "very Shelah Richards" – so Grips and Young Doctors to you!)'

Predictably, the Hope of the Gaels section of the press did not appreciate *Youth's the Season – ?* at all, and did not care to believe that the characters in it could possibly be Irish; what may also have been upsetting to them – for they tended to belong to that peculiarly unsophisticated troupe which equates the actor with the part portrayed – was that the Gaelic-speaking MacLíammóir, who had now produced or acted in more than a dozen plays in the first national language, was letting the side down badly by appearing (as he described the character himself) as 'a youthful invert in a cyclamen polo jumper . . . I painted lampshades in designs of a rather dubious Greek origin, got tight at a party and slapped a boy-friend's face, wept and said how hard it was to be called Flossie at school, and ended up with a lament for a young suicide after the manner of the page of Herodias in *Salomé*.' The Ballsbridge and Rathgar section of the audience appreciated the play very much indeed: there was a strong element of recognition in their laughter.

Motley made its first appearance in March 1932. There was an introduction by the Earl of Longford, describing the Gate as a 'national asset' – 'where else,' he enquired, 'would we ever have seen new plays by Irish dramatists such as *The Old Lady Says 'No!'*, *Youth's the Season – ?* or *Juggernaut*? Without these, the dramatic standards of Ireland would be lower, her intellectual life poorer . . . The Gate declares war upon the ghosts and demons that have haunted the Irish drama!' He thanked the Minister for Finance for removing the tax on theatre tickets. C.P. Curran gave an lucid analysis of the MacLíammóir *Hamlet*, and Christine Longford contributed a compendium of remarks overheard in the foyer, such as, 'Meriel Moore lives in Ailesbury Road. I heard she was so keen on acting, she gave up everything. She even gave up her golf!'. There were articles and poems, not necessarily on theatrical topics, by very eminent writers, among them Sean O'Faolain, Frank O'Connor, Austin Clarke, Donagh Mac-Donagh and Francis Stuart. Mainie Jellett wrote convincingly on the topic of modern art in a later issue. The inclusion of reviews of Gate plays by independent critics shows the Gate's confidence in its own product – Marcel Pagnol's *Topaze* 'repeated neither its Paris success nor its London failure'; and Richard Goddard's *Obsession in India* was 'a real thriller which succeeded in boring us for its first dangerous quarter of an hour'.

A later issue gives a detailed report of a Symposium held at the Gate on the rhetorically posed question, 'Should the Theatre be International?' Lord Longford was in the chair, and the theatre was crowded – this latter is remarkable, for there was no internationally-celebrated guest speaker. As is usual on such occasions, the precise subject of the debate was hardly adhered to, but many pithy opinions were given on a variety of theatrical topics; the hoary matter of Synge's inability to understand the Irish peasant because he was a member of the landed gentry and a Protestant, was raised by one ultra-nationalistic member of the audience, who was immediately put down by a genuine Irish-speaker, who said that Synge was the *only* dramatist who knew the people of the Gaeltacht and could give expression to their culture! Hilton Edwards made the most germane speech of the evening when he said that his interests in the theatre were 'neither national or international: they are theatrical. The whole danger to drama in Ireland lies in [the people's] consciousness of their national drama, which was so well developed by the Abbey Theatre during the last three decades. I would prefer that Irish drama was incidentally national rather than consciously national. If an Irishman decides to write an Irish play he usually – instead of producing something original – writes a bad Abbey play, a pseudo Synge or an imitation O'Casey.'

Motley for 5 September 1933 contains *A Proposal for the Strengthening of the Censorship* in the manner of Swift's lacerating *Modest Proposal*. 'Censorship should be increased,' it begins, 'because it will give employment to clerks, up to the number of thirty; financial rewards to the state, as each publisher must pay to have books scrutinised . . . ' The article is unsigned, but must surely have been written by Samuel Beckett, who was in Dublin at the time – his father had just died – and was a close friend of Mary Manning. It bears a strong resemblance to the much fuller *Censorship in the Saorstat* (Free State) of 1936. It was a subject which became increasingly vexing for Edwards and MacLíammóir.

INTERLUDE AT STRATFORD

In the summer of 1933 'the Boys', as they were now generally spoken of, visited Seville, Paris, London and Stratford-upon-Avon, according to an interview which Hilton gave to the editor of Motley. As the Gate was running into further deficit, how they managed to pay for the trip is a matter for some wonderment. Hilton enjoyed the Spanish cabarets – 'they are all finished artists', he said, thinking perhaps of his own career with the Cabaret Kittens. In Paris he liked Jouvet's production of Giraudoux' *Intermezzo*, recommended by Owen Sheehy-Skeffington; of the Comédie Française production of Sophocles' *Electre*, he said their techniques had not moved since the time of Sardou. Of Gordon Daviot's *Richard of Bordeaux* in London, he said it contained 'nothing one could not read between the lines of *Richard II*' – but he thought John Gielgud gave 'a superb performance', and he produced it four years later. They then went to Stratford, where Anew McMaster was playing Hamlet, Coriolanus, Macduff, Leonato, Escalus and Petruchio – an extraordinary range of rôles.

Christopher McMaster, now six, played Coriolanus' son. 'His physical likeness to me,' McMaster recalled on radio, 'brought out the terrible poignancy of the famous pleading scene. His small brave figure and clear child's voice affected me extraordinarily.' It was quite a family reunion when Micheál and Hilton arrived to visit Mac and Marjorie in the cottage which they had taken for the season. Mary Rose was five; she, and Sally Travers, were the two nieces Micheál remained fondest of throughout his life. In the town, and at the theatre, Micheál and Hilton made contact with a number of people with whom they would work in the future – Rachel Kempson, the current Juliet, Virgilia and Ophelia; Tyrone Guthrie, who was directing *Richard II*; and W. Bridges-Adams, the most important influence on the Gate Theatre's foreign touring. The production which most excited Hilton was Komisarjevski's *Macbeth*, which was also the one that had caused the strongest outcry in the British press. 'He did not treat the play in the usual manner as a supernatural drama,' Hilton told Motley, 'but simply as a tragedy of the mind.' The setting, which was of polished aluminium bent to catch the light, and the costumes with spiked helmets suggestive of the Prussian troops of 1914, displayed 'the fertility of this wonderful Russian's imagination. I left the theatre full of admiration for Komisarjevski, but not having received one single impression of Shakespeare's *Macbeth*. Two or three more productions like this and it will be the Komisarjevski Memorial Theatre!'

ILLINOIS IDYLL

'Like a wax-flower under a bell of glass, in the paisley and gingham county of McHenry, is Woodstock, grand capital of mid-Victorianism in the mid-west.' These are the opening words of the brochure which Orson Welles, now genuinely eighteen, wrote as introduction to the Todd School of the Theatre and Theatre Festival, which he instigated. He was supported by Mr Roger Hill, described by Welles as his 'mentor', headmaster of Todd boys' preparatory school, of which Welles was a former pupil. The centre of Woodstock is still preserved as a charming relic of nineteenth century provincial America, all spruced up with that sense of historical pride in townscape which is a feature of American life. The idea was that students should enroll at $250 in a 'practical rather than theoretical' course, which would enable them to take part in the three professionally produced plays at the local Opera House – one of them, *Trilby*, directed by Welles, the other two, *Hamlet* and *Tsar Paul*, directed by Hilton Edwards, with Micheál MacLíammóir playing in all three.

Harry Fine, a Trinity College graduate who played supporting parts at the Gate and also wrote press-releases and looked after publicity, and who soon became so indispensable that he was taken on as the company's first official business-manager at £3 a week, had been in correspondence with Orson Welles from the autumn of 1933 about an American tour for the company, on Welles' suggestion. The idea came to nothing, probably because Welles' enthusiasm outstripped his knowledge of theatre business. Welles then gave his energies to the less ambitious project at Woodstock. He wrote to Edwards from the Andrew Jackson Hotel in Nashville on 12 April 1934, saying, 'You cable me a little plaintively for particulars. What particulars?' In Edwards' language, 'particulars' meant 'financial arangements'. Before enumerating these, Welles explained that Mr Roger Hill 'is kindly turning over the entire campus with its submarine-lit swimming pool, its riding stables, its machine and print shops, cottages and dormitories, private experimental theater . . . to the Festival Company for its sole use in July and August. Here, three minutes from Woodstock's Opera House and town square, we will live and work, and, as there are only two performances to be given a week, it is also safe to say, play . . . Each production will have careful, painstaking and leisurely consideration, so that by the time the critics get at them they won't need either the old apology of the summer repertory theater, or the older apology of the first night . . . '

The 'particulars' were that the partners' passage from Dublin to Woodstock and back would be paid, and 'all your expenses during your stay with us . . . Your names will be featured, and you will receive nation-wide publicity.' He added that 'because the theater company can't afford a penny more, you are offered a few dollars, very literally pin money, a week.' It is clear that Edwards and MacLíammóir decided to consider the trip as a holiday; after all, they had done the plays before – and so they accepted. They enjoyed themselves thoroughly, as Welles' biographers are not slow to point out. Hilton, characterised by Welles as the 'straight' man of the partnership in Dublin, now appears in rather different guise, joining his partner in the pursuit of attractive male students from rehearsal-room to swimming-pool to dormitory, with what evidently amounted to gay abandon. Though publicity may not have been exactly 'nation-wide', they certainly did receive a great deal of friendly (if uncomprehending) attention from the gossip columnists – 'Seeing him

[MacLíammóir] sitting at the head of the table, so handsome in his dinner-clothes, it was easy to believe he was the last actor ever invited to speak at a certain girls' boarding-school in Dublin!', swooned one lady journalist; and they received a not uncritical, yet very fair assessment from the Chicago critics. Gail Borden in the Daily Times took MacLíammóir to task for failing to note 'the Dane's own line, "Do not saw the air with your arms thus, but use it gently"'. MacLíammóir thought that if Welles had achieved the promise shown at rehearsal he would have been 'the finest Claudius I have ever seen, but Orson in those days was a victim of stage intoxication: the presence of an audience caused him to lose his head; his horses panicked, and one was left with the impression of a man in the acute stages of delirium tremens.'

As to the Todd campus, MacLíammóir was reminded of Louisa May Alcott's American dream of an idyllic education, and thought how logical, sane, kind and clean it was; he wondered if 'logic and sanity are not destined to rob us at last of intensity'. Unlike the visit to Stratford-on-Avon, he found that nothing resulted from the new contacts, and he learned nothing about the theatre. They visited the Chicago World's Fair. MacLíammóir later recalled to the readers of *All for Hecuba* that one night, in a movie-house on Michigan Avenue, they were startled by shots outside: they were told that the notorious gangster, Dillinger, had been killed by the police. However, as the killing took place two miles away on Lincoln Avenue, both he and Hilton must have had very sharp hearing. While at Woodstock, the partners were approached by representatives of an Irish-American society, which was producing a *Pageant of the Celt* at the end of August, and who eagerly solicited their help – Edwards for his directorial skills, MacLíammóir as writer and narrator. When the Todd season had finished, they moved to Chicago, where the committee of Irish Historical Productions Inc. installed them in great luxury in the Congress Hotel.

In *All for Hecuba* MacLíammóir makes it appear that he wrote the script of the pageant, but the copy preserved in a private collection in Chicago is credited to a John V. Ryan. MacLíammóir's name is printed on the programme as Narrator, and it is possible that he wrote the narration (rather than the script) as well as speaking it, or perhaps he re-wrote John V. Ryan's narrative section to suit his own delivery. The text has that Hibernian bargain-basement style which affects so much of Irish-American utterance, as if the imagery had been lifted from the heroic nineteenth-century boys' adventure novels of Standish O'Grady and mingled with the jargon of a south Boston grade-school. If any of the passages are by MacLíammóir's hand, he was surely writing to order, as any professional script-writer might. Lines like 'they walk as gravely as though they walked in the white courts of heaven' is very much in his 1930 neo-Celtic style of *The Ford of the Hurdles*, taken up again in 1956 in the *Pageant of St Patrick*. Hilton Edwards' name is given on the programme as 'Technical Advisor', though one forms the impression from *All for Hecuba* that he was the director.

The pageant played its two nights in the magnificent Soldier Field stadium, home of the Chicago Bears, with its Fascist style colonnades and seating for many thousands – but to a small attendance. 'I wound my black velvet voice through the convolutions of my script,' MacLíammóir wrote, 'while in dumb show St Patrick plucked huge shamrocks from the grass of Illinois.' The committee of Irish Historical Productions, so generous with their hospitality, failed to pay the partners' fees, which did not seem to cast too much of a gloom over the proceedings. (Hilton remarked that they had been 'hit below the Celt'.) There was an *al fresco* farewell party at Woodstock, where they drank Orson Welles' health and swore lasting friendship. If Welles absorbed anything from his professional encounters with Hilton Edwards, it was his great interest in and understanding of lighting; from both Edwards and MacLíammóir he probably derived his theatricality in performance, something which in turn had come *via* Forbes-Robertson and Tree – having to feel the part on the stage, as Edwards was continually stressing to younger actors, 'a hundred times larger than in life'.

When Hilton Edwards, Micheál MacLíammóir and Orson Welles next worked together, fifteen years and a world war would have intervened.

Chapter 6
Flight into Egypt

On 9 July 1934 Hilton Edwards wrote from the Todd Theatre Festival, Illinois, to Denis Johnston, who had sought private clarification on a matter, as a member of the Gate board. Johnston reported that Mrs Isa Hughes, the Gate secretary, had been suspended by Lord Longford for engaging in correspondence with the Ministry of Education in Cairo without the board's approval. He wanted to know the background.

Hilton replied breezily that, as the Egyptian plan was so vague, there had been no reason for him to raise it formally with the board – 'until I had a definite offer to put before them I have handled the details myself with the help of Isa.' In the light of what followed, it is easy to see that both Hilton and Micheál knew perfectly well that the board, and particularly Edward Longford as its chairman, would not countenance anything so rash as a foreign tour, which might land the company in greater financial difficulties – especially as Longford was now paying theatre bills from his private purse. (It is extraordinary that he should have paid sundry accounts as they became due, instead of providing a set annual subscription as patron, with the stipulation that if the company did not remain within its budget it would have to find additional funds elsewhere.) Hilton continued chattily to Denis: 'We are working hard here at Woodstock, which is quite a charming place. We are very comfortable, but the work is not of good standard . . . You are well known, and the people are full of interest and desire to see your other plays.' (This kind of flattery would not have taken Denis Johnston in at all.) 'Orson is in great form and is really much improved. With love to Shelah and many thanks to you, Yours ever, Hilton.'

When Hilton and Micheál returned to Dublin in September, they learned that Edward had turned down the 'invitation' to play in Cairo. (It was not an invitation: Hilton had originally written proposing a season, knowing that English companies had played there, and the response from Cairo had been favourable.) Mrs Hughes was reinstated; she became a prominent figure in the subsequent anti-Longford faction.

There was a genuine invitation to the Gate from Anmer Hall to play at the Westminster Theatre in London. Hall was a wealthy impresario, whose policy was to provide a London venue for plays which would not otherwise be seen except in 'art' theatres like the London Gate. He had read The Times review of 23 September 1933, in which Longford's *Yahoo* was praised, and had been interested in the work of the Dublin Gate ever since. It appears, among the board tensions, that there was a shared desire for the Gate's work to be exposed elsewhere, for the company had received widespread press coverage outside Ireland, but had not even played in Cork or Belfast. Anmer Hall's invitation was accepted.

When they returned from Chicago, Micheál and Hilton relinquished their flat in Harcourt Street and moved to what they rather grandly spoke of as 'a service flat' in Dartmouth Square, just across the Grand Canal. It was what the previous generation would have described as 'rooms' – services such as fuel and hot water were supplied as part of the renting agreement: in effect it meant that you did not have to carry coal up the stairs, or feed pennies into the gas-meter. From this location they planned the season for the remainder of 1934 and the first half of 1935. Determined that they should not continue to suffer from the (entirely justifiable) accusation that they kept all the best parts for themselves and that the female leads invariably went to Betty, Coralie and Meriel, they brought Ria Mooney back into the company, and engaged James Mason as a result of an interview in London.

They were at last taking the trouble to ensure that their supporting players were 'right'. The celebrated actress, Sara Allgood, who had created Juno in *Juno and the Paycock* at the Abbey with great distinction, before moving to London and Hollywood, had been cast two seasons previously in *The Cherry Orchard* and *The Way of the World* with embarrassing lack of success, for the rôles of Madame Ranevskaia and Millamant were ouside her range. She should not have been offered the parts, but Hilton Edwards believed her name would be a draw, and she certainly should have had the self-knowledge not to accept them. Shelah Richards may have had an axe to grind as a fellow actress, but her words in her unpublished memoirs sum up what the critics stated rather more diplomatically. 'She was awful. Ghastly! Her marvellous Juno voice was very near her natural way of speaking, but when she was being grand she had, you noticed, a singularly unpleasant Dublin accent. Perhaps it seemed so frightful in Chekhov because it was so incongruous.' (She was, however, very good as Zola's Thérèse Raquin, where 'grandeur' was not required.) The same problems could have occurred with Ria Mooney, who came from rather the same school, and who barely got away with Gwendolen in *The Importance of Being Earnest*, but by all accounts was superb as an earthy heroine in Ibanez' *Blood and Sand* and as Catherine Earnshaw in her own adaptation of *Wuthering Heights* – in which Geraldine Fitzgerald was Isabella, the part she was later to play in Hollywood with Laurence Olivier. Ria Mooney was given the lead in *Lady Precious Stream*, for which Hilton Edwards took great care in studying Chinese stage conventions. The author, Shih Hsiung, arrived from London, where the first English production of the play had recently opened; he told the press that he had seen many plays by Irishmen translated into Chinese, especially those of Mr Shaw and Lord Dunsany; his smiles suggested that he was enchanted by everything he saw, but when the partners asked for his comments on the production, he kept repeating 'Wery bad!'.

James Mason caused just as much interest in Dublin as Orson Welles had done, and received a very good press, which is undoubtedly the reason why there was a coolness between him and MacLíammóir. He was twenty-five, somewhat gauche in manner, and exceedingly handsome. Geraldine Fitzgerald said 'he had that curious quality of a man with an eternal secret.' In 1992 the actor, Patrick Brock, who joined the company for the same production and in whose home Mason stayed for a short time, said 'the two men were not sympathetic'. Harry Fine was more open: 'Micheál hated his guts, and did everything to make his life miserable.' Mason confided to Fine that Micheál's treatment nearly made him give up the theatre, for in 1934 he was still unconvinced about his future in the profession. Terence de Vere White, a Dublin solicitor who later acted for Edwards and MacLíammóir in their most difficult period of financial instability, told Mason's biographer, Sheridan Morley, that he was 'desperately worried about whether he had enough talent for the theatre. To cheer him up I told him that if all else failed he could always go into films and become the English Clark Gable!' In 1946 Mason won the Daily Mail award as the most popular film actor of any nationality.

Julius Caesar, with James Mason as Brutus, Micheál MacLíammóir as Mark Antony (wearing, for no reason which anyone could fathom, a leopard-skin leotard) and Hilton Edwards as Caesar, was one of the most successful productions presented since the opening of the theatre. The set was emblematic – the imperial eagle surmounting immense militaristic banners which converted into the tent at Philippi. Roy Irving said that when Mason played Brutus on film with Brando and Gielgud a quarter-century later, he had not changed one inflection – 'I know, I stood under him for one month drenched in his spittle listening to every word.' Irving also recalled a joke perpetrated on the rest of the cast by Edwards, who became bored lying dead under the robe, and one night during a scene-change substituted another actor; 'When Micheál as Mark Antony swept the robe off the body there was a momentary shocked pause, and then a bigger scream of terror from the crowd than he could get at rehearsals.' Liam Gaffney, another young actor who joined at the same time, had to be carried off as a corpse; 'one night the two extras dropped me before they had reached the wings, and thinking I was offstage I sat up – the audience exploded!'

In *The Provok'd Wife*, according to an unidentified reviewer, 'Mr Mac-Líammóir and Mr Mason were the two bright young sparks, and the former gave a familiar picture of mincing vivaciousness. Mr Mason's deliberate and nicely calculated style produced a sort of ratiocinative gallantry.' The Times of London noted that 'Mr James Mason made an almost ideal Heartfree – gay, witty, satirical, affectionate by turns.' *Ascendancy*, a new play by Edward Longford based on incidents in the life of his grandfather, which, according to John Cowell, fared badly, was 'remembered principally for the young James Mason's performance as a wicked, attractive Irish rake.' Mason's last appearance was in a revival of Ria Mooney's verson of *Wuthering Heights* in February 1935.

LONDON

The London season was to consist of three plays. One was to be *Yahoo*, the cause of the original invitation. The Cambridge Festival Theatre produced *Yahoo* in May, with Betty Chancellor as Stella. It was so well received that Edward Longford, who had been genuinely hesitant about agreeing to a Gate transfer to the Westminster Theatre, was now convinced that it would not appear too obscure to the English audience. He was touchingly keen for London to see Micheál's Hamlet, while Hilton felt that would be 'coals to Newcastle'. The third choice would be either Denis Johnston's *The Old Lady Says 'No!'* or his new play *A Bride for the Unicorn*, which relates the life and death of Mr Phosphorus, a Peer Gynt figure, who yearns for the romance which seems to elude him; it contains melodrama, farce and opera, and the word which is most in evidence in the press comment is 'expressionism'. Johnston was keen that it should be seen in London, and it was revived with alterations at the Gate in April-May 1935 with *Yahoo* and *The Old Lady Says 'No!'* as a kind of six-week dress rehearsal.

After an inspection of the Westminster Theatre, Hilton Edwards wrote to Denis Johnston to say how disappointed he was to find that technical consider-ations prevented *A Bride for the Unicorn* from being presented on its stage. The size and shape of the Gate set was the difficulty. 'I know you will be upset by this,' he concluded. 'So are we.' If Johnston was upset – it is quite usual for an author to wish to promote his latest work, even if an earlier one may be more in demand – it is likely that he divined the real reason behind the letter: Micheál wanted to play the *Old Lady* in London, for his part in *A Bride for the Unicorn* was much less showy.

Denis Johnston must have given his agreement, for the Westminster season was shortly announced as opening on 4 June with '*Yahoo* – a Fantastic Com-mentary on Jonathan Swift by the Earl of Longford', '*The Old Lady Says "No!"* – a Satiric Review of everything Irish by Denis Johnston, Author of *The Moon in the Yellow River*' (the latter had been produced by the Abbey Players in 1931 and also seen in Birmingham, Malvern and London; it remains Johnston's most frequently performed play), and *Hamlet* – which is given no introductory billing, save the name of the leading actor. This programme was a reasonably well balanced compendium of what the Dublin Gate Theatre had been engaged in during its first eight years: two quirkily 'Irish' plays, very much in advance of what was being written in England insofar as stage technique was concerned, and an international classic. There was much murmuring both in the company and in the Dublin press about the choice of *Hamlet*; no doubts were expressed regarding MacLíammóir's interpretation, but it seemed to some to be less representative of the Gate's repertoire than modern European or American work, like Kaiser and Capek, or Rice and O'Neill; but on the other hand the Gate had established 'modern' readings of Shakespeare.

A company of forty-seven travelled – Anmer Hall had provided a financial guarantee; eight performances of each play were given, and if the reports are correct (no box-office returns survive) both the modern plays sold out after their openings, and *Hamlet* did better than some had predicted; it was presented last, by which time the Gate's reputation had established itself, and Londoners who had seen the play many times were probably attracted by the enthusiastic reports of the liveliness and flair of the company. MacLíammóir's Speaker/Emmet also received universal approbation. In *All for Hecuba* he speaks with unusual modesty, indeed with a tinge of bitterness, of his 'failure' as Hamlet, but the reviews do not all bear this out – they are generally condescending rather than negative. Betty Chancellor's auburn hair as Ophelia was thought appropriate to an Irish interpretation, and the references to MacLíammóir's 'brogue' are numerous and not at all pejorative. The thought must have struck him that here he was in his native city, not half a mile from the Duke of York's and His Majesty's theatres, where he had triumphed under his real name, yet now believed to be a visiting Irish star. Oliver Twist and Michael Darling had matured into Hamlet and the Speaker/Emmet: but the London public did not know.

Someone did call at the stage door of the Westminster, enquiring loudly for 'Mr Willmore' – it was rumoured that this was Anew McMaster, being 'naughty'. (He attended the opening nights in an opera cloak.) News spread backstage that Willmore was Micheál's real surname – the newer members of the company were not aware of it – and its Englishness caused much amusement. Harry Fine remembers some of the younger players walking home up the Buckingham Palace Road after the performance, shouting the name 'Alfred Willmore!' with late-night merriment, to the puzzlement of the local residents.

*

Edward Longford, now paying theatre bills like a sower broadcasting seed far and wide, was quite determined that the proposed Egyptian tour should not take place. The potential profit did not strike him as realistic – what if the audience did not measure up to expectations? – and the fact that the travel costs were not covered struck him as preposterous. There was also the problem of the Gate and its audience: if the company was absent for two months during the spring, the theatre would be 'dark' and the public might forget there was such a thing as the Gate. In spite of the board's decision, however, Hilton Edwards resumed negotiations with Cairo, and the composition of the Gate's programme for the autumn and winter of 1935-36 must have looked, with hindsight once the players had departed for Suez, not much more than a preview for Cairo and Alexandria.

Welcoming the announcement that the Dublin Gate Theatre Company would be playing at the Royal Opera House, Cairo, from 10 March 1936, the Egyptian Gazette said that the Ministry of Education 'in choosing a company for this year's English season has departed from its practice of recent years. Instead of a cast of uneven quality got together [in London] it has selected a well-known repertory company whose members are accustomed to act together and to getting up a number of plays at once. Theatregoers who were in London last summer will remember the excellent season the Gate Theatre Company gave at the Westminster Theatre.' The programme for Egypt was *Berkeley Square, Hamlet, The Provok'd Wife, Romeo and Juliet, Heartbreak House, The Taming of the Shrew* and *Payment Deferred*. All of these plays were already in the repertoire, except for *The Taming of the Shrew*, to which Hilton Edwards gave a bouncing production, with the Christopher Sly scene in modern dress, on 15 October 1935, and *Payment Deferred*, a popular English thriller by Jeffrey Dell. Henri Ghéon's *The Marriage of St Francis*, which provided Micheál MacLíammóir with a part full of wide-eyed spirituality, Elmer Rice's *Not for Children*, notable for the set which he designed in the cubist manner of Mainie Jellett, and an adaptation of Dostoievski's *Crime and Punishment* were the remaining plays of the Dublin season.

The board of the theatre remained divided on the question of Egypt, when it was raised time and again throughout the autumn. Lord Longford and Norman Reddin were opposed, Hilton Edwards and Micheál MacLíammóir militantly in favour; Denis Johnston, who seems to have sided with the opposition, came up with the proposal that Edwards and MacLíammóir should proceed under their own management, provided they undertook to take responsibility for whatever expenses were not guaranteed by the Egyptian authorities, as well as any unforeseen losses. In effect, he was proposing an official 'splinter group', and it was deeply resented by the Boys. This course was reluctantly agreed; and in this unpropitious atmosphere Hilton Edwards, assisted by Isa Hughes, made the arrangements for a company of thirty, with settings and costumes for seven productions, to travel in early February.

Their greatest problem was the fare. It is not recorded who thought of the solution, and it was probably put to the company in a way which suggested that they had been 'let down' by the Earl – 'the wicked Earl' was one of Edward Longford's unearned *soubriquets*. Each member of the company should pay his or her own fare – if not, there would be no tour. Harry Fine, the business manager, was quite sure he could not pay his own fare, nor could other company stalwarts such as Robert Hennessy (which meant a new Horatio and other important parts would have to be recast) and Edward Lexy (Polonius and six other parts). Naturally, this caused contention; overseas touring was very rare, and as far as Irish companies were concerned non-existent, except for occasional visits to Britain and the United States; holidays overseas were virtually unknown too, and there was the promise of a few days off at

Alexandria at the end of the season. To compound the disappointment of some of the regular members of the company, there were others from well-off families, who could afford to travel, even though they were only playing walk-on parts. One of these was Edward Ball, a young man of nineteen, assistant to Cecil Monson, the stage-manager, and, according to Harry Fine, 'a charming fellow'.

*

Edward Ball lived with his mother, whom Mary Manning remembered as 'a fiend'. Her son always referred to her as 'Medea'. Edward's father, a leading physician, lived apart. On leaving school, young Edward expressed an interest in the theatre; he found work as an unpaid extra at the Gate, and a little later was taken on to the stage crew. He had a small part as an organ-grinder in *Crime and Punishment*, and each night was standing beside Micheál MacLíammóir when, as Raskolnikov, he declared that he had 'killed the woman with an axe'. Edward imagined that his mother would advance him the fare to Suez, but it seems she refused to do so. When she was reported missing, and when bloodstained garments were found by the police in a suitcase which Edward had left in Cecil Monson's flat, suspicions were aroused. Edward was questioned by detectives several times, but always had appropriate alibis.

Hilton Edwards was sure that Edward had disposed of his mother – a bloodstained axe was reported to have been found at their house – and when he was arrested, no one was surprised, for in spite of his outwardly pleasant personality, it was recalled that he had been known to have sudden outbursts of temper. All were deeply shocked, and, in an extraordinary way, very much on his side when the case came up. Harry Fine remembered that there was a photograph in the Gate foyer showing Raskolnikov holding the axe; he quickly removed the picture, when he read in the paper of the alleged murder weapon being found. Edward Ball's defence was that his mother had committed suicide. He had found her in bed with her throat cut, and, due to irrational fears, had panicked, and dumped the body in the sea at Shankill, a few miles down the coast. Denis Johnston, as a lawyer, was of the view that Edward would not be sentenced, because, unless the body were found there could be no positive evidence of murder. At the trial, however, it was disclosed that letters were found to his father, expressing remorse at the trouble which he had caused; this was taken as a confession. There was a typical 'Gate rumour' to the effect that Hilton Edwards had been so angry with Mrs Ball for not letting Edward travel that he had seized an axe and chopped her up, smuggling the remains out of the country in Ophelia's coffin . . .

In this macabre atmosphere the Gate Theatre Company completed rehearsals for Cairo, travelling to London before the case was heard. Cecil Monson had to remain in Ireland as a character witness for the defence, for Edward Ball had shared his flat, and they were believed to be lovers. The players embarked on the P & O liner, Strathclyde, at Tilbury on 20 February. Betty Chancellor wrote from Gibraltar to Denis Johnston to say they had bought the English papers and read the latest court evidence. She was feeling 'uncomfortable', for she had just had a row with one of the actors, Blake Gifford. 'I had the temerity to say that I thought Cecil might know more about the Ball case than he cares to say. Cecil is a very bad influence on people, and living with a hysterical boy and having rows all day would have some effect . . . I didn't mean to be vicious, but I'm sorry for that poor queer boy. The whole thing gives me nightmares.' The musical director, Bay Jellett, wrote to her mother: 'It's awful about Edward Ball. The whole company are *fearfully* upset. He was a great friend of Cecil Monson's'. Edward Ball was subsequently committed to the Central Criminal Lunatic Asylum in Dundrum, where visitors, including Harry Fine, who played cricket with Lord Longford's team against a team drawn from the inmates, found him to be as pleasant and 'normal' as always. He was discharged after a few years, probably due to representations made to Eamon de Valéra by Dorothy Macardle, who would have received a colourful account of the case from Micheál MacLíammóir.

Hamlet was rehearsed on shipboard, as there were important parts to be filled, and there were line-calls every afternoon for the other plays. The ship called at Tangier; Betty Chancellor wrote to Denis Johnston: 'Everyone warned me not to go ashore as it was dull, dirty and uninteresting. I loved it'. Bay Jellett wrote to her mother: 'When we got on shore Hilton and Micheál rushed into the arms of a guide who was here when they were here before . . . The men had on things like the brown Moorish cloak that Aunt Moll gave me. Then we went into the garden of the Governor's House. It was just like a fairy tale . . . After that we went to a grand Moorish café. We had *lovely* coffee, and the band played queer African music. Coralie's grandfather came from Tangier, she looked quite at home in it . . . ' Bay was determined to savour and enjoy every minute of the trip, while Betty carried her critical faculties with her, unallayed.

Betty wrote to Denis from the National Hotel: 'The stars, Hilton and Micheál, are being grand and are staying at the Continental-Savoy! . . . We rested last night and then some of us went to the Opera. I wore my silver coat and white billowy dress, just to make a splash . . . I am the only one who is properly equipped for summer. Hilton and Micheál and Coralie were put in a box by Walter Humphries [Harry Fine's replacement as business manager] and he gave *us* back stalls! The theatre is marvellous: it is old-fashioned and very elegant! Row upon row of boxes, with two great royal ones, one of them veiled heavily for the king's wives. He is coming to *Berkeley Square* on Tuesday.'

Bay Jellett reported to her mother that the Seaforth Highlanders were deployed to provide the incidental music during the Gate season – 'they really were very good on the whole . . . The bandmaster stands beside me and takes the tempos and all from me, and gives them the beat. The barracks is away up on a hill. I was sent up in a taxi and we drove through the poor parts of the town – so picturesque . . . ' On 8 March, two days before the opening night, she wrote to her mother to say that they had had a 'wretched time' because the Italian Opera would not allow them to rehearse on the stage. 'It was in Hilton's contract that we were to have six clear days to rehearse *in* the theatre and they broke their word.' Evidently 'in the theatre' was interpreted as 'in a room in the theatre'; Betty Chancellor wrote that they had barely time for dress rehearsals – 'the poor management is in a frenzy and so are we!'

Micheál MacLíammóir does not dwell on the difficulties in *All for Hecuba*, simply noting Hilton's dedication – 'He shut himself up in the theatre from morning till night . . . In desperation at his spartan behaviour I, too, spent the greater part of my days in the theatre watching the sets go up, editing and correcting the angles of sets and rostrums, supervising the repainting where the long journey had wrought havoc . . . But when I could I wandered away, drawn irresistibly through the cool corridors, the dim, tented stage entrance with its robed and turbanned guards, to the unending fascinations of the town, ambling contentedly for hours among the jostle of water-sellers and the hawkers of cakes and incense and carpets and perfumes and beads, the fortune-tellers, the holy men, the pimps and dervishes and guides and donkey-boys . . . '

On 10 March the company rehearsed *Berkeley Square* until 7.30 p.m., and at 9.30 the curtain rose on the opening performance in the presence of King Farouk. Bay Jellett led the Seaforth Highlanders – 'dressed in a lovely Russian blouse uniform' – in the national anthems of Egypt, Ireland and Great Britain. 'The Cairo audiences are well known to be very sniffy, but after the second act they melted, and when the end came they gave it a great reception . . . Micheál, Meriel and Coralie did beautifully . . . ' Afterwards there was a party 'to introduce the company to the Cairo *beau monde* and press. I really enjoyed it, everyone was so agreeable.' The pattern during the first week was setting and lighting in the morning, a dress rehearsal at 3 p.m., and the performance at night; after the first week the schedule became less onerous, and the sightseeing and social life more hectic. 'Cairo had decided, from the opening night of *Berkeley Square*, that we were a success,' MacLíammóir later wrote. He did not exaggerate. 'A brilliant opening,' proclaimed the Egyptian Gazette. 'MacLíammóir instantly conquered the audience . . . One thing must be said of the entire company, the diction was beautiful and there was no trace of an exaggerated accent – indeed of any accent at all.' The critic of the Egyptian Mail was at a loss as to how to apportion the success of all the productions – to Hilton Edwards or to the company as a whole: 'I do know that they are a vindication of repertory in the best sense of the word.' La Bourse Egyptienne was especially taken by *Romeo and Juliet* with MacLíammóir and Moore, comparing the troupe to that of Copeau. The Gazette remarked that 'Impartial public opinion . . . high, low, middle and almost no-brow, is unanimous that this is the finest company of players the capital has seen in many a year.' As to the players, they were fêted everywhere. They were given free access to the Gezira Sporting Club, with its gardens and swimming pool, they were conducted on archaeological expeditions and trips on the Nile, and in more serene moments they took afternoon tea on the terrace at Shepherd's Hotel.

CROOKS AND EMBEZZLERS

A cloud, however, appeared on the brilliant blue horizon in the form of a London newspaper which found its way to the manager of the Royal Opera House. On reading it, he enquired of Edwards and MacLíammóir if they were, genuinely, the directors of Dublin Gate Theatre? – for the article stated that the same company was about to open at the Westminster Theatre, London, in the British premiere of O'Neill's *Ah, Wilderness!* Endless explanations probably convinced the manager that theirs was the 'real' Gate, but, had the season not opened so triumphantly, controversy could have crept into the papers. Both partners were completely taken aback. They knew that Edward Longford planned to keep the Gate open during their absence, starting with a comedy, of which they did not approve, called *Three Cornered Moon*, but they had no idea he had booked another London season with Anmer Hall, and they wondered how it had been possible for the negotiations to have been kept secret from them. The fact that Lord Longford was chairman of the board did not seem to Edwards and MacLíammóir to give him the right to produce plays elsewhere, bearing the Gate name.

Lord Longford announced his Westminster season under the title of 'Longford Productions', and the plays – *Ah, Wilderness!* and his own *Armlet of Jade* – as having come direct from the Gate Theatre in Dublin; but the London press naturally believed this was the company which had been seen the previous year, and referred to it constantly as the 'Dublin Gate'. Hilton Edwards sent a telegram to Edward Longford insisting that the press be formally corrected, to which Longford replied 'Hear you are having a wonderful season. So are we.' The partners took this as a declaration of war.

A letter from Alexandria dated 3 April reached the Irish newspapers on the 9th: 'Sir – Our attention has been drawn to paragraphs in the newspapers announcing the second visit of the Dublin Gate Theatre to the Westminster Theatre. The company of the Dublin Gate Theatre, including Hilton Edwards and Micheál MacLíammóir, is at present on tour in Egypt at the invitation of the Egyptian Government and has no connection with any other company from Dublin which may intend to visit London. We will be obliged if you will correct any statement which you have made to the contrary, Yours etc, Isa Hughes, Secretary, Dublin Gate Theatre Company Ltd.' Hilton Edwards wrote to Edward Longford in London and Denis Johnston in Dublin, and received a prompt reply from the latter, explaining that after the departure of 'your' company for Egypt and the confirmation of Anmer Hall's invitation to 'our' company – which revealed the side of the fence on which Johnston had finally decided to station himself – it was inevitable that 'in the case of any company so geographically situated, a certain number of unofficial and unauthorised references to the Gate Theatre Company may have appeared . . . '

Johnston went on to refer to the 'rather far-reaching step of writing to the press', to the 'hostility' which Edwards and MacLíammóir had created towards those who would not go to Egypt on their terms, and to the received feeling that 'any play that is put on not by you and Micheál is likely to be bad for the Theatre.' He continued, '"L'Etat c'est moi" carries its responsibilities as well as its advantages . . . so if you feel that the theatre is yourselves, and you don't like either your Backer or your Board . . . then take the Theatre and (with all sincerity) good luck to you.' He then reiterated his support in the past for Edwards and MacLíammóir's policies, and for the Egyptian visit 'to make some money for yourselves that you certainly deserve. To this end you have shut down the Theatre's regular activities four months before the proper time, have had free pick of both cast and staff on your own terms. You have been allowed to buy and build your scenery on the Theatre's credit . . . you have been allowed to put on play after play at the Theatre's expense with the sole object of rehearsing them for Egypt . . . ' He concluded by wishing both partners a nice holiday, and, hoping that they would be able to 'accept this very frank letter as a sincere expression of an honest opinion, offered without the slightest malice towards anybody'.

Denis Johnston certainly had several points. There was another, which he did not choose to make, and which the partners in their present mood would not have recognised, which was that his play *The Old Lady Says 'No!'* had placed Edwards and MacLíammóir on the theatrical map. There is no extant correspondence or memorandum on Johnston's reaction to the partners' decision not to stage *A Bride for the Unicorn* in London the previous year, but the incident certainly would have coloured his attitude to the present *débâcle*. Lord Longford's company (now managed by Harry Fine, with Shelah Richards, Eileen Ashe, Cyril Cusack and Fred Johnson) was so well received at the Westminster, it transferred to the Ambassador's. Anmer Hall, who probably did not know about the Egyptian tour, then requested an extended season, and *A Bride for the Unicorn* was chosen. Johnston directed this himself in settings by Norah McGuinness which caused no difficulties on the Westminster stage. In a bold move he wrote to Cairo, inviting Edwards and MacLíammóir to take their original rôles, but both declined. MacLíammóir wrote, 'I am sure that as a theatre man you will see that just as it is impossible for Hilton to return to the very company he has twice produced in your play, as the actor of a part he always felt bad in, it is equally impossible for me in the present circumstances either to leave him to join the organisation which is trying to render useless eight years of our work, or to ask him to accept a position which I'm convinced you can see is humiliating. Curiously enough' – he could not forebear to add – 'it was my design which would not fit into the shallow space of the Westminster stage, so from a practical point alone I would be the wrong man for your purpose . . . Please forgive me for much bitterness and sentimentality, but as you probably know I am incurably nineteenth century in temper . . . '

The season at the Alhambra Theatre in Alexandria was as successful as that at the Royal Opera House, Cairo. Micheál and Hilton then went on a short holiday to Greece, before returning to Dublin to face the Gate board, and the prospect of having no professional home.

Edward Longford, for his part, found Hilton completely irrational when they met. 'When he called me a murderer,' he wrote to Denis, 'I walked off . . . There is just a chance, a very remote one indeed, of Hilton's and Micheál's resigning this week. In that case Norman [Reddin] thinks liquidation should be avoided: I am not inclined to agree, and I don't think you are either. If I am right about your view, I am sure Norman can be talked over, and in any case he realises we must act in unison. Hilton and Micheál appear to regard your offer to them for *The Bride* as an insult, and say they are not getting fair play, and that thanks to our action they are being accused of being crooks and embezzlers all over Dublin. I offered to deny this rumour publicly if they really want me to . . . They threaten to publish everything in the press after the meeting. If they get it in, it should be funny reading!'

The meeting of the board proved to be an anti-climax. The bitter words had already been written and spoken in a kind of round-robin of accusations and denials, some of it reaching the press, where rumours of the theatre's imminent closure were fair copy. By the time the matter came to be formally discussed the heat had gone out of the arguments. Norman Reddin would probably have been delighted to see Edwards and MacLíammóir resign. While Lord Longford was weary of them, he was an exceptionally fair-minded man, and he acknowledged that without their peculiar genius there would be no Gate at all. The result was that liquidation was ruled out, but an uncomfortable compromise was put in place. The Gate Theatre Company remained as the lessees of the building. Arrangements were made for two other self-sufficient companies to be formed: Edwards-MacLíammóir Dublin Gate Theatre Productions Ltd., and Longford Productions. These would each lease the theatre for six months of the year, with the option of sub-letting to other reputable managements at times when neither was in a position to fill their half-year either in whole or in part.

The disadvantage for Edwards-MacLíammóir was that they would have to find their own funding, now that they had lost a generous, if erratic patron. The advantage was that they would not have to grind out a full year's programme. They issued an unusually aggressive leaflet seeking patronage, outlining their programme, and announcing that their season would run 'from Horse Show Week (early August) until 20 January'. This period was selected because they were hopeful of being invited back to Egypt annually in the spring: the profit had been considerable, and without that additional guaranteed income they had no source of revenue other than their own box-office. Another reason may have been that they realised they would probably have to eke out their year with touring in Ireland – Longford had already announced that his company would be devoting half its time to bringing the best of theatre to the provinces. Edwards and MacLíammóir knew from experience of the rigours of winter tours, with unheated halls and damp beds – *their* Irish tours would take place in the summer, while the Longfords would discover for themselves what winter touring was like. The new arrangement gave rise to a symbolic annual ritual concerning territorial rights: when the Longfords took over the theatre for their six-month occupation, down came the photographs of early Gate productions and the framed designs by Micheál MacLíammóir, and up went dozens of watercolours signed 'Longford' – for Edward had taken up another hobby. These works of art were sold for figures ranging from five shillings to £2; they made the foyer and staircase look like the entrance to a sale-of-work by Sunday painters. Unfortunately, they also set the tone; the stage productions were often of high quality – when an expert director was employed – and the leading actors were invariably highly skilled; but there was always a pervasive sense of amateur do-gooding, of 'bringing culture to the masses', and this derived from Edward himself. He was totally sincere in his endeavours, but he lacked the common sense to understand that the patron should stand apart.

The Boys very quickly came to realise that although they could not now make use of Longford's money, they could benefit from it in kind. They rarely troubled with maintenance work – if stage lighting needed repair or replacement, they left this to be attended to by the incoming Longford crew, while they swept off to further foreign assignments. When threatened by an angry note, they either did not trouble to reply, or pleaded inability to pay. It took them some time to understand that when actors who had played with them accepted parts from Longford, it was pointless snubbing them in the street, or making impassioned speeches about 'loyalty'; actors, as they should have known, and in fact did know, must find work where they can get it, and no repertory actor could afford to sit at home unpaid, hoping that some time there would be another part with Edwards-MacLíammóir Productions. The coolness with Denis Johnston continued for some years; there was coolness with his wife, Shelah Richards, when she directed *Three Cornered Moon* for Longford; and an icy cloud descended when Betty Chancellor decided to join the first of Longford's provincial tours: but the Boys had failed to offer her good parts in their 1936-37 season. ('*She* won't be coming with us to Egypt in the spring!') In the fullness of time these and many other ruptures were healed – but never completely.

There were other changes. Mary Manning went to the United States, where she subsequently married Professsor Mark Howe of Harvard. She became a co-founder, with Denis Johnston, of the Poets' Theatre in Boston, and an important force in establishing a broader understanding of Irish art and letters in that quintessentially Hiberno-American city; Micheál MacLíammóir performed in Boston in the 1960s on the invitation of one of the cultural bodies with which

(*Above, left*) George Relph as
Joseph and Alfred Willmore
(Mícheál MacLíammóir) as
Benjamin in *Joseph and His
Brethren*, His Majesty's
Theatre, London, 1913.
(*Above, right*) 151 Purves
Road, Kensal Green, London
N.W.10., birthplace of Alfred
Willmore. (*Right*) Alfred
Willmore in 1911 when
acting for Sir Herbert
Beerbohm Tree.

(*Above, left*) Hilton Edwards in a
photographer's studio about 1912,
in costume for an unidentified
school play. (*Above, right*) Hilton
Edwards in *Love on the Dole*,
Dublin Gate Theatre, 1942.
(*Right*) Netherwood, High Road,
East Finchley, London N.2., home
of Thomas Cecil Edwards.

(*Above*) Orson Welles at
Woodstock, Illinois, where he
played Claudius in *Hamlet*, directed
by Hilton Edwards, with Micheál
MacLíammóir as Hamlet, 1934.
(*Right*) Anew McMaster as
Coriolanus at the Shakespeare
Memorial Theatre, Stratford-
upon-Avon, 1933.

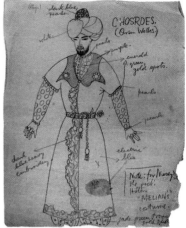

(*Above, left*) Costume design by Micheál
MacLíammóir for his own play *Diarmuid
agus Gráinne*, Galway, 1928. (*Above, right*)
Costume design by Micheál MacLíammóir
for Orson Welles as King Chosroes in Padraic
Colum's *Mogu*, 1931. (*Right*) Caricature of
Micheál MacLíammóir, Hilton Edwards and
Coralie Carmichael by Brigid O'Brien, 1934.
(*Below*) An early revival of *The Old Lady
Says 'No!'* by Denis Johnston.

(*Above*) Members of the Dublin
Gate Theatre Company on the
terrace of Shepherd's Hotel, Cairo,
1937. (*Below*) Micheál
MacLíammóir (*left*) as Byron in
Portrait in Marble by Hazel Ellis,
1936; and Hilton Edwards (*right*) at
the time of the first Mediterranean
tour, 1936.

(*Top*) Micheál MacLíammóir as Algy and Cyril Cusack as Jack in *The Importance of Being Earnest*, Gate, 1933. (*Above*) The Opera House, Valetta, where Dublin Gate Theatre Productions played in 1938 and 1939. (*Right*) Poster for Hilton Edwards' production of *Macbeth*, Belgrade, 1939.

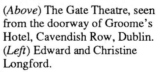

(*Above*) The Gate Theatre, seen from the doorway of Groome's Hotel, Cavendish Row, Dublin. (*Left*) Edward and Christine Longford.

(*Above*) *Not for Children* by
Elmer Rice, design by Micheál
MacLíammóir in the manner of
the painter Mainie Jellett, 1935.
(*Below*) *Marrowbone Lane* by
Robert Collis, Gate, 1939.
(*Right*) Denis Johnston.

she was associated. Her departure from Dublin meant the end of Motley; its pages remain as the most pungent and scintillating deposit of the heterodox artistic society which centred round the Gate Theatre, the United Arts Club, the Buttery in the Hibernian Hotel, and a small coterie in Trinity College in the early 'thirties – not extensive enough to be given a neighbourhood name like 'Bloomsbury' or 'Barbizon', yet much more influential than those outside its tolerant circle realised at the time.

An influential newcomer to the Gate in 1935 was the young Scottish designer, Molly MacEwen; she was engaged initially as a scene-painter and then, as her talent made itself manifest, she began to design sets and costumes, taking the strain off MacLíammóir. He found her unassuming and shy at first, but 'Molly blossomed like a garden with the people she liked, and her talent was remarkable. Her temperament and tastes were all different from mine; she liked Jane Austen better than the Brontës, Mozart better than Chopin, the colour blue was prized above green, Matisse was higher on her list than Picasso . . . ' Her first work was, appropriately enough, on a play about Mary, Queen of Scots, *Three Leopards*, written by Cecil Monson, where her huge Gothic inscription 'In my end is my beginning', which flew right across the stage, was much admired. (Betty Chancellor referred to *Three Leopards* as 'Maisie Monson's play'; she told Denis Johnston it was 'most expensive as well as poor, and will probably ruin the theatre'; her remarks were typical of a certain tone which encompassed the Gate and its adherents.) Molly MacEwen designed almost fifty sets for the company in Ireland and abroad over the next thirty years.

Inspired, perhaps even alarmed – both are always denied – by the Gate's now unassailable superiority in the visual and technical aspects of stage presentation, the Abbey Theatre engaged the Welsh director, Hugh Hunt, and the English designer, Tanya Moiseiwitsch to mount almost all the new productions from 1936 to 1939. One of Hunt's first actions was to invite Micheál MacLíammóir to play in a revival of Yeats' *Deirdre*, with Jean Forbes-Robertson. Hunt later wrote that one of 'my happiest memories of the Abbey is producing Micheál as Naisi'. He found himself in trouble immediately, for he gave billing to the two leads, a thing unheard of in the democratic National Theatre; and the absence of a declamatory style in the speaking of the verse annoyed the directors of the Abbey so much they passed a resolution that Mr Hunt should direct no more plays by Mr Yeats. (Yeats himself evidently ignored this, and gave Hunt his script of *Purgatory* in 1938.) MacLíammóir chose to accept the Abbey enagagement because an appearance in any Yeats play there was prestigious for an actor, and also because he knew he would enjoy working with Jean Forbes-Robertson, the latest in the series of Peter Pans. He was not, therefore, in the Gate production of *When Lovely Woman* – , one of the very few of Lennox Robinson's plays to be first performed outside the Abbey. 'We liked Lennox Robinson's *When Lovely Woman* – less than anything he has written,' declared the critic of Dublin Opinion, and The Times of London felt that 'Mr Robinson has not found the inspiration he needed'. It was later referred to as 'the Abbey's revenge on the Gate'. It seems that MacLíammóir had made a judicious choice in deciding not to be in it.

A Playgoers' Circle was inaugurated by Andrew Ganly, author of *Murder, Like Charity*, in the autumn of 1936. Patrons paid £5, members £1 or associates ten shillings; they could identify themselves with the work of the theatre, obtain certain booking privileges, and be confident that their subscriptions would help to subsidise the programme. A number of lectures and discussions, which appear to have been very well attended, were held on Sunday nights in the theatre, in spite of the increasing popularity of radio in the dissemination of cultural comment and opinion. Distinguished authors took part, and for no fee. Financial constraints nonetheless, Hilton Edwards was still choosing plays with very large casts, and some of the plays did very poor business – notably the Robinson play, Ibsen's *Brand* and Henri Ghéon's *The Marvellous History of St Bernard*, which did not attract the crowds hoped for after the popularity of *St Francis*.

The unexpected success of the season was *Portrait in Marble*, which appears to have been a fairly straightforward and certainly uncontroversial study of Byron by Hazel Ellis, a member of the company; Moore, Hobhouse, Lady Caroline Lamb and Miss Milbanke all appear – the latter, according to the press, giving a splendid opportunity to a young English actress, Diana Vernon, whom MacLíammóir described as having an 'excited conspiratorial manner' offstage and on. Byron had not yet been treated *ad nauseam* by stage and film writers, and the subject matter would have been quite novel. Housman's *Victoria Regina*, a series of harmlessly amusing sketches of life at Balmoral and Buckingham Palace, which had displeased the British stage censor and which MacLíammóir recalled as bringing in a 'densely-packed display of Protestant millinery, even at matinées', was a box-office hit, as were J.B. Priestley's homespun north London drama, *Laburnum Grove*, and the first Gate production of *The School for Scandal*. Ann Clark – 'small and brown as a thrush, reminiscent as mignonette and inexorable as an oleograph', as MacLíammóir rather ambiguously described her – whom they had first met on the McMaster tours, played Queen Victoria and stayed with the company for the Mediterranean tour the following spring. McMaster himself joined the company for *The School for Scandal* and a revival of *The Importance of Being Earnest*, because *Othello* and *Twelfth Night* were specially requested by the Ministry of Education in Cairo, and also no doubt because McMaster was in need of a little change, after a winter of Holy Faith Halls and Majestic Cinemas from Balbriggan to Ballyporeen.

PLAYING BEFORE CROWNED HEADS

The Mediterranean tour of 1937 followed the pattern of the previous year, with an additional three weeks at the Royal Opera House in Valetta, a huge mid-

Victorian theatre, built by local enterprise with the approval of the British colonial administration of the day. The architect, Edward Middleton Barry, did not visit the site until after his plans had been drawn; and the building, when completed, bore no resemblance to anything previously seen on the island of Malta. The members of the Gate company seem to have thrived in its opulence and splendour, buoyed up no doubt by the reaction of the audience. 'To appear before the Maltese people is the nearest thing an English-speaking actor can know of the ferocious pleasure that must be the lot of the Italian singer,' MacLíammóir wrote ten years later; 'a pulsing melodramatic silence holds the audience during the playing of a scene, a taut apprehension like that which hangs in the air over the bull-ring in Spain, and then, as in Spain . . . the long-drawn sweet gush of applause . . . ' Bay Jellett's letters to her mother in Fitzwilliam Square are full of gardens – and garden parties; it would seem that the small island was an exotic extension of Kent, and almost the entire population either titled or engaged in some high-ranking and probably rather hush-hush commission on behalf of His Majesty. MacLíammóir, while making himself the centre of the lunches and cocktail parties, was rather less impressed by this aspect of Maltese life; he noted the inherent philistinism of the British character in the attitude to the arts of these friendly people – something to be vaguely encouraged, but which did not affect your life. When lunching at the palace with the governor, his wife, Lady Violet Bonham-Carter, enthusiastically suggested a performance of *A Midsummer Night's Dream* in the entirely appropriate setting of Greek portico and cypress trees of her garden, but could not understand that 'the production of a play was a matter of some weeks of plodding methodical preparation, and that the apparently universal idea that actors were magicians capable of shaking a new and unique performance out of the empty air was but a dream.'

The Gate players seem to have been in a relaxed mood when they arrived for the first time in Valetta, for the season at Cairo and Alexandria had been free of troubles, though not entirely free of incidents that in retrospect read somewhat strangely. They played to two thousand Egyptian students in what must have seemed, to that audience, a most puzzling work, *Laburnum Grove*: can there have been a mistake, and can the young audience have come expecting to see *Othello*? Hazel Ellis's play about Byron and his circle was received with much interest, as if it were an important new literary work. (It vanished from the stage thereafter.) McMaster, according to MacLíammóir, 'was a brilliant success as Othello and Malvolio', but he does not mention Jack Worthing or Charles Surface, in which Mac was probably no more than adequate; he 'went wild over Cairo and must have spent hundreds of pounds in the Musky, where he was the idol of the Arab dealers with his great height, his fair hair, his disarming smile and his indifference to bargaining.'

The profit made from the 1937 Mediterranean tour meant that Edwards-MacLíammóir Productions had a small surplus at the end of the operating year, and this was the cause of smug rejoicing. What the partners did not disclose in their public pronouncements was that the figures did not take into account the staffing and maintenance of the Gate Theatre building, and a perennial internal wrangle with Lord Longford on this issue ensued. As far as the partners were concerned, foreign touring would have to play an important part in their programme.

In the autumn and winter of 1937-38, Emlyn Williams' *Night Must Fall* with MacLíammóir as Danny and May Carey as Mrs Branson, broke the Gate attendance-record and inevitably drew cries of 'commercialism', which were countered by other cries that questioned whether the truly commercial theatre could produce such performances. Hilton Edwards added Macbeth to his list of major successes. There was the sequel to *Victoria Regina*, billed simply as *Victoria*, with Ann Clark again as the queen; and several revivals of what were now seen as 'Gate staples' – *Hamlet*, *Berkeley Square*, *The Drunkard* and *The Old Lady Says 'No!'* – for which Denis Johnston granted permission without demur. The 'artistic' success was Cocteau's *Infernal Machine*, with the Gate's child-actress discovery, Peggy Cummins; and the 'controversial' work – there always seemed to be one – was Elmer Rice's anti-fascist play of almost *grand-guignol* horror based on the Reichstag fire trial, *Judgement Day*; letters appeared in the press acccusing the author of being anti-German, and the producers as insulting German residents in Ireland, but one writer probably summed up the feeling by saying that 'such occurrences are beyond the comprehension of people in this country.'

Disappointingly, there was no return invitation to visit Cairo for the spring of 1938. The British Council was becoming active in promoting English music and drama in countries where it was felt the British influence might be at risk, and Egypt was one of these countries; the Royal Opera House was a beneficiary of the Council's policy – but it is also quite possible that the management felt two successive visits from the Irish company was enough for the time being. The municipality of Alexandria, however, provided enough funds to make another Gate season worthwhile, and the Royal Opera House in Malta issued an invitation on a guaranteed commercial basis. On the suggestion of Anew McMaster, who knew that W. Bridges-Adams, the producer of the season in which he had appeared at the Shakespeare Memorial Theatre in Stratford-upon-Avon, had just been appointed drama advisor to the British Council, Edwards and MacLíammóir called on him at his office in Hanover Square on their way home from Valetta to Dublin in the spring of 1937. Bridges – he was never referred to as Walter – did not see any reason why an English-speaking company, even if it were based in the Irish Free State, should not be eligible for financial support; and throughout the summer and autumn he was in constant touch with Hilton Edwards about possible plays and venues. It was agreed that Italy and Greece would be mutually suitable; but in that year relations with the Mussolini regime dwindled, and Valetta-Athens-Alexandria became the itinerary. There was only one problem, as Bridges-Adams wrote to his superior in a memorandum of 16 February 1938, and that was the fact that the Dublin production of *Victoria Regina* was uncensored. He suggested that a copy of the play be sent to 'His Majesty's Minister in Athens'. Hilton Edwards had agreed, he said, to consult Mr Lawrence Housman 'for details of any variations from his printed text which have been made in deference to the British censor. I feel this step to be particularly necessary in view of certain lines in the "Proposal Scene" which have some reference to the question of Prince Albert's legitimacy.'

It is to be assumed that Sir Sydney Waterlow (described by MacLíammóir as being 'as full of surprises as a Viennese Apfelstrudel') did not feel that the British censor had a rôle to play in Athens, and *Victoria Regina* was included in the programme. British Council staff very efficiently made the theatre and travel arrangements for the Athens part of the trip. The Royal Theatre received numerous beautifully typed instructions, including one saying that the Gate's 'normal orchestral requirements were two first violins, two second violins, viola, 'cello, double bass, clarionet [sic], tympani, piano. For *The Provok'd Wife* they require also a flute and an oboe. For *Macbeth* and *Hamlet* they require, in addition to the aforesaid, two trumpets and a trombone.' Presumably Bay Jellett did not reveal that she was used to an orchestra of three: herself (violin), Cathleen Rogers (piano) and Gretta Smith ('cello).

The company travelled from Valetta – where, according to The Times of Malta, a controversy was raging as to whether Mussolini had personally made an aerial reconnaissance of the island from a 'high-powered bomber' – by ship to Syracuse, thence by train to Brindisi *via* Messina, and from Brindisi to Athens by plane. Few of the players had ever flown before – there was a company called Irish Sea Airways, which ran regular flights from Baldonnell Aerodrome near Dublin to Croydon and Bristol, but only the wealthy and the intrepid made use of it – and their excitement was childlike. Bay Jellett wrote to her mother from the Acropole Palace Hotel in Athens that it was the most wonderful experience she had ever had in her life; she said much the same of a trip to Delphi with Ann Clark, Lionel Dymoke and Tyrrell Pine; it seems that the whole company felt enriched by the externals of the season as much as by the rapturous response of the Greek public. King George attended the opening performance of *The Provok'd Wife*, and received the ladies of the company during the second interval. 'He is charming,' wrote the impressionable Bay Jellett, 'so simple, and made us feel quite at our ease. He said he had always hoped to take his car over and tour Ireland.' The king also came to *Macbeth*, unannounced, and shook Hilton Edwards warmly by the hand afterwards; but the most 'exciting and alluring' person the company met was Katina Paxinou, who came to every play: after *Victoria Regina* she told Micheál MacLíammóir that she could see he was 'charming, accomplished and sympathetic', but she was waiting to see him 'acting seriously', and in *Hamlet* she was not disappointed.

The English-language papers in Egypt were full of complaints about the Royal Opera House not presenting the Gate in Cairo that year. After the final night in Alexandria an additional performance of *Night Must Fall* was given at Port Said, with Roy Irving as Danny, for Micheál MacLíammóir was suffering from 'a boil'. All the members of the company were presented with a bonus of £5 because the tour had been such a success – Bay Jellett wrote that this was 'very generous' of Micheál and Hilton, and deplored the attitude of some members of the company who felt it should have been more!

MacLíammóir and Edwards stayed on in Egypt with their friends the Heathcote-Smiths after the other members of the company sailed for home, and then they travelled by a leisurely route through Italy to Paris, where they were joined by Aunt Craven and Molly MacEwen. They found the military rallies in Italy ubiquitous and disturbing; it may have crossed their minds that the marching jackboots were measuring out the final steps of foreign theatrical touring as they had come to know it.

Chapter 7
Agamemnon, Hecuba, and the Theatre of War

In Paris Hilton took his scripts to the Luxembourg Gardens each morning, while Micheál did a round of museums in search of material for the Byzantine sets which they had agreed upon for *The Comedy of Errors* – presumably imagining the city of Seljuk would replace classical Ephesus – 'houses like gilded tea-chests with rounded windows perched up on narrow pillars, walled-in gardens like minute fives-courts, and sloping roofs chequered in puce and silver' as Micheál reported Hilton saying, though the choice of words is much more like his own. They went with Craven and Molly to the Théâtre de l'Athenée to see Jouvet in Marcel Achard's latest play, the poetical romance *Le Corsaire*, and decided there and then to choose it as their second work for the Dublin season and to negotiate the rights. Micheál added the task of translating it to his already voluminous portfolio of projects, while Molly joined the daily *enclave* in the Luxembourg and started her sketches for sets and costumes.

Spurred on perhaps by the enthusiasm of Owen Sheehy-Skeffington, they called on Jean Giraudoux, but nothing resulted from the encounter, and, most surprisingly, the Gate never produced a Giraudoux play in all its fifty years of existence, though MacLíammóir appeared in *The Madwoman of Chaillot* at the Olympia in Dublin in 1956. He also went to see the elderly playwright Henri-René Lenormand, whose work he had come across when it was given by the Pitoëffs in the 1920s, and their meetings ended with Lenormand agreeing to a transposition of *Les Ratés* into an Irish setting. They visited libraries and museums and, in the evenings, cabarets: Mistinguett had returned to Paris after a long absence, and Micheál found her 'as ancient as the stage itself, as careless as a child'. They agreed that the Don Juan in Hell scene from Shaw's *Man and Superman* would make a complete play in itself and would contrast well with *The Comedy of Errors*, shortened to make a challenging double-bill (too challenging, as it turned out). They decided that the centrepiece of the season should be O'Neill's *Mourning Becomes Electra*, which had rarely been performed outside the United States. There would also have to be some classical revivals, the choice depending upon what might be required by the British

Council, if Bridges-Adams proved receptive to another overseas tour. With so much still in the melting-pot for the autumn, they took train and boat for London. Here they went about the annual business of finding new players. Diana Vernon had left in an aura of mystery; and a sensitive young actor would be needed to play Orin in *Mourning Becomes Electra*.

A succession of interviews and readings resulted in very little and it was not until they were introduced to Christopher Casson, 'in fly-away tweeds and a butcher-blue shirt that made his eyes almost as dazzling as his mother's', that they knew they had met the right actor for the younger parts. His mother was Sybil Thorndike, and his father Lewis Casson, keystones in the British theatrical establishment. His experience was astonishingly wide and varied: he had played at the Old Vic, the repertory theatres in York and Perth, and on one occasion, while on tour with his parents in the Middle East, he took the part of the Bank of the River Loire in *St Joan*, when the scenery failed to arrive. He was wrapped in a length of canvas on which the actor who played Dunois not only sat but stood. All this emerged over the next few months, as Christopher Casson settled into the life of Dublin, the city which became his home, where he married, and where he and his wife, Kay O'Connell, the stage designer, brought up their children. She had been an ardent Gate-goer while at school, and was very soon helping Molly MacEwen with scene painting. When Christopher arrived for his first rehearsal, The Irish Times stated that 'he might pass for an Irish boy. He plays the harp, sings Irish songs, and is delighted to have the chance of working here.' The harp had been acquired when playing in Scotland, and he gave innumerable recitals on Radio Eireann over the years.

The Gate had never had a full-time publicity officer because the budget would not stretch to one, and the duties had usually been undertaken by someone whose real interests lay elsewhere – principally in acting. The imposition of writing and public-relations work on a supporting player had never proved satisfactory. When Edwards and MacLíammóir interviewed Toska Bissing, who had acting experience at the repertory theatres of Cambridge and Manchester, and had appeared in the London Gate production of Schauffer's *Parnell*, they realised that she was more a 'theatre person' than an actress, and that her immense vitality and charm, as well as her deftly witty way with words, would make her ideal casting for the neglected off-stage rôle of Press Representative, with the occasional acting part. Toska Bissing was a niece of General Baron Freiherr Moritz von Bissing, who had ordered the execution of the British nurse, Edith Cavell, in Belgium in 1915 for helping allied prisoners of war to escape. Toska Bissing's father was a naturalised Englishman and she went to English schools, but her striking appearance, her elegant capes and furs, her suavity, and her effortless command of several European languages, created suspicion in many quarters, not least with officials in the countries which the Gate Theatre visited in 1939, for the fact was she completely answered the description of the Glamorous Spy of fiction.

THE MOST PROBLEMATIC CREATURES IN EUROPE

The opening of the Gate's new season coincided with a twelve-day Festival at the Abbey designed to celebrate the thirty-fifth anniversary of the founding of the Abbey Theatre. Thirty-fifth birthdays are not usually considered to be specially noteworthy, but it is possible that the directors of the National Theatre Society wished to make some kind of official statement of achievement at a time when W.B. Yeats was still there (he was in very poor health, and died the following winter). No less than seventeen plays were presented, from the early stage work of Yeats, Gregory and Synge, via O'Casey to Paul Vincent Carroll, whose *Shadow and Substance* had opened the previous year. Yeats' *Purgatory* was given its first production during the Festival, and the aged playwright attended the performance.

The burden placed upon the actors and crew proved too great at times – Cyril Cusack had to appear in nine different parts – and the programme had to be altered slightly during the run. A series of lectures on the history and evolution of the Irish theatre was planned to take place in the Aberdeen Hall at the Gresham Hotel each morning at eleven o'clock. Lennox Robinson, the organiser, was warned that lectures at the Shaw Festival at Malvern were very sparsely attended, and he might be saving his speakers some embarrassment if he were to omit this element from the programme. Robinson, however, knew his public, and divined rightly that talks by the literary notables of the day would prove as much a draw as the plays themselves. He decided to speak on Lady Gregory, and thereby was able to set right the record of his admiration for her work, for it was known that there had been private animosity between them. Frank O'Connor spoke on Synge, making a savage and unfair attack on Daniel Corkery's book *Synge and Anglo-Irish Literature*. Controversy was in the air. Robinson's invitation to Micheál MacLíammóir to speak on the subject of Problem Plays was provocative, for all the other lecturers were either a part of the fabric of the National Theatre structure, or were closely associated with it. MacLíammóir had acted on the Abbey stage only three times – and none of the celebrated senior Abbey actors – such as F.J. McCormick, Barry Fitzgerald, or Arthur Shields – were asked to air their views in any capacity whatsoever. The choice of MacLíammóir was an astute one, for it showed an awareness of another type of theatre and another audience, and there was the obvious attraction of the matinée-idol.

MacLíammóir's lecture was planned for the final morning of the Festival. The Aberdeen Hall had seating for over four hundred, but, as Robinson later wrote, the interest was so great 'we could not drag in enough chairs'. MacLíammóir, who was rehearsing *Le Corsaire* across the road in the Gate, arrived in a flurry with a minute to spare, and began on a note of mock modesty, saying that a man who can speak seriously before lunchtime is not a lecturer but a hero, and that he was neither lecturer nor hero 'but a wretched actor and a designer of stage settings and costumes, and I am full of the defects of my tribe, among the worst of these being that I hate the morning and that I dread a dry-up more than anything else in the world, so I have artlessly written out my talk'. He said that when he came to consider his subject, he was forced into the bewildering conclusion that all Irish plays were problem plays, that the Irish people 'are possibly the most problematic creatures in Europe' and that Ireland is 'one long unending problem whose solution may conceivably be lying in the womb of time'.

He presented a list of plays which had been written since the time of the formation of the Irish Literary Theatre, on the assumption that the Festival was not concerning itself with the work of earlier Irish playwrights like Farquhar and Goldsmith and Boucicault, and it is clear that he picked those for which he had either a great admiration or a great dislike, so that he could discourse fluently about them, detecting 'problems' in each, in order to justify the subject of the lecture. The first was Yeats' *The Countess Cathleen*, which, as the audience knew, had created archiepiscopal displeasure. He recalled in lengthy parenthesis his discovery of the play as a boy – he could only have seen it in London, though he did not say so – 'its fascination for me lay not merely in the fact that it had the romantic colour and the supernatural interest that I have always loved, or even that it was the first play that I had come across that revealed to me the light, the climate, the very perfume of the Irish countryside, in a noble and tragic mirror' – and then proceeded to empathise with Yeats' view of the heroine's certain redemption, where 'many a lesser playwright would have pulled down a cowardly curtain on an unanswered question, and sent his audience home agog about the fate of a misguided philanthropist'.

Of *John Bull's Other Island* he remarked that Shaw, 'who set out not only to solve a problem but also to explode several outworn superstitions concerning Irish and English people, one of them that the Irish are possessed of a fatal and overwhelming charm, was himself caught away into the maelstrom and emerged with a handful of characters who . . . showed themselves to be undeniably charming.' MacLíammóir had never acted in either *The Countess Cathleen* or *John Bull's Other Island*, which were both recognised as 'Abbey' plays, but not many years passed before he appeared in both of them – not at the Abbey, but at the Gate.

MacLíammóir's entertainingly allusive approach was quite different to anything the audience had experienced over the previous two weeks, for the style and delivery of most of the other lecturers was fairly pedestrian, even if their arguments may have carried greater weight. Here, too, was the Abbey Theatre being looked at from the outside, in flattering terms which savoured not of a younger and respectful institution at the other end of the street, but a younger institution with a much wider perspective. He spent several minutes discussing the plays of Lennox Robinson, especially *The Big House* in which Shelah Richards had played the part of the survivor of a long line of planter stock when the family mansion is burned to the ground during the 'troubles'. The play had first come out in 1925 and had been hailed as 'Chekhovian', and MacLíammóir, five years later, said that he disliked it 'so passionately, and was so passionately moved and excited by it, that the seeing of it remains to this day in my mind as one of the theatrical events of my life. I hated its perfect presentation of what to me was then the most maddening of all human beings, the intelligent West Briton. I hated its sympathetic handling of our national disease of rapt self-analysis, practised with such skill by the West British heroine. I hated the tolerance and understanding with which the, to me, intolerable and incomprehensible figures of the play were drawn; and all this because, like everyone else in the country, I was consumed with emotions of love and rage and burning contempt for various schools of thought not shared by myself.'

His avowed hatred for *The Big House* was articulated in such a way that its fine qualities were subtly exposed and his own absence of appreciation amusingly denigrated, and the audience was left with what was in effect a most delightful and undoubtedly genuine vote of thanks from the speaker to the organiser of the lecture. It was probably no accident that Lennox Robinson's next play (a much more interesting work than the hapless *When Lovely Woman – *) was produced two years later by the Gate rather than the Abbey; it was to cause a scandal of a kind which no one could possibly have imagined in 1938.

*

Le Corsaire was renamed *Hollywood Pirate* for Dublin. Its cinematic technique, and its somewhat Pirandellan transitions from reality to fantasy did not greatly appeal to press or public. *Les Ratés* (literally, *The Failures*), translated as *Juliet in the Rain* and reset in a dismal Irish provincial town, was described by the Independent as 'depressing' – a lethal word at the box-office. Halfway through its two-week run Neville Chamberlain returned from his meeting with Adolf Hitler in Munich, and announced that there would be 'peace in our time'. The world, as everyone knows, trembled with relief; and the chief consequence, as envisaged backstage at the Gate, was that the spring tour of Balkan countries might still be a possibility. On 5 October – the day following the opening of *Night Must Fall*, hastily revived to restore financial equilibrium – the Czechoslovak cabinet resigned, and the Irish Times published a photograph of a platoon of Gordon Highlanders standing 'in readiness' at Aldershot, which suggested that the message of Munich might not be worth the paper it was written on. *Night Must Fall* did excellent business, but revealed a tendency in the programme planning towards the sombre and indeed spectral, which was to continue with *Mourning Becomes Electra*: yet this play proved to be the most popular of the new productions offered. (It was, of course, a much better play.)

The diarist Joseph Holloway had been warned that the new pianist at the Gate, Patricia Victory, had been shocked by O'Neill's use of language. The fact that Holloway bothered to note this suggests that he attended the opening prepared to be shocked himself, for he was of a prim disposition. Contrary to expectation, he did not find any crudity at all. 'One of the most remarkable performances seen in Dublin in recent years,' he confided to his journal with the air of a man who expected to be widely quoted, '*Mourning Becomes Electra* is a play worthy of the great tradition in which it had its origin. Its Americanisation is an integral part of it. From the first lifting of the curtain until the last closing, a unity of atmosphere and dramatic tension was preserved. The actors never loosened the taut string.' The design by Micheál MacLíammóir (who did not appear) took as its motif the great classical columns of the Mannons' southern mansion, suggesting to those receptive to the idea the columns of Mycenae. As is so often the case when work of real quality and excitement is provided, the public was not deterred by the early start at 7 p.m. and the late close at 11. 'For their great courage,' The Times of London remarked, 'no less than for the splendour of their accomplishment, the director and cast deserve all the support which packed houses for the duration of the run can give them.' David Sears wrote in the Independent, 'For the first time in my life I heard the Gate audience cheering, when Meriel Moore and Coralie Carmichael came out last night to take their curtain calls. The quiet understanding and insight of Hilton Edwards' portrayal of the Agamemnon figure, General Mannon, pleased those who perhaps had expected histrionics'.

Bridges-Adams came to Dublin during the run of *Mourning Becomes Electra* and said that events in central and eastern Europe had persuaded the British Council to increase rather than abandon its activities there. No English company seemed able or willing to provide the kind of repertoire required – this caused some raising of eyebrows: did the English managements know something, perhaps? Questions of nationality and cultural credibility were again discussed, as they had been prior to the visit to Athens. How would an Irish company be received, when specifically British drama was requested? Would the host theatres object to a company from Dublin, when they probably expected one from London? The informal view, it appeared, was that very few people in the countries concerned would know where Dublin was situated anyway, in the way that few people in Dublin, or in London for that matter, knew where to place Ljubljana or Salonika on the map. As to repertoire, the two revivals planned to bring the programme up to Christmas, *Julius Caesar* and *The Importance of Being Earnest*, were clear contenders for the tour. Volleys of letters and telegrams were exchanged between Bridges-Adams and Raymond Percy, Hilton Edwards' colleague from his first Charles Doran tour, who was now the Gate's manager. There was the further complication of the Edwards-MacLíammóir company having to vacate the theatre at the end of January, in order to admit Longford Productions; this would mean a dreaded Irish tour in February and March, since the Balkan arrangements could not be completed until April. Fortunately, Raymond Percy was able to organise a season at the Cork Opera House at short notice, followed by a week in Belfast – the company's first visit to Northern Ireland. J.B. Fagan's popular musical, *And So To Bed*, with Hilton

Edwards as Samuel Pepys, was produced at the Gate for Christmas, with astonishing lack of success (it did very well in Cork); it was unceremoniously taken off and replaced with revivals of *Wuthering Heights* and the thriller, *Death Takes a Holiday* – all part of the immense preparations for the tour which would take the players from Cork to Sofia.

Toska Bissing organised a backstage party for the press after a performance of *Death Takes a Holiday*. The novelty of the idea pleased the theatre correspondents, particularly Nuala Moran of The Leader, who responded warmly to Toska's suggestion that she should send extracts from her tour journal for publication. 'I am glad that the company realise,' she wrote in her column the following week, 'that it is necessary to keep in touch with their Irish public, recognising the wisdom of the proverb, *"Nuair a bhionn duine amuic, fuarann a chuid"* '['When a person is abroad, his portion grows cold']. She wrote that 'Hilton Edwards was forced to take the pipe out of his mouth, leave his Balkan maps down, and say something' – which he then did at some length. During the informal question period, when the possibility of war was being discussed, he flippantly asked her if she would prefer to be shot in Belfast or Belgrade, and she voted for Belgrade because she had been to Belfast and would like to see somewhere else before she died. Hilton said he had never really believed the Balkans existed outside novels. 'Remote and impenetrable as the Balkans appear from Dublin,' he continued, 'it is easier to get into Bulgaria than across the frontier of the six counties at the top of our own map. Mr Percy is all entangled in forms and documents in an effort to get the scenery across the border – when the company of twenty-four turns up in Ljubljana in Yugoslavia, their stuff will all be there waiting for them.'

After the fall of curtain on 19 January, the final night of the Dublin season, Micheál MacLíammóir came forward to thank the audience. He also thanked the actors, and said they were all looking forward to Cork – he did not mention Belfast – and, 'weather and war permitting, we shall make a European tour.'

SWEET CORK, OF THEE

Next morning Toska Bissing travelled with the other members of the company to Cork on the Great Southern Railway, as press representative and also as small-part actress. Like many another discerning traveller, she realised that in spite of the preconceptions, and in spite of the fact that the English language was spoken, Ireland was as unlike England as France was from Belgium or Austria from Hungary. She was entranced by Cork, and 'blessed the Opera House for being beside the river. To no other Stage Door that I know does one come such an enchanting way. In wet weather there are screaming gulls and the water swirls muddily away; and on fine days it twinkles and flashes and the houses and churches rise Greekly from its far bank, for all the world like some city of Mediterranean culture; and at night the river is black, pitch black and mysteriously inviting, and secretive swans criss-cross majestically; the Quays are silenced, and little candle-lit interiors glow like coals among the embers of the eighteenth century.' There were after-show parties at the Neesons', and receptions at the Opera House for the members of the Little Theatre and for friends of the company from University College, where MacLíammóir gave a talk on Gaelic Drama to the Arts Society. Toska spent most of one Sunday morning typing out his script, and that evening went to hear it. 'Much impressed by the matter and manner of delivery. He spoke of the theatre in Ireland, and of his own passionate belief in its future; of colour and design, and of the subtle and almost hypnotic bond between audience and players, and of the necessary part taken by author, actors, producer, designer and audience to achieve of the theatre's best . . . '

MacLíammóir's Cork lecture is revealing, for in it he stated publicly for the first time what he had said to Lady Gregory ten years before, that there really was no future for professional drama in the Irish language. 'I have come to the stern conclusion that the salvation of the language in the theatre lies not in the attempt to make professional Irish-speaking actors, but in extensive amateur activities. These should be directed by professional producers.' The Cork Examiner reported a lively discussion, and the Chairman, Professor Aloys Fleischmann, spoke of Cork's indebtedness to the Gate Theatre as the only professional Irish company bringing full-scale productions to the city.

HORSEMAN, PASS BY

Micheál MacLíammóir wrote in *All for Hecuba* that it was in Cork he heard of the death of Yeats – but this can not have been so, for the poet died on 28 January before the six-week season in Cork opened. What he probably recalled was his inability to leave Cork for the memorial service in St Patrick's Cathedral some weeks later. His thoughts were full of despondency as he re-rehearsed the over-familiar plays. 'What was to come to Ireland now, I wondered, striving to visualise the future of the arts in this rain-sodden country, turning restlessly from side to side in its dream-haunted sleep? Would the era born in the turmoil of 1916 replace the creative energy of his labour?' Hilton Edwards unsympathetically remarked that the real tragedy of the Abbey Theatre was that its players could not understand the plays of their own prophet. He certainly had a point. His own highly ritualistic staging of *The Countess Cathleen* and *The King of the Great Clock Tower* revealed these works for the gems which they are, in a way which few Abbey productions had managed to do. For the present, however, he had more practical matters to think about. As Toska Bissing did not have a part in *Macbeth*, which closed the Cork season, he suggested that she travel to Belfast in advance of the company to meet the press, for he was apprehensive that the unknown Gate might not draw an audience. He had decided not to give any of the Shakespeare plays, because Donald Wolfit's company had just given a week of Shakespeare there, and so he selected *Wuthering Heights, And So To Bed* and *Night Must Fall*.

The Northern Whig – Ireland's longest established daily newspaper – was enchanted with Toska – 'tall, good-looking, surely born to be a mannequin, Miss Bissing delights in self-effacement and enjoys placing other people in the public eye.' Her presence in Belfast may certainly have helped to secure the full houses, and all went well until the Friday of the run when Hilton's chance remark about the Northern Ireland frontier being more difficult to cross than any European one was proved correct, for the *Night Must Fall* sets were still held in customs on the morning of the performance. A disconsolate crew sat on the stage with nothing to do, and the manager was consulted as to whether they should cancel, or perform without scenery, or repeat the previous night's play. The set was released in the afternoon, and the players frantically helped to erect it, while Hilton fumed in the stalls, shouting directions to the lighting supervisor up to the moment when the crowd had to be admitted. The Irish News reported next day on a totally satisfying evening, finding the Danny of Micheál MacLíammóir to be 'complete with an astonishingly convincing Welsh accent'. When asked how he had acquired it, Micheál replied without a bat of his mascara'd eyelid that he had taken instruction from a Welsh docker in Dublin.

Toska Bissing left Belfast for London to supervise the arrangements with the British Council, and to welcome the guests at a reception given for Hilton Edwards and Micheál MacLíammóir at the Hyde Park Hotel on 21 March. As might have been expected, the Gate's visit to eastern Europe was linked in the papers to more alarming matters, for Hungary had invaded Carpatho-Ukraine, and German troops had crossed the Czech frontier. The Irish Independent's London correspondent referred darkly to 'Irish theatre as British propaganda'. The Observer printed a complete history of the Gate and expressed surprise at the absence of theatre censorship in Ireland, where, in its view, a state of cultural repression prevailed; and upon enquiring how these actors could manage the English accents required, was given the stock answer about Dubliners speaking the best English in the world. (Nobody ventured the opinion that the audience in Zagreb would hardly appreciate any difference.) The Daily Telegraph reported without comment that the tour to the Balkans was taking place, and informed its readers of the much more important intelligence that the Duke of Kent had done a morning's shopping at Harrods.

EASTERN APPROACHES

The members of the company duly assembled, as May Carey had promised, 'dead under the clock' at the Gâre de Lyon in time to board the Simplon-Orient Express on the evening of Good Friday. Her son Patrick – who, with his twin brother Brian, was causing much amazement playing one of the Dromio twins in *The Comedy of Errors* – had taken advantage of his fare being paid to spend a few days in Paris; he had read the afternoon papers and was able to announce to those who had been travelling for twenty-four hours from Ireland that Mussolini had invaded Albania that morning. A Russian passenger wagered Toska Bissing a bottle of champagne that they would be turned back at the Yugoslav frontier. Next morning, as the train emerged from the Alps and slid by the brightly sunlit waters of the Lago di Maggiore, Bay Jellett wrote to her mother in Fitzwilliam Square that everything was 'perfectly lovely', and the man from Cook's who was travelling with them as courier, a Mr Earlham, was 'very agreeable', though La Bissing was 'very much to the fore', indeed, she was 'too frightful'. La Bissing spent the afternoon at her typewriter, pausing to note in her diary that they only stopped for two minutes in Venice, after which there was 'the delicate silver and orange Adriatic breaking gently on a shore that swept up to the coloured true-to-type houses'.

At the border with Yugoslavia the immigration officials no more than glanced at passports. (Toska Bissing did not record whether she received her bottle of champagne or not.) At 10 p.m. they reached Ljubljana, where, according to Patrick Carey, 'a tweedy lady descended on us all, announcing that she was "the English colony".' This was Miss Copeland, who immediately told MacLíammóir 'of course there's going to be a war – but we islanders are not going to be frightened off by that sort of business, are we?' A 'distracted notability' begged him not to allow anyone to speak German in public, because 'these people think that England may join up with Hitler any moment, and if they hear an English actor talking German they will be sure of it!' He then handed out roses to the ladies of the company, and was never seen again.

Mountain-girt Ljubljana, capital of Slovenia, was a prosperous city adorned with picturesque public buildings in the Austro-Hungarian manner. It seemed the last place on earth where a war, except perhaps in a Ruritanian comic-opera, could be remotely contemplated. The whole of the next day was spent preparing for *Hamlet* in the spacious Opera House. The cast found the huge audience astonishingly attentive, and wondered if it was because they were straining to comprehend the language and if they would tire before the end, but they did not, and the applause was far greater than anything they had experienced before. After MacLíammóir had made a brief speech of thanks, the applause continued so that Edwards, as director, in the attire of Claudius, came forward and thanked them again. The critic of Slovenski Narod wrote that 'although we have seen some excellent Hamlets, last night's performance was a revelation because of its original staging, and above all by the powerful creation of the name part by Mr Micheál MacLíammóir'. He was pleased to see so many young people in the theatre – 'Our youth marches sturdily in line with our adult public' – and this was a tendency which the players noticed throughout the tour. After the Ljubljana *Hamlet*, members of the cast went to a nightclub, and one of the dancers came down from the stage and, as MacLíammóir described it later, 'gave me a little pair of wooden doll's shoes, then bursting into tears she asked me to sign my name on eleven programmes, made the sign of the cross over my head, and returned to her work.'

It was in the National Theatre in Zagreb, however, that he gave the performance of Hamlet which both he and his colleagues remembered as his finest and most magical. The theatre, splendidly situated in a park in the Donjigrad, or Old Town, contains an extraordinary sculptural caprice in that the caryatid figures which support the upper circle all, from their different vantage-points, turn their faces towards the stage, as if they were watching the performance. MacLíammóir does not mention this in his memoirs, but he describes the stage as giving 'a huge sense of freedom and power, it was beautifully shaped and seemed to carry one with pleasure and response as though one walked miraculously on water.' As he rehearsed the *What's Hecuba to him or he to Hecuba?* speech, 'in the echoing twilight of the stage, bare of deception and effect, stripped of all trickery', he said he came to understand that in the speech 'lay an analysis of the despair that slept at the back of every actor's mind. It was the Irish despair too, for who was Hecuba to us but Ireland herself, queen or harlot, angel or vampire?'

In Zagreb the company was joined by J. Kendall Chalmers from the British Council, who reminded MacLíammóir of Anew McMaster, because nothing but the future could hold his attention and so he was 'as full of wild conjecture as a horoscope'. Patrick Carey was astonished when this highly educated and well-travelled representative of British officialdom, asked very politely by a local functionary if he spoke French or German, replied brusquely 'No! I speak the only language worth speaking – English!' The British consul and his wife, Mr and Mrs Rapp, gave a party for the company and two hundred other guests. The columnist of Jutarnji List reported that 'a short artistic programme was given'; but the Gate players who, like most actors, had a dread of 'party pieces', did not feel it was in the slightest bit artistic. Roy Irving performed a series of impersonations – including one of a female assistant in Clery's department store in Dublin, discussing bolts of cloth – which had his friends in paroxysms, the more so as the Croatian guests looked so utterly bewildered. Christopher Casson came to the rescue with his harp, which pleased everybody, and then Micheál and Coralie – 'valiantly' according to Toska Bissing – played the closet scene from Hamlet, to much applause. A leading member of the Croatian National Opera, Madame Podvenic, sang what Bay Jellett described as 'some lovely wild songs from this country'; she introduced herself to the singer, who in turn introduced her to a man who exported oak to Dublin for the manufacture of Guinness casks. Bay sent this information to her sister, whose husband was a Guinness executive; but the real point of the letter was to reassure those at home about the safety of the company, for the consul had told them that if there was any 'trouble', he would guarantee to get them all back to Dublin.

Toska Bissing went on in Zagreb as the Courtesan in *The Comedy of Errors* for the first time, and found herself to be very nervous. Afterwards she crouched in an unoccupied corner and watched 'my beloved *Don Juan*. Admired especially Hilton Edwards as the Devil, and in particular his brilliant rendering of the very long speech'. The newspaper Hrvatski Dnevik, echoing the opinion of the Dublin press, thought that the Shakespeare – for which 'the experimental décor inspired by old Byzantine church mosaics glowed brilliantly' – was quite enough without the Shaw, and so Edwards and MacLíammóir reluctantly decided to drop the piece once the company arrived in Belgrade.

The Importance of Being Earnest was performed in a smaller theatre, because the organisers believed that as Wilde's name did not mean as much in Croatia as Shakespeare's, it would be less of a draw, and Hilton was driven to distraction because half the people he wanted in one theatre always seemed to be rehearsing in the other. The organisers were proved wrong, for the demand for seats far exceeded the number available. Hrvatski Dnevik described Wilde as 'an Irish sceptic and rebellious spirit, a master of paradox and a refined aesthete who received wide but injudicious advertisement in his day . . . With stylised décor, the Irish players, symbolically wearing Wilde's sunflowers, gave us a really ideal interpretation . . . ' The critic of the Obsor thought it 'the most perfect interpretation of Wilde's comedy which could be seen anywhere in the world'.

The hospitality was almost overwhelming – not, as MacLíammóir observed, anything like American hospitality, but much more informal. On the Saturday after their arrival in Zagreb, the actors of the Royal Theatre invited all the members of the company (as Bay Jellett told her mother) 'to a heavenly place in the mountains – a châlet. First of all we were taken to see the sucking pig being cooked over a wood fire. This was outside. Then we sat down at a huge table on the verandah looking out on a wonderful view down through the trees to Zagreb in the plain below. There were wild flowers everywhere.' Toska Bissing was interested in the peasants they passed on the road, each dressed 'in a costume worthy of a museum . . . Over blouses and full swinging skirts of white they wore aprons, and neck and head kerchiefs of the most wonderful brilliant colours; on their feet, over thick white stockings, they wore little bootees of plaited soft leather; on their heads they carried bright bundles, or huge round baskets of coarse shining yellow or red straw, filled with produce, or things wrapped in more brilliant cloths. And they walked like royalty itself . . . Added to the view and the food were lovely Dalmatian wines, and we were soon toasting each other in Irish and Croatian, to say nothing of English, German and French, and telling each other that languages do not matter to actors. Over the whole world there is an almost "secret society" of the stage and all who belong are beyond the barriers of nationality. The vast majority of our own countrymen are more foreign to us than were these enchanting Croatian actors . . . Mercifully, and because our hosts were actors, we had time for a rest before playing *Night Must Fall*.'

The next afternoon Coralie Carmichael went to a peasant operetta and said that never in her life had she seen anything to equal it. She looked at the stage filled with costumes as beautiful as any in opera or ballet, and then back at the ornate auditorium and found it filled with costumes and colours and faces even more beautiful than those on the stage. She joined the others in the Hotel Esplanade 'dazed with the beauty of it', and praying that it would survive. On 17 April the company was seen off at the railway station by the Rapps and their friends, and by actors from the two theatres, who thrust huge bunches of lilac through the windows. Toska had lunch in the buffet-car with two journalists and kept thinking that they were 'in the middle of the danger-spot of the world. But it does no one any good to think of such things, so we had Serbian wine and discussed anything but "The Situation".'

Bay Jellett found Belgrade 'ramshackly'. In 1939 it was still a comparatively small city, with neither the charm of Zagreb and Ljubljana nor the metropolitan grandeur of the capitals the company was still to visit. They stayed at the Srbski – the writing paper was pretentiously headed Hotel Roi Serbe – and performances were again split between two theatres; *Macbeth* was rehearsed in one and *Night Must Fall* in the other, which meant endless journeyings for actors and stage management with make-up and personal props. The day following their arrival, there was the mandatory formal visit to the Tomb of the Unknown Warrior at Avala, twenty miles from Belgrade, but as this had been designed by the sculptor Mestrovic the expedition to the wooded hill-top site was a pleasure rather than an inescapable penance. Eight colossal female figures support the domed tomb, which was built by soldiers under Mestrovic's supervision. The company was then taken in buses a further fifty kilometers into the country to the royal mausoleum at Oplenac, where the lately assassinated King Alexander was interred.

Princess Olga, wife of the Prince Regent (and sister of the Duchess of Kent), attended the opening performance of *Macbeth*, and received Hilton Edwards and Coralie Carmichael in an ante-chamber off the royal box. She particularly praised the lighting – whether she had studied her programme and discovered that Edwards had designed it and therefore thought that a royal comment would be in order, or whether she genuinely noticed, is a matter for conjecture; but the actor Gerard Healy, in an interview with the Independent on his return to Dublin, said that Edwards' lighting was as much a talking point in the Balkan press as among members of the profession. He said that the director in the Balkan theatres 'did not consider lighting the plays as part of his duties. He left it to the chief electrician who was often content merely to flood the stage with light.' (Fifty years on, the same generally applies.)

There were receptions at the British Legation and the Anglo-Yugoslav Club, at which the members of the company as usual had to bear in mind the fact that they were travelling by courtesy of the British government and that protestations of their Irishness, which had been so well comprehended at private parties among theatre people in Slovenia and Croatia (where the British designation was immediately paralleled with the Serbian) would have been highly inappropriate. There was a Mayoral banquet at which the dishes were named in honour of the company – Potage *Macbeth*, and Omelette Surprise *à la* Dublin Gate

Theatre – causing explosions of suppressed laughter, especially as the Raspberry Flummery was named after MacLíammóir.

Princess Olga unexpectedly made a second visit to the National Theatre, this time to see the final performance of *Hamlet*. The critic Vladimir Subotic commented that many members of the Diplomatic Corps had done the same, and there was the air of an impromptu Gala Night. 'The enthusiasm of the reception given to Micheál MacLíammóir had to be seen to be believed. The whole house stood up and cheered. It was *Hamlet* with an Irish impulsiveness.' This time Micheál MacLíammóir and Meriel Moore were conducted to the royal presence, and thence to a reception given by the Artists' Association of Belgrade, at which the President of the Association gave what Toska Bissing described as a charming speech, immediately translated by an interpreter. She was delighted by MacLíammóir's reply, in which he thanked 'all the artists of Yugoslavia for their welcome to us, and remarked on the non-nationality of artists, and their understanding among themselves, irrespective of race or language. – I turned to the interpreter. No sound! To my horror I learned that as the President's speech had been written before, a translation had been prepared. As Micheál had spoken extempore, nothing was going to be done.'

MacLíammóir later wrote that he had never come across so many reporters since their visit to the United States, but that the Yugoslav variety seemed genuinely anxious to know what their victim believed and felt, instead of noting comments and getting the job over as quickly as possible. He was even asked his opinion of British and Irish actors whom the Yugoslav public could hardly expect to see – and certainly did not see, on account of the war and the descent of the Iron Curtain. In *All for Hecuba*, he describes the journey across the Greek frontier to Salonika on 24 April – it is curious to note how at that time the term 'Balkan' was automatically understood as including Greece; the alteration in popular nomenclature probably dates from the beginning of Soviet influence. 'It was good to cross the border as the mist lifted at twilight, to breathe the cool spice of the air and see the white-kilted sentries, silhouetted against a ridge of mountain as tenderly coloured as a hyacinth. It was good to smell wet wild flowers and hear the streams running through the dusk. *You are in Greece*, the wheels said, bearing us lightly over the bounding earth . . . ' How he managed to smell the flowers and hear the streams from the interior of a rackety steam-filled compartment is a question which can never be answered; but nostalgia for Greece had clearly set in, and not only that but nostalgia for the early McMaster tours in Ireland – for the representative of the British Council had not indicated that they would be playing in a cinema, and that only *parts* of the sets for the three Shakespeare plays would fit on its stage. This was all very pleasant and romantic and reminded MacLíammóir of places like Cappoquin and Dungarvan – but not at all so to Hilton Edwards and the technicians, who were forced to improvise as best they could, in order to give the appearance of large-scale richly designed productions.

The company had two days described on their timetable as 'free', and free it was to the actors, but those who doubled as stage management and wardrobe spent the two days with the crew sweltering inside the cinema, contriving means of adapting the sets without destroying them, devising ways of storing fifty costumes, and hanging and focusing lamps in an auditorium devoid of spot-bars or brackets. When the audience came in each night they found their local cinema transformed, its little stage spilling out Mediaeval and Renaissance pictures of a kind they had never imagined outside frescos or mosaic or illuminated manuscripts. What was left of the painted setting for *The Comedy of Errors* provided a special frisson for the people of what had once been Macedonia, and it is to be assumed that some of them supposed this Byzantine design had been specially created in their honour.

Toska Bissing, with her Baedeker-like penchant for crumbling churches, took Coralie Carmichael to climb to a monastery, which had a breathtaking view of Mount Olympus, set on a crag above the city. 'The place was hallowed: it had about it the glow and fervour and simple mystery of the early churches. The flowers and the sun outside, the nobility of the priests' faces – priests who tended their gardens and their church under the eye of Olympus – all seemed part of some life of peace and order and beauty beyond the struggling bewildering belligerent world.' English newspapers must have been available, or the British consulate may have been able to pick up the BBC, for it was in Salonika the company heard the news of Chamberlain's imposition of compulsory military training. 'I wish I could hear Chamberlain speaking now,' Bay Jellett wrote to her sister in London. 'He is wonderful, and I have every confidence in him.' It is reasonable to suppose that Micheál MacLíammóir's thoughts turned – between swimming in the bay and receiving laurel wreaths from dedicated admirers – back to 1917 and Alfred Willmore's flight from British conscription to smouldering, two-faced Ireland. What way would Ireland turn this time, should war come again, and would one be safe there?

NIGHT MUST FALL

The Ivan Vazov National Theatre, named after the Bulgarian novelist and revolutionary, was built in 1904 in that curious mixture of neo-classical and baroque which characterises so much municipal architecture from Paris to Cairo, with Vienna as its epicentre. It stands today very much as it must have done when the Dublin Gate Theatre performed there in 1939, except that it is now fronted by rows of magnificent fountains. It was certainly the most splendid theatre building encountered on the tour, and a complete contrast to the cinema in Salonika. The spacious stage and luxurious dressing-rooms, and the latest marvels of technical equipment impressed the Dublin visitors somewhat less, however, than the information that the actors were on annual salary and that once a young actor had successfully completed his or her training, there was automatic entry to the State artists' payroll – an enviable development of the court patronage of the previous centuries and a preview of the much more widespread official recognition of the arts, which was to come into being within a decade under the Communist régime. Hilton Edwards, suffering from laryngitis, felt he might be unable to get through an extra matinée of Macbeth audibly, and asked for a doctor to be called; he was surprised to find himself beckoned along a corridor and down a flight of stairs, where a gleaming surgery revealed itself, complete with two throat specialists whose ministrations enabled him to accomplish the performance in perfect voice.

A reception was given for journalists in the sitting-room, which was part of Hilton Edwards' suite at the Ivan Vazov Theatre. One scholarly critic enquired, quite seriously and without malice it seemed, why *Night Must Fall* had been included in the programme, for it was neither a classic nor a worthwhile contemporary play – he had read it (to everyone's surprise) and this was his view. The usual glib and intentionally disarming answers were given, the Gate representatives skirting round the fact that the British Council had specifically asked for a modern English play, and J. Kendal Chalmers tactfully omitting to add that *Night Must Fall* was the only modern English work in the Gate's repertoire. Emphatic declarations were made concerning Emlyn Williams' secure position in the scheme of contemporary English drama, and how it had been felt that audiences in the Balkan capitals should be given the opportunity of seeing an example of the kind of play which the ordinary London citizen regularly attended. Micheál MacLíammóir was astonished when the same critic sought him backstage after the performance, saying that he could not have believed the play he had read could come alive to such an extent, nor the character of Danny mean so much; to which MacLíammóir muttered some conventional words about there being more to a play than what was printed on the page, which was evidently a satisfactory reply.

This critic may have been the 'Str. Dimov' who wrote an article in the 16 May issue of the Bulgarian National Theatre Journal in which the Dublin Gate Theatre is complimented for acquainting the Sofia audience – 'which knows almost nothing about the contemporary English theatre' – with 'the principles of modern English theatrical art'. He reserved special praise for the 'style, simplicity and dynamic action' of the productions, and picked out *Hamlet* as the supreme example of Hilton Edwards' directorial technique. *Hamlet* was, again, the popular success. Toska Bissing noted that the house was sold out and 'people were offering fantastic sums and being turned away. In the wings, stage hands and interpreters listened in rapt silence among artists of the National Theatre who, unable to obtain a seat, watched from the side. Every single member of the company was at his or her best before that intense and enthralled audience. At the end, the applause and cheers and the curtain-calls amid armfuls of tulips, in a country where people seize their hats and fly almost before the curtain falls, was an experience to have witnessed.'

After *Macbeth*, Hilton Edwards was presented with a laurel wreath almost as big as himself, and he, with May Carey, Toska Bissing and Micheál MacLíammóir was conveyed to a party at the British Legation in 'a little carriage drawn by horses hung with blue beads to keep away the Evil Eye'. Sir George Rendel, the British Minister in Sofia, attended every performance and must have been greatly pleased at the impact made on Bulgaria's consciousness of British culture. The dispatches sent to the Foreign Office from the Balkan countries were destroyed in a systematic clearance of papers at the Public Record Office at Kew in 1956 and only the titles of the files remain. One of these is tantalisingly headed 'Criticism of the off-duty conduct and appearance of members of company', and this may refer to 'complaints' mentioned by Bay Jellett to her sister, passed on by J. Kendal Chalmers in Belgrade about the 'appearance of some of the girls, that they must dress better!' Snapshots suggest that the ladies were very smartly dressed, though often with short sleeves, and hatless. However, Bay Jellett only heard of complaints made about 'the girls', and as the heading of the file does not differentiate between men and women, it is possible that the boys may also have caused a scandal, in the same way they had shocked some of the citizens of Woodstock, Illinois, wearing very short shorts in public places.

Sir George Rendel made arrangements for the whole company to sit with him on the official stand for the parade on May 6, St George's Day by the Orthodox calendar. Toska Bissing wrote in her journal that she hated 'all the modern armies in their field uniforms' and could only bear to 'look at troops when they are in fancy dress – and the fancier the better'. There were other, much more lavish, parades in Bucharest a few days later, at which Toska Bissing's idealised operatic soldiers were very much to the fore in a ceremonial display, which Christopher Casson described as 'totally camp – they had glittering uniforms, and plumes and swords, and their eyes were flashing because they wore make-up. On the second day there were tanks and armoured cars and the atmosphere was disagreeable. It was a frightening display of militarism.'

There was a party at the British Legation in Bucharest at which Princess Bibesco (daughter of the former British Prime-Minister Herbert Asquith, and sister of Anthony Asquith, the film director), who disliked the Gate's interpretation of Macbeth, spoke to Hilton Edwards as if she were not aware that he had played the title part. They had a spirited argument about the theatre in general, which developed into what Christopher Casson described as 'a frightful row', and Micheál MacLíammóir said it was as if two full orchestras were being 'conducted against each other, one of them engaged perhaps with the *Damnation of Faust*, and the other almost certainly with the *Walkyries' Ride*.' As her journal was intended for publication, Toska Bissing did not mention this incident – nor another which occurred in Micheál MacLíammóir's salon-like dressing-room, where Royalty was expected, and the dresser, Lennie, piqued because he had been too busy to go sightseeing, and complaining that he might as well never have left the Tottenham Court Road, appeared dressed in a white suit, his face made up just as generously as the Romanian soldiers, and smelling all too obviously of the contents of a *parfumerie*, expecting to be presented. He was pushed behind a screen just as the major-domo was opening the door, and had to remain there, like Lady Teazle in *The School for Scandal*.

After the party in the theatre on the final night, when the members of the company were feeling sad that their Balkan tour was now at an end, and hoping that there would be more and even longer tours in the future (for the company had undoubtedly distinguished itself), and after further declarations of artistic solidarity and international friendship had been made, and more champagne drunk, Hilton Edwards prophesied *sotto voce* that 'Night Must Fall', and 'all the countries the British Council have sent us to will without hesitation join the Axis'. But – 'Next year, when you come back!', newly-made Romanian friends were calling – and it really seems that they believed in the possibility.

Of all the places the Dublin Gate Theatre, or any Western theatre, was least likely to visit in the future, Romania and Bulgaria were those countries. Irish companies did not perform in Yugoslavia or Greece until another quarter century had passed. By this time they would be travelling under the banner of the Cultural Relations Committee of Dublin, and not the British Council; yet the British Council's paternalism would again be generously if illogically brought to bear on a further Dublin Gate Theatre enterprise as far away as Argentina and Peru – but that was quite undreamt of, as Hilton Edwards and Micheál MacLíammóir said goodbye to their players at the railway terminus in Bucharest and strode out, incredibly, for the mountains of Hungary, bearing knapsacks, and, no less improbably, dressed in *lederhosen*.

Chapter 8

In a State of Emergency

When Dublin Gate Theatre Productions reassembled for rehearsal in late July 1939, war seemed inevitable. Recently recruited English actors in the company wondered if they ought to return home. Which side would Ireland be on? Would Hitler invade Britain by way of the undefended Irish west coast, as was commonly predicted? Hilton Edwards and Coralie Carmichael – and Micheál MacLíammóir, had it been known – were English; would they still be welcome in Dublin? The play they were preparing, too, was quintessentially olde worlde Tudor: *Will Shakespeare*, Clemence Dane's verse exercise in bardolatry, a recent West End success. The next production, *I Have Been Here Before*, by one of middle-England's most revered authors, J.B. Priestley, might turn out to be the wrong choice. Sudden changes in cultural attitudes had been noted throughout Europe; authors and artists could be discredited, and quite suddenly find themselves classed as subversives.

Hilton Edwards, who had never been known to stop a rehearsal and was always impatient with the statutory tea-break, allowed a pause on the afternoon of 1 September so as the company could listen to Neville Chamberlain's broadcast informing the world that England was at war. Sally Travers said she wanted to stay in Ireland, come what may; but the older players kept their thoughts to themselves. On 3 September Senator William Quirke, addressing the Senate, moved that 'arising out of the armed conflict now taking place in Europe, a national emergency exists affecting the vital interests of the State'. The term *Emergency* was taken up by the other members in the debates which followed, and in due course was adopted as the official designation for what very quickly became known elsewhere as the Second World War. Thus, as far as the people of Eire were concerned, the war did not exist. The material hardships caused by neutrality were mere irritations compared to what was experienced in Great Britain and Northern Ireland. De Valéra's doctrine of puritanical self-sufficiency created a pervasive xenophobia, unmatched in history, even at times of armed rebellion – for the 'oppressor' of the past had been simply, and often romantically, identified as the 'Saxon foe'. Here was something quite different: communication with all other countries severed, supplies cut due to foreign naval action and reliance on the pitifully tiny Irish merchant service, and a subliminal feeling of guilt at having opted out of the fray. This in turn created a falsely justified sense of moral superiority, described by MacLíammóir as 'the ingrowing process of virtuous self-esteem'.

By 11 September legislation had been passed requiring permits for those who wished to travel outside the state, even into Northern Ireland. The B & I steam-packet service from Dublin to Liverpool was discontinued, due to difficulties over war risks pay. A strict régime of censorship was placed on the press to the extent that war news could not be printed except in a ludicrously general way – The Irish Times, unable to report that an Irish-born officer had been saved from a torpedoed British warship, and anxious to provide his relatives with the information, headlined the story 'Dublin Man Rescued In Boating Accident'. Radio Eireann news bulletins had to be submitted to the Government Information Bureau prior to broadcasting. Censorship of literature became much more severe, yet, paradoxically, censorship of plays was never proposed, though fear of its introduction caused managements to select their scripts with caution. When the Gate Theatre found itself in difficulties over the content of a Maupassant play in 1940, the pressure from two government sources was so severe that it had to be withdrawn.

Curiously, very few British nationals fled. One of the few was Christine Longford's mother, Amy Trew, who had been living at Pakenham Hall and was pressed by everyone, including the butler, to stay. Edward Longford told her that there would be far more food in Ireland, and that to remain would mean that there would be more for the needy in England. She replied that she could not be 'neutral', and that anyway Oxford was unlikely to be bombed. She waited until Longford Productions visited Mullingar with Christine's comedy, *Mr Jiggins of Jigginstown* and then she left on the Mail Boat, which was still running, for Holyhead. Christine later told her biographer, John Cowell, that she never saw her mother again.

Even more curiously, within a few months of the outbreak of war Dublin had become a city with a rakish international life. There were genuine refugees, helped by philanthropic organisations to escape from Nazi-dominated countries; many of these people made a distinguished contribution to the cultural and commercial development of Ireland. There were also refugees by choice – conscientious objectors, artists and musicians in the main. There was an élite tourist trade, principally of wealthy Britons of the class who would normally have patronised Cannes or Monte Carlo, who were able to obtain travel permits through influence, and who patronised the larger hotels where the kind of food which could not be bought for any money at home was abundantly on the tables. Later, after Pearl Harbour, there were the high-ranking U.S. military personnel stationed in Northern Ireland in preparation for the Normandy landings; and there were the ordinary folk of Belfast who travelled to Dublin on the resilient Great Northern Railway, which managed to maintain its schedules in spite of fuel shortages, just to see the lights: for Dublin was a blaze of glowing gas and electricity and neon, while Belfast, like all British cities, was dismally blacked out at night.

There was a further element which made Dublin unique. This was the element which centred round the Diplomatic Corps, for Dublin was one of the few capitals of Europe where the German and Italian ministers could meet their British, French and American counterparts, socially if not on official terms. Espionage was widespread. The Irish government maintained an internment camp at the Curragh, in which suspected spies of all nationalities, as well as the survivors of naval actions, forced landings of military aircraft, foreign parachutists and British soldiers who strayed across the Border on reconnaissance, were housed in remarkably open conditions. The consular coterie brought a sparkle and gaiety to theatrical first nights, the staff of diplomatic missions glad not to be in their home cities of London, Berlin, Paris, Rome or Brussels, and grateful for whatever evening diversion might be to hand. The Gate Theatre was a far more likely venue for such outings than the Abbey, for its repertoire savoured so much of Britain, Europe and America.

Britain's 'war-effort', and the need to economise, brought the name of the Dublin Gate Theatre to notice in the House of Commons. In a written reply to a Parliamentary question posed by the Honourable Member for Stourbridge, the Prime Minister stated that the British Council had 'never granted any subsidies to theatrical companies', but had 'from time to time contracted with companies to perform abroad, and defrayed their expenses'. The distinction was academic, and provoked a not unreasonable outcry. The Daily Express looked back through its files and found that in 1938, 'when there wasn't much money allowed by the Treasury for the re-armament of this land', the Dublin Gate Theatre 'was sent to perform in Athens'; this was the company, the editor protested, which had 'produced Sean O'Casey's anti-British plays'. (The facts that the Gate never performed an O'Casey play, because MacLíammóir disliked them so much, or that O'Casey had never written an anti-British play, though he had written anti-war plays, did not trouble the Express. The same paper also inveighed against a production of *Candida* in Paris, because 'Shaw was always a bitter critic of Britain!') – 'The Council lost all restraint and reason,' the Express continued. 'The Dublin Players went hither and thither round Europe . . . most of their audiences could not understand English. Any more than you can understand the language of Ljubljana.' Having been attacked in some Dublin papers for accepting British subsidy, the Gate players were amused to see the London papers attacking the British government for giving them that subsidy; whether their injection of English-language culture to the Balkans had had its desired effect or not was hardly worth speculation. They thought sadly of the beautiful cities which had responded so warmly to their work, and of the friends they had made there; but Ireland's problems, clearly, were now to be of more immediate concern.

Of the English actors, almost all remained – notably Christopher Casson, who continued as a leading member of both the Edwards-MacLíammóir and Longford companies. Emmerton Court – on being introduced to another member of the company he was asked if that was his name or his address – came from London to join the company and told the press 'I have not been here before, but I have come to act in *I Have Been Here Before*.' He was cast in parts which called for displays of British phlegm and tight upper lips, excelling as cabinet ministers and generals. During his sojourn at the Gate, he made a practice of borrowing costumes from the wardrobe, for city wear. Lea Holinshed, who also joined for the season, was called up without warning; when he applied to the War Office for leave to play until the final night of Auden and Isherwood's *The Ascent of F6*, he was allowed only twenty-four hours to cover the opening night, and his part had to be hastily recast. Cecil Monson, who was Irish, surprised some (but not all) of his friends by expressing a great desire to join the British navy; he surprised everybody by being accepted. In 1943, the Reverend Brian Kennedy, who had been involved in several Gate productions while a student at Trinity, met Cecil on a tour of duty as a naval chaplain; by this time Cecil was an officer-cadet and well-known on board as a writer of sketches which were broadcast on ship's radio. When asked by a superior to catch a rope thrown to him, he exclaimed, 'Oh Peter! It's all *wet!*'

THE POOR OF DUBLIN

During the war Ireland was never short of beef, mutton, pork, poultry and dairy produce, but only the well-to-do could afford meat of any kind, and the diet of the poor had not changed much since famine times. Imported foods were a rarity; children brought up in the early 'forties did not know what bananas or oranges looked like; tea was rationed to half an ounce per person per week – about enough to make one pot. Those who lived in the country were better off, because vegetables could be grown in small gardens, but in Dublin distribution was ill organised, and the people of what were still said to be the the the worst slums in Europe simply did not understand that milk and vegetables were more suitable for children than bread and watery tea. Poverty was sustained by ignorance.

In deciding to produce Robert Collis's play *Marrowbone Lane*, the Gate became involved in a national controversy which in the course of time led to major social reforms. It also drew the theatre to the attention of a section of the public which might have regarded playgoing as a frivolity of the leisured classes – if it was aware of playgoing at all. Robert Collis was a young paediatrician who came from a well-to-do Protestant family with a long tradition in medicine. He played rugby for Ireland, and was 'capped' seventeen times. He was precisely the kind of person whom Edwards and MacLíammóir were unlikely to meet under normal circumstances. In 1932 he became Physician to the recently established National Childrens' Hospital. He was appalled by the conditions which he found in the homes of his patients, but, unlike the majority of his profession, he was not content to accept the *status quo*. Dr Patricia Sheehan, an early colleague and supporter, recalled that 'he bulldozed his way through everything. Before a committee meeting you would be summoned to his rooms in Fitzwilliam Square and every item would be gone through, so that he was completely briefed.' He happened to meet Frank O'Connor, at that time one of the most internationally admired of Irish authors – and also one of the most frequently banned – who was a member of the Board of the Abbey Theatre. O'Connor said, 'If you feel so strongly about the Dublin slums, why don't you write a play about them?'

Collis considered the idea, and one evening sat down to write some notes. 'I wrote as fast as I could; I wrote all night. At last as the dawn began to lighten the sky I found that the story of the play was finished. This is the only time in my life I have experienced something completely outside myself containing emotions and other factors of which I had no previous conscious knowledge.' He had a strong belief in the dramatic content of his play, but both O'Connor and Lennox Robinson understood that although there was a good plot – that of a girl from the west of Ireland who comes to Dublin, marries, and is destroyed by the slums – it was a social tract in dialogue, rather than a piece of theatre. Both gave him structural advice; and then O'Connor resigned from the Abbey board – it is extraordinary to recall that such were the moral pressures of the era, his liaison with the wife of the actor, Robert Speaight, was considered so damning he had to give up his public appointments – and Robinson did not pursue the work because it was generally felt that the topic was 'too controversial'. Urged on by Shelah Richards, Collis passed the script to Hilton Edwards.

Edwards saw immediately and gleefully that *Marrowbone Lane* was indeed controversial. Collis, whose autobiography reveals a man whose self-belief is paramount and who rarely gives credit to others outside his immediate family, generously acknowledges the help of both Edwards and MacLíammóir – 'by far the most talented pair of actor-producers in Dublin or indeed in Europe . . . with their experience we succeeded in making it actable. The evening before the first night the dress rehearsal went on till 4 a.m. It did not seem possible that it could be produced the next evening. But such was the skill of the Gate players that in fact it went on in time the following night. MacLíammóir himself only took the small part of the brother from the west . . . but he was such a consummate actor he stole all the male parts in the few minutes he was on the stage. I have only seen this done on one other occasion, when Olivier came on as the Button Moulder in *Peer Gynt* and stole the whole play from everybody, including Ralph Richardson . . . '

The Irish Independent's reviewer noted that in *Marrowbone Lane* 'the Gate company struck a blow for housing reform'. The Irish Times found the play 'propagandist – yet it moved the audience by its intensity and truth'. Shelah Richards as Mary was universally praised, and some astonishment was expressed at Micheál MacLíammóir appearing so credibly as a country boy, her brother, Martin. (In fact, this performance opened the way for a series of engaging young rustics, mainly in parts which he wrote for himself when he was in his forties.) The Evening Mail commented that Dr Collis 'frankly proclaimed himself on the side of art for truth's sake'. There was an immediate reaction to the play from the Housing Section of Dublin Corporation, pointing out that new blocks of flats were being built, even in the neighbourhood of that same Marrowbone Lane which the author had taken for his setting. A Councillor Milroy pointed out that there were now only 17,759 condemned houses in the city – to which Dr Collis replied that this was an *increase* since 1914! Only a week after the opening, a public meeting was held in the Metropolitan Hall, at which Dr Collis described the pitiable condition of thousands of families, and drew attention to the fact that there wás a total of only 225 beds for children in the city hospitals. 'I have not exaggerated anything in *Marrowbone Lane*, believe me,' he said.

The effect on the Gate was capacity business, once again emphasising how a theatre with only three hundred and fifty seats could not adequately cope with success, nor make a substantial profit from it. The standard run of two weeks was extended to four, after which the company had to revert to its announced programme of *Third Party Risk*, *The Ascent of F6*, and *A Hundred Years Old*. *Marrowbone Lane* was brought back for the notoriously unreliable fortnight before Christmas, and was booked out again.

The play inspired the formation of the Marrowbone Lane Fund, the object of which was succinctly stated as 'to feed the starving children of Dublin'. In 1949 Robert Collis launched the National Association for Cerebral Palsy. At one of the entertainments given by the Marrowbone Lane Fund for underprivileged children, he had noticed a 'twinkle in the eye' of a 'dumb', crippled child of twelve carried on his brother's back, and felt that there must be some way of releasing his trapped spirit. The child was Christy Brown, who, under Dr Collis's care, wrote his own autobiography *My Left Foot*, holding a chalk between his toes, though many people refused to believe that Collis had not written the book. Exactly two years after *Marrowbone Lane*, the Gate presented Collis's second play, *The Barrel Organ*, in which the leading character is the playwright son of an Italian café-proprietor in Dublin. The young man is of morbid disposition, and this is put down to 'artistic temperament', but in fact he is dying of tuberculosis. There are affinities with *The Doctor's Dilemma*, which no one seemed to notice at the time; it was Collis's concern for the dread disease, still 'unmentionable' in Ireland, which caught the public attention. The reviews were mildly favourable, though critics felt the play lacked the passion and conviction of *Marrowbone Lane*. The theatre correspondent of Sean O'Faoláin's militant journal, The Bell, perceptively noticed how the players often cover up inadequacies of authorship: 'I take my hat off to all the actors and actresses. They will get a play full of ham parts and throw their very hearts into it. Hilton Edwards revelled in the part of the Italian ice-cream man. Cyril Cusack was loyal to his part as if it was all the last act of *King Lear*. And the new "discovery", Maureen Kiely, was like a dewy violet, as sweet and charming as nature itself.'

Cyril Cusack played the consumptive playwright. It was at the first rehearsals that he met Maureen Kiely, the 'dewy violet' of The Bell's review, whom he was later to marry, and who was to be the mother of Sorcha and Sinéad Cusack. Micheál MacLíammóir was originally cast in Cusack's part, but, according to Betty Chancellor 'funked it'; she said of the play, 'it positively stinks', and did everything possible to stay out of it. She wrote to Denis Johnston, now a BBC war correspondent in the vaguely designated 'Middle East': 'There is a frightfully heroic doctor, so obviously meant to be Bob himself it is downright embarrassing.' Betty's liaison with Denis was now quite well known. It was said that he had accepted the war correspondent post so as to be away from both Betty and Shelah.

Robert Collis does not appear to have written another play. *Marrowbone Lane* was revived, again successfully, at the Gaiety Theatre, Dublin, in 1941, and there was an independent and evidently ill-funded production at the Lyric, Hammersmith, with Shelah Richards again in the leading rôle; she lent the author £26, which he did not repay, and she found it ironic that her family kept referring to 'that nice Dr Collis'. Nice or otherwise, he was one of the first doctors to treat the victims of Belsen, when the concentration camp was liberated (Denis Johnston was one of the first journalists to report the atrocities to the world, via the BBC) and he adopted two Belsen children whom he and his second wife brought up in county Wicklow. He established the Department of Paediatrics at the University of Ibadan, where he is recalled as a great humanitarian. He died following a fall from a horse near Newtownmountkennedy in 1975.

WHERE STARS WALK UPON A MOUNTAINTOP

The winter of the first year of the war was particularly severe. Coal was scarce, and would soon be almost unobtainable, for it had to be imported. The turf bogs were exploited for fuel, and in the following years many Dubliners took turf-banks in the mountains near the city and cut their own supplies. Fortunately the economic policy of the State since its foundation in 1922 had been towards the development of water power, which now supplied most of the country's needs, though when the coal burning generating stations were forced to close, electricity was rationed. It was gloomily predicted that the absence of electric trams in the evenings would restrict theatregoing – but somehow citizens refused to be daunted; the bicycle became the chief means of transport, and the city still being comparatively small (with under half-a-million inhabitants) it became the natural thing to walk to the theatre from the not too distant suburbs of Ballsbridge, Rathmines, Phibsborough and Drumcondra, on evenings when the trams were 'off'. Contrary to what was expected, the theatres and cinemas flourished, and more plays – as distinct from music-hall variety, opera and dance – were presented annually in Dublin than at any previous period in the city's history.

The Gate's Christmas programme consisted of *The Merry Wives of Windsor*, designed by Molly MacEwen, with Hilton Edwards as Falstaff. He told Nuala Moran of The Leader that he could never be too fat for Falstaff, but Molly designed a heavily padded costume, so voluminous that on the opening night, when hurrying round the back of the stage, he got stuck at the narrowest point between the set and the plaster cyclorama. Actors on one side pulled him, and those on the other pushed, while their colleagues anxiously invented Shakepearian dialogue on the stage. Then, with a report reminiscent of Winnie-the-Pooh being ejected from the rabbit-burrow, he was suddenly liberated, falling over a heap of helpers, while the Garter Inn appeared to be the victim of an earthquake. *The Merry Wives of Windsor* was followed by a modern-dress revival of *Hamlet*. Traditionalists railed against this novel idea, but when the production opened in mid-January 1940, they had to admit that Micheál MacLíammóir's costumes added vitality and significance, for he had set the tragedy in a contemporary Balkan court, where all the Ruritanian trimmings of regality still, anachronistically, prevailed – as he had noted in Sofia and Bucharest the previous spring.

This year, however, there was to be no foreign tour to keep the company together, and in funds, while Longford Productions took over the Gate for its annual six-month tenure. What fairy godmother would provide a home, and work?

MR LOUIS

The fairy godmother turned out to be a godfather, and as far from resembling any kind of fairy as one might imagine. He was Louis Elliman, whose family owned a chain of cinemas, as well as the vast art-deco-Moorish Theatre Royal which seated over 4,000 persons, and the 1,200 seat Gaiety Theatre, which, for seventy years, had been Dublin's 'No. 1' receiving-house for cross-channel dramatic and operatic companies. Hilton Edwards had performed there with Charles Doran, when he was eighteen.

Louis Elliman was a tall, dapper man, never seen in anything but a very well-cut suit. He smoked cigars with an air of nonchalance. Of Russo-Jewish descent, the Ellimans had run a theatre-seating business in Camden Street, where, after taking his degree from University College, Dublin, 'Mr Louis' – as he was known to staff – opened his own cinema, the Theatre De Luxe. He obtained the agency for First National Films, and subsequently became Managing Director of Odeon (Ireland) Ltd. During the autumn of 1939, it became quite obvious that no amount of lobbying at the highest government level would result in a continuation of visits from entire London production companies to the Gaiety, though individual performers could, with difficulty, negotiate permits to travel to Dublin for solo appearances at the Royal. The Gaiety could not be kept going on Christmas pantomime and the annual productions of the Rathmines & Rathgar Musical Society. Something more substantial was needed.

Mr Louis discussed all this with Hilton and Micheál. Their seasons at the Opera Houses of Belfast and Cork, and more especially their prestigious productions on the national stages of the Balkans and the Middle East, had demonstrated that they could no longer be paternalistically regarded as the purveyors of an 'art' genre of limited appeal. The popular success at the Gate of new plays like *Marrowbone Lane*, and imaginatively designed productions of classics like *Hamlet*, begged a wider public. Mr Louis believed that, under certain circumstances, he could promote their work to such a public, and he proposed that they combine to present an initial six-week season of six plays, for which he would guarantee an agreed figure. If this season attracted a large enough attendance, it would be followed by others.

Louis Elliman professed that he knew nothing of legitimate theatre, but he was constantly on hand during the runs of *Marrowbone Lane* and the Shakespeare plays at the Gate to discuss their programme. It was explained to him that it was not physically possible to rehearse six new productions and create settings and costumes for the large stage, and open on six consecutive Mondays; some of the plays would have to be taken from the Gate's repertoire and this might cause difficulties: who was to tell if a production which had done reasonably well in the smaller theatre could draw four times as many people per night? There were huge risks in logistics, economics and artistic credibility. Edwards was keen to restage *Peer Gynt*, the first play the company had ever put on and which had only been revived once at the Gate; it also gave him an important leading rôle. MacLíammóir wanted to appear in *Berkeley Square* again – here was a play which had never failed to attract audiences. He was also writing a part for himself – 'Martin', his country-bumpkin *alter-ego* – in a romantic comedy to be called *Where Stars Walk* (a quotation from Yeats). There was a severe risk for a new play by an inexperienced playwright. Denis Johnston's new piece on Jonathan Swift based on his own radio drama *Weep for Polyphemus*, which members of the company had broadcast from the BBC in Belfast the previous July, was also available: was all this too much to ask of a 'popular' house?

Mr Louis did not seem to think so. They decided to include Patrick Hamilton's thriller *Gaslight*, the current hit of the West End, and *Wuthering Heights*, in the version by Ria Mooney; but the advance interest, once the programme was announced, seemed to be weighted in favour of the first play of the season, *Where Stars Walk* – which seemed a good augury.

There were six weeks of general rehearsals when Hilton Edwards plotted all six plays. After each play opened, rehearsals for the next in line were intensified. The sets were built in the Theatre Royal workshops under the supervision of Molly MacEwen; Patrick Perrott, a native of Bray, Co Wicklow, who had worked with the company before and had been designing dresses for Liberty's of London, came home to avoid the call to arms and was put in charge of costumes. As the opening night approached, the advantages of working with a well-staffed organisation became apparent. Louis Elliman took a special interest in publicity, and invited a distinguished first-night audience. Government ministers, members of the diplomatic corps – among them Sir John Maffey, the British minister, and John Betjeman and Osbert Lancaster who were members of his staff – as well as several Irish literary figures recently returned from exile, thronged the pretty foyer of the Gaiety. A dark blue Rolls Royce brought Ireland's first President, Dr Douglas Hyde, founder of the Gaelic League, a genial scholarly man, whose translations of almost-forgotten Gaelic poetry were the chief influence on the Irish literary revival at the turn of the century. Here he was, fifty years later, smiling from his box in the theatre where his early plays had been produced in the Irish language, eagerly absorbing a play which, in spite of its modern setting, clearly derived from that movement.

Where Stars Walk uses the Celtic legend of the lovers Etáin and Midhir as *leitmotif* for a society comedy set in a Dublin drawing-room. A celebrated actress's new housemaid and houseboy, who come from different localities in the country, seem to recognise one another. At an evening party, the actress and her *demi-mondaine* friends play with an ouija-board, which summons up spirits from the past. At the end of the play the actress returns from an early morning walk to find that both her young servants have vanished; she observes two beautiful swans flying into the dawn, but fails to make the connection. The mixture of romantic Celticism with the smart epigrammatic dialogue of Miss Sophia Sheridan and her theatrical friends in contemporary Ireland delighted the audience. This was something quite new in inspiration and technique, as far as the Irish theatre was concerned. President Hyde might have wondered if it was a debasement of the culture which he and his friends had been trying to reinstate; yet in spite of the play's prevailing comic spirit, the Celtic myth which supplies its motivating force is treated seriously – MacLíammóir was too much in love with the genre to consider mocking it for theatrical effect.

Had anyone queried MacLíammóir's 'Irishness' at this period, it should have been obvious that the almost besotted way in which he embraced the literature and visual art of the Celtic Revival was the admiration of the discoverer from another bourne. By the time he settled in Ireland the Revival was over; and certainly in 1940 no serious Irish writer was going to recreate the stories of Diarmuid and Gráinne, or Etáin and Midhir, or place them on canvas or tapestry, in the sensuous romanticised manner of the 'nineties. The writers who were of his own exact generation – O'Connor, O'Faoláin, MacNeice, Kavanagh, Beckett – and the artists MacConghail, Keating, McGuinness and Jellett, had their own highly individualistic views of an Ireland in which neo-Celticism had little or no place. Yeats had moved on from his Celtic Twilight to a sterner, sparer and more concentrated vision.

Where Stars Walk was produced five times in Dublin over the next forty years and was taken on numerous provincial tours as well as to Britain and North America. It was produced by the Pitlochry Festival company in 1957. MacLíammóir's other play which deals with the supernatural in the present day, *Ill Met by Moonlight*, first produced at the Gaiety Theatre in 1946, offers less of the Celtic twilight and more of rural superstitions. It concerns the notion of the changeling bride, so prevalent in Irish mythology. A highly sophisticated French professor of folklore, Sebastien Prosper, settles in Connemara with his daughter, and there entertains their recently married friends, the Mallaroes. The charming Catherine Mallaroe is wont to take walks in the moonlight, and true to the changeling pattern, is 'removed' by the people of the other world and replaced with a being who resembles her physically but is of spiteful character, turning everyone in the household against one another. It transpires that the Prosper house is built on the site of an ancient ring-fort, known in the country as a 'fairy fort', and matters will not come right until he moves out and leaves the place to the people of the Sidhe.

The play is lighthearted in tone and does not attempt to explore the psychological implications of *Doppelgänger* or *bean-sidhe*. MacLíammóir created another rustic part for himself, the ingenuous house-servant, Lee, who, very much in the manner of 'Anyone for tennis?', enters at fraught moments to make announcements of urgent domestic import, such as 'The dinner's boiled!' Roger McHugh, one of the highly perceptive reviewers of The Bell, wrote that it was 'a very entertaining piece of hocus written with an admirable sense of theatre'; he also found it 'reminiscent of J.M. Barrie, J.B. Priestley, of Yeats Without Tears, of J.W. Donne, of many Gate successes, and at times of Jimmy O'Dea and Roddy the Rover'. *Ill Met By Moonlight* proved to be MacLíammóir's most successful play, achieving more performances than any of his others by companies outside the Gate. J. Kane Archer of the Irish Times, reviewing a new production after the author's death, felt that most of the new cast simply did not understand the style, taking it much too solemnly; he believed it was a masterwork of its era.

The Gaiety Theatre provided the launching platform for two other successful MacLíammóir plays, *Portrait of Miriam* in 1948 and *The Mountains Look Different* in 1949. In *Portrait of Miriam*, announced as 'the blending of legendary superstition into a modern setting', he used the device of a collection of travellers held up by a blizzard, who seek shelter in a lonely country house, where events occur which force each character to examine his or her life anew. The mysterious 'portrait' in the hallway, swathed in dust sheets, is revealed to be a mirror. In reviewing the play for The Bell, Con Leventhal opened with a short appreciation of MacLíammóir's special genius, counting him 'among that rare band whose activities are essentially aesthetic and who must find self-expression in varying forms of art'. He found that in *Portrait of Miriam* he had 'rid himself of the burden of his aesthetic experience. I cannot agree with those critics who insist that his borrowings are plentiful . . . The play does not derive from established models but breaks new ground technically.'

The Mountains Look Different is 'constructed in the main from a Greek model', according to a handwritten note of MacLíammóir's. 'That is to say, it is concerned with the lives of three people, a wife, a husband and a father, who are thrown into conflict by certain events that have passed before the rise of the curtain . . . The play is a morality in the sense that, like the plays of Greece, it tells of sin and its atonement, and I wrote it in that way because I wished to experiment with a modern theme in an approximation to a classic form.' A young farmer, Tom Grealish, returns from England with his bride, an Irish girl who has been living there for some years. Tom's father immediately recognises her as a prostitute with whom he spent a night on his only visit to London, and tells her she is no fit wife for his son. She declares that she has relinquished her old life, and will start anew. He agrees to her staying, and attempts to make an obscene bargain. She resists his advances, and ultimately sets fire to a shed in which he is burned to death. The play ends with her admitting the murder, and giving herself up to the police. The press found the theme unnecessarily vicious. The performances of Helena Hughes as the girl, Micheál MacLíammóir as the young man and Denis Brennan as his father – if age had entered the casting process, these rôles should have been reversed – were praised, but the play was altogether too steamy for the Ireland of its day. Hilton Edwards foolishly wrote to the Editor of the Independent, complaining of an unfair review, forgetting that the journalist always has the last word, which in this case was that 'the attempt to protect a poor play by equating artist to dramatist and critic to ostrich or escapist is just tiresome'. During the intermission the following night two young men addressed the audience, denouncing the play for representing the people of Ireland as 'tramps and undesirables'. They asked those who agreed with them to leave the theatre and a man in the gallery did so. MacLíammóir received an unusually cordial ovation at the end of the night, but did not come forward to speak. He told a reporter that it was a pity the protesters had not waited to hear what the play had to say in its final act, for it was 'a drama of expiation and repentance'.

BOTTOM'S DREAM

The Gate's first Gaiety season of 1940 proved that Louis Elliman had been right about the company's drawing power. It also proved that Hilton Edwards and Micheál MacLíammóir were now stars in the Irish theatrical firmament, joining that small but sparkling constellation which included F.J. McCormick, Barry Fitzgerald, Liam Redmond, Maureen Delany, May Craig and Eileen Crowe. Further, it proved that the Gate was capable of treading on Abbey ground in presenting popular new plays by Irish dramatists – but giving them much better-mounted productions. (Johnston's *The Dreaming Dust*, which concluded the season, for all its scholarly theorising on the subject of Swift's relationships, was described by the Irish Times as 'a triumph'.) It was agreed that thenceforth Edwards-MacLíammóir should occupy the Gaiety twice a year for a total of at least twelve weeks. Elliman made a point of not providing a written agreement; he said his handshake was sufficient.

In April the company left the Gaiety for a tour to Cork, Limerick, Waterford and Belfast with *Where Stars Walk, A Hundred Years Old, Gaslight, Night Must Fall* and *Marrowbone Lane*, not returning to the Gate until November, for Louis Elliman requested an additional run of *Where Stars Walk* 'by popular demand', and rehearsals for the second Gaiety season began in August. It was Hilton Edwards who had the ingenious idea of inviting the comedian, Jimmy O'Dea, to play Bottom in *A Midsummer Night's Dream* at the Gaiety, the theatre where he and his partner, Harry O'Donovan, presented the annual pantomime and a summer revue. To many Dubliners O'Dea *was* the Gaiety. O'Dea had often acted in the legitimate theatre before, though the public seemed to have forgotten, and so his appearance in Shakespeare was eagerly awaited. His was an exceptionally expressive face ; he had huge eyes, brimming with astonished merriment. Dermot Tuohy, a junior member of the company, recalled that when Bottom wakes from his dream, takes off the ass's head and declares 'I have had a rare vision,' O'Dea's voice and face 'took on a magical sense of wonderment'. Hilton Edwards remarked that the only problem was having to place the ass's head on O'Dea at all, when the effect of the wonderful eyes was lost.

The 'rude mechannicals' of Athens were played with Dublin accents; there had been a tradition inherited from the English touring companies that members of the Shakespearian lower orders should only speak in 'Mummerset' – Hilton Edwards, an Englishman, thought this ridiculous, and substituted whatever Irish accents he thought appropriate to the work. One night O'Dea introduced a piece of impromptu business which caused such laughter that Edwards begged him to keep it in. Approaching the moment in the play-within-the-play where Bottom as Pyramus has to kiss Thisbe through a chink in the Wall (which is played by Snout), O'Dea looked puzzled, sidled over to the proscenium, took the prompter's book, checked the text, shrugged, and then very tentatively spoke the line, 'I kissed the wall's hole, not your lips at all'. The other actors had difficulty maintaining their poise; the laughter seemed to go on for ever.

During the war years, Jimmy O'Dea and Harry O'Donovan presented a comedy show on the BBC Home and Forces Programme. This had to be recorded at a studio in North Wales, to which the company travelled each week by Mail Boat, at some considerable danger because of German submarines. The curious venue was selected due to official objections from the Unionist-dominated BBC studios in Belfast – only a train-ride away – where the title 'Irish Half Hour' was felt to be insulting to the people of Northern Ireland. Micheál MacLíammóir had a similar experience with *Ill Met by Moonlight*, which Val Gielgud, Drama Director of the BBC, said he found 'enchanting', and the producer, Noel Iliff, wished to broadcast with the original Gate cast. Between September 1946 and July 1951, the script shuttled to and fro between the London and Belfast studios. A number of criticisms were made on artistic grounds. Eventually, after several reports had been written and studied – 'Has freshness, invention, charm and humour' – 'The characterisation is not subtle' – 'Atmospheric subtlety suggested by the text, and sound effects dramatic and organic' – it was left to the drama producer in Belfast, James Mageean, to make a recommendation. First Mageean said he was reading it. Then he was on sick leave. Then Raymond Percy sent another script, as the original seemed to have been been 'mislaid'. Finally Mageean wrote to Lance Sieveking, a BBC producer in London, who was also keen to produce it, to say that it could not be broadcast in Northern Ireland 'for policy and other reasons'. The Celtic Twilight element would have upset the Unionist listeners, who had to be shielded from such subversive stuff! The irony for MacLíammóir was that *The Dancing Shadow*, his only work which did poor business at the Gaiety and was never revived, was produced by the BBC in 1950. The theme of incest did not upset anyone in Belfast.

UNDIPLOMATIC INCIDENT

As well as *A Midsummer Night's Dream*, the second Gaiety season included Maxwell Anderson's Meyerling play, *The Masque of Kings*, Daphne du Maurier's *Rebecca* and Bertha Selous' *No Traveller Returns*. Joan Reddin, daughter of Tony Reddin of the Capitol Theatre, joined the company as a juvenile. Years later in London, in less happy circumstances for Hilton Edwards, she became his efficient and supportive agent.

During the extended run of *A Midsummer Night's Dream*, rehearsals started for a new play by Lennox Robinson, based on Maupassant's story of the Franco-Prussian war, *Boule de Suif*, which he retitled *Roly Poly* and set in contemporary war-riven France. The opening was announced for 19 November 1940 – the company's much-delayed return to the Gate. The story tells of a group of French refugees – a wine-merchant, a banker and an aristocrat, with their wives, two nuns and a prostitute, fleeing from their home town of Rouen before the invading German forces. At Tours, they find the hotel is in enemy occupation. The German lieutenant keeps them in confinement, suggesting that if one of the women of the party agrees to sleep with him, he will release them all. The bourgeois members of the group, conferring among themselves in dire anxiety, insist that this duty should naturally be fulfilled by the prostitute, Roly Poly. After she has 'sacrificed' herself, much against her will, to the enemy of France, the group is allowed to continue on its journey, and the 'respectable' folk again shun her.

Shelah Richards' performance as Roly Poly drew enthusiastic reviews, but it was the searing topicality of the piece which caused the most excitement.

Christopher Casson, who played the wine-merchant Rousseau, said it was 'so topical, it was as if it was all happening in the next room'. On the day following the opening Hilton Edwards was startled to receive a telephone call from the Department of External Affairs to say that the German Minister, Herr Hempel, had protested strongly at the content of the play, for no Nazi officer would behave like the Lieutenant portrayed on the stage. The official of the Department requested that changes should be made to the script, as Mr de Valéra (who, as well as being Taoiseach [Prime Minister] had assumed the External Affairs portfolio for the duration of the war) was greatly concerned. Frantic discussions took place in the office-dressingroom, but it was a foregone conclusion that if the central incident in the action were excised, there would be no play left. In any case, most of the press reviews that morning had contained a synopsis of the plot. Matters took a turn for the worse when a further *communiqué* indicated that the French Minister, Monsieur de Laforcade, had complained that the French citizens in the play, who persuaded Roly Poly to act as she did, were not in any way representative of the people of their nation. The presentation was a travesty, and should be withdrawn. An apology would be insufficient.

Heated affirmations by Edwards that the work was a straight transposition of a story by a renowned French author were useless in the circumstances, for it was pointed out that the playwright was Lennox Robinson, and it was quite possible that a new 'interpretation' had been given to the story. No one could find a copy of Maupassant's original. In any case, there was also the German point of view, and that was that Maupassant was quite definitely anti-German. The fact that he had been dead for fifty years did not seem to signify.

The press did not report this *débâcle*, and the second performance proceeded without anyone in the audience being aware of the turmoil backstage though a member of the French diplomatic corps left at the interval; it was believed that he had been sent by his superiors as an observer. Edwards and MacLíammóir were terrified that their theatre might be closed, and that the authorities might use their influence in the insidious way they knew was prevalent in central Europe to discredit their work as professionals. Next day there was a message from the Department of Justice requesting that further performances be cancelled.

There is a long-standing inveteracy in the theatre to the effect that once officialdom starts tampering with what theatrical practitioners believe to be their right to present reasonable portrayals of human behaviour, compliance with such interference must be fiercely resisted. The play must go on! The actors were prepared to continue with *Roly Poly*, and when evening came, they put on their costumes and waited. They, however, did not hold responsibility for what might happen. What made it even more difficult for Edwards and MacLíammóir, as managers, was that Lennox Robinson was quite determined that that night's performance should take place. The audience was admitted –

there was still no public inkling of the affair – and Robinson came before the curtain and told them what had happened. He announced that he had agreed with the management to buy out the house, and the performance was therefore a private one, as everyone present was his guest.

Shelah Richards wrote in her unpublished memoir, 'I remember Hilton and Micheál looking at each other, and Hilton saying "Oh! my God! What does he think he's going to use for money to pay the expenses?", meaning the actors' wages, the electricity, and so on.' As it happened, a collection was being taken, as had been agreed by all the theatres for that night, for the survivors of a fire at the Poor Clare's Orphanage in Cavan. Edwards ruefully expressed the view that the collection should have been taken up for *him*.

Next day the incident was fully reported. Edwards and MacLíammóir issued a one-sentence statement to the effect that the play had been withdrawn 'at the request of the Department of Justice'. Edward Longford and Norman Reddin were not slow to disassociate themselves from the choice of work. Longford wrote, 'I am in no way responsible for the production of this play or of any other play presented at the theatre, except those presented by Longford Productions . . . ' Edwards and MacLíammóir, in the throes of getting together yet another revival of *Night Must Fall* to replace *Roly Poly* for the following Monday, replied immediately with 'We notice with pleasure that Lord Longford and Mr Norman Reddin have at last found a suitable moment to state the fact of their dissociation with our work on the stage, a fact which we ourselves have endeavoured to make quite clear to the public since 1936 . . . '. Reddin then wrote another letter to say that he was 'shocked at their attitude towards my colleague and fellow director Lord Longford, who came forward voluntarily when the Gate Theatre was on its last legs and poured thousands of pounds into the enterprise without the hope of ever receiving back a single penny. Were it not for that money, spontaneously given by Lord Longford, those two gentlemen might now be enjoying the delights of London and not of Dublin.' The last sentence was designed to convey the message, which readers would have instantly understood, that Edwards and MacLíammóir should by rights be suffering the effects of the blitz, or even serving in the forces. The acrimony of the 'Longford split' was thus revived.

A PLACE OF BREADTH AND DIGNITY

The new pattern was now established. A spring and autumn season in the Gaiety, with a summer provincial tour in between, and then what were supposed to be holidays, but became a series of urgent planning meetings. Mid-winter in the Gate always included a Christmas revue, made up of satirical sketches written by MacLíammóir, Casson and other members of the company, cabaret numbers in which Roy Irving and Tyrell Pine excelled, one-act plays and scenes adapted from novels, all collected under umbrella titles like *Snapdragon*, *Harlequinade*, *Jack-in-the-Box* and *Masquerade*. There was an air of almost decadent fun as Europe crumbled into rubble, British cities were bombed from the air, and then Belfast became the target of appalling Luftwaffe raids in which over two thousand people died in their own homes. Yet Belfast continued to welcome the Gate on its now annual visits to the Grand Opera House, possibly as a response to the bravery of the actors in engaging to come north at all. The Opera House also maintained a repertory company called the Savoy Players, in which several Gate players including Coralie Carmichael took part when not required at home – the only permanent drama company ever to occupy a large theatre in Belfast. 'It's an ill wind . . . ', people in the theatre were saying.

For Edwards and MacLíammóir, the Gaiety became home-from-home. During the war the company gave fifty-four productions there and only twenty-three in the Gate. MacLíammóir liked the Gaiety because it was 'a real theatre, a place of breadth and dignity, with room to move in and plush to sit on, and a flock of ghosts over one's head in the air. To us, who have spent most of our lives on the stage, the height and space alone of a theatre is essential. It was at the National Theatre in Zagreb I realised this. In those halls, cranky or macabre, that have been adapted in so many countries by experimentalists like the Pitoëffs or Peter Godfrey or Hilton and me, not from intellectual preference but from the necessity arising from the lack of this in the public, one may gain intimacy, but one loses, however skilfully one works, majesty, nobility, comfort and depth.'

The Gaiety's 75th anniversary was celebrated in November 1941 with a production of Shaw's *Caesar and Cleopatra*, with Hilton Edwards and Betty Chancellor. Much was made in the press of the appropriateness of a play by a truly celebrated Irish dramatist, and it was recalled that the theatre had opened in similar vein with Goldsmith's *She Stoops to Conquer*. John Betjeman wrote a stirring prologue in rhyming couplets which was spoken by Anew McMaster, and which ended

> The great tradition she has known before
> Goes on – with Edwards and MacLíammóir!

The Gaiety seasons introduced several other young players who were to proceed to the international stage and to films as actors and directors – among them Daniel O'Herlihy, Wilfred Brambell, Patrick Carey and Jack McGowran – the latter to create important rôles for Samuel Beckett. Cleopatra's younger brother, Ptolemy, was played by a child actor, Milo O'Shea. Eithne Dunne, Ginette Waddell, Noëlle Middleton, Aiden Grennell, Patrick McLarnon, Godfrey Quigley and Denis Brennan, whose work was later to dominate the Irish stage, all took part in Hilton Edwards' productions at this period.

During a revival of the modern-dress *Hamlet* in May 1941, Sybil Thorndike came to Dublin to meet her son, Christopher Casson's fiancée, Kay O'Connell; she also gave an afternoon recital of Shakespeare in the Gaiety. Christopher and Kay were married on 11 June, with Micheál MacLíammóir as best man, the bride and bridesmaid's dresses designed by Patrick Perrott. When MacLíammóir opened an exhibition of Kay's work at the Country Shop, he said 'Christopher and Kay have a trick of looking at things through the eyes of childhood. Their world is intoxicated with gaiety as a bee is intoxicated with honey.'

Sybil and her husband Lewis Casson gave further recitals in the Gaiety and at the Cork Opera House, while the Gate was in residence in those theatres in 1942, and in 1943 Sybil Thorndike joined the company to play Lady Cicily Waynflete in *Captain Brassbound's Conversion* and Mrs Alving in *Ghosts*. None of the critics suggested that MacLíammóir, at forty-two, might have been a little too old for Oswald. Christopher Casson felt this was because the production was in the romantic tradition, and his Oswald was seen as a successful artist who had spent some time in the Paris of *La Bohème*. He believed that Mrs Alving was one of his mother's truly great rôles – the others were St Joan and Medea – and Dublin resoundingly agreed.

Betty Chancellor's return to the Gate was much welcomed by the press, but caused difficulties for Edwards and MacLíammóir, for Shelah Richards, who now shared the leading rôles with Coralie Carmichael and Meriel Moore, would not perform in the same plays, or even enter the same room as Betty, who was living openly with Shelah's husband, Denis Johnston. The antagonism between these two highly talented women continued until their deaths in the 1980s, and, apart from the genuine heartbreak which seemed more pronounced on Shelah's side, gave rise to trivial social problems as well as intractable professional ones. 'We all loved Shelah, and we all loved Betty,' said Harry Fine – and while there certainly was a Richards camp and a Chancellor camp, it was extremely tricky for those who were in both, or subscribed to neither. Even when they were all considerably advanced in years, Mary Manning had to invent excuses, if Shelah heard she had been seen attending the theatre with Betty. Denis Johnston, who from a very early age kept all the letters ever written to him, as well as copious copies of letters he wrote himself, was the recipient of Betty's usually entertaining and often penetrating views on the Dublin scene while he was working as the BBC's Balkan and Middle Eastern correspondent, and as a producer in New York in the later 'forties. They were married in 1945 'outside the jurisdiction' – in fact in Dungannon, Northern Ireland, a town often used by MacLíammóir as an illustration of spiritual as well as architectural dullness.

Betty Chancellor's letters give a fairly frank picture of the Dublin she was living in. ' . . . Life is so drab here, and the country does get one down a bit. Things like scabies, a skin disease got from dirt, are rife in Dublin . . . The gas goes off at 7 at night. The buses stop at 9.30. We have barley flour which is nearly white and madly constipating . . . ' In another letter she says, 'This city is dying. The frightful censorship and narrowness is sapping the life out of everything, and there is nobody to fight a battle because the place is full of drunken Blitz Gaels and Queens . . . ' (This was an uncharacteristically female-chauvinist reference to Irish people who had returned from Britain, and homosexuals, several of whom were close friends.) Of Hilton Edwards' affair with a young man whom everyone referred to as 'Miss S', she wrote, 'Meriel and I think Hilton has something in his head. I mean that he is going Potty. He is getting more and more panicky and uncertain. Miss S apparently is still in the ascendant . . . In fact went to the Arts Ball with Sally as a chaperone. Of course they only met at the ball by accident! Oh yes! Strange, there was a table ordered. Miss S complained to Sally that H. was too old, that she liked to be surrounded by youth. Sally's suggestion that she should have a baby was not well received . . . '

Material shortages became more prevalent as the war progressed. Locomotives were adapted from coal to turf, and it was known for trains to stop in the middle of the countryside where passengers were asked to help gather fuel among the heather. The summer tour of 1942 was fraught with late arrivals and departures. The journey from Sligo to Dublin, which normally took four hours, on one occasion took thirteen. Betty wrote to Denis, 'After waiting in Mullingar for three hours, the train gave a jerk forward and then stopped. Hilton rushed out of the carriage and up and down the corridor angrily shouting "Who moved that train?"'

*

The Gaiety also played host to several Gate productions of West End and Broadway comedies and thrillers, which in normal times would have been part and parcel of the now defunct world of cross-channel touring. These were judiciously slipped into the programme between works of greater literary, though not necessarily greater theatrical, merit. MacLíammóir was of the opinion that Irish actors never really understood the texture of American comedies like *Arsenic and Old Lace* (which was seen by 54,000 people in five weeks) and *The Man who Came to Dinner* (in which Edwards was described by the normally iconoclastic student magazine, TCD, as 'quite the best actor on the Dublin stage' and MacLíammóir as giving 'a perfect little character sketch in a five-minute appearance'), but they were great fun to perform, they employed huge casts, and they undoubtedly convinced first-time attenders to try other Gate offerings. The Gate was enlarging the theatregoing sector in a way no Dublin company had ever done before.

'A DIRTY TIRADE'

The Christmas show of 1942 included a short comic play, *Thirst*, by the Irish Times columnist, 'Myles na Gopaleen', later celebrated internationally as the novelist 'Flann O'Brien', though his real name was Brian O'Nolan. O'Nolan contributed a surrealist programme-note on the subject of Rain in the Theatre, which had nothing to do with the play, ending, 'Yes, I'm going to write a play about rain. I am off to Connemara to get some local cholera.' (He did no such thing, but later published the novel *The Poor Mouth* in which rain and Connemara are inextricably linked.) Hilton Edwards suggested that O'Nolan should adapt Karel and Josef Capek's *Insect Play* to an Irish setting. His response was immediate, and the script, adapted much more radically than Edwards had anticipated, was ready for production at the Gaiety on 2 March 1943.

The original work takes the form of an allegorical revue and seeks to demonstrate that the insect world is more intelligently organised than our own. O'Nolan's adaptation lost much of the play's bite. His amusing transpositions – the Capek's beetles were given Dublin accents and attitudes, his crickets those of Cork – obscured its main thrust. The Irish Press suggested that the Capeks would have been surprised to find their play used ' . . . to burlesque the divisions of this country . . . to mock the movement for reviving a national language and to sneer at the people of Ireland, north and south.' This over-solemn judgement was nonetheless echoed by Gabriel Fallon, critic of the Catholic Standard, who found the adaptation salacious, not to say obscene. A bizarre correspondence ensued in the same paper – O'Nolan obviously enjoying himself, and Fallon bursting journalistic blood-vessels.

O'Nolan responded to the original critique by stating that he and the producers were 'content to endure the implication that as Christians and Catholics we are very inferior to Mr Fallon. We claim, however, a sense of aesthetic delicacy, and we protest very strongly against a dirty tirade which, under the guise of dramatic criticism, was nothing more or less than a treatise on dung. "There will always be a distinction", Mr Fallon says, "between the honest dung of the farmyard and the nasty dirt of the chicken run." Personally I lack the latrine erudition to comment on this extraordinary statement, and I am not going to speculate on the odd researches that led your contributor to his great discovery. I am content to record my objection that his faecal reveries should be published . . . ' Fallon had objected, among other things, to 'sex'. O'Nolan pointed out that there was 'no reference as such to sex anywhere; it is true that there are male and female characters, but very few people nowadays consider that alone an indelicacy.'

Gabriel Fallon wrote to the manager of the Gaiety Theatre, Hamlyn Benson, to say that, as a protest at the content of the play, he intended to 'refrain from attendance at any subsequent presentation which this company may offer'. As the readership of the Catholic Standard was believed to be small among theatregoers, his threat did not appear damaging.

Among the most successful revivals – and revivals of revivals – at the Gaiety, were MacLíammóir's version of *Jane Eyre* and Ria Mooney's of *Wuthering Heights*. These heavy dramatisations also became a staple of the provincial tours. MacLíammóir's Rochester struck Con Curran of The Bell as 'the true aristocratic-republican swarthy-volcanic creation of the Yorkshire moors, the swollen beck and the cabined Parsonage parlour'. Betty Chancellor was not of the same mind; she wrote to Denis Johnston that Micheál 'plays it as a romantic martyr with tears flowing down his cheeks – that cruel, sadistic, interesting man. Oh my God!' – but the audiences loved it, and the company, including Betty, played the melodrama for all it was worth. Neither Brontë work was included in a summer tour of Northern Ireland during the last months of the war, however, for neither Betty, the Catherine, nor Eithne Dunne, the new Jane, was free to travel. Early in 1945 an invitation had been received from the newly-formed Council for the Encouragement of Music and the Arts to perform for three nights each in Bangor, Ballymena, Ballymoney, Portstewart, Derry, Omagh, Newry, Armagh and Portadown. The invitation was clearly intended in part as a formal vote of thanks to the Gate for its unsolicited visits to Belfast at the time of the worst wartime troubles. The plays chosen were *Where Stars Walk*, *Othello*, and *A Hundred Years Old* by the Quintero brothers. Micheál and Hilton felt it was like being back with McMaster 'in the smalls', except that this time there was a subsidy, and the booking and transport arrangements were looked after by energetic young people from Belfast, one of them Betty Lowry, who later became Ulster's leading theatre critic.

The opening in Bangor followed soon after Victory in Europe Day and 'Ulster's premier seaside resort' was still decked with little union-jacks and pictures of George VI and Queen Elizabeth. Dublin, naturally, was not celebrating, though many citizens thought there should be some acknowledgement of the cessation of hostilities, no matter how distant they had been. Micheál said to Betty, 'Really, dear, trying to love this country is like trying to love a very beautiful woman with B.O.' In Bangor there was a late start as Hilton Edwards was not satisfied with the lighting, and irate citizens banged on the door exclaiming that tardiness might be acceptable 'down there' – meaning 'in the south' – but the people of Northern Ireland were not going to put up with it; however, they did put up with it, and the County Down Spectator reported that 'the Dufferin Memorial Hall proved altogether inadequate for all who sought admission.' In Ballymena the Observer, in the middle of its review of *Othello*, could not forbear to omit the fact that Daniel Wherry, who was playing a minor part, was the son of the proprietor of the Adair Arms Hotel; and in Derry the Standard noted that Aiden Grennell, who doubled Montano and the Duke, was 'the son of Mr A.P. Grennell, who was the manager of the Hibernian Bank, Derry, for fifteen years', and that Aiden had been educated at St Columb's College in the city. 'His many friends in Derry will be pleased to hear of his continued success,' it added, before resuming the critique.

The company arrived in Newry on a very wet Sunday and could not gain entry to the Town Hall because the caretaker was said to be 'at church'. When he eventually appeared, Edwards' vituperation quickly removed the smile of welcome from his face. That night the audience was again kept waiting in the rain, and when they were allowed in, cold and bedraggled, Edwards went on stage and publicly berated the town of Newry for treating visiting artists in this way. He then told them they could wait until he had dressed and made up for Iago, which they meekly did; but there was no reaction to the performance throughout the whole evening and the actors realised they were being silently snubbed.

The Northern Ireland tour showed that there was still a theatre audience in that province, in spite of war and the cinema; the comfort of a guaranteed income, thanks to British government support through CEMA, reopened the debate about the continued unlikeliness of Irish government support for the Gate in Dublin. The actors were aware that Edwards and MacLíammóir had 'creamed off' a percentage of the CEMA grant, which was calculated on a *per capita* basis, and that the members of the company did not each receive the figure which the Gate management had applied for on their behalf; but if officials of CEMA were aware of this, they did not record it.

When the partners were once more established in the No.1 dressing-room at the Gaiety for a seven-week autumn season, the thought was constantly in their minds as to how long this satisfactory arrangement with Louis Elliman was likely to last, for the cross-channel companies would probably return now that the war was over. Personal savings arising out of the Gaiety engagements had placed them in a position where they could move out of their flat in Dawson Street and buy a house. The purchase of No.4 Harcourt Terrace, a three-storey over basement stucco town residence, built in 1840 but looking more like a London house of the Regency period, gave them a greater sense of security. More significantly, it provided social *cachet*. Here they could entertain – and they did so, lavishly. Here they could be looked after by a devoted (but ill-paid) domestic staff.

The founding of an actor's union in Dublin, in 1942 – a precursor of Equity – presaged agitation for increased salaries. Should that occur, the Gate company, if confined to its own small auditorium, certainly would not be able to survive. It was with this in mind, that Hilton Edwards started on his quest for a new theatre.

Chapter 9
Broadway at Last

Christopher Casson believed that while the Gate Theatre's most 'interesting' phase was that of its innovative years, from the end of the 1920s into the 'thirties, its best productions were those which took place at the Gaiety during the 1940s and early 'fifties, when techniques had become tempered by time and experience, and there was money – not much, but some – with which the partners were able to measure out their bright designs. During the war years Hilton Edwards had planned and directed sixty-three productions. Micheál MacLíammóir – who never settled by the fireside to read novels or listen to the radio or contemplate the back yards of Dawson Street or the gardens of Harcourt Terrace unless it was to further some theatrical or literary project, and always seemed to have a sketchpad or notebook in his hand – had created twenty-six stage settings and written four plays and two dramatisations of prose fiction. During the winter of 1942-43 he had contributed a series of memoirs entitled *Eachtraí Aisteóra* (*Tales of an Actor*) to the Irish-language periodical, Comhar. He submitted them in translation to the London publishers, Methuen & Company, who in due course commissioned a full autobiography.

All for Hecuba was published in 1946. Patrick Perrott had said to him of one of his plays, 'You are such a good conversationalist, and such a terse and, so to speak, intelligent actor, what a pity that when you write your style is like a herbaceous border.' *All for Hecuba* is more than a herbaceous border, it is a thick and resplendent shrubbery of evasions, and an expansive lawn of omissions. As for what is included, the Cork actor Maurice O'Brien described the contents as 'A major work of fiction – he wasn't born within sound of Shandon bells – it was Bow bells!' Yet if *All for Hecuba* is weak on bare fact, it is exceedingly strong on social comment and atmosphere, and gives an artistically accurate picture of the times through the actor's highly receptive eyes. The myth of his birth in Cork is strengthened, there is very little about his London upbringing and (strangely) of his brilliant juvenile career there, not much about his wanderings through Europe with 'Máire', nothing about the nature of his relationships with other men – this was to be expected in the climate of the period – and no suggestion of his and Hilton Edwards' emotional interdependence. His early mentor, Wilfred Rooke-Ley, is not mentioned (what can he have thought of such ingratitude when the book came out?), neither is Harry Fine, the Gate's earliest manager, nor is Edward Ball, whose fate coloured a whole Gate season. James Mason, who generously attributed his rise in the profession to his period at the Gate, is dismissed in one sentence.

The book was rightly praised for its positive points and received a generous welcome in the quality British press. Christine Longford was invited to review it for The Bell, and wondered if she *ought*. In the end she decided that she *should*. She overcame the instinct which must, even for a few fleeting seconds, have suggested a hatchet-job; but Christine was more at home with the hatpin. She described MacLíammóir as 'the second best actor in Ireland' (McMaster was the best). She thought he should have expanded on his acting – 'there is something about his Hamlet, but I want more'. She would love to have been told about 'the child-actor who sent London into raptures'. She was confused by the flash-backs and flash-forwards – 'Sometimes he refers to a thing that happened before, when he has forgotten to tell what it was.' When she reached the chapter on the 'Longford split' she said, 'I remember things differently . . . The theme-song of a certain drama seems to be "We were poor, but we were honest, Victims of a rich man's whim." The drama, of course, is the quarrel with the Longfords. It is in no sense a tragedy, nor a comedy or a farce either, but a sad little melodrama which is now out of date. The Longfords once wept over it too.'

THE GREAT ORGAN VOICE

The 1946 spring season at the Gaiety lasted ten weeks and included a production of *The Merchant of Venice* set in the period of Canaletto, with incidental music arranged by Hilton Edwards from Scarlatti, and presented in the manner of a harlequinade. The last play of the season was the first production of MacLíammóir's *Ill Met by Moonlight*: it immediately transferred to the Gate. Then Louis Elliman presented a summer revue, *And Pastures New*, written by Dick Forbes of the Queen's Theatre, with sketches by Micheál MacLíammóir and Tyrell Pine, operatic arias from the popular soprano Renée Flynn, and dance numbers devised by Alice Dalgarno of the Theatre Royal, with the Royal's high-kicking chorus-line, The Royalettes. Hilton Edwards directed it in the manner of Ronald Frankau's Cabaret Kittens, but the public would not be wooed by such a *mélange*. The Gate's autumn season at the Gaiety reintroduced Anew McMaster, who had been on tour 'in the smalls' of the south for almost the entire war period. Mac appeared as Svengali in a new adaptation of *Trilby* by his brother-in-law (with his son as Little Billee), and as *Oidipus the Tyrant* [sic] in a translation by Edward Longford, which was played as a double bill with the Don Juan scene from *Man and Superman*. McMaster had first asked Longford for a version of Oedipus, in blank verse with rhyming choruses, in 1938, but then his plans changed and the play was given a student production at All Hallows College. In 1942 Mac joined Longford Productions for the first professional performance of the play, and it was he who suggested it for this Gaiety season, and who made the arrangements with the author, which Hilton was reluctant to do. The Independent was pleased that 'there was neither the limitations of naturalism nor the exaggeration of rant', rather supposing that McMaster might have been expected to provide both. The Irish Times' newly-appointed theatre critic, who signed himself 'K' – Seamus Kelly, from this time onward a staunch upholder of the Gate and its policy – said 'It is rare that we have a chance of seeing three of the country's best actors in two of the world's best plays at one sitting.' (It was he who coined the phrase 'McMaster's great organ voice', which was quoted many times on playbills.) In the Shaw, MacLíammóir played Don Juan and Edwards the Devil, as before; 'salvo after Shavian salvo rocked a house, harrowed by Sophocles, back to self-critical laughter.'

McMaster's portrait by Gaetano Gennaro in the National Gallery of Ireland shows him in the rôle of Oedipus, wearing a laurel wreath on his head. The actor Colm O'Doherty, who joined McMaster's company in 1944, said that the wreath was something thought up at the last minute. 'I know it's not right, dear, but I have to put something on me head, and besides, laurel leaves look so dignified!' Christopher Casson, who did not appear in any of these plays, remarked that 'actors like Mac, Micheál, Hilton, my mother, can play two thirds of a performance indifferently, and suddenly they give a *revelation*. Mac's *Oidipus* was weak and ham until the blinding scene, which was so magnificent that you remember it as being better than, for instance, Olivier's.'

At the end of 1948 the McMasters sailed for Melbourne with a company made up almost entirely of newcomers, except for Christopher (who had recently played the juvenile lead in Saroyan's *The Beautiful People*, at the Mercury in London) and Colm O'Doherty who had been a childhood companion of his when the McMasters played in Strokestown, County Roscommon. Mary Rose joined them the following year. When they reached Perth, a little girl of twelve, Margaret Anketell, whose forebears had come from County Monaghan – where McMaster claimed to have been born – approached him in the dining-room of the Shaftesbury Hotel and said 'Please, Mr McMaster, may I have your autograph?' 'Little did I know,' she wrote later, 'that before the end of the year I would be on stage asking, "Please, sir, may I have some more?" as Oliver Twist to his Fagin; nor could she know that she would be cast to play Desdemona to his Othello with the Gate Theatre company in Dublin when she was twenty-five.

SEARCH FOR A NEW STAGE

Hilton Edwards was obsessed with the notion that the Gaiety engagements could not go on for ever, and the company would not be able to mount the kind of productions it wished in the Gate, due to rising costs. In the summer of 1945, through the company's lawyers, Hoey & Denning, and with the co-operation of the architect Michael Scott, he investigated the possibility of buying the 800-seat Queen's Theatre, a charming but ill-maintained building of 1823 in the city centre, which was the home of melodrama and variety. It was specially notable for its Celtic Revival plasterwork, installed during a refurbishment at the turn of the century and, though its backstage accommodation was cramped due to the nature of the site, the stage itself was excellent and had the advantage of a fly-tower. Scott and Edwards learned that £30,000 was the figure needed for the purchase and the renovations required by the Dublin Corporation fire department. Edwards-MacLíammóir Productions could provide £2,000, and the balance would have to be raised by sponsorship and public subscription. The partners soon came to realise that money of this order simply was not available in Dublin for such a project, and they did not pursue the matter for the time being.

Louis Elliman, through the Dublin Theatre Company Limited, also had an interest in the Queen's, and this fact made for difficulties of a diplomatic nature when serious negotiations began a year later. How would Mr Louis react if he learned that the Gate was likely to pull out of the Gaiety before the Gaiety had even indicated that the existing arrangement might not go on for ever? On 12 August 1946, Edwards wrote to Elliman, squarely outlining their position. ' . . . As you know, our associations have always been very pleasant and, I think, mutually profitable (this sounds like a desperate threat, but it is my unfortunate phrasing) what I mean is – with all the desire in the world to maintain the status quo, Micheál and I feel that we must have a permanent theatrical home (which was our original policy in Ireland and which we succeeded in having for some years at the Gate until circumstances foiled us) or change our entire theatrical programme . . . ' Edwards also spoke to his friend Erskine Childers, then Parliamentary Secretary to the Minister for Local Government (and subsequently President of Ireland), for there was a rumour that the government was concerned that so many cinemas and theatres were becoming part of the J. Arthur Rank chain, represented in Ireland by the Ellimans. Childers wrote to Edwards under confidential cover to say that 'the Government has been taking an interest in the growing monopoly of the Rank Companies, though this is for your private ear. They are not prepared to intervene directly, but the Minister for Posts and Telegraphs has indicated his willingness to say an unofficial word to Mr Elliman . . . '

Some months later Childers again wrote to Edwards, 'The Minister for Posts and Telegraphs has informed me that as the result of an entirely unofficial discussion, it would not now be opportune for you to discuss with the Rank interests the leasing of the Queen's Theatre. Certain *démarches* were made in connection with the general policy of the Rank Company in regard to the acquisition of cinemas and theatres here . . . ' Edwards was not daunted, and continued over the next three years to investigate any possibility of the eventual purchase of the Queen's, and also the Forum Cinema in the same street –

originally the Ancient Concert Rooms, where Yeats' *The Countess Cathleen* had been first performed. On 7 January 1951, at one of a series of Sunday night discussions at the Gate, he announced – somewhat prematurely as it turned out – that he was going to open a new theatre. Edward Longford, who was also present on the platform, was completely taken aback and cried out 'I will keep this place going as long as I can, though the ruins of it fall on me!' Longford's emotional assertion was to have an entirely beneficial bearing on the future of Edwards-MacLíammóir Productions, for he did keep the Gate going, and when Edwards and MacLíammóir at length failed to find an alternative venue they were very glad to continue the arrangement of sharing the theatre for half of every year.

The Queen's was leased to the National Theatre Society in 1950, following the burning of the Abbey Theatre, and was demolished in 1966, during a severe epidemic of office development, when many fine old buildings were similarly destroyed. Edwards' searches for a new theatre continued sporadically, while the Gaiety seasons continued, gradually becoming single engagements until 1964 when the first production of Brian Friel's *Philadelphia, Here I Come!* set the partners on a new course of creativity.

NEBULOUS MOONSHINE

The restless partners started searching for overseas outlets almost as soon as the war was over. The Cairo Opera House was approached, but the message which came back was that the presentation of plays in English was 'too arduous a project in view of the present state of civil unrest'. The London papers which had reviewed *Ill Met by Moonlight* in 1946, caused enough interest there for Hilton to feel he could approach West End managements; the Vaudeville responded favourably and a date was set for the following spring. On 10 November 1946 he made his first trans-Atlantic flight – from Rineanna, as Shannon Airport was then called – to discuss taking the same play to New York, and to try and secure the rights of new American plays which up to this time he had had to negotiate through London. 'Do you not have censorship in Ireland?' asked a naive Broadway agent when Hilton facetiously described *Ill Met By Moonlight* as being a play about fairies.

London, however, was far from entranced by a play about fairies from that island which had been so disloyal as to remain out of the war – 'Out of the war on which side?', Edwards had to stop himself from enquiring. The Sunday Express said that the pixies had run away with the play, and the News Chronicle felt it was no more than 'a bit of nebulous moonshine'. W.A. Darlington in the Daily Telegraph took the opposite view, finding the play 'full of imagination, atmosphere, Celtic magic and sense of beauty'; and Harold Hobson of the Sunday Times found it a 'memorable experience, dramatic, suggestive, frightening and funny'; but, as the members of the cast asked each other, of what use were so few among so many? There was a snowstorm during the first week, which affected all the theatres, but when the fine weather returned, *Ill Met by Moonlight* had been frozen out.

At the close of the same year, the Glasgow Citizens Theatre requested a visit from the Gate, to form part of an Irish Season. The plays chosen were *Where Stars Walk*, *The Old Lady Says 'No!'* and the production of Shaw's *John Bull's Other Island* which had concluded that autumn's Gaiety programme. All three had been selected with a view to the United States and Canada, for a tour ending in New York was now a certainty. In the meantime, the British Arts Council, undeterred by London's reception for *Ill Met by Moonlight*, agreed to underwrite a week each of these plays at the Embassy, Swiss Cottage, then a theatre with an adventurous programme. It was decided to travel to Glasgow and London via the Grand Opera House, Belfast.

GLASGOW

Glasgow was rainswept and dirty, and seemed not to be even thinking of recovering from the war. There was still food rationing, and the theatrical digs did not have fires or even the means of making a cup of tea after the performance. Hilton and Micheál were accommodated in a small hotel where the conditions were slightly better, but they found themselves reduced to slipping bread-rolls from the lunch table into paper bags so that they would have something to eat late at night. Some members of the company felt guilty about the comparative luxury of touring in Ireland, where there were always huge plates of mutton and potatoes or eggs and black-puddings, and Shannon Scheme electricity and aromatic turf fires; and sorry for the people who lived in the neighbourhood of the theatre, which seemed to be more deprived than any Dublin slum: a Bob Collis was urgently required here. Helena Hughes, the Eileen in *Where Stars Walk*, wrote of 'fog that never lifted – darkness and penetrating damp cold – the awful smell of soot and coal dust – everything grimy from coal, everything streaked with black. A Gorbals-Italian family who had a shop-café where you could have a big plate of *minestrone* for 6d, passed us all sorts of tins and rations from under the counter and we were all able to live mostly in the theatre – there was nowhere to go except the cinema and the matinée of Redgrave's *Macbeth* (we were on the same tour and we met again in New York).'

If the city was sadly uninviting, the audiences were warm and friendly. All three plays received excellent reviews, and there was much discussion about the sheer amount of drama which Irish writers were able to produce, contrary to the situation prevailing in Scotland. 'As for the productions,' said the Glasgow Herald, 'no praise can be too high.' The playwright and founder of the Scottish National Theatre, James Bridie, came to see *The Old Lady Says 'No!'* with his biographer, Winifred Bannister; she subsequently wrote, 'I have never seen him so enthusiastic about a performance . . . We came out of the theatre together, and he said: "Wasn't that wonderful! When we have a production like that in the Scottish theatre we shall have got somewhere"'.

Where Dublin and Glasgow had chuckled at Hilton Edwards' Broadbent in *John Bull's Other Island*, London felt his portrait of the eternal Englishman was farcical: the play was 'not a revival, but a corpse'. As with *Ill Met by Moonlight*, the 'quality' papers praised *Where Stars Walk*, while the others did not. The Arts Council's patronage helped considerably in the public relations aspect. There was a widely reported reception, attended by the Gate 'discovery', Peggy Cummins, now working at Elstree and described as 'the film star', Shelah Richards, and Lord Killanin – later to become chairman of the Dublin Theatre Festival. On New Year's Day 1948, a week after the Embassy Theatre season, the company left Southampton on the Mauretania, bound for New York.

THERE'S NO BUSINESS

The company consisted of Edwards and MacLíammóir, Helena Hughes and Meriel Moore, Norman Barrs, Denis Brennan, Liam Gannon, Edward Golden, Brian Herbert, Roy Irving, Reginald Jarman, Pat Nolan and half a dozen others; extras were to be recruited locally. The 'half dozen others' meant it was not a strong company – certainly not nearly as strong as that which had visited the Mediterranean and the Balkans. Betty Chancellor, who remained in Dublin with her and Denis Johnston's two small children, said they should have engaged the Cusacks, the Cassons, Maureen Delany – she did not mention Shelah Richards. It was like the kind of replacement company one might send out round the Irish smalls, she thought – certainly not right for Broadway. She felt that Hilton and Micheál were depending too much on their own charisma, which was unproven in America, where nobody there had heard of them.

The North American tour was masterminded by a Toronto agent, Brian Doherty, who had been in the Royal Canadian Air Force during the war and visited the Gate when on leave in Dublin 'to see the lights'. He was joined by Richard Aldrich and Richard Myers for the New York part of the visit; Paulette Goddard, whom they had met when she and Burgess Meredith had played in *Winterset*, in Dublin, was one of their backers. Raymond Percy travelled as Company Manager, as he had done in the Balkans. The theme was Four Irish Comedies – *John Bull's Other Island*, *The Old Lady Says 'No!'*, *Ill Met by Moonlight* and *Where Stars Walk*. After landing in New York following a very stormy crossing, the company was accommodated in the Markwell Hotel, which sold rooms by the hour; after one night the ladies removed themselves to the Taft. Some of the players took part in radio chat-shows, on one of which the host explained their accents as being that of 'cultivated Dubliners – a far cry from the brogue of the ordinary Irishman, or the speech of the average New Yorker'. After a few days they were transported in first-class parlor cars on the New York Central to St Thomas, Ontario, where they were met by members of the London Little Theatre and brought to London, Ontario, which turned out to be a bustling city with a very fine old theatre, the Grand. Here they again said 'Hello' and 'Goodbye' to Michael Redgrave, who was travelling a week ahead of them.

Liam Gannon recalled that Micheál MacLíammóir tore a ligament descending from his parlor car at St Thomas, and had to sit in a wheel chair for the dress rehearsal of *The Old Lady says 'No!'*, but was miraculously cured in time for the opening performance. London, Ontario, had no reservations about Edwards' Broadbent, nor about the plays from the twilit tradition, and Ottawa was equally successful. The doyen of Canadian critics, Herbert Whittaker, wrote of the Gate's 'brilliant playing' at His Majesty's Theatre in Montreal; and of the two weeks at the Royal Alexandra in Toronto, J.A. McNeil wrote of Brian Doherty's judgement and enterprise 'in bringing this splendid troupe across the Atlantic'. Addressing the Heliconian Club, Micheál MacLíammóir spoke of the long tradition in Irish playwrighting, starting with Farquhar; a Lucy Van Gogh in the Toronto magazine Saturday Night summed it up by saying that 'these two weeks have been a revelation of what intelligent and co-operative artistry can do in the theatre even in this cinema-ridden era'.

A week before the Gate company was due to open on Broadway, Denis Johnston wrote from New York – where he was directing a production of St John Ervine's *John Ferguson* – to Betty Chancellor in Dublin, that 'there is a very funny row going on now between the Dramatists' Guild (the American authors' trade union) and the Gate in Canada – principally over my royalties! No manager is allowed to put on any play here or in Canada without the Guild approving of the author's contract and terms . . . So of course the Gate never having given me a contract at all has raised a stink at once. Hilton hasn't answered my letter on the peculiar grounds that he has a "sore throat" so I have had Romping Raymond at the other end of the post.' The Dramatists' Guild insisted that Johnston be provided with a formal contract, or the company would not be allowed to perform the play in New York.

Romping Raymond quickly set matters right, and *The Old Lady Says 'No!'* opened as scheduled at the Mansfield Theatre (now the Brooks Atkinson) on 16 February, in the presence of the author, as their second production of the season. Johnston spent a great deal of his time over the next month in the company of Gate personnel, listening to their problems and helping them with advice, and sending ironic bulletins to Betty. *John Bull's Other Island* had opened the season on 10 February. 'It was quite good – no better,' he wrote. 'They liked Hilton (Broadbent) a lot, and some of the bit players, but Micheál was atrocious – not only fluffing but inaudible as well. Meriel (Nora) was very good but far too small in her playing (and too subtle) for that big theatre. This morning the notices were almost word for word what I'd said. Not rude but not very good.' Johnston can not have read the notices through, for though there were strong reservations about the age of the play, the production and performances were much admired. Howard Barnes in the Herald Tribune summed up that 'the Dublin Gate Theater deserves a rousing welcome', and Brooks Atkinson in the Times found the evening 'long but rewarding'. A feature of much of the press comment on all the plays was how much more impressive the staging was, compared to what Broadway audiences were used to. Brooks Atkinson picked out Molly MacEwen's neo-realistic cloths for the Shaw as 'worth the attention of a theater like ours where scene-design has become cumbersome'; and Hilton Edwards' lighting and massed movement in *The Old Lady Says 'No!'* appeared to New York to be quite as innovative as it had in Dublin almost twenty years before.

On 17 February, Denis Johnston wrote to Betty about his play: 'A packed house – naturally for a first night – and the usual people going out before the end. But naturally it was much better than London and got lots of curtains and shouts for author (which I didn't respond to). I have only seen three papers this morning. Brooks Atkinson in the Times is really quite nice – not a rave but a good intelligent notice praising its poetry and saying that of course it wasn't written for New York, but that it is exciting . . . Much the same in the Herald Tribune, and one of the usual wise-cracking "What's this all about?" pieces in the other paper – a tabloid . . . On the whole it seems I don't have to leave town.' Two days later he continued, 'I saw the *Old Lady* right through last night – a lovely house, not of the regular Broadway kind at all – that really thoroughly enjoyed it on the whole and made me like it too. Micheál was far better than in London as a result of various lectures . . . '

Some of the ladies of the company complained to Raymond Percy that Helena Hughes seemed to be getting all the publicity. The fact was that Hilton hoped that her extreme beauty, as well as her performance as Eileen in *Where Stars Walk*, would interest Hollywood, and it was his intention to state that she was on contract to the Dublin Gate Theatre, so that if she were cast in a picture, the Gate would receive a percentage. She did in fact have several film offers which she would not consider, because they were mostly for parts which she found 'ridiculous', including a 'stage-Irish colleen in a sickly film with Bing Crosby'. She was in due course brought to Hollywood by David O. Selznick, on a contract in which the Gate was not involved, but she only stayed for two months and then returned to Dublin, the Gate, and marriage to Liam Gannon. Their wedding present from Micheál MacLíammóir was the young parts in *The Mountains Look Different*, which he wrote specially for them. Liam Gannon later said that one of the most magical moments for him was seeing Helena's picture on a huge display in Times Square, one snowy night during the New York run of *Where Stars Walk*.

Denis Johnston went to see *Where Stars Walk* and wrote to Betty that it had been 'a flop financially, but it got quite good notices in the tabloids – the papers that razzed me!' It was retained for a second week, after which Doherty proposed to end the season, as he was losing money, although the contract specified an eight, rather than a four week run in New York. Hilton hurried to Denis, believing that his legal training would be of help, but Denis had to explain that he knew little of American law, and introduced him to 'a nice tough lowbrow lawyer'. Doherty had the option of substituting a short tour of one-night stands in Canada, plus a lump sum and their fares back to Ireland, and this was agreed upon, to the annoyance of the players, who were pleased with the audiences, did not believe the business could be as bad as the management stated, and liked being in New York.

So, indeed, did the partners, engaging in a succession of receptions and parties, and meetings with old friends. Toska Bissing, now married, appeared full of enthusiasm backstage, and Burgess Meredith and Paulette Goddard came to the opening of *Where Stars Walk* and gave a party at a cabaret called the Persian Room. Denis Johnston told Betty Chancellor that Goddard was 'really a nice simple creature with a sort of honest schoolgirl smile – but *what* emeralds!' Master Noël Coward's *Tonight at 8.30* was running on Broadway. He went to the same party with Elsa Maxwell, who at that time was writing a society column in the New York Post, to see Master Alfred Willmore's *Where Stars Walk*, and they both found it 'delightful'. She continued, 'The other night at a party given by the Duke di Verdura for Noël, Gertrude Lawrence and others, Richard Aldrich, who sponsors the Gate Theatre, brought Micheál MacLíammóir along. On meeting him, MacLíammóir whispered, "Noël Coward, I sang the Goldfish duet with you in Manchester when we were both nine years old!" Noël's eyes danced as he took up the refrain, remembering it word for word.'

'I don't think they did *Where Stars Walk* badly at all,' Denis wrote to Betty. 'It wasn't any better filled than the *Old Lady*, but had the same nice intelligent audience that the Boys are still trying to grumble at and say "How stupid New York is". They are now fully convinced that it is not their fault at all and that the standard of intelligence here is far beneath them, and that nobody appreciates anything above *Abie's Irish Rose*, and needless to say I haven't the nerve to continue the argument by telling them what is painfully obvious, that New York wants and expects something better than what will do for Belfast.'

The second Canadian tour opened in Brantford, Ontario, on 9 March. Roy Irving recalled that there were 'no more parlor cars', and their reappearance at London, Ontario, was less enthusiastic than before, because the audiences had read the New York reviews. Some members of the company were wondering if they ought to return to New York and take their chances, but in the end only Irving, Barrs and Herbert stayed.

At the end of the tour, Hilton Edwards and Micheál MacLíammóir returned to New York to fulfil engagements in radio drama – Edwards in Daphne du Maurier's *Rebecca*, MacLíammóir in Shaw's *Great Catherine* – having seen off the main body of the somewhat disgruntled company for Cóbh on 9 April. On the night before their departure, Denis Johnston took them to dinner, and Hilton asked him to take whatever steps were necessary to sue Brian Doherty for the money which was still owed. 'Just before they sailed on the Mauretania, H. rang up to say he had had a wire promising to pay before the end of the month. I don't somehow see myself having a good time starting a lawsuit on H's money between this and Monday!'

Before they left, the New York Critics Awards were announced, on 5 April. *The Old Lady Says 'No!'* took third place for Best Foreign Play, with *Where Stars Walk* in fourth – 'which isn't bad for a flop season,' Johnston wrote. (First place went to Rattigan's *The Winslow Boy*, and second to Sartre's *The Respectable Prostitute*.) A few days later Johnston met Roy Irving, who was looking for work in New York. 'He has decided to stay on here and is living in great squalor with Norman Barrs in a low Broadway hotel.' Forty-four years later, Irving recalled, 'I will never forget the feeling of seeing the ship pull out from New York City Pier, and I turned around to look at the skyscrapers and thought, "Now you've done it, now you are really on your own!".' He was thirty-six, and had devoted most of his working life to the Gate. He found a considerable amount of work in radio, and subsequently in television, and also directed for university and community theatres. 'I amazed myself that I could, if pushed to it, design the set, light it, dress the cast, make them up and direct the whole she-bang . . . when I had only acted under Field-Marshal Edwards and a much gentler Micheál's direction; but I suddenly was aware of what had gone in by osmosis in my years at the Gate.' He became the resident director for the Argus Eyes Drama Club at St Peter's College, Jersey City. In the course of time this work developed into a full course, and a new theatre building was opened. He did not know it was to be named the Roy Irving Theatre until the moment when the brass plaque was unveiled. 'I was overwhelmed. I must have done something right.'

*

In Dublin, Betty Chancellor sent the latest news about the new Gate season at the Gaiety to Denis Johnston. The first play, *Abdication*, was by an author whom Hilton and Micheál had met in New York, a Mrs H.T. Lowe-Porter. It was set in Elizabethan times, and written in a kind of blank verse, but clearly dealt with the abdication of Edward VIII in 1936. Mrs Lowe-Porter said she had been in England at that time and had been writing the play ever since. All the present members of the British royal family appeared, very thinly disguised, and Dubliners, now that they were no longer part of the United Kingdom, were able to indulge their passion for royal-watching at this discreet remove. It was also patently clear that the author had provided financial backing. Betty wrote: 'It was beautifully presented and produced, but a crashing bore of a play. M. and H. boring in the extreme. The only time I kept awake was a little scene with Mary Rose McMaster and Helena Hughes as Princess Elizabeth and Margaret. They looked so lovely, and were enchanting. I had lunch with H. and M., it was so nice, they were not boring at all, but quite their old selves. M.'s new play *The Mountains Look Different* is next week.'

The critic, Gabriel Fallon, who had vowed never to go to another Gate production after *The Insect Play*, not only attended the opening of *The Mountains Look Different*, but wrote that it was MacLíammóir's best work. It transferred to the Gate, and was revived again there, after an interruption of four weeks, during which the company made its second visit to Glasgow, bringing *The Mountains Look Different* and Ladislas Fodor's *The Vigil*. Remembering the cold of the Citizens Theatre, Helena Hughes brought a hot water bottle, and, taking advantage of the concealment of wooden panelling in the courtroom setting, kept it by her on the stage.

A revival of *The Drunkard* brought the Gate from Christmas into the new year of 1949 in rousing fashion. During its run the Gaiety rehearsals started – this time for Strindberg's *The Father*, with Hilton Edwards in the title rôle, followed by Victor Rietti's *To Live in Peace*, with a flock of hens, and a donkey which refused to trot up the hill specially created for it, until Signor Rietti, the embodiment of St Francis of Assisi, shouted 'Avanti!' from the wings.

*

Two seemingly fortuitous events of the previous year had an unusually far-reaching influence on the fortunes of the partners and of the theatre. Hilton was cast in a supporting rôle in the film of Robert Hitchins' book, *Call of the Blood*, which was shot in Sicily, where he was joined by Micheál for a summer holiday. He had brought with him a new novel by Maura Laverty called *Lift Up Your Gates*, and he wrote to her to say how much it had impressed him – so much, in fact, that he had given it to the director of the film as a possible subject. The book did not become a motion picture, but it did become a play, and its author's resulting association with the Gate was the only factor which prevented the company from disintegrating completely during the financially fraught 1950s.

The other event was the resignation of Everett Sloane – the American actor whose finest rôle was Bernstein in Orson Welles' *Citizen Kane* – from the part of Iago in Welles' *Othello*. Shooting began in 1948, but Sloane could not tolerate the delays occasioned by the speculative nature of the backing, and resigned his part. Welles tried to get James Mason, who was not available (or did not wish to be). Carol Reed then suggested Micheál MacLíammóir, and a series of telegrams was dispatched to Harcourt Terrace. MacLíammóir had been replaced in a revival of *The Drunkard* due to influenza (described to Welles as 'a nervous breakdown') and did not feel like accepting. In the end, after much persuasion, he did. Filming continued off and on, from the spring of 1949 for almost a year, which prevented MacLíammóir from taking other engagements. Then Edwards was cast as Brabantio in the same picture, which he accepted 'for the money', and so for the time being, Edwards-MacLíammóir Productions ceased to function as a performing company.

Chapter 10
Tush! Never Tell Me

The story of the filming of *Othello* was later told by Micheál MacLíammóir in his published journal, called *Put Money in Thy Purse*, a very different kind of book to *All for Hecuba*. Precise where the autobiography is vague, it follows a strict chronological course. The style is almost too terse – a natural trait with books which purport to be diaries; and as in many diaries, there is that irritating shorthand which dispenses with the definite and indefinite articles, and the personal pronoun – 'Jingled receiver like comic manservant in farce, also shouted to exchange, but no good. Have spent rest of evening in isolation and despair but will now sally forth to visit town'. He must have been reading E.M. Delafield's *Diary of a Provincial Lady*, for his style is almost a parody of that work.

Welles was annoyed by *Put Money in Thy Purse*, even more than with *All for Hecuba*, which he said he had hurled across the room in disgust, when he came to the section that concerned his first visit to Dublin. As he is described in *Put Money in Thy Purse* as 'cranky as a dromedary', 'dropsical as a black panther', 'a *fête champêtre* in a haunted valley', 'a thunderstorm' and a whole lot of other things by implication (such as schoolboyish, immature, irresponsible and moody) it is no wonder he gave a highly jaundiced picture of MacLíammóir to his biographer Barbara Leaming, four years after MacLíammóir's death. Yet he kept coming back to the Boys, like a prodigal nephew to two rather disapproving aunties. Perhaps it was only to Hilton he returned, for he told Ms Leaming that Hilton loved him, and it is reasonable to suppose that he would not have said so unless he had loved Hilton, in his way.

Micheál went to Paris for a week in early February 1949 to meet Orson, and arrangements were made for him to return for rehearsals a month later, which he did; and as rehearsals seemed to be few, he started writing a new play. One day Orson vanished to London, and without telling Micheál, went on to Dublin to see the re-opening of *Ill Met by Moonlight* at the Gaiety, an incident MacLíammóir does not record. Hilton went on stage during the curtain calls and introduced Orson Welles, who bowed to the throng from a box.

Othello then took MacLíammóir from Paris to Rome for costume and wig fittings; and there he remained, with some other members of the Welles organisation, for two weeks, waiting for the master who did not return, and attending parties at the two Irish embassies – Rome and the Vatican. On 9 April he flew back to Ireland in time to join his company in Belfast, in the unusual capacity of a member of the audience. 'Impossible,' he wrote, 'to fathom why I like this city, but I do. Admittedly a cold, ugly sort of place, even in this radiant northern April, its setting of windy mountains and dark shipyards, blotched with *fin-de-siècle* mansions and fussy streets full of plate glass and cake shops and trams, but there's something about it all, its fantastic predictability, its bleak bowler-hatted refusal of the inevitable – what is it? To arrive here from Rome within the space of two days is a fabulous experience; from that languorous immemorial embrace one passes to Brooke's 'rough male kiss of blankets'; Virgil and the Palatine Hill make way for the Bible and the bottle of Bushmills, and its air is that of a Business Man stepped right out of Alice's Wonderland and marching side by side with the Jabberwock through yards of bunting and a gritty northeast wind to the rolling of drums . . . '

The company moved on to Cork, where MacLíammóir went back into his part as Lee, but only for three nights, for a cable from Welles informed him he should be in Ouarzazate, which, upon investigation, appeared to be in the desert, some distance from Casablanca. Liam Gannon again took on the part of Lee – and the mystery of a missing round of applause. He found that, when he wore a dark jacket – as Micheál had done – he received the customary round of applause on an exit line; but when he wore a white one, there was total silence.

The Cork run of *Ill Met by Moonlight* and *The Drunkard* proved to be the last occasion when the company would play together for eighteen months. Louis Elliman had to look elsewhere for dramatic attractions for the Gaiety, for economic times had changed and cross-channel companies were now largely unable to risk a Dublin date. (In a letter to Welles, Edwards referred to 'a certain amount of Boat-burning' which was embarrassing him.) There was some resentment in the profession at the partners 'swanning off' to the Mediterranean, and if the Gate had been in receipt of a state subsidy they could not have done so. The point was, they were not in receipt of subsidy, and believed that the money earned from the film would help them to maintain the company when shooting was complete. They were wrong. If they had continued the arrangement with Elliman they would have been much better off: but how were they to know?

EVERYONE LOVES THE FELLOW WHO IS SMILING

MacLíammóir's contract for Iago had been negotiated by his agent, John Findlay, of Linnit & Dunfee, and was for 1,500,000 French francs, to cover three weeks rehearsal and ten weeks shooting. The document prudently stipulated that 'for any further work over and above this period, the artist shall receive payment *pro rata*'. All expenses were to be paid, and neither MacLíammóir nor Edwards were slow about charging bottles of wine or cigars or long-distance telephone calls to Welles' account in the numerous expensive hotels from Paris to Mogador, the more so as the stipulated ten weeks gradually became ten months and the matter of fees was expansively and continuously laughed off.

MacLíammóir arrived in Casablanca, as bidden, to find that no hotel had been booked for him, for Welles had taken on a rôle in the film, *The Black Rose*, (in order, it transpired, to help pay for *Othello*) and was not expected for three weeks; a message from Welles said that his second telegram cancelling MacLíammóir's trip had clearly not reached Cork in time, but why did he not visit Fez, Rabat and Marrakech to fill in the days? This he did, at Welles' expense, feeling lonely but admiring the architecture, and being taken by emissaries of Welles to places of evening resort, among them a '*closerie d'amour*, where we were entertained for more than reasonable sums in a series of dazzlingly lighted marble rooms on long puce or sky-blue divans by a bevy of unveiled houris smothered in *maquillage* and moles, and dressed, obviously, by Henri Matisse'; and to a series of cafés to see Berber dancing boys – 'these, dancing in long white night-shirts with bracelets on their ankles, proved as quiet and docile as if they had been brought up at St Margaret's Hall (which they probably had, or a Schleu equivalent). After the dancing was over, they squatted in the corner to drink mint tea, never taking their eyes off us, and a sort of Mussulman Santa Claus explained in French that they admired our ties and would like them as a souvenir. (Of what, I should like to know?)'

He was then requested for a costume fitting in Rome (whence he flew *via* Paris) and thence back to Casablanca, after several days delay in Paris caused by his not having a Moroccan visa – how, he enquired, without receiving a satisfactory answer, had he been admitted to Morocco three weeks before? In Paris Hilton Edwards appeared, on his way to Morocco for the long awaited holiday, and they went to the *Folies Bergères*. At length the visa arrived, Hilton set off in a new car for the south of France where the car was to be garaged, and thence to Casablanca – to which Micheál flew, in the expectation of doing some work at last. At Ouarzazate he was welcomed by Orson, who told him he had put on too much weight. By moonlight they inspected a Portuguese citadel which was to become 'the whole island of Cyprus'. Orson, singing snatches of a song he had written when at school in Woodstock, Illinois, *Everyone loves the fellow who is smiling*, dilated on the endless difficulties with money, and the cost of labour. Next day the drinking scene was rehearsed, but shooting was delayed because the costumes had not arrived from Rome. In due course Iago was fitted out locally with 'a workmanlike but unattractive jerkin in yellow leather' and 'some extremely painful armour and greaves', rendering the two trips to Rome a total waste of money. The murder of Roderigo was shot over several days, in a tower contrived to look like a Cypriot steam-bath, as there were no suitable costumes for the participants. The glare of the lights rendered MacLíammóir temporarily blind; in later life this worsening condition necessitated a number of operations. It was attributed to what the film technicians called 'Klieg eye'.

After two weeks Hilton arrived by bus, swathed in bandages, having had a car accident in Nice. He was also in possession of a case containing sundry medicines, which rarely left his side from this time onward. In the midst of hectic shooting on ramparts, beaches and cliff-tops, and dinners at which Hilton excelled in dealing with savoury mutton with his fingers and Micheál was confined to salads, Orson disclosed that his next subject would be *Julius Caesar*, with Hilton directing and Micheál playing Brutus, and a film of Joyce's *Ulysses*; the proceeds of the Irish rights for both would be donated to financing the new theatre in Dublin, which Hilton was still pursuing. Hilton became much excited, and started sending off telegrams to his bank in Dublin, while Micheál by turns studied the jealousy scenes and made notes for a booklet to be called *Irish Theatre*, which the Department of External Affairs had just commissioned. Then Hilton went down with what the doctor called 'une forte bronchite' which developed into 'une legère congestion' and then 'pneumonie' – all alarmingly reminiscent of Cóbh in 1927. At that point Orson announced that there was no more money, and production must cease forthwith; within two days the whole crew and cast had vanished, but Hilton was too ill to move. Then a message came from Orson in Paris, to say that the crisis would be resolved in ten days, when they should all reconvene in Venice. The period specified in MacLíammóir's contract had long ago expired, only a quarter of the film was in the can, and the Desdemona had not even been cast.

They reconvened, as requested, at the Hotel Europa, but Orson was nowhere to be seen, until a week later Micheál met him 'wandering like a thunder-cloud in indigo overalls among the streets behind the Frezzaria'. Suzanne Cloutier, the Desdemona whom Orson had just engaged in Paris, joined the company. Two weeks later work started again in earnest, with crowd scenes on the Piazza San Marco, and the Brabantio scenes with Hilton in voluminous robes, and a grey beard. A month of this, and then the unit moved to the Scalera studio in Rome, where Hilton, thinking over the idea for *Julius Caesar*, began to have misgivings about film direction, and asked Orson why he thought he would be any good at it; and Welles replied it was precisely because he had *no* experience that he would be good at it. (Orson Welles, who had directed *Citizen Kane* without prior experience, was the prime example of the efficacy of this theory.) He then said Hilton could take over some of the direction of *Othello*; but another financial crisis intervened, and the partners found themselves on the plane for Dublin (*via* Paris as usual). Once back home in Harcourt Terrace, the whole escapade seemed never to have happened, except that everyone remarked upon how well they were looking.

Surprisingly, there was a small cheque as an interim payment awaiting them, but they needed £2,000 immediately to pay off debts on the previous season and help finance the next, and Hilton wrote to Orson requesting this figure. 'The intolerable part of the whole business,' he added, 'is that we are forced to appear tough with you, whereas we are only asking you to fulfil a portion of your undertaking so that we, in turn, may keep faith over here.' He also asked for a written proposal about *Julius Caesar* and *Ulysses*. Welles replied from Claridges in London on 5 October, confirming that Hilton Edwards would direct *Julius Caesar* 'for the same weekly compensation as received by Micheál MacLíammóir as an actor playing in my film of *Othello*'. The fact was, MacLíammóir had not received his 'weekly compensation'. *Ulysses* was not mentioned. On 16 October there was a telegram requesting MacLíammóir in Viterbo the following day, and Edwards three weeks later.

In Dublin, Edwards found that Maura Laverty had done some useful work in altering her novel, *Lift Up Your Gates*, for the stage. She proposed calling the play *Liffey Lane*; having read the draft, Hilton expressed what she took to be genuine concern as to whether he would ever work in the theatre again. In Viterbo, there was no sign of Orson Welles; but he was found at the location, an eleventh-century church in Tuscania, 'dragging his forbearance about him', MacLíammóir noted, 'like a cloak, as he emerged wild-eyed from a car in heavy garments suggesting an Eskimo chief.' Edwards was called from Dublin for a scene to be shot on 27 October but, when he arrived, found he was not needed. All the acrimony of letters on financial matters evaporated as he and Welles discussed *Julius Caesar* and a putative season at the Gaiety where Welles would play *Othello* and *The Emperor Jones*. On 27 October, Welles vanished again, and the company was summoned back to Rome. On 30 October the location was changed without warning to Venice, where work began at once with unprecedented intensity. Michael Scott appeared for a day from Milan, and further plans for theatres in Dublin were discussed in a small restaurant in the Spadaria, Hilton nursing another severe cold. Orson Welles then decided that the Venetian senate scenes would look better if filmed in Perugia, and disappeared to inspect several *palazzi* there, leaving the shoot in charge of others.

During his absence, Edwards, MacLíammóir and Suzanne Cloutier were given instructions to proceed to Marseille; on arrival, there was a message to say they should be in Bordeaux; so Mademoiselle Cloutier returned to Paris, and the partners stayed where they were, attended a recital by Cortot, saw Jouvet in *Dr Knock* (which MacLíammóir later adapted as *An Apple a Day*, in a rural Irish setting), an opera, and the film of *Bicycle Thieves*; and then they received a very kindly-worded message from Orson asking them to join him at St Paul de Vence: the bad news was that a film of *Julius Caesar* was to be made in Hollywood with Brando and Mason. It was now December, and Micheál MacLíammóir had been working since March on a film which should have been completed in June.

In St Paul de Vence, the partners found that their rooms facing the sea were changed for others at the back of the hotel; then they were moved to smaller rooms, and then to a shared room. They knew better than to enquire the reason. They spent whatever little money they had 'on impressive teas at the Negresco' in Nice. Messages from Welles in Paris suggested that the next location would be Mogador, but the partners were now immune to planning of any kind, and were not at all surprised when they were at length asked to proceed to Paris, where they were met by the film's scenic artist, Trauner (who appeared to have no first name, and also appeared to be in charge of Welles' business affairs). Trauner gave them money towards expenses, but no salary, and placed them in the Hotel Royal at Montparnasse. Orson turned up, full of financial woes, but soon he and Hilton were, according to Micheál, 'screaming at each other all day to their own great enjoyment. Their new topic, the fact that *Othello* was once more on financial rocks – how like recurring nightmare the situation has become – has spurred O. to grand new scheme for six weeks' tour of *Importance of Being Earnest* (slightly cut) and Marlowe's *Dr Faustus* (exceedingly cut) to be performed on the same night in – ' and a list of the chief cities of Europe followed. Welles already had the casting worked out: he would play Algy and Faustus, Suzanne Cloutier Cecily and Helen of Troy, Edwards Canon Chasuble and the Prologue, MacLíammóir Ernest and Mephistopheles. Instead of regarding this amazing piece of eyewash for what it was worth, Micheál rushed out and bought a copy of Wilde, in order to make the necessary textual changes. They went to the Folies again and were surprised to be asked for their autographs by a group of Bulgarian boxers: it emerged that the boxers had seen them in *Hamlet* in Sofia in 1939!

A few days later Micheál burned his back on a hot water pipe, and Welles suffered blood poisoning from an incision made by an enthusiastic Spanish lady who shook his hand so warmly that one of her exquisitely pointed nails entered the flesh. While they were receiving medical treatment, Hilton studied Maura Laverty's script and suggested that, if *Julius Caesar* were out of the question, Orson might direct *Liffey Lane* in Dublin, as a film. In this atmosphere of almost cosmic unreality, the trio parted on 18 December. 'Not *still* doing *Othello*?', Hilton and Micheál were asked at every Christmas party in Dublin, and the fact was they truly did not know whether they *were* still doing *Othello* or not.

LOBSTERS, TURKEYS, AND EARTHA KITT

After Christmas, Orson Welles wrote from the Hotel Lancaster, in the Rue de Berri: 'Dearest Hilton and Micheál: As 1949 prepares to die of old age I want to acknowledge that I've made it pretty awful for both of you. Come what may (and it probably will) you deserve to know how earnestly I'm going to balance the budget before next Christmas . . . ' Before next Christmas! – the exclamations in Harcourt Terrace may be imagined. 'We'll be starting in Mogador about the twelfth . . . '

A 'definite' call informed the partners that they must travel to Mogador (*via* Paris) on 20 January, Edwards in the rôle of voice coach for Suzanne Cloutier. MacLíammóir hastily recorded the sound-track for a Department of External Affairs film on Yeats, and they went on their way. Weather this time turned out to be the main difficulty, as the shots could not be matched with those taken during the summer, for Morocco was steeped in rain. When work resumed with the reappearance of the sun, Micheál admitted that acting, even in films, was better than not acting at all. This was quite a major admission, for in one of the scenes he was placed in an iron cage and hauled up the exterior wall of a tower on a cliff top – Iago's punishment, which in the theatre takes place after the audience has gone home. As it turned out, this scene became the breathtaking opening of the film, often quoted by cinema historians as one of the 'great' moments in movies. The clear black-and-white photography, too, which did not arouse special commendation when *Othello* was released, because technicolor was then all the rage, was acclaimed when the film was reissued in 1992. Micheál MacLíammóir's performance as Iago surprised theatregoers in Ireland who had made up their minds that he would mouth the words and indulge in pouts and *moues*: that he did not, and that his speaking of the lines came though with unusual sharpness and a real sense of every underlying *nuance*, was a tribute to Welles' direction as much as to his own intelligence.

Apart from the dubbing, MacLíammóir's scenes were finally completed on 1 March 1950. Nine months' salary was still due. All talk of stage productions of Wilde and Marlowe had been forgotten, though Welles was now considering a film of J. Sheridan LeFanu's Gothic novel *Carmilla* (which Edward Longford had dramatised in 1932), and a play which he was threatening to write himself on the Faust legend – as well as an amalgamation of Shakespeare's Henry plays as a single evening's entertainment.

A reminder about payment must have been sent from Harcourt Terrace early in April, for an undated letter from Welles, posted in Messina on the 20th of the month, was clearly written as a response to something very urgent and, to him, vastly irritating. This response is typed by Welles himself, and runs to nine pages. It starts, 'Dearest Gents:' and ends, 'I kiss your hands', after which there is a large pencilled O and three hearts. What happens between the greeting and the subscription can best be described as notes for a stream-of-consciousness work of fiction on the theme of how a very famous producer-director has been doing a huge favour to a barely-famous-at-all actor and his cohort. It is full of sub-clauses ('I'm sure I don't need to say that *seldom* is hardly the word; on the other hand, never, honestly *never*, is such a chance given to an artist (no matter what his theatre position) without the producer covering his investment . . . '), parentheses ('I'm raising a lot of secondary issues here, I know you're ahead of me, but I want to be sure I'm being clear even if boring'), and declamatory queries ('Are you cross with me already?'). The tone is High School Campus pique, and the content may be reduced to something like: Please don't bother me about money and I'll make it up to you on our next collaboration.

Instead of leaving the matter for Linnit & Dunfee to deal with – indeed, the agents seem to have been unprofessionally by-passed on almost every issue – Edwards wrote back in much the same vein: 'My very dear Orson', he calls him, ' . . . Now, if I have you aright, it reveals that Micheál's past year's work was done under a misapprehension and makes our present position a nightmare indeed.' The crux was this: 'Leaving aside your casting Micheál in an important part, a gesture which I assure you we appreciate thoroughly, leaving aside, too, our mutual feelings towards each other, and dealing on a purely business basis (after all we are all pros and ultimately do what we do not only for our health) I think you should remember this: Micheál has worked and waited and turned down three lengthy seasons at the various theatres here on your advice, and in the belief that the continuance of the film, after the finishing date originally suggested by you (July last)' – in fact it was June – 'and the loss of the further Dublin seasons etc., would be compensated by the fact that he was earning his salary all the time. Now . . . it looks as if Micheál is only to receive payment for the weeks during which he has been on actual location . . . '

Unlike Welles, Edwards is able to observe the situation with some sense of proportion, for he adds as a postscript, 'Oh God! for the gift of brevity, but the Fairy who dispenses that was not at my christening; strange, because all the other Fairies were there and have reversed the process by taking gifts from me ever since!'

A third potential Gaiety season had now been passed over, and this would have been one of the reasons why the partners agreed, within days of this frank exchange of views, to take part in Welles' latest theatre project, in Paris. Another reason may quite likely have been that they felt if they did so, the money owed on *Othello*, calculated by their agent as upwards of six thousand pounds, might be more readily forthcoming. Edwards received a contract from Paris, to play 'Mephisto' in *Time Runs* and 'L'Archeveque' in *The Unthinking Lobster*, two plays by Orson Welles, 'presenté par La Compagnie Les Pléïades (animateur Georges Beaume)', in English at the Théâtre Edouard VII. MacLíammóir suddenly discovered that he had an inescapable commitment to adjudicate at the Kerry Drama Festival in Killarney, and, much to the annoyance of the author of these two Paris *premières*, declared that he could not take part, as everyone in Killarney would be dreadfully disappointed – and there *was* the little matter of his having signed an agreement. 'So you honestly prefer sitting around looking at amateurs in Killarney to acting with Hilton and me in Paris in the Spring, do you?' Welles roared down the telephone. MacLíammóir demurely replied that if required, he would join the company at a later date for the tour, which Welles was now proposing to follow the Paris triumph – not believing that any such tour could possibly materialise.

Edwards was engaged to design the lighting as well as perform, a doubling of duties which came as second nature to him, but, as Helena Hughes found when she arrived at his invitation to rehearse the part of 'L'Archange', he was staging the plays as well, for Welles was so full of ideas and theories he rarely bothered to give any direction, and the actors were becoming alarmed.

Time Runs was described on the bilingual programme as 'an interpretation of the Faust legend'. *The Unthinking Lobster (La Langouste qui ne pense a rien)* was a modern morality, set in Hollywood. Duke Ellington was engaged to write incidental music, and Eartha Kitt, then a relatively unknown dancer with the Katherine Dunham troupe, played a chorus part, which was quickly enlarged to suit her talents. Hilton Edwards, a man rarely out of his depth in any theatrical situation, was treading water in this one. He was very thankful that Helena Hughes had agreed to join the cast, for here was a person he could trust, a professional among what turned out to be a company containing a surprising number of amateurs. When he met her at the airport, he said 'Please don't forget you represent the Gate. Don't let the side down!' She behaved in her naturally professional way, and found that as a result she was the only person to whom Welles was never rude. He called her a 'great trouper' when she stood in at fifteen minutes notice on the opening night in an extra part, which had remained vacant due to his own inefficiency.

Helena Hughes recalled that 'le tout Paris' was present at the opening. The productions were not a success. (The actor Patrick Bedford described *The Unthinking Lobster* as 'the greatest turkey of all time'.) MacLíammóir said that it had not occurred to Welles that the French simply have no time for anything in English. Welles asked him to investigate theatres in London, where the very obvious consensus was that the public *would* come out to see Welles on the strength of his Harry Lime in *The Third Man* – *if* the show was any good. Back in Paris at the Hotel Royal, the dreaded tour was being discussed by Edwards, Welles and his French associate Pierre Beteille. MacLíammóir learned to his horror that he was to play a rewritten version of Mephisto in a shortened *Time Runs*, to fill the first half of the evening; and, in the second, short scenes from Wilde and Shakespeare – after which Welles and Kitt would provide further divertissements of the kind the former believed suitable for 'the chief cities of Europe'. Edwards was to direct, but not play. MacLíammóir felt there was a mild kind of conspiracy against him; and the subject of the money owing on *Othello* was not raised.

While the tour scenes were being rehearsed, the possibility of returning to the Dublin routine was very much in the air, with Rodney Ackland's adaptation of the Hugh Walpole novel *The Old Ladies*, Maura Laverty's much-postponed *Liffey Lane*, *Richard II* in a setting inspired from mediaeval illuminated manuscripts, and *Death of a Salesman*, for Arthur Miller was hardly known on this side of the Atlantic. These more peaceful deliberations were broken by boisterous incursions from Welles, during one of which he announced quite seriously that as part of the touring evening he would be performing conjuring tricks. When asked in 1970 by Peter Bogdanovich, who was contemplating a book on Orson Welles, about the star's associations with the Dublin Gate Theatre, and in particular about his claim to have played *Richard III* and *The Importance of Being Earnest*, MacLíammóir replied by letter, concluding with a paragraph on *Time Runs*: 'The second half of the programme was a hotch-potch or variety show which included songs by Eartha, conjuring tricks by Orson himself, a scene from *Henry VI* when I, as Henry, was stabbed by Orson as Gloucester (later to become Richard III) wearing a sort of gym-frock with the largest hump that was ever known on land or sea. Undoubtedly it was this that made him think he played Richard III: he did, for ten minutes. Later in the same evening he dazzled German audiences with a brief *précis*, lasting for about a quarter of an hour, of the first act of *The Importance of Being Earnest*, with me as Algernon and Orson as John with several cracks from Lady Bracknell added to the rôle. Undoubtedly it was this that made him think we played *Earnest*; we did, for a quarter of an hour.'

'The only thing,' MacLíammóir continued, 'that has really saddened and maddened me . . . was and is his continual trumpeting of the fiction that Hilton and I ever believed him when, as a boy, he told us he was an experienced actor and had played with Cornell and others. Not for one single second did this touching invention convince us, but, as our poet Yeats once remarked, "we must be tender to all budding things". After all, he was only sixteen.' Welles perpetuated the same story to his biographers, and also emphasised MacLíammóir's predilection for swarthy soldiers and policemen, giving the impression that the pursuit of sexual encounters in the barracks and *gendarmeries* of Morocco were his sole preoccupation while working on the *Othello* film.

The *Time Runs* tour opened in Frankfurt during the first week of August, where large numbers of people in the audience bore with them copies of Goethe's *Faust*, assuming that they would be able to follow the text. There was a great deal of page-rustling, and then an ominous silence. Eartha Kitt's songs and Orson Welles' conjuring tricks were apparently the highlights of the evening. Eartha Kitt, of whom both Edwards and MacLíammóir had become instant devotees, found that, as soon as it became apparent that she was the star of the evening, Welles would stand in front of her on the stage, and so vast was his frame that she was completely hidden, and her voice seemed to be coming out of him. The large portions of the audience which did not carry texts of Goethe were identified as officers of the American Rhine Army and their families; it was they who entertained the cast after the performances. One of them took MacLíammóir on daytime trips to Wiesbaden and other nearby towns which were being reconstructed in replica of what had been there before the war. He wrote in his diary that evening: 'Maybe the psychoanalysts are right when they say that even in friendship there is some hidden sexual emotion: to me it seems that only great friendships, only great loves, can survive a passion that has found complete fulfilment.'

It was in Hamburg that MacLíammóir learned that a German translation of *The Mountains Look Different*, entitled *Feuer*, had been successfully produced at Innsbruck. *Ill Met by Moonlight* had already been given in Italian in Milan; and an adaptation of *Dancing Shadow* was broadcast by the BBC on 24 July with Cyril Cusack and Máire O'Neill, which he attempted to listen to in a German hotel, but, as is so often the case – especially when wellwishers are sitting eagerly round the wireless set – it could not be heard so far from London. It received very favourable reviews in the British and Irish press where there were still weekly columns devoted to serious discussion of radio drama – much more favourable reviews than the play had inspired in Dublin.

Hilton Edwards travelled ahead of the players to each city, in order to acquaint himself with the technical hazards of each new theatre – which seemed in his current mood of irritation to be insurmountable, but were always surmounted. In Munich, Welles said he was thinking of extending the tour to Italy, and was not impressed when both Edwards and MacLíammóir expressed an immediate wish to return to Dublin. As recorded by the latter, Welles' resulting monologue went as follows: 'What in God's holy Name has Dublin ever done for you in return for the work you've both done for it in the last – how long is it now? – twenty-four years? Twenty-four years, Goddammit, and in that time you've both made an international theatre, and you've given them everything from Aeschylus to Cocteau, and new experiments in production and décor and realism and surrealism and Shaw and Denis Johnston and – oh, I don't know, I just think you're *lacking*, that's all, working like that for nothing . . . A new theatre? *Have* they given you a new theatre? But if you *don't* get a new theatre pretty quick, my opinion, and it's everybody's opinion, you poor silly Pronk, is that you will be Utterly Crazy to stay in Ireland or go on working yourselves to death for that Very Tough little country of yours any longer.' These home truths solved absolutely nothing. Edwards left for Düsseldorf, and the Italian plans remained floating in the air.

Düsseldorf was followed by Berlin, where MacLíammóir, walking amid rubble-filled alleyways that once were handsome streets, was beset by melancholy thoughts of carefree visits in 1923 and '31. These were compounded by the gloomy matter-of-fact remarks of his dresser, whose father was a prisoner of the Russians. 'They took him away one day three years ago. We have heard nothing of him since then. Not one word. Perhaps he is dead. I hope he is dead. It is better in these times to be dead and have no more pains to bear.' He finished the play he had been writing for most of the past year and decided to call it *Home for Christmas*, partly because they would be home at the Gate for Christmas, Italian tour or no Italian tour; and started to learn Richard II, now agreed with Louis Elliman. Then Welles announced that he would not be adding Italy to the tour, but Brussels instead; so they could return to Dublin and in two weeks MacLíammóir would rejoin what was now known as *Der Dritte Mann Personlich*, for *The Third Man* was at the height of its popularity.

Hilton Edwards, who was not needed in Brussels, wrote to Welles from Dublin on 30 September, regretting that his first letter 'must be a moan. The Bank and the Income Tax people promised to hold off until the middle of July last when we undertook definitely to have £2,000. The bank has stopped all payments of course and a writ of attachment on our personal belongings is to be issued in fourteen days . . . ' Welles responded by sending £800, but, as

Edwards stressed in a letter dated 13 October, this did no more than 'stave off the more voracious of the wolves'. Welles then agreed to narrate, and make a token appearance, in a short film which Edwards hoped to direct, Orson's name to be used as a bait for backers; but this did nothing to stave off the wolves.

Louis Elliman generously agreed to provide financing for the film. *Return to Glenascaul* was based on a ghost story which a police sergeant had told MacLíammóir while he was at the Kerry Drama Festival. Edwards wrote the script, 'so that I could ruin nobody's work but my own'. He engaged the cameraman, Georg Fleischmann, who later told Brian McIlroy, the author of a book on the Irish cinema, that Hilton Edwards could never distinguish 'camera right and left' from 'stage right and left', and was always short of money – 'I had to buy the film and pay for the processing myself.' Shelah Richards and Helena Hughes were cast in the principal parts, and shooting took place, usually late at night, in an empty and very cold old house in Dundrum, made all the more eerie by Fleischmann's atmospheric lighting. By day Edwards was preparing the production of *Home for Christmas*, MacLíammóir's revue-style melodrama, set in Victorian times on a Grand Tour of Europe. When, in late November, MacLíammóir was suddenly called to Rome for pick-up shots in *Othello*, Edwards felt himself in duty bound to adjudicate at the amateur Drama Festival in Newry. He had originally accepted this engagement believing himself to be totally free; when shooting started for *Return to Glenascaul*, he suggested to the Newry committee that MacLíammóir would replace him, and this was readily agreed to; when MacLíammóir had to go to Rome, he felt he could not let the committee down – so he drove the 140-mile round trip each evening for a week, saw the play, gave his public adjudication from the stage of the Town Hall, and returned to the 'haunted house' in Dundrum to continue filming. He could easily have found a deputy for Newry, but the £5 fee per night was too valuable to turn down.

Had *Return to Glenascaul* been conceived twenty years later, it would have commanded a commission from any of a number of television companies, but in 1950 the commercial cinema was still the only possible outlet for 'shorts'. It was distributed by Associated British Cinemas, where it supported Delbert Mann's *Marty* on the circuit. It is sometimes screened as 'a forgotten master-piece' at arty film and television festivals.

The press gave no inkling of the desperate financial straits of the partners and their company when *Home for Christmas* was reviewed at the Gate, and the spring season announced for the Gaiety. The Meath Chronicle proudly noted that young Patrick Murray from Kells had composed the musical numbers for Micheál MacLíammóir's new comedy, and the Sligo Champion was happy to provide the information that Noëlle Middleton from Collooney would now be playing regularly with the company; Coralie Carmichael was welcomed back from her long stay in Belfast with the Savoy Players. The critic of The Stage

(London) wrote that *Home for Christmas* was MacLíammóir's 'best play to date' – an opinion which surprised the author as much as the cast, but it was certainly one of his most successful at the box-office, running until *The Old Ladies* with Coralie Carmichael, Marjorie Hawtrey and Dorothy Casey opened at the Gaiety in mid February. During the run of *The Old Ladies*, MacLíammóir saw a Sunday night performance at the Gaiety of *St Joan*, with the company from the Taibhdheardhc playing in Irish, in a translation by a young actress from Belfast called Siobhán McKenna, who also took the lead. (His old friend, Liam O Bríain, was Cauchon, Bishop of Beauvais.) There was a huge and enthusiastic crowd, and remarks in the papers the following day about a 'resurgence' of Gaelic drama (even though the play was far from new), but he was pleased that the work he had started in 1927 was continuing, even if by fits and starts, and he was so impressed by Miss McKenna – whom he had seen in less distinguished rôles at the Abbey – that he re-read the play for the Gate.

Richard II was now in rehearsal. The idea for settings, based on motifs in the Harleian manuscripts, had been given to a young designer, Micheál O'Herlihy, who achieved a glowing image of the Middle Ages in one of the most brilliant designs seen on the Gaiety stage within living memory. Noëlle Middleton as the Queen had difficulty with her entrances, for her head-dress, which resembled two draped dunce's hats, was so wide, and the Gothic doorways so narrow, she had to enter sideways, the left-hand horn of the hat proclaiming her arrival by about two feet. Niall Carroll, in the Independent, thought MacLíammóir's Richard an original interpretation – 'an artist of France completely out of place in the England of his time; a man of many doubtful qualities, but who faced the tragedy which his own failings brought upon him with more courage than self pity'.

Orson Welles, still working on *Othello*, did not come to Dublin to appear as Willy Loman in *Death of a Salesman*, as had been hoped, so Hilton Edwards played the part. Noëlle Middleton felt that 'his alleged "Jewishness" – the hooked nose and the mobile mouth, which was like rubber' helped the physicality of the performance. Seamus Kelly of the Irish Times wrote of his 'anguished clown's face'; 'when it comes to the death of the flabby, ageing, broken-down commercial traveller, he catches the dignity of classical high tragedy.' Here was the Gate company back again at the top of its form. It was also back again with its familiar trappings of controversy, for members of the Catholic Cinema and Theatre Patrons Association – of which no one seemed to have previously heard – distributed leaflets outside the theatre, quoting an American publication, which stated that the play was 'one of a type which are hot-beds of left-winged agitation'. There was a list of 'red' organisations in the United States, to one of which Arthur Miller was said to belong. Six members of the Garda Siochana were on duty in South King Street on the opening night, but their services were not needed.

The saga of *Othello* was far from over, even though the film was now being edited. In fact, its financial implications were such that it overshadowed Edwards' and MacLíammóir's very existence for the next two years; and the figure of Orson Welles would loom as large as ever in their professional and private lives exactly a decade later.

Chapter 11
Maura My Girl

Although all the plays did well in the Gate's spring season of 1951 at the Gaiety Theatre, the one which was most eagerly awaited – and which, in the event, was the greatest commercial success – was Maura Laverty's *Liffey Lane*.

Maura Laverty was born in County Kildare in 1907. After leaving her convent boarding-school, she found employment as a governess in Spain, became secretary to Prince Bibesco, and then wrote for El Debate in Madrid. She returned to Ireland before the 1939-45 war and married a staff journalist with the Irish Press. She ran the Housewife's Half Hour for many years on Radio Eireann, dealing as far as was possible at that time with what were later to be known as 'women's issues'. Her first novel, *Never No More*, came out in 1942. Her next, *Touched by the Thorn*, was banned under the Censorship of Publications Act, although published in Britain – but it won the Irish Women Writers' Award. Her next, *Alone We Embark*, was also banned. She was guest of honour at the Women Writers' Club on 4 May 1944, when Senator Donal O'Sullivan said he understood the book had been banned because it was deemed to be 'indecent in general tendency'. 'I am astonished,' he said, 'that any group of men could find that this book comes under that definition'. Dr Robert Collis, in a highly emotional speech, said, 'Mrs Laverty has been insulted, and there should be legal right to take the censors to law to prove it.' When *No More Than Human* came out in 1944, she had to apply to the Minister of Justice for permission to import two copies of the book from her London publisher, and had to show that they were intended 'for her own use'.

Lift Up Your Gates (1946), which had so impressed Hilton Edwards, was also banned shortly after publication. It was set in a laneway at the back of two grand Georgian terraces, where the abandoned stables and servants' quarters had become the homes of the very poor. (Thirty years later, the same mews buildings were being sold as *bijoux* residences.) The life of the lane – which can only be described as 'teeming' – is viewed through the eyes of one of its inhabitants, a little girl called Chrissie Doyle; her innocence and wonder is one of the most engaging elements in the book. Micheál MacLíammóir was on a visit to Paris when he heard it had been banned. He wrote to Maura Laverty, ' . . . It fills me with despair to think of us all in this country, as poor and bad as any other, with all the material for the artist, and with artists like you to use that material, a country slowly being transformed by a pack of ignoramuses into a dank, damp little nursery . . . '

When Hilton Edwards approached Maura Laverty about the possibility of making the novel into a play, he said she should forget about breaking it into conventional scenes, and simply allow the action to flow. He thought she might use a narrator, and suggested one of the minor characters, Billy Quinlan, a well-educated man who had come down in the world: he could be the outside observer of life in the lane. It was all rather Brechtian in concept, although the term was not then current, and Edwards, like most directors in the British Isles, had yet to see a Brecht play in performance.

Had *Liffey Lane* been produced by any other Dublin management at that time, it would undoubtedly have been given a series of solid, realistic settings, but Hilton Edwards felt the atmosphere of urban poverty could be achieved in more interesting and subtle ways than the easy provision of the externals of squalor – peeling wallpaper, tattered curtains, overflowing garbage cans, broken pavements. The presence of these externals would be witnessed in the faces of the deprived, in their stance and gesture, and in their clothes. The actors would operate in spaces defined by light, and the noises of the city – distant tram-cars, church bells, hooters at the docks, seagulls – would be discreetly pervasive. In discussing this with the designer, Tony Inglis, they came to the conclusion that there should be some kind of appropriately monumental form as a point of focus, and this eventually took shape as a larger-than-life neo-classical doorway with Ionic pillars, the archetypal centrepiece of thousands of Dublin's domestic façades. This feature could be lighted at times, as characters were seen to enter or exit from the tenement, but the main action would take place downstage where a bare deal table and four wooden chairs would stand for one of the interior rooms, or a lighted lamp-standard suggest the corner of an alley.

This kind of visual treatment was new to Dublin, where MacLíammóir's suggestive or 'expressionistic' settings had tended to make use of painted gauzes, angular flights of steps and rostra, or silhouettes against a lighted cyclorama. Here was something which, by comparison, could be said to be uncompromisingly drab. Some of the players were perplexed and wondered, when they were seen disappearing into a doorway upstage-centre, and five seconds later walked on from the wings into a pool of light containing nothing but a battered armchair and a radio, whether the audience would 'understand' that they were now in a room in the same house. They need not have worried, for the audience did not seem to notice anything strange, and Edwards said that was a good sign, as it meant the idea had been unobtrusively effective. Niall Carroll of the Independent asked if 'we are going to lose a great deal of the inherent charm of the theatre when with one fell swoop this theatrical wizard . . . has turned the stage into a mere cinema screen across which shadowy figures chase one another under ghostly lights in the rapidly-changing manner of the motion picture . . . The more conservative will throw up their hands in horror at Mr Edwards' action . . . Those who genuinely want to see a natural evolution of technique will tell Mr Edwards he went much too far and much too fast.' Neither of these agitating reactions occurred, for the method was supremely well suited to the play.

J.J. Finegan of the Evening Herald predicted the production would 'set the town talking'. He, too, noted its cinematic quality, but did not believe that the theatre should discountenance the cinema, for the cinema had taken so much from the theatre and there was a need for a lively trading of techniques. Edwards' use of a group of street-urchins collecting money for Hallowe'en, singing snatches of traditional street songs as they go, was seen by the more acutely scholastic as a modern-day Greek chorus, just as the pillars of the old doorcase gave a notion of the background for a classical drama. These elements had all been carefully contrived, and they all seemed to coalesce.

The chief character, Chrissie Doyle – whose determinedly innocent campaign to prevent her four-year-old brother from being placed in an orphanage (because their parents simply could not afford to feed the whole family) brings her up against all the insidious barriers of the adult world, social, civil and religious – was played by a youngster called Joan Lappin. She presented a character that was, as Seamus Kelly remarked in the Irish Times, 'ingenuous, moving, never overplayed, and never, thanks be to Thespis, showing a trace of that monstrous theatrical infliction, the Infant Prodigy.' He also admired another young actress, Laurie Morton, who played Nannie Buckley, Chrissie's opposite in every respect, a 'termagant of the tenements', already at the age of fourteen putting on the 'posh' accent which her deluded mother thought would get her somewhere. Micheál MacLíammóir, as Billy Quinlan, the narrator who enters the action every so often, played his first elderly character rôle in a modern play: it was this which astounded the public, as well as his friends in the profession. Seamus Kelly wrote that 'as the drunk fallen from near-episcopal respectability,' he gave 'a performance of impeccable sincerity, particularly in his lyrical roadside scene with the disenchanted child'.

IT SUITS YA, CHRISSIE!'

Liffey Lane introduced a number of jargon phrases into the theatrical lexicon of Dublin. A 'chrissie' became a word for a lower-class person with delusions of grandeur; and the phrase 'It suits ya, Chrissie!' (spoken by Nannie Buckley in the play) it still used to compliment someone wearing an item of clothing which patently does *not* suit them. Most of the critics compared Laverty with O'Casey; Seamus Kelly praised the 'genuine ring' of the dialogue, and made the very obvious point that 'Mrs Laverty is writing in an era when we have passed the high revolutionary phase, and have merely our poor to work on.' The same might have been said of Robert Collis's *Marrowbone Lane*.

The play had scarcely opened, and Maura Laverty had barely had time to consider the fact that her first work for the stage was a success, when Hilton Edwards asked her if she had any other ideas. She did, in fact, have something in the back of her mind about a city-centre family which had been moved by the Housing Department to a bleak new council estate. She even had a provisional title – *Dodder Terrace*, the Dodder being a river which flows through the south of the city. Edwards asked for a treatment, which she provided in a very short time. The company then went to Cork with *Home for Christmas*, *The Old Ladies* and *Liffey Lane*, returning in the second week of May to resume the triumphant run of *Liffey Lane* at the Gaiety. As Edwards and MacLíammóir had failed to make use of their allotted number of months at the Gate over the past year and a half, they were obliged to take part of Longford's summer period, so *Liffey Lane* subsequently transferred there, while they rehearsed a new play by L.A.G. Strong, which left not so much as a ripple on the surface of the theatrical stream and was quickly forgotten. Maura Laverty's second play, now entitled *Tolka Row*, after yet another Dublin river, was announced for the autumn of 1951 in the Gaiety, along with two other plays which, as it turned out, were never performed, for *Tolka Row* swept away everything else in its path.

Tolka Row is more conventionally structured than *Liffey Lane*. An old-clothes dealer calls at a council house in north Dublin and is given a worn-out jacket which belonged to Rita Nolan's father: 'That's the last of him now,' Rita says, the little incident reminding her of the final year of the life of Dan Dempsey, a retired bargee from County Kildare. The rest of the play is a flashback exposing tensions in the Nolan home, after the roguish old man comes to live with the family, and Rita's venomous and pietistic spinster sister-in-law, Statia, is deprived of her 'position' in the household. The play is a study of old age, and what the old view as ingratitude in the young.

Tolka Row was, in the five years following its first production in 1950, the Gate's 'great reliable', when financial difficulties became overpowering, as was frequent, or when other productions failed and a quick replacement had to be found. It gave Micheál MacLíammóir, as Dan Dempsey, one of his most famous parts – a part he was reluctant to take on, because it was entirely lacking in glamour of any kind; at the same time, the adulation heaped upon him as a 'character' actor for *Liffey Lane* was a compensation, now repeated. Those members of the audience who sat very near the front were aware of the heavy make-up which MacLíammóir used to age himself for the rôle; any of the cast who happened to enter his dressing-room noticed that he did not remove the toupée which covered his bald patch, but gummed a bald-wig over it. When Orson Welles came to see the play after it had been running for two months, he said, 'Michael, you're now appearing as you are. Don't ever go back on it, honey!'

Orson Welles' much-publicised visit to the Gate gave a further opportunity to the Catholic Cinema and Theatre Patrons' Association to place a picket, for its members had heard that Welles was 'a communist' and were even attempting to sell copies of a publication entitled *Red Stars over Hollywood* to prove it. A spokesman for the association said they were 'interested in keeping the cinema pure, and that Orson Welles had never repudiated many of the statements made in the Report of the California Legislature on Communist Front Organisations'. Maura Laverty, with her two student daughters Maeve and Barry, joined the party given by Hilton at the theatre. During the interval they had drinks in the office-dressing-room which overlooked the front entrance, where the demonstrators had gathered and where a second group was forming, anxious to catch a glimpse of the star of *The Third Man*.

There was an atmosphere of excited amusement backstage; Maura Laverty was exasperated that a very famous actor who had travelled from the continent to see her play should be treated with discourtesy by a section of the Dublin public, no matter how unrepresentative, and, glass in hand, she sang a few lines of *The Red Flag* through the window. This was taken as a serious token of defiance rather than as a joke, and when Welles gave a friendly wave there were boos. At the end of the performance, Welles was ushered on to the stage by Edwards. He said that the only scandal was that there should be any interference with the tribute to such a fine play. He recalled that it was twenty-one years since he had acted on that same stage, and that it was a moving experience to be there again. There was prolonged applause. Highly respectable members of the audience, annoyed in the same way as the author, shouted highly unrespectable epithets at the demonstrators as they left the theatre, adding to the confusion. Welles left by the fire-escape into the garden of the Rotunda Hospital, and Edwards told a reporter that 'so far from being a communist, Mr Welles has been trying to be a capitalist all his life!'

Orson Welles gave a different account to his biographer. Where the Dublin press reported 'about twenty youths and girls', Welles described 'a hundred'. He also said that the picketers hurled bottles at the police, who unsuccessfully tried to disperse them. In fact, a bottle was smashed in the roadway, but it is unlikely that it had anything to do with the picketers.

At the end of 1951, it was announced that Maura Laverty would be completing her trilogy on the 'Human Comedy of Dublin' the following year. The third play would be called *A Tree in the Crescent* and would deal with people who lived in a neighbourhood one further step up the socio-economic ladder. (The poet Donagh MacDonagh wrote to Denis Johnston giving his preferred wording of the announcement as 'From Monto to Mount Merrion, a sexology by Maura Lavatory'.) As Maura Laverty was badly off – her husband was an unresolved bankrupt when he died – she wrote to Hilton Edwards asking for an advance payment on her new play, mentioning in passing that she had two girls at college and a boy at school. Edwards wrote back to say that he could not possibly comply with her request. 'In spite of one of the best seasons we have ever had, because of the debt with which we opened the season – for which our non-payment during the Orson Welles film was solely responsible – we have only just enough money remaining to ensure our opening next season at all . . . The royalty you receive is about equivalent to the profit we make ourselves; and the cost of rehearsal money for cast, and the multitudinous expenses of production are so enormous as to make the theatre hardly worth while from the financial angle . . . I know how many family and other obligations you have, but remember, we, too, have a family of some 25 to 30 people . . . '

Mrs Laverty was too good-natured to point out that the sole reason for 'one of the best seasons we have ever had' was her playwrighting, and too innocent, at this stage, to comprehend the hypocrisy of Edwards' statement about the number of people he had to support, for she did not know that Edwards-MacLíammóir Productions did not have a permanent company, and that when a so-called Gate player or technician was not required, he or she went off the payroll. Neither Edwards nor MacLíammóir appeared in *A Tree in the Crescent*, believing, rightly, that there were no suitable parts for them. Denis Brennan and Peggy Marshall (who had played the middle-aged Nolans in *Tolka Row*) played the Farrell couple, covering, in a series of flashbacks, their lives from courtship in 1925 to approaching old age in 1952. Seamus Kelly wrote in the Irish Times that 'in crossing the Liffey from Cabra to Rathmines, Mrs Laverty endorses, more than ever, her already proven ability as a social commentatory of percipience, humour and compassion . . . ' R.M. Fox in the Evening Mail thought *A Tree in the Crescent* superior to her two earlier plays. 'It will add,' he ventured, 'to the repute of Irish drama'.

'DON'T QUARREL WITH HILTON!'

Maura Laverty's trilogy, and Donagh MacDonagh's verse comedy *God's Gentry*, which was the Gate's Christmas offering, certainly added to the Irish drama's repute in so far as they were substantial, well-constructed and highly performable works, but they were not of the calibre to create much attention abroad. Yet that was not R.M. Fox's point – he was indulging in Abbey-bashing, the critics' favourite sport at times when there was little else to write about. The same week Niall Carroll in the Irish Press asked, 'Is the centre of influence in the Irish Theatre gradually shifting from the Abbey to the Gate? – I would not call *Tolka Row* great drama, but it has many touches of genius . . . The pertinent question is why all such new and interesting plays about any phase of Irish life should not be collared immediately on being written for the National Theatre, which has lapsed into a sorry, anaemic position for want of nourishment. The Gate partners got this play and *Liffey Lane* because they were alive to their responsibilities . . . '

Tolka Row was in fact produced by a number of repertory companies in Britain and the United States. It was broadcast on BBC radio in 1957 and on BBC television two years later, with MacLíammóir as Dan Dempsey on both occasions; after the television recording he wrote from London to Maura

Laverty to thank her for 'one of the grandest parts I have played' – using the term 'grand' in the Irish sense of 'first-class'. As was the case with the partners' relationship with Orson Welles, they managed to work together in a generally amicable frame of mind, leaving the very real business problems to correspondence. Following visits of *Tolka Row* to Limerick and Belfast in 1954, Mrs Laverty had to write requesting the royalties which were due; Edwards replied that 'our complete season though most successful, has barely covered our increasing cost of production, and – in confidence – we are in real trouble and for the first time in our 24 years in existence we are not in a position to meet all our obligations, of which we acknowledge your royalty to be among the first . . . The humiliating facts are as I have stated.' A seven-week revival of *Liffey Lane* took place in the spring of 1955, but still there was no 'cheque in the post' and Mrs Laverty felt constrained to write, 'Dear Hilton, I know that you have been having difficulties, but I doubt if they compare with mine. If you want the play for the next seaosn, I must have the peace of mind which an immediate cheque would provide. *Please,* may I have it?'

Hilton did send an immediate cheque – for £25, 'as a token of our good intentions'. Maura gave the necessary permission for a further revival of *Tolka Row* at the Olympia Theatre for July 1955. 'It is a risk,' Edwards wrote, 'putting on the show at this time of year after so many revivals', but his stated reason of inviting representatives of London managements to see it seemed a good one, because 'reading the script has only inclined to fog them'. His letter of 1 July promised that the accumulated debt would be paid on the Tuesday after the opening. It was only £190, but in 1955 would have represented, for example, three months' salary for the average actor. When a cheque did not arrive on the date specified, Maura wrote in a much firmer strain, and this resulted, not in a further reply from Hilton, but from Micheál. – 'My dearest Maura – Don't quarrel with Hilton! Darling Maura, I ask this in a way very difficult to describe – there's no reason why you should like him or be nice to him – but just don't quarrel at this moment. He is a very tired and very ill man: twelve years of really hard slogging at something that didn't come off have taken everything away from him but an over-easy irascibility and a feeling of hurt – and at the moment not one thing is going right – not one! I think that if just one thing did, or if one person were to say a nice warm encouraging word to him it might save him from the cold emptiness of the hell he's making for himself – his own fault I dare say, but it makes it no easier for him. Please forgive this – I've no right to say it at all but our mutual affection, yours and mine, your warm friend, Micheál.'

The 'hard slogging at something that didn't come off' was an exaggeration in point of the number of years – Hilton had been trying to find a new theatre for ten rather than twelve, but his disappointment was enormous when, having seen the Queen's Theatre go to the Abbey, he then failed to find enough backing to enable him to lease and renovate the Forum in Pearse Street. The building was available, but by now Edwards-MacLíammóir Productions did not have any financial resources at all with which to secure a bank loan. The Laverty plays had kept them afloat for four years, and had indeed enabled them to present several other fine productions; but Dublin, indeed the whole of Ireland, had by now been saturated with revivals, and Maura Laverty did not appear to have any new plays in mind. The partners' fortunes were now at their lowest.

GRAND PRIX

The awarding of the Grand Prix de Cannes to Orson Welles' film of *Othello* on 11 May 1952. and the appearance of Micheál MacLíammóir's face in close-up on the cover of Movie News, seemed nothing more than an insulting irony to The Boys, for it was generally supposed that they had reaped considerable financial emoluments from the engagement, MacLíammóir was by now writing *Put Money in Thy Purse* for Methuen, another of whose authors, the Dublin lawyer Terence de Vere White, was introduced to him over lunch in Dublin by Methuen's representative, Fordie Forrester. When the conversation turned to the subject of *Put Money in Thy Purse*, it naturally emerged that the lighter side of the *Othello* saga would be chronicled, and the monetary suppressed. De Vere White offered to see what he could do through legal channels to secure the sums owed by Welles, and in so doing, without realising it, he immediately became the financial and legal adviser to the partners, who from that date called upon him in moments of crisis – and very often in moments of crisis which had nothing to do with money or the law. It was through his unceasing efforts that Edwards-MacLíammóir Productions eventually achieved state recognition and an annual subvention from the Arts Council.

As far as the general public was concerned, the period later to be sentimentally known as the Laverty Years was resplendent with a number of equally brilliant productions of works by other authors, living and dead, Irish and foreign – Donagh MacDonagh, Liam O'Flaherty, Bernard Shaw, Arthur Koestler, Jean Anouilh, Marcel Maurette, Jules Romains, Luigi Pirandello and, of course, William Shakespeare. The cancellation of some projected plays due to the long Laverty runs – Maura Laverty still over-generously countenancing late payment of royalties in every case – allowed the partners to take single engagements elsewhere, though they had a way of saying that they were 'forced' to accept these because they could not afford to keep presenting handsome productions in a theatre where, even with full houses, expenses could not be covered. The first of these 'away' engagements for Edwards was a return to the scene of his early appearances in twenty plays of Shakespeare, the Old Vic, and to work with one of his oldest comrades, Donald Wolfit.

Chapter 12
The Old Vic, Elsinore,
and Croke Park

During the early 1950s, the Old Vic was running two companies under the artistic surveillance of Tyrone Guthrie, with Hugh Hunt as Administrative Director. 'Company A' was headed by Donald Wolfit, who had just enjoyed a huge success as Tamberlaine and now wanted to out-do Olivier's much lauded tragic-comic combination of Oedipus and Mr Puff, by balancing a showy comedy rôle against Tamberlaine. He decided upon Lord Ogleby, the ageing *roué* in Colman and Garrick's *The Clandestine Marriage*, but objected to the names of a series of directors put forward by Guthrie and Hunt. The latter eventually suggested Edwards, believing that anyone who could cope with MacLíammóir could cope with Wolfit – later to be known as the 'unruly knight'. During the period of rehearsals, he was engaged in a bitter dispute with the management, which he felt was in breach of contract over a number of issues, and in fact he and his wife, Rosalind Iden, gave notice of their resignation before *The Clandestine Marriage* opened, thus causing the cancellation of a planned continental tour, which Hilton Edwards would have welcomed.

The Clandestine Marriage, nevertheless, opened with Wolfit at Stratford-upon-Avon on 5 November 1951, reaching London on 5 December. Edwards had to work his rehearsals round *Tamberlaine*, a massive pageant-like production which was tiring to both actors and technicians. He and Wolfit got on famously together, constantly recalling the 'old days' with Doran on three-month long Shakespearian tours. No sense of a company exhausted by overwork or internal squabbles was apparent at the London première, the 'smoothness' of which was remarked upon by both the Morning Advertiser and The New Statesman. Kenneth Tynan in The Spectator thought that the company offered 'their best all-round display of the season . . . Mr Edwards moves as racily as if on roller skates.' All Hilton Edwards' reviews were either good or excellent, and it would have been reasonable to suppose that he should have been invited back to the Old Vic; but, as with McMaster at Stratford in 1933, there was a change of management personnel, and new brooms inevitably swept in, accompanied by vessels of their own choosing. In any case, Dublin was waiting for *God's Gentry*, Donagh MacDonagh's romantic satire on the Tinkers' Republic, and there were intimations of the Gate being honoured by the Danish government with a production of *Hamlet* at Elsinore.

Donagh MacDonagh was the son of the executed leader of the 1916 Rising, Thomas MacDonagh. He was a considerable lyric poet, and a witty, indeed rollicking, raconteur and broadcaster. He made much of the fact that his first verse comedy, *Happy as Larry*, had been rejected by the Abbey Theatre and was subsequently produced at the Mercury in London, under the direction of Denis Carey, where it ran for three months. *God's Gentry* was another Abbey rejection, initially taken up by the Belfast Arts Theatre, where it came to the notice of Edwards and MacLíammóir, and of Denis Johnston, who directed it in a community theatre at South Hadley, Massachusetts. On 22 November 1951, Mac-Donagh wrote to Johnston, 'Hilton is working overtime on his production which opens here on December 26th with grand settings by Micheál . . . Balor is really any politician . . . ' – this was a reference to Balor of the Evil Eye, one of the ancient demi-gods, who is summoned from the past and delivers what amounts to a superlative parody of a modern politician's platitudinous and vacuous speech. Edwards, in a letter to Johnston shortly after the opening, said that he had not cast himself as Balor, 'as I think that the part requires two things that I lack, slightness of stature and a very definite Irish voice: however Godlike we English are to them now, I feel that the ancient gods should at least be Irish.' (The part was played by Robert Hennessy, raised to the height of ten feet with stilts up his trouser-legs, and a make-up giving a very distinct impression of Eamon de Valéra.) Edwards continued: 'Micheál is too old for the part of Mongan [the jaunty tinker lad] which he didn't particularly want to play . . . Frankly I am very glad to have him, and in spite of the play's success with both yourself and us, and in spite of all my admiration for one or two exquisite lines and a couple of delightful lyrics, I think there is some very poor stuff in it after the lovely first act, and no sense of character whatsoever. Please treat these remarks as confidential, as I have learnt how dangerous it is to be on the receiving end of criticism, and I don't want to cry Stinking Fish when we are doing so well with the show.'

Hilton Edwards' gratuitous comments are somewhat off the mark, for *God's Gentry* is packed with allusive language and possesses a bursting theatricality; it could not otherwise have passed muster with critics and public in the way it did. MacDonagh wrote to Johnston after the opening: 'As you will read in the reviews, Micheál had old tin cans, cartwheels, dirty linen, old socks and all the rubbish of a tinkers' camp . . . covering the proscenium arch. Pretty drab it looked until the curtain went up on the wonderful set, and then it all fell into proportion.' The set was 'Rouault and Jack B. Yeats blue, with the Reek dominating both scenes from the background.' MacLíammóir's idealised tinker costumes in bright purples, magentas and reds created an extravagance and richness entirely in keeping with the text. The poet, John Montague, writing in The Bell, took a somewhat jaundiced view of the play, which left him with 'the uneasy feeling of having seen it all before, and at first hand, in the plays of Synge and the stories of O'Flaherty and O Conaire'; he also saw it as 'a falsification, a colourful artistic lie that has lost its kick, and is fast becoming period, like the early romantic pictures of Jack B. Yeats'. In fairness to MacDonagh and the Gate, he might have added that there was a deliberate element of exaggeration, almost to the point of parody, in both writing and staging. 'But how much better,' Montague continued, 'than the Abbey Pantomime, and, indeed, than the majority of plays shown in Dublin this year!'

SOMETHING ROTTEN

An official invitation from John Brunnick, the director of the Elsinore Festival, followed hard upon a number of exploratory letters and telephone calls, requesting the honour of the presence of the Dublin Gate Theatre Company in a production of *Hamlet* in the courtyard of the Castle of Kronborg, for two weeks in June 1952. Eleven foreign Hamlets had been seen there; the last English-speaking one had been Olivier's in 1937. The Festival would pay for rehearsals and performances in Denmark from the 6th until the 24th and the Danish Tourist Board would sponsor thirty first-class berths on the Harwich-Esbjerg ferry, but the company would have to find the cost of travel from its own resources. As the company did not have any resources at all, an application was made to the Cultural Relations Committee of the Department of External Affairs for a travel grant, and the Minister for Foreign Affairs, Mr Frank Aiken, was invited to become Patron of the enterprise. His letter of acceptance suggested to Edwards and MacLíammóir that his department would respond favourably to the request for funds. On 1 February Messrs Thomas Cook were asked to quote for the return trip.

The Cultural Relations Committee decided at its February meeting *not* to recommend the department to provide a grant. Seamus Kelly, the Irish Times theatre critic, in his guise as the daily columnist 'Quidnunc', published the story, and immediately there were letters of protest at the 'miserly' and 'lamentably short-sighted' attitude of the government. A lady in Blackrock wrote to say that she would contribute £2 to a fund to help Ireland to be represented, as other countries had been represented, at this prestigious event. The department must have been surprised at the extent of the outcry, for it relented, but not until there had been an embarrassing report in the Danish press. Members of the company were astonished to be welcomed by the festival director and his assistant before they had even set foot on Danish soil, for they were met at Harwich, where flowers were presented to the ladies, and a banquet which included generous quantities of *schnapps* was given on board the ferry. The highly formal hospitality shown throughout the visit was in marked contrast to the jolly parties in the Balkans, and the society teas with pretzels and cookies in sumptuous suburban homes in Canada and the United States. When they arrived at Kronborg – which is situated by a pleasant sandy beach quite unlike the beetling cliffs imagined by Shakespeare – Michael O'Herlihy had already erected the platform stage, which was dominated by two huge portraits of Hamlet's father and Claudius: 'look here upon this picture, and on this'. There was consternation when the cast learned that the Danish custom was for critics to attend the dress rehearsal – all the more alarming when the play was to be given in daylight. Rain poured down daily so that no rehearsal was ever completed, and the critics were sent back to Copenhagen on 11 June without so much as hearing the opening lines. They reappeared the following evening, the official opening having been postponed. MacLíammóir wrote that they were 'clearly visible in spite of drizzle'; they sat 'in a wedge-shaped phalanx and seemed, by the majority of their facial expressions, pleased'.

There were showers every evening, on two occasions starting on cue at the line 'this brave o'erhanging firmament'. During the worst gusts of wind, Hamlet was seen holding on to his *toupée* with one hand, while prodding Laertes with a rapier held in the other. There were nine Danish reviews, five of them very favourable, the remainder ranging from non-committal to bad – nothing unusual in that, it was just like being at home. One, on the subject of accents, described Hilton Edwards as sounding like 'an Irish bull', upon which he commented during yet another *smorresbrot* and *schnapps* party, that if he'd been described as a Hereford bull he wouldn't have been nearly so flattered. All the Swedish reviews turned out to be favourable. There were banquets and speeches every day; the Mayor presented MacLíammóir with a medal inscribed 'Spetacula in Cronburga Helsingore'. Eithne Dunne was given a special award for Ophelia, the only Ophelia – a dignitary called Knud Klem announced – ever to have been so honoured. 'She is,' he continued, to suppressed explosions of laughter from the company at a farewell dinner, 'the maddest Ophelia I have ever seen!' Sensing the atmosphere, he neatly added, 'you are mad in a sympathetic and charming way!' Her madness, in fact, was wonderfully composed. She did not wear the traditional rags, but a black velvet dress with a diamond cross, as mourning for her dead father.

Denis Brennan, who played Horatio, was sent the Irish press cuttings by his wife, Daphne, in Dublin. These were passed round the company, who thought it 'typical' that the Dublin papers should reprint only the unfavourable reviews, which were greatly outnumbered by the favourable. 'Danish critics slate Irish "Hamlet"', the Sunday Independent proclaimed. 'Danes call Hamlet "Irish Stew"' announced the Sunday Press. The Danish authorities were greatly upset – so much so, that when the company returned to Dublin on 26 June they found that a letter from John Brunnick had been printed in some of the Irish papers, in which he said he wished to contradict so false an impression, and quoted from the excellent reviews which had been ignored; but the damage had been done, for denials always draw attention to the negative aspects of the case. Gerard

Healy, who played Rosencrantz and directed a short cinema film about the visit, remarked that there was 'something rotten' in the state of Ireland, for this was not the first time an Irish company abroad had been misrepresented at home.

*

Terence de Vere White was now devoting much of his time to helping the partners retrieve the money owed to them by Orson Welles. He sent a series of telegrams, which greatly irritated Welles, and he drafted letters for the signature of the company's new manager, John Bools. On 23 June 1953, Welles retorted to one of these, 'I must take the gravest exception to your statement that "our present position has its roots in the absence from the Gate, for such a long period, of Mr MacLíammóir, in your Othello film" . . . ' On 5 May 1954, de Vere White wrote a letter in his capacity as legal advisor, addressed to MacLíammóir, specifically for him to pass on in desperation to Welles: 'Dear Sir, We are sorry to tell you that having examined the affairs of your Company, we can offer no other advice but that you should go into liquidation. This is very serious because it will injure your credit in Dublin. We notice that you are personally owed £6,000 by Mr Orson Welles, which he acknowledges in a letter which appears in the file. If you are prepared to bring this amount into the Company, it will of course make the Company solvent . . . We are now taking the necessary proceedings against Mr Welles . . . '

Orson Welles responded by writing to his distributors, United Artists: 'This is an irrevocable authority to you to pay from the first receipts of my picture *Othello* in the United Kingdom, the sum of £6,000 to Messrs Hilton Edwards and Micheál MacLíammóir . . . ' Sums gradually arrived, in small moieties, which were quickly submerged in the maelstrom of the Gate account books.

De Vere White also prepared a series of memoranda to the Arts Council. He drafted a submission to the Council for its March 1953 meeting, which was signed by both Edwards and MacLíammóir, in which the company's financial position for the years from 1947 was carefully tabulated. In this he was only doing what the theatre's managers over the years ought to have done; the trouble was that Edwards and MacLíammóir's managers were recruited from the stage-management and acting sector, and had very little understanding of book-keeping, let alone accounting. De Vere White's explanatory paragraphs attached to the figures potently demonstrate the difficulties posed for any professional company attempting to mount productions of high standard entirely from the box-office takings.

'The 1952 season was disastrous,' he added, 'but certainly not through lack of success. Indeed, it included for *God's Gentry* £5,692 gross takings, and £9,404 for *Tolka Row* [a revival], but the tour to Elsinore in spite of a subsidy from the Cultural Relations Committee resulted in a loss pf £297. An effort to bring the company to Limerick and Ennis resulted in a heavy loss in spite of good houses . . . ' The submission goes on to mention that 'the directors have mortgaged their house to the extent of £1,600.' A cumulative deficit of over £4,000 was declared, and the Council was asked to consider making a contribution of £2,000, 'to enable us to carry on.'

The Secretary of the Arts Council, Dr Liam O'Sullivan, replied on 24 March, agreeing, for the first time in the Gate's history, to a grant of £2,000 'to offset losses', with a promise of a further £1,000, to be made available during the financial year of 1953-54, conditional upon the provision of certified accounts. There was a further paragraph: 'It is a generally understood condition in grants of this kind that plays by Irish dramatists should, as far as reasonably possible, be performed by your company.'

The actual promise of state money caused the wildest astonishment and delight at Harcourt Terrace; what the partners probably never did understand was that they might have received similar grants in the past if their requests had been less haphazard, and had been backed up with precise figures. The clause about Irish dramatists gave reason for much pondering, for the Gate had been founded principally to present foreign work, and it now looked as if the state was asking them to duplicate the policy of the Abbey Theatre.

For the moment the financial pressure was somewhat alleviated, though by no means removed. Terence de Vere White probably did not have a hand in the four-page letter which Hilton Edwards wrote to the Arts Council in August 1954 seeking the further £1,000, for it rambles considerably. The result, however, was the figure promised – but the rider about the repertoire was stronger this time: 'Plays by Irish dramatists should form a larger part of the company's productions than heretofore.' What 'plays by Irish dramatists' had they done? – and on looking at the progamme they realised that in spite of the Arts Council's admonition the previous year they had done fewer than usual – in fact none, if *St Joan* and *The Countess Cathleen* were discounted on the grounds that Shaw and Yeats were dead.

HOW LONG, O LORD, HOW LONG?

The idea of producing *St Joan* was formed when MacLíammóir saw Siobhán McKenna play the part in Irish. Siobhán McKenna was first invited to appear with the company as Anna Christie, and, proving herself in such a very different rôle, Edwards was convinced that she would be able to carry one of the longest and most arduous women's parts in the modern theatre – for he was not convinced that the reception which she had received when playing in Irish with a semi-amateur company, to an audience of language-enthusiasts, necessarily qualified her for the manner in which he would require her to perform it. She had played it in Connacht Irish and suggested that she should use a Connacht accent, now that they were performing in English. Edwards thought this, like Jimmy O'Dea's Dublin Bottom, would be entirely plausible to the Irish public. (The public in other countries found it plausible too, as it turned out.) Edwards also wanted to experiment further with a production in a setting which did not suggest any place or time – simply a kind of grey limbo, to which the sense of period would be conveyed entirely by the costumes. He would play the Archbishop, MacLíammóir the Earl of Warwick, Denis Brennan Dunois, and Jack McGowran the Dauphin.

St Joan opened at the Gate on 18 November 1953 and ran for three months with a break at Christmas – the longest single run in the company's history. It could have continued, were it not for Siobhán McKenna having to fulfil a prior engagement in March. She rejoined the company in May for a tour to Limerick, Cork, and then Belfast – a triumphant return to the city of her birth. Her Joan was an absolutely innocent and unpretentious peasant – there was none of the other-worldliness which many Joans suggest in the earlier scenes. At her trial she was still a country girl, believing implicitly that the voices she heard came from God, and that she was bound to obey them. Leslie Scott, who had come from the Abbey Theatre and was now assisting Edwards on the lighting, asked her to wash her face free of all make-up for the later scenes, so that she looked literally washed out. The epilogue was retained after much argument – there was a view that it was merely tacked on to make a topical point shortly after Jeanne d'Arc's canonisation; it also added to an already lengthy evening; but those in favour won, and audiences may well have been grateful, for Siobhán McKenna's speaking of the final lines – 'Oh God that madest this beautiful earth, when will it be ready to receive Thy saints? How long, O Lord, how long?' remained in many memories; and critics who were wont to declare that Shaw had no feelings or emotions were obliged to think again.

The short Christmas break, which was a condition of Siobhán McKenna's contract, caused a disruption in the company which was to have repercussions involving the trade union, Equity, and which led to a greater awareness of the power of the union in future years. On the Friday before the break, the actors found that their pay-packets did not contain the usual weekly sum. No one expected a Christmas bonus, but they did expect that their salaries would be paid during the few nights' rest. Denis Brennan, who was on contract for the season at £12 per week, and had a young family to think about, was shocked when he opened the envelope to discover that it contained three pound notes. He immediately wrote to the manager: 'Dear Sir, As the result of the insult offered to me by your company in the form of £3 by way of salary this day, and as a protest against such *mean* behaviour, I wish to terminate my employment with your company as from Friday 1st January 1954.' This was an extraordinarily brave step to take, for Brennan had little prospect of finding alternative work. He continued, 'I feel that I, as an old and trusted member of the company, should receive better treatment . . . If this company cannot afford such a human gesture as to pay one full salary in Xmas week, then it should cease to operate. In fact, it has ceased to operate as far as I am concerned.'

Instead of allowing the manager to deal with the issue, Hilton Edwards entered into correspondence with Equity, giving it as his understanding that

Christmas and Easter were considered under a *force majeure* clause, and that payments were not in order when theatres were closed at those times. The General Secretary, Dermot Doolan, replied to disabuse him of this notion, and also wrote to Brennan to say that, as a contract player, he should have given two weeks' notice instead of one. Edwards also wrote for legal guidance from Terence de Vere White, who advised that indeed the *force majeure* should apply. The absence of clarity in the Equity contract was called into question, and Equity in due course amended the wording. Brennan was quite determined to leave, having made the point that his protest was about the impersonal nature of the management's action, just as much as about his loss of earnings; but Siobhán McKenna implored him to reconsider, for he was giving the most stable performance in the production, and she depended upon him for the full effect of the scene on the bank of the Loire. So Brennan stayed; but after the tour he only once played with the company again, and the loss was theirs. From this date there existed an uneasy relationship between Edwards-MacLíammóir Productions and the actors' union – of which both Edwards and MacLíammóir were members – and, unfortunately, with their own actors.

*

Following the establishment of the Dublin International Theatre Festival in 1957, it became the practice for the festival to send a production which had attracted special interest on a tour of European theatres, usually in association with Brendan Smith Productions of Dublin and the Jan de Blieck management in Amsterdam. Brendan Smith, the festival's director, found that Siobhán McKenna's name was often mentioned at meetings in continental cities. The Irish ambassador in Paris, Mr William Fay, told the festival's chairman, Lord Killanin, that he would like to see the Gate Theatre represented at one of the annual Paris festivals, so it was natural that an attempt should be made to combine two objectives by arranging a Gate tour to Paris and other cities in a play with Siobhán McKenna. *St Joan* was the obvious choice, and Smith set about co-ordinating the various elements. He wrote to Edwards on the last day of 1958, confirming the result of a meeting in Paris: 'I recommended that this should be a Dublin Gate Theatre production with your good self directing and Micheál responsible for design – and both of you playing too, of course. It was on this basis that I approached Siobhán and obtained her agreement on what I consider to be favourable terms . . . ' The proposal was for the new production to open at the Gaiety Theatre, as part of the Dublin festival in May 1959 and then proceed to Paris and elsewhere; though nominally a Gate production, the financing would come from the festival, and European sources. He continued, 'I have had the project of *St Joan* with Siobhán McKenna in the title rôle endorsed by the Department of External Affairs, supplemented by a helpful guarantee . . . ;' this was to make it clear to Edwards that a production would take place whether the Gate co-operated or not.

Edwards and MacLíammóir felt that Smith was being high-handed in making arrangements for them without detailed consultation, and when MacLíammóir said that he wished to play the Dauphin this time, as Jack McGowran was not available, and McKenna intimated to Smith that she would be uncomfortable with MacLíammóir in that part, it became obvious that the Gate was merely the vehicle for the star. A heated correspondence ensued. McKenna stated *via* Smith that Joan's relationship with the Dauphin should have a tinge of the maternal, and she did not see how she could achieve this with MacLíammóir in the part. In other words, she wanted a younger actor, though she did not name one. (Smith suggested Donal Donnelly.) Smith also knew that the terms offered, £100 per week to both Edwards and MacLíammóir, were of an order which they would be unlikely to turn down in their present circumstances. MacLíammóir then sent a memorandum to Smith which stated: '1. Siobhán McKenna is a first rate actress but not Ireland's only product. 2. Eithne Dunne is also a first rate actress and has scored a great success in Ireland and abroad with extremely moving performance of "St Joan" in Anouilh's "The Lark" . . . . 3. Siobhán McKenna should not be allowed to dictate casting and thus undermine the confidence and trust in her directors . . . '

Brendan Smith must have outlined the reality of the case – that Paris wished for Siobhán McKenna – to MacLíammóir, for on 6 January 1959 he signed a declaration, 'Re: Saint Joan – Paris Festival and Tour: In order that the Company should not lose the distinction of playing in Paris and other European cities, I, under great protest and entirely against my artistic conscience, relinquish my ambition to play the Dauphin and instead will play the Earl of Warwick as this seems to be one of the conditions which would make it possible for Siobhán McKenna to appear.' When it came to the first reading in the dress-circle bar of the Gaiety Theatre at the end of April, there was no Dauphin present; it was rumoured among the cast that Miss McKenna had approached Richard Harris and that he was due to arrive at any minute, but he did not. Edwards announced, 'My partner will *read* the part of the Dauphin for the time being!' – which the partner instantly did. When no actor suitable to Siobhán McKenna seemed to be available at this late stage, she relented, probably on the principle that it was preferable to have an experienced player opposite her than someone cast from the rank and file of Equity; she was soon to regret her decision. Godfrey Quigley then took over the part of the Earl of Warwick.

MacLíammóir, who was designing settings for a projected *Tristan und Isolde* at Covent Garden, wrote to Christopher West of the opera company on 28 April, 'Now we plunge into *St Joan*, God help us, and take it to Paris with La McKenna. Oh dear. I am playing the Dauphin, and as it is to be at the Sarah Bernhardt, I've decided to do it in the tradition of that promising young actress, with a hat right over the eyes and a collar nearly meeting it, so that as few centuries as possible may be visible. To this pretty effect, a false nose *à la* Valois is added . . . ' He also added a voluminous nightcap for the epilogue, in the shape of a turban, and comprised of many strands of cloth, which he said research had shown to be *de rigueur* as bedchamber attire in the early 15th century. When Edwards first noticed this eyecatching millinery at the dress-rehearsal, he bellowed, 'For Chrissake, Micheál, you look like bloody Scheherezade!', to which a voice from the depths of the four-poster replied, 'I can assure you, Hilton, it's absolutely authentic.'

The BBC producer, Jeremy Swan, who at the time was a pupil of the Brendan Smith Academy of Acting, appeared as a page in *St Joan*. He recalled that in Paris, MacLíammóir hoped to have 'the divine Sarah's' dressing-room but supposed it would be allocated to Miss McKenna; on arrival at the theatre it was found to have been turned into a museum, which saved an unseemly tussle. He said that MacLíammóir's playing with a cup-and-ball – introduced to suggest the unfortunate Dauphin's juvenile traits – became obsessive. One night, during a poignant and well-delivered speech, Siobhán McKenna was conscious of a slight ripple of laughter but was unable, in the tension of the moment, to look upstage to discover the reason; afterwards she learned that the Dauphin had introduced further distracting variations with the cup-and-ball. The following night, sensing similar upstaging, she turned abruptly and drew her sword on him. The Paris audience, absolutely *au fait* with what was going on, and not quite sure that they agreed with the critic who thought M. Edwards' idea of having their Dauphin portrayed as an 'homosexuel ravissant' was altogether *comme-il-faut*, signified their approval with with prolonged laughter.

The tour continued to Utrecht, The Hague, Amsterdam, Florence and Zurich. Micheál MacLíammóir's upstaging nothwithstanding, he and Siobhán McKenna conversed affably in Irish in all public places. Queen Juliana attended a performance in The Hague and was introduced to the cast backstage during the interval; when taking their individual curtain calls, Reginald Jarman bowed to the wrong box. In Amsterdam, MacLíammóir took the opportunity of calling on Frans Boerlage, who was to produce *Aroldo* at the 1957 Wexford Festival, for which he had been commissioned to design the sets and costumes. In Florence, when crying 'I command the army!', Reginald Jarman's false teeth flew out on to the stage. In Zurich, a locally recruited monk, overcome by the excitement of being on stage, screamed hysterically and had to be carried off. The company disbanded in Switzerland, Edwards and MacLíammóir travelling south to Rome for a reunion with Orson Welles, their difficulties with him resolved for the moment, and curiously eager to learn what new antics he might wish to share with them.

AR AIS GO DTI AN dTAIBHDHEARDHC

Siobhán McKenna's appearance in the Irish-language version of *St Joan* at the Taibhdheardhc may have awakened a nostalgia for the early days of that theatre, for Micheál MacLíammóir accepted an invitation with a modest fee, to direct and design his own play *Diarmuid agus Gráinne* for the company's twenty-fifth anniversary. He went to Galway to see a production of *Iníonn Rí Dhún Sobhairce* and to familiarise himself with the players, among them the young actress, Treasa Curley. When MacLíammóir was introduced to the audience and came on stage to take a bow, and, as was his wont, took the hand of the leading lady to kiss it, Treasa, not understanding the graceful gesture, involuntarily withdrew her hand in fright. He cast her as Gráinne nevertheless, and cast a young army officer, Padraig O Cearbhall – for the Taibhdheardhc still depended on part-time players – as Diarmuid. Treasa Curley found him extremely helpful as a director, where characterisation was concerned; later, when she joined the Gate, she realised that Hilton Edwards' *forté* was ensemble, and that in the direction of individuals, his notes were technically, rather than psychologically, apt. MacLíammóir made a number of cuts in his own text, finding that a quarter of a century previously his writing had lacked economy. His design this time was less 'Celtic', starting with a sunlit palette, moving to autumnal colours, and finishing with sombre browns and umber.

President Seán T.O'Kelly attended the opening night on 13 August 1953, having been installed as a Freeman of the City of Galway that afternoon. There were speeches and congratulations; but MacLíammóir admitted privately that he did not feel the theatre, which he had helped to found (with such enthusiasm for the revival of the Irish language), had progressed at all in its twenty-five years. 'Thersites', the acid anonymous commentator of the Irish Times, wrote in the issue of the day prior to the anniversary, 'When the Taibhdheardhc tomorrow night does Mr MacLíammóir's play, it will have admitted its own failure.' Val Mulkerns, writing in The Bell the following month, said that *Diarmuid agus Gráinne* was 'the best play ever written in the Irish language'. MacLíammóir felt that this was a cause for concern, rather than for celebration.

Diarmuid agus Gráinne was translated into Welsh in 1955 and broadcast on BBC radio. Radio performances, for which free-lance actors could earn ten or twenty pounds, occasionally supplemented both Edwards' and MacLíammóir's incomes. When MacLíammóir was in Galway, Edwards played Sir Anthony Absolute in *The Rivals* in an unusual venture for Radio Eireann, when two of England's most revered radio actors, Gladys Young and Valentine Dyall, were guest artists at the studios in Henry Street. Six month later he played Othello, when the guest producer was W. Bridges-Adams, now retired from the British Council.

In May 1954 MacLíammóir went to London to take the leading part in Yeats' *King Oedipus*, with Meriel Moore as Jocasta, and Charles Doran, now almost eighty, as the herdsman. In August 1955, he played in Elizabeth Boyle's *The Exiles*, which was produced in the Belfast studios by Ronald Mason, for which he received £25, plus the return fare from Dublin and £3.10.0d for two days' subsistence, which was considered a very good rate, enabling him to stay in the Grand Central Hotel, then the best in the city. When Mason mentioned that someone would be taking a picture of the cast at the microphone for the Radio

Times, he asked to be released from the studio for an early lunch, and turned up afterwards in what resembled a film make-up, and, as the actor, Denys Hawthorne, recalled, 'a gangsterish suit'. Mason, who later became Head of Drama in London, remembered MacLíammóir in *Exiles, Tolka Row* and *Weep for Polyphemus* – listening very carefully to his directions, nodding agreement and making notes on the script, and then reading the line exactly as before. Maurice O'Callaghan remembered him deliberately forgetting Mason's name – 'Yes, Roland, I quite understand you'; Mason would then press the intercom key and say 'Ronald'; and a minute later MacLíammóir would address him again as 'Roland'.

Adjudications at Amateur Drama Festivals also became a staple of free-lance employment. MacLíammóir shone at the social gatherings, praising bishops in flowery speeches for their generous patronage, flattering councillors, and keeping the attendance enthralled with his reminiscences. What should have been concern with the technical and artistic achievements of the play of that night became intimate one-man shows round the fire of the local hotel parlour until the early hours of the morning. He took pages of notes during the performances, but had surprising difficulty in committing his reports to paper, or in supplying the committee with a list of marks and awards. (Anew McMaster had the same disability.) The chairman of the Ballyshannon Festival spent a whole Sunday trying to get him to make up his mind on the results. He also liked to be taken on afternoon drives – which members of the committee were very pleased to arrange – and on one occasion, feeling that the sedentary life was detrimental to physical well-being, requested the services of a masseur. There being none in Ballyshannon, the trainer of a neighbouring Gaelic Athletic Association football team was sent for; but he retreated in consternation after only one session. Edwards, on the other hand, found small-town social life irksome, and though his speeches of thanks and congratulation were superbly delivered, there was an overriding note of fulsomeness in his utterance. He had no difficulty in filling in the marking sheets and announcing the lengthy lists of medallists and cup-winners, and was much in demand for his quick and fair decisions – and described at Ballyshannon, where he was engaged in 1952 and '62, as 'the daddy of all adjudicators'.

THAT CAN'T BE THE DAWN, DEARS

Anew, Marjorie and Mary Rose McMaster returned from Australia in 1950 and resumed the life of the Irish road. The going was tougher than it had been, but young actors were keen to join them for the experience, and a number of these, who played the Salanios and Salarinos, and borrowed properties from hotels, and lugged chairs into the Daniel McGrath Memorial Hall in Bagenalstown and the Magnet Cinema in Monaghan, became, before very long, leading figures of the Irish stage, drama directors in radio and television, and administrators in the film business. Some became better known outside Ireland – Pauline Flanagan,

Pinter, who later wrote a monograph vividly recreating McMaster's character –
'evasive, proud, affectionate, mischievous, shrewd, merry' – entitled *Mac*.

When, in 1954, McMaster told Edwards and MacLíammóir that he intended
to present two weeks of Shakespeare in the Gaiety Theatre, playing five leading
rôles, there was much shaking of heads at Harcourt Terrace. He was sixty-one;
while he might certainly play Lear and Shylock, surely Petruchio, Othello and
Hamlet were out of the question for the metropolitan audience; MacLíammóir
had been fifty-one when he played his last Hamlet, at Cork and Elsinore, and
there had been unfavourable comment, though muted; the era of the star
continuing in the star rôle, no matter what his or her age, was past, like it or not.
McMaster persisted, however, and Edwards reluctantly agreed to contribute a
new production of *The Taming of the Shrew*. Friends in the press doubted
whether anyone in Dublin would want to see Shakespeare nowadays; but
McMaster had saved money from his Australian tours and was willing to risk a
loss. Besides, as he pointed out, Dublin had never seen his Lear. The Boys
decided to go to Ennis to attend a performance, and were, for once, at a loss for
words. (Pinter said that in this part McMaster achieved the heights of 'terrible
loss, desolation, silence'; and Pauline Flanagan recalled that the exit line, 'O
Fool, I shall go mad', spoken almost as a question, was terrifying.)

The Gaiety was booked out for all fourteen performances. Evidently youthful
graces were not expected, and even the sixty-one year old Hamlet held their
attention, for McMaster's speaking of the part was wonderfully illuminating –
the clarity of delivery, the variation in pitch and tone, the effortless
comprehension of the iambic: but much more, for it was the emphasis he placed
on the meaning of the text which was so revealing, and so exhilarating. 'Thank
you! Thank you!', cried McMaster in a curtain speech, 'For coming to see old
mutton dressed up as lamb!'

PATRICIAN PAGEANT

In the same year, Hilton Edwards and Micheál MacLíammóir were invited by
the Irish Tourist Board to produce a Pageant of St Patrick, designed to form the
centrepiece of a springtime festival called *An Tóstal*, or 'Ireland at Home', with
McMaster as the national apostle. McMaster had already appeared in the rôle in
a pageant in county Meath, when, disembarking from a property boat on the
banks of the River Boyne, several spectators felt constrained to rush forward
and kiss the hem of his garment. Croke Park, the Gaelic Athletic Association's
stadium in Dublin, was selected as the venue, and the sodality and confraternity
of Drimnagh – reputed to be the largest Roman Catholic parish in Europe –
agreed to supply the huge crowd of druids, warriors, shepherds, monks, princes
and persons of noble birth. There was a very definite sense of *déjà-vu* to the
Pageant of the Celt in Chicago in 1934.

Rehearsals took place in May 1955 in a community hall in Drimnagh, where
the extras were drilled scene by scene – the whole cast could not be fitted into

the space – by 'crowd marshals' working to a plan devised by Edwards, who visited these sessions and then returned to the railway-engineers' recreation-hall in Inchicore, where the principals were rehearsing, loudly complaining that the whole thing was going to be 'a bloody shambles – chivvying four thousand horrors round Croke Park'. MacLíammóir was not present to offer solace, for he was in Belfast on one of the many Maura Laverty tours; his script was much admired by the cast of the pageant, and had been written in a declamatory style which was pre-recorded and played over the amplification system, while the actors mimed in huge gestures somewhat resembling semaphore.

The great surprise to Edwards was that the public turned up in such numbers over the six performances; his second surprise was that the heavens, probably in deference to the subject-matter, did not open as he had predicted; what did not surprise him at all was that the members of the sodality and confraternity diminished in numbers each evening, so that by the final night the hosts of newly-converted Christians from the four provinces of Ireland looked like an ill-attended Lenten mission in a country parish.

When the pageant was over, McMaster went back to 'the Irish smalls'. Returning to Skibbereen in the early hours of a summer morning after a swimming party at Tragumna strand, he drew attention to an orange glow in the sky, exclaiming, 'That can't be the *dawn*, dears!'. It was not indeed the dawn, but the Town Hall in flames, with the sets and costumes for seven plays. It was said later that the McMaster lighting equipment had overloaded the electrical system, but this could not be proved, and he received substantial compensation. On the morning after the fire he left for Dublin, announcing to the disconsolate company that they would re-open in Bantry the following Monday night, as advertised.

At noon on Monday, Mac stepped out of a huge pantechnicon containing curtains, properties and costumes from the Gate store in Harcourt Terrace. 'All thanks to Mickey and Hilly,' he said. 'The Boys have been *so* kind!'

Chapter 13

Contagious to the Nile

'You can't imagine what it's like to have been someone who literally turned heads in the street', Micheál MacLíammóir said to Simon Callow, then a student at Queen's University, Belfast, as he regarded himself balefully in the mirror of the makeshift dressing-room of the McMordie Hall, where he was to perform *The Importance of Being Oscar*, in the fall of 1968. He was nearly seventy. When he was approaching fifty, and appearing as romantic leads with Helena Hughes in *Portrait of Miriam* and *Where Stars Walk*, he had already had his face lifted (most people thought unnecessarily), wore a toupé to cover a bald patch and receding hairline, and had taken to wearing panstick make-up and eyeshadow offstage (which Helena Hughes thought made him look like an Egyptian painting). 'Offstage', she said, 'we made a slightly surprising couple – but on the stage, no! not at all. And furthermore, he was really marvellous at playing love scenes, and, just as has been said of Bertrand Russell, he looked at you as if you were the only person in the world.' His almost psychopathic determination to retain a youthful appearance had quite the opposite effect: the wig and the make-up drew attention and, at a close glance, the tout-ensemble was too obviously a fabrication. On one occasion in Paris, Orson Welles told him he looked like an unemployed gipsy fiddler.

Hilton Edwards took no such pains with his physical appearance. Pudgy as a young man, in his forties he became portly, though not obese. He dressed neatly, on occasions even wearing a suit at rehearsals. His anxieties about growing old were more about money, and where it was going to come from. When MacLíammóir spoke of ageing, it was often in a wryly self-deprecating fashion, as if to make a mock of his own silliness. The reality of the passing of the years was brought home to him in a more forceful way with the death of Aunt Craven, on 23 August 1954. She had remained in her cottage on the hill of Howth until a few weeks before her death in hospital. Micheál wrote to a mutual friend: 'We buried her in Howth in the little cemetery between the sea and the mountain where Máire's ashes are, and I feel very happy about her but sad at the same time, and quite dread the knowledge of how much I will miss her at Christmas.' She was his last remaining older relative – although an adopted one – and he now found himself placed firmly in the the oldest generation, for there was no one left ahead of him.

*

During Craven's last illness, Micheál was appearing at the Olympia Theatre as Judge Brack in *Hedda Gabler*, produced for H.M. Tennent Productions by Hugh (or 'Binkie' as he was universally known) Beaumont, and directed by Peter Ashmore. It was conceived as a vehicle for Peggy Ashcroft, who wished to show Hedda's actions in an ironic light, almost as a comic character, and very much against the grain of the traditional interpretation. The engagement occupied him from June to December of that 'ghastly year', rehearsing in London, opening in Dublin, and then, after a short English tour, coming to rest at the Lyric, Hammersmith. He then had the option of remaining for the presumed transfer to the West End. Hilton Edwards made much of the story that he had accepted the engagement only because they could not afford to play continuously in Dublin. As usual, MacLíammóir was a distinct social success while away from home, and captured a great deal of the publicity. 'We were bowled over by his charm from the moment we met him,' Peggy Ashcroft wrote. 'He came into my life for such a short time, alas! but his effect on all of us was very strong, and I think we all found the shared experience unforgettable. We were all exploring Ibsen for the first time – and Michael Mac, as we called him, George Devine [Tesman], Rachel Kempson [Mrs Elvsted], Alan Badel [Lovborg] and myself found it a fascinating adventure. We were all buoyed up by Michael Mac's wit, ebullience and – perceptiveness.'

While on the *Hedda Gabler* tour, MacLíammóir was writing a new comedy with music, rather in the style of *Home for Christmas*, sending the script back to Dublin by instalments. When he became bored with Ibsen he decided to return to Dublin and take part in it, foregoing the West End run, but making sure he could rejoin the cast for a continental tour starting at the end of February; he had told Binkie Beaumont that there was a possibility of his 'starring' in his own play, and now that it had been 'accepted for production' it was his wish to do so. The title decided upon was *A Slipper for the Moon*; the action takes place backstage in the hours between the end of a matinée performance of *Cinderella* and the beginning of the evening show – starting with the final chorus and walk-down, and ending with the overture and opening number. The relationships between the actors offstage reflect the traditional relationships of the characters in the pantomime. MacLíammóir must have been reading Pirandello, for he seems to be asking: What is real? What is merely theatrical illusion? Or is the illusion the reality? – but he does not investigate the possibilities of a potentially exciting variation on the theme, throwing in a comic bit of rehearsal here, or an audition there, more to keep things lively than for any tellingly dramatic effect. The character which he played himself, the actor-manager, Mr Lacey, reads rather like MacLíammóir in a bad mood; but it allowed him to do an Ugly

(*Above*) Hilton Edwards'
production of *The Clandestine
Marriage* by Colman and Garrick at
the Old Vic Theatre, London, 1951.
(*Right*) Sybil Thorndike as Mrs.
Alving in Ibsen's *Ghosts*, directed
by Hilton Edwards, Dublin Gate
Theatre Productions at the Gaiety
Theatre, Dublin, 1943.
(*Below*) Shelah Richards.

(*Above*) Orson Welles as
Othello and Micheál
MacLíammóir as Iago in
Welles' film of *Othello*, on
location in Morocco, 1949.
(*Right*) Eithne Dunne as
Ophelia at Kronborg Castle,
Elsinore, 1952.

(*Above, left*) Patrick Bedford.
(*Above, right*) Patrick McLarnon.
(*Above, centre*) Sally Travers.
(*Right*) Maura Laverty.

(*Above*) Micheál MacLíammóir as
Brack and Peggy Ashcroft as Hedda
in Ibsen's *Hedda Gabler* directed
by Peter Ashmore, Lyric Theatre,
Hammersmith, 1954. (*Right*)
Siobhán McKenna as Joan in
Brecht's *St. Joan of the Stockyards*,
Dublin Gate Theatre Productions at
the Gaiety Theatre, Dublin, 1961.

(*Above*) Aiden Grennell,
Christopher Casson, Micheál
MacLíammóir, and Déirdre Maher
in the Don Juan scene from Shaw's
Man and Superman, Gate, 1973.
(*Left*) Brian Friel. (*Below*) Eamonn
Morrissey and Fionnula Flanagan in
Lovers by Brian Friel, Gate, 1967.

(*Left*) Hilton Edwards at Harcourt
Terrace at the time of his
appointment as Head of Drama,
RTE Television, 1961.
(*Above*) 4, Harcourt Terrace, Dublin.
(*Below*) Micheál MacLíammóir at
Harcourt Terrace designing
Anouilh's *Ring Round The Moon*,
1952.

(*Above*) Costume designs by Micheál MacLíammóir for *The Taming of the Shrew*, 1974, and *An Ideal Husband*, 1972. (*Below*) Backstage group at the opening of Desmond Forristal's *The True Story of the Horrid Popish Plot*: Hilton Edwards, Aiden Grennell, Brian Tobin, Desmond Forristal and, seated, Micheál MacLíammóir, 1972. (*Below, left*) The sleeve of the record of Micheál MacLíammóir's *The Importance of Being Oscar*.

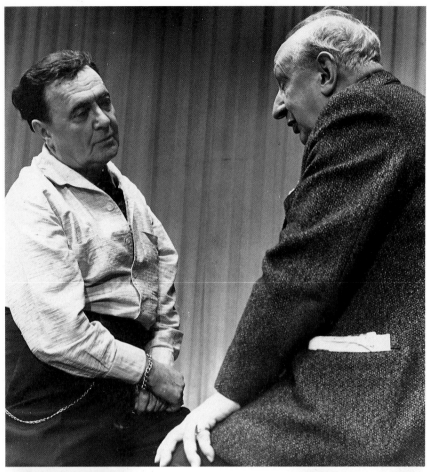

(*Above*) Hilton Edwards and Micheál MacLíammóir rehearsing for Brian Phelan's *The Signalman's Apprentice*, the last play in which they appeared together, 1971. (*Below, left*) Micheál MacLíammóir as Adolf Hitler in *The Roses are Real* by Patrick Paterson, Vaudeville Theatre, London, 1963. (*Below, right*) Hilton Edwards as Herod in *King Herod Explains* by Conor Cruise O'Brien, Gate, 1969.

Sisters double-act with Milo O'Shea, who, as well as being one of the leading younger actors in Ireland, was also well known as a comedian and mime. Critics and audiences expected more from O'Shea than this production allowed him, and MacLíammóir kept saying, 'I'm going to write a little number for you!' – but he never did. His words for the prologue, spoken by Hilton Edwards, certainly reflected his own growing sense of disillusionment: 'Which plays,' the pantomime prologue enquires, 'Have had the longest runs?' and then he answers his own question,

> Why, those that in some way or other
> Remind us of the tales that mother
> Told us when our minds were fresh,
> 'Ere cynicism, in its mesh
> Entrapped us, in its smirking way,
> And made us fear to praise a play . . .

A Slipper for the Moon was not greatly praised, but it provided seasonable entertainment and looked as if it might run for some time. The members of the company were cynical – whether in a smirking way or otherwise – in their comments when the notice went up announcing that the final night would be Saturday 26 February, for they knew that MacLíammóir was to re-join the cast of *Hedda Gabler* at Heathrow on the following day, for rehearsals in The Hague.

The *Hedda Gabler* tour was managed by Jan de Blieck of Amsterdam and covered a number of cities in Holland, as well as Copenhagen and Oslo. Peggy Ashcroft and Rachel Kempson had been speculating as to whether MacLíammóir's hair was real or not, and conspired as to which of them should dare burst into his bedroom 'by mistake' to see if it sat on a wigstand by night, which caused a great deal of mirth. When the tour finished in Oslo on 19 March, they went to wave him goodbye from the berthing-place of the ferry, which was to carry him to Newcastle-upon-Tyne (thence by train to Liverpool and boat to Dublin) – 'I expect to be abandoned to my fate amid the irresistible attractions of Newcastle,' he said – and as the ferry pulled away they saw him gesticulating and pointing frantically from an upper deck. On the quay beside them there was a small case: his make-up! They wondered how he would manage without it amid the irresistible attractions of Newcastle, before they entrusted it to the parcel post.

Immediately on returning to Dublin, MacLíammóir went into rehearsal at the Gate for Pirandello's *Henry IV*, which the publicity stated he had translated himself, though in fact he had written a 'version' from existing English texts which, as Pam Pyer told Kitty Black of the literary agents, Curtis Brown, were not 'suited to the requirements of our theatre or the taste of this country'. He described the play as 'a masquerade . . . enriched by the hero's fragmentary revelation of an eight-hundred-year-old anguish'. The modern-day hero has so absorbed the rôle of the emperor Henry IV that he virtually becomes him, and lives surrounded by an entourage whose members wear mediaeval costume. It was an ideal play for the Gate, allowing for a visual interpretation by Molly MacEwen which artfully accounted for past and present simultaneously, provided Edwards with an opportunity for the most ingenious Masaccio-like pictorial grouping and lighting, and a part for MacLíammóir which combined elements of the fanciful with the grotesque. No one could describe the choice, as many of the productions at the Gaiety had been described, as 'commercial'. It was indeed so un-commercial that audiences were conspicuously sparse, and this was a huge worry for the partners, now that all players and staff were on union rates.

When the company went to Belfast for the annual season at the Grand Opera House in May, the unseasonable *A Slipper for the Moon* did poor business, a revival of *Not for Children* with Rachel Kempson did even less, and *Henry IV* was cancelled at the last minute due to an unprecedented absence of advance bookings. 'If people walk out of *Not for Children*, they are going to be bored stiff with Pirandello's play,' Edwards pessimistically told members of the Young Ulster Society, to whom he gave a talk in the Union Hotel. George Lodge, the managing director of the Opera House, was reported by the Belfast Newsletter as saying that he had 'no objections to experiments in the presenting of plays, as long as John Citizen wants to go and pay to see them.' John Citizen demonstrably did not want to see them, so frenzied telephone calls to Dublin were made, which succeeded in rounding up actors who had been in *Liffey Lane* and *Tolka Row*, and these two plays alternated in the final week, though to disappointing houses, owing to the lateness of their announcement. Senator Roger McHugh, who had reviewed earlier Gate productions for The Bell, wrote to congratulate the company on *Henry IV*, which he had seen in Dublin. 'Afterwards I thought of the days when both of you and Miss Carmichael and the rest gave us *Peer Gynt* and *The Power of Darkness* and the other great plays which were like rain from heaven upon the imagination, which was parched at that time. A quarter of a century carries its own attrition. It is good to see you have survived it and have not been choked by the detritus which necessity, sworn brother to the arts, enforces as a condition of survival.'

With the Gaiety closed for renovations ordered by the fire officer, there was nowhere available in Dublin for productions which might show even a modest profit. During this period the new secretary at Harcourt Terrace, Pam Pyer, was constantly taking letters from Edwards suggesting film or television productions of MacLíammóir's plays, and proposing foreign tours with the company's current repertoire. She wrote persistently to the Education Ministry in Cairo following a communication which suggested that visits from foreign companies might once again be considered.

It was an extremely depressing time. Coralie Carmichael, who had not been well for some months, was found to have cancer. After a period of treatment, she bravely returned to work in Cyril Cusack's two-week production of Hamlet, in which she played Gertrude opposite MacLíammóir's Claudius, a part for which he was now eminently suited. At the same time, Edward Longford threatened to place the parent Gate Theatre Company in liquidation. In March of the previous year he wrote to Hilton Edwards to say that he was 'not going to lift a finger under the circumstances to keep the present state of things going any further unless you promise to allow me to occupy the theatre until the two years' rent you owe the Limited Company is paid.' Edwards and MacLíammóir did not pay – they could not pay – and, following the Belfast *débâcle*, Longford proposed buying the (valueless) Edwards-MacLíammóir shares and taking control of the Gate Theatre himself, allowing them the option of renting it from time to time. In a memorandum to Terence de Vere White dated June 1955, MacLíammóir wrote, 'I feel we must say "yes" to this if there is no help forthcoming. However, I do wish to make it clear that my fear of having no theatre is not merely sentimental: it is the fear of a solicitor having no office or a doctor having no surgery . . . I do know that material is available for a very strong appeal to the public and the Arts Council. I cannot imagine that the disappearance of say the Old Vic for a comparatively modest debt would be allowed to pass without somebody doing something . . . Our present acute position, indeed, is partly due to Pirandello and an insistence on first rate casting, an extravagance that perhaps may have to be curbed . . . I cannot believe that public opinion and support, which saved us from the first attempt of Lord Longford to blot us out of existence, would fail us now.'

A sum received from United Artists on behalf of Orson Welles helped to delay a confrontation with Longford, in that John Bools, as company manager, was able to advance the rent for the forthcoming autumn-to-winter season. There was an exchange of letters about who should have paid for what over the past year – Longford acceding that Edwards-MacLíammóir were due reimbursement for six broken seats which they had replaced, but demanding that they should pay for 'half the new carpet on the stairs' – 'Which half?' Hilton enquired. Longford also asked what had become of a 'small green table' from his office, which he had reason to believe had found its way to Harcourt Terrace. To make matters of normal administration even more difficult, the Harcourt Terrace telephone was disconnected because the bill had not been paid. A pay-phone was applied for, and residents and staff had to keep a little pile of coins. Then the sheriff telephoned Terence de Vere White to say that he had three decrees of execution. He was quite friendly, de Vere White said, but it would be his duty to send a bailiff to seize whatever belongings could be carried away. When, at a later date, two bailiffs did arrive, Hilton took whatever silver he could lay hands on and made his exit through the back garden, while MacLíammóir descended the stairs to the front door wearing a Chinese kimono and silver eye-shadow. The bailiffs fled at once.

This farcical dicing with debt could not continue indefinitely. As in stage farce, it was compounded of real anxiety and desperation. De Vere White and his legal partner, Alexis Fitzgerald, decided to speak to the Taoiseach, John A.

Costello, in the hope that he would influence the Arts Council towards the provision of a regular subvention. The news which came in the autumn, that the Cairo Opera House would provide certain guarantees for a season there and in Alexandria (both theatres now being under state control), was met with misgiving by de Vere White, who felt that such a venture might well prove unstable; he also thought the Arts Council might take the view that they should not assist a company which was spending much of its time abroad. On de Vere White's advice, Edwards wrote to the secretary of the Council, to assure him that reports of their projected tour did not rule out their usual autumn season in Dublin.

CAIRO AND ALEXANDRIA

'Of course you have realised by now that I am one of those cads who never writes until he wants something,' Hilton Edwards wrote in his assumed Public School style to Helen and Adrian Holt. The Holts were old friends from the British diplomatic service; Adrian was now a Queen's Messenger in Cairo. 'We are trying to negotiate another season at the Opera House, Cairo, and later on at Alexandria. My top contacts are Soliman Bey Naguib, now secretary of the Heliopolis Jockey Club but late intendant Opera House; Sedky Pasha, present boss of Opera House; and, if still in the land of the living, Jules Morris, who was, and perhaps still is, box-office manager at the Opera House . . . My remembrance of Cairo prompts me to believe that we haven't an earthly without influence and pressure in Cairo. "Would-ja-ever" do what you can for us? If Adrian, or you Helen, your lovely self, would care to constitute our representatives for the negotiations, I would be delighted to come to terms with you, confirm them and make a proper business deal . . . It might even be possible to extend beyond Egypt to East and South Africa . . . '

'Darlings!', replied Helen Holt on 3 February, 'When do you wish to come to Cairo – for how long – and what plays are you bringing? Let me know as soon as possible and give me all details, and then I will see Abdel Rahman Sedky. – GLORIOUS here – and we all adore it, have spent the day at Mena House eating, drinking and sitting in the sun! Longing to see you and do hope your trip comes off. We are here for another 6/9 months . . . '

A correspondence in which Helen and Hilton vied for 1920-ish expressions of enthusiasm and pleasure had begun. In due course she called on Abdel Rahmed Sedky and confirmed that the Egyptian government were now disposed to receive English-speaking companies, and that the more spectacular the productions were the better. *Antony and Cleopatra* was proposed as being most suitable, but this suggestion did not even merit coffee-break conversation at Harcourt Terrace because of the question of the casting of Antony. The engagement of a local impresario was proposed by Sedky, to make 'all the financial arrangements'. (A decade later it would be quite normal to make an advance trip by air and dispose of all contingencies at one meeting.) Helen Holt offered to contact friends in Beirut, Baghdad, Cyprus, Nairobi and Malta – 'The more engagements we can lay on for you, the better.'

Hilton was surprised to learn that the visiting company now took the entire box-office receipts at the Opera House, after only 20% expenses a night had been deducted. 'The use of the Opera House is free – being subsidised by the government – the same thing in Alexandria where the Municipal Theatre is free,' Helen explained; against this, there could be no state subsidy for visiting companies. The matter then, as Hilton saw it, was to arrange such effective publicity that the theatre would be full every night, and to attempt to obtain a guarantee of an agreed figure per night from Sedky. On the Holts' recommendation, he wrote letters of goodwill to a number of dignitaries. He also sent an application for a travel grant to the Cultural Relations Committee in Dublin, and when this was refused – on the grounds that the Department of External Affairs did not have sufficient funds – he set about organising a supporters' list, inviting subscriptions towards the cost of the company's sea and rail expenses, promising to repay after the tour was over. Before the company left for Egypt, Miss Tinney of the Cultural Relations Committee wrote to advise Hilton Edwards that there had been second thoughts, and a travel grant of £200 would be provided; this was 10% of the figure sought, and was interpreted at the Gate as conscience-money.

Adrian Holt went on a business trip to Iraq, and his wife reported that the King Feisal Hall was 'somewhat primitive, as no company has ever been as far as Baghdad.' Istanbul was then mentioned, where the Holts had another friend, Sir James Bowker. In a subsequent letter to Pam Pyer, Adrian Holt said it would be a very good idea if Orson Welles were to join the company 'if only for one or two performances'; but Hilton knew it would be impossible to tie Welles to any date. At the end of May, the Holts reported that Sedky was very ill but had received Adrian at his bedside and had promised a guarantee of £2,000; he suggested that the Minister for Education should now be approached for a further guarantee of £4,000, which would make the trip viable. Sedky believed the minister might agree, if it were suggested that prices be lowered in order to accommodate students, and further suggested that the company should number not more than fifteen – Edwards had proposed thirty-four – in order to reduce expenses. (Eventually sixteen players and four technicians were agreed.) In August Helen Holt had a meeting with the Minister for National Guidance, and after some time, he agreed to make a cash grant to the Dublin Gate Theatre company. She was working extremely hard on the Gate's behalf, receiving and dealing with letters and telegrams from Edwards almost daily. There were many conflicting suggestions about the repertoire – *The Merchant of Venice* was suggested in some quarters as especially suitable because it was 'anti-Jewish'; *Oedipus* would 'please the Greeks'; an interested Egyptian wrote that '*St Joan* would be good because it is anti-British'! Edwards and MacLíammóir took note only of titles which would suit them for a pre-Egypt season in Dublin.

The autumn 1955 season at the Gate was made up entirely of the plays finally agreed for Egypt. These were Anouilh's *The Lark* and *Ring Round the Moon*, Yeats' *King Oedipus* in a double bill with Shaw's *The Man of Destiny*, Wilde's *The Picture of Dorian Gray* in the adaptation MacLíammóir had made in 1945, Chekhov's *The Seagull* and Shakespeare's *The Merchant of Venice*. With the help of Pam Pyer, the partners made out a complicated chart of the characters in all six plays, so that these could be cast in such a way that each player would have a part in every play, and that no player would appear in only three or four productions, thus wasting salaries with evenings off. As it turned out, several actors not only appeared in every play, but often in more than one part in some of them. There was absolutely no allowance for accident or illness: if an actor were to become seriously indisposed, a crisis decision would to be taken on the spur of the moment.

Realising, perhaps, that an insufficiently gifted group had been chosen for America, Edwards drew up a list of what he considered to be the best actors in Ireland. Even those with whom the partners were not on particularly easy social terms were approached, including Denis Brennan – 'he wouldn't know how to put a foot wrong on the stage if he tried', said Hilton, regretting the incident during *St Joan*. He also spoke to Maurice O'Brien, undoubtedly the most stylish actor in the country, who normally worked with Longford Productions. There had always been a coolness between MacLíammóir and O'Brien, since the latter was a genuine Corkman and took pleasure in voicing his disbelief in MacLíammóir's claim to a Cork background. Edwards also approached Christopher Casson, Helena Hughes, Laurie Morton and Peggy Marshall; but none of these indicated interest or availability. A company was subsequently chosen which was unusually strong in its women – Eithne Dunne, the most versatile Irish actress of the day; Anna Manahan, who already had a range extending from the crazily scatterbrained to the fiercely emotional; Marjorie Hawtrey, who came from London to play the parts in which Coralie Carmichael would have been cast; Maureen Toal, whose talent, beauty and vivacity were a talking point; Deirdre McSharry, who excelled in brittle, sophisticated parts; and Finola O'Shannon, who had joined the company as an assistant-stage-manager for *St Joan* and was making her name as a spirited juvenile lead. Among the men were Milo O'Shea, whose potential was far greater than what he was given to display; Patrick McLarnon, established as a *jeune premier* of Grecian good-looks and bearing; Liam Gaffney, veteran of previous Egyptian tours; the young Patrick Bedford, who was quickly extending his range from demotic to classical rôles; Leo Leyden, one of the original members of the Radio Eireann Players; Reginald Jarman, the solid British character-player *par excellence*; Colm O'Kelly, the stage director who had proved himself as a useful supporting player and had recently married Anna Manahan. Two other young actors completed the company. Headed by MacLíammóir (as Oedipus, Lord Henry Wotton and Trigorin) and Edwards (as

Shylock) it was a company which could have passed muster on any stage of the world.

Two letters arrived from Helen Holt which gave a vivid insight into the nature of her involvement in promoting the Gate's interests. 'Darling Hilton and Micheál, Typing with a bandaged hand and one finger – left my hand in a car door!! but this note is so terribly important I must get it off to you. Adrian tells me you are planning to go to Israel. If one teeny PEEK of this gets out here – you will not get into Egypt. And, if this is even BREATHED whilst you are playing here, you will be shown the frontier and lose whatever is left of the subvention. The Egyptians, somewhat naturally, will have NOTHING to do with Israel. If you should try to get in here with Israel stamped on your passport, you will not be allowed entry . . . This, darlings, is much more serious than you could possibly imagine . . . '

Hilton Edwards had mentioned the possibility of playing in Tel Aviv in a note to Adrian Holt, but he had done no more than that, so there were no delicate knots to be untied. Then Helen wrote in a panic on 13 December to say, 'The typist told me IN CONFIDENCE that the Comedie Francais [*sic*] found last Holy Week – in her own words "disastrous". The only way, darling, to get over this, is to INSIST that ALL students take their seats THAT WEEK . . . and that it is all advance booking . . . The new Minister – has been in power only 2 weeks, and WHY Chiaty did not show him the proposed programme before Sunday last, is a mystery. The Minister is, however, in COMPLETE CHARGE, and his word is law. I wish to heavens we had been dealing with him all along, he is intelligent, and Chiati drives one QUITE MAD . . . ' Then Helen wrote to say that Chiati, who appeared to be the deputy manager of the Opera House and 'a moron', insisted on two copies of each play – one for the censor, and one for the library. She enclosed information on seating, tickets, matinées, a gala opening, drapes, hotel accommodation, and the man who had been retained to look after publicity, a Romanian with the unlikely name of Monsieur Raphael. She had done everything she possibly could, and was now joining Adrian in London, where their address would be The United Hunts Club . . . Before travelling to Southampton to embark on the *Oranje*, the company played in Limerick and Clonmel to very poor business indeed. It had been the intention to present a pre-Egypt season at the Cork Opera House, following the pattern set before travelling to Denmark and the Balkans, where each production would be taken out of its hampers (there were fourteen of them, and four tons of scenery), given a metaphorical dust over in front of an inveterately lively public, and packed up again for that other opera house on the Nile; but the opera house on the banks of the Lee was accidentally burned to the ground, and there was nothing for it but to take whatever else was available. The cinema in which they played in Limerick was cramped, could not accommodate the sets satisfactorily, and the dozens of costumes could not be adequately pressed and hung. It rained every day. Audiences were sparse and unenthusiastic. In order to gain publicity and achieve a little goodwill, Hilton Edwards agreed to a request for a midnight performance of *The Picture of Dorian Gray* in aid of a local charity; it was announced for a Saturday, when the company was already giving a matinée and an evening performance. No one could recall any theatre company ever having played three different major classics within a space of twelve hours; the galling aspect was that very few charitably disposed patrons turned up for the midnight show. It was soon apparent that it would have been less expensive to place the company on retainers for a month, and not perform in Limerick and Clonmel at all.

The only compensation was that Limerick allowed the opportunity to open *The Merchant of Venice*, which had not been played in Dublin. Maureen Toal's Portia was a triumph of beauty and wit combined; Hilton Edwards' Shylock was said to be as good as ever; and Micheál MacLíammóir gave what each night turned out to be a hysterically funny appearance in the small part of the Prince of Aragon, all castanets and swirling cloaks and stamping feet. Not one member of the now quite demoralised troupe could envisage this production as being anything but a huge success in more propitious surroundings. However, John Bools, the first manager trained in accountancy which the company had ever had, gave in his notice: it is probable that he felt the odds against the company ever recovering its financial equilibrium were too heavily loaded, even if money were made in Egypt – and that was another imponderable. Pam Pyer was about to leave for London for a short break at home before embarkation. She was approached by Edwards and MacLíammóir and asked if she would take on the manager's work as well as her own. She thought she had no other choice – as she said, 'it was that or no tour!' As a result of this doubling of duties, there was an unfilled place in the travel budget; Edwards asked Charles Roberts, whom he had first met as a highly resourceful crowd-marshal on the Pageant of St Patrick, and who had been recruited to the stage staff at the Gate that autumn, if he would stay on for Egypt. When Colm O'Kelly was playing Salerio in *The Merchant of Venice* in Limerick, Roberts took over the 145 sound cues and 170 lighting cues as if he had been doing it all his life, and this impressed Edwards enormously. Roberts' attitude was typical of the genuine professional: 'I'll be seeing the world and being paid for it!' Later Edwards remarked, 'If you get Roberts on your side he'll bite you to the elbow, but he'll leave the rest of your arm!'

*

Edwards, MacLíammóir and Gaffney, the only members of the company who had been in Cairo before, were pleased to find that many members of the Opera House staff of twenty years ago ('was it really twenty years?') were still employed, in spite of war, revolution, and time; several stage-hands cried with emotion at this undreamed-of reunion. The population of Cairo had doubled, they were told, since their last visit. Anna Manahan, looking from the window of the train from Port Said, saw numerous mounds of earth and exclaimed,

'Imagine keeping animals in those!' Liam Gaffney corrected her in his gentle way: '*People* live in them.' War was in the air again – quite literally, for there were air-raid precautions every evening, when all the lights in the city had to be extinguished for a few moments after a hundred sirens sounded.

The news that the French company which had played in the Opera House some weeks before had lost £13,000, created a state of almost catatonic fright in Edwards, MacLíammóir and Pam Pyer. This intelligence had to be kept from the company, and evidently was, for with the exception of two official complaints, one of them trivial, the other serious, everyone seemed to be enjoying themselves. Some of the actors complained about not having been properly prepared for all the tipping which was evidently necessary. (Had none of them ever been abroad before? MacLíammóir sarcastically enquired.) This problem evaporated when members of the cast noticed slung microphones, of the kind normally used for outside-broadcasts. Leo Leyden, the seasoned radio actor, who happened to have been elected Equity representative for the tour, saw a commentator behind a glass panel and asked Hilton Edwards about it. Hilton replied that it had 'nothing to do with the company – every opening night is being broadcast in full.' No one believed that Egyptian State Broadcasting would not be paying a fee for these transmissions, and a lengthy correspondence was carried out *via* Equity in Dublin; in the end, the company – which meant Edwards and MacLíammóir – was required to pay each actor for every broadcast, but only if all the members of the cast signed a request. Two members refused, on the grounds that if they did so they would never be employed again, and so none of the players received the moneys due. Leyden determined never again to allow himself to be cajoled into becoming Equity representative.

The opening night – *Ring Round the Moon* – proved an undoubted hit, and minor tensions vanished. Two nights later, *The Picture of Dorian Gray* was received with hardly a laugh (which upset the cast very much) but exultant applause at the end (which perplexed them); the reviews were excellent, and the booking for its two further performances immediately prospered. MacLíammóir wrote in his journal: 'So many jokes, so many epigrams having slipped by totally unheeded during course of evening. Am convinced that the vast majority of these people, both Egyptian and European, have passed so far from the backgound of that strange period we call *fin-de-siècle* and of that strange writer O.W. in particular, that they can no longer understand it or him. Remembering our past season in Dublin and in a couple of Irish country towns, and recalling that *Dorian Gray* was by a long chalk the most popular thing we did, it strikes me more sadly than forcibly that . . . the appreciation of wit, humour, of that nimble yet stately juxtaposition of words essential to the reader or spectator of Wilde, depends not only on time but on place as well.' Yet who could have expected, in a society where Arabic and French were as much the *linguae francae* as English, that there should be peals of delighted laughter when Lord Henry comments on Basil Hallward's mysterious disappearance, 'I dare say that what really happened was that poor Basil fell off an omnibus into the Seine and the conductor hushed up the scandal'?

Eithne Dunne received a tumultuous reception as Jeanne d'Arc in *The Lark*, as did Maureen Toal and Hilton Edwards for *The Merchant of Venice*. It became obvious that they should have taken advice and brought more Shakespeare; but the season was going well financially. What irked amid the general adulation, and seemed to follow the partners like a cloud of hot desert dust, was the increasingly threatening news from Dublin, which arrived enclosed in letters from Terence de Vere White, who felt he had to apologise 'for being such a Jonah'. The literary agent, Jan Van Loewen, wrote threateningly about the Anouilh royalties, which had not been paid; Frau Kettner, the housekeeper at Harcourt Terrace, had received a cheque from Cairo, which she said was barely enough to buy food for the cat; the Electricity Supply Board advised that the current would be cut off – but de Vere White managed to speak to a higher official and a two weeks' extension was allowed; the sheriff delivered a note, stating that the scenery housed in a store off Merrion Street would shortly be seized; the bailiffs called and removed the refrigerator from the kitchen – 'they were decent enough,' de Vere White wrote, 'to say it was a shame to take it for the amount that was due'. De Vere White continued: 'To be sending you all these miserable messages is only to discourage you, but, on the other hand, Frau Kettner and I are bearing the brunt of it here and it all makes it abundantly clear to me what I have thought all along, and that is that the only basis to operate in Dublin is to do so as free lances, and to rid yourself once and for all of this huge set up which, as far as I can see, can only operate at a loss of £1,500 a year . . . You have no idea how much goodwill there is, because I ring up all the sheriffs, the Corporation and the bailiffs, and they all hold off and do everything they can to meet the situation. I assure you in the the case of the ordinary professional man there would be no redress at all. I say this to encourage you, when I am sending you such a discouraging letter.'

MacLíammóir was particularly sad that the bank had said there was no money to cover the small cheque he had written for Coralie Carmichael, who was now unable to work. He used to give her regular presents, which were never discussed, and now de Vere White reported that her husband, Denis McKenna, had come looking for money. MacLíammóir had never 'approved' of her marriage, especially to a person whom he considered to be her inferior in every way, but he had never let this private consideration darken their friendship.

Personal affairs and theatre business were inextricably and confusingly mingled. Very shortly after their return to Dublin, Edwards wrote formally to de Vere White to state that they had decided upon the liquidation of Edwards-MacLíammóir Dublin Gate Theatre Productions Ltd; it is reasonable to suppose that much of their conversation between rehearsals, performances, receptions, and parties in the homes of the Egyptian elite, was taken up with this spectral topic. One thing however was clear: their professional standing in Cairo was undiminished. The final performance, on Saturday 7 April, was *Ring Round the Moon*; the British, French and Soviet ambassadors came backstage to congratulate the company – the Soviet ambassador had attended three productions; having come initially to be present in a box for *The Seagull*, he became a Gate addict, and entertained the players lavishly; one of his presents was a gigantic wreath of red roses, another a barrel containing bottles of vodka for every actor. He especially admired Micheál MacLíammóir's Trigorin and Maureen Toal's Masha, and said, in the outwardly sincere manner of ambassadors, that the Gate must assuredly come to Moscow; MacLíammóir thought to himself that he would not mind being barred from the United States for ever if this were to come to pass.

FUNERAL IN ALEXANDRIA

Members of the technical crew, as is their sacred custom, do not go to parties after the last performance until every drape, flat, door-piece, ground-row, stage-brace, teaser, lamp and skip has been removed from the theatre and loaded into the trucks. On the final night at the Cairo Opera House, Colm O'Kelly complained of aches in his limbs, and thought he might be sickening for 'flu. Charles Roberts told him that as they had plenty of help from the theatre staff he should sit in the manager's office, and they would all go back to the Union Hotel together when the get-out was completed. He and his wife Anna sat there, but when they left, Colm walked very slowly. In the morning, Anna said he had been very restless, but he would not see a doctor because they were all about to leave for Alexandria. Everyone thought he looked dreadful, and his condition was not helped by the very slow and very hot train, in which he unaccountably felt cold. At Alexandria, Charles told Hilton he thought Colm was seriously ill, and a doctor was sent for once the party arrived at the hotel. Hilton took on part of the stage management duties as well as the lighting, and there was discussion as to how to distribute the small parts which Colm played, as it was obvious he was not going to able to work for some days.

The logistical difficulties were increased when a letter arrived from Malta stating that a fortnight's engagement starting on 30 April was now definite; a contract signed by Mr E. Baldacchino of the Radio City Opera House was enclosed. All the approaches made by Helen and Adrian Holt in middle-eastern countries had proved fruitless, probably because they were not themselves present to press the cause with governors and ministers in their graciously persistent way, but in Malta the Gate was remembered with affection from 1937 and '38. The contract included a guarantee which made it possible to pay salaries to the company for the two weeks between closing in Alexandria and opening in Valetta – a holiday with pay for everyone.

Anything *less* like a holiday Pam Pyer had never experienced. First, having confirmed the company's travel arrangements back to Southampton, she then had to return to the agency to cancel them, 'to my great embarrassment and the agent's annoyance. I was in a turmoil – I was only in my early twenties – and it all happened in a haze of pain because I had caught my finger in the hotel lift-gates and in the end had to have my finger-nail pulled off.' On the Monday morning of the opening, Eithne Dunne and Patrick McLarnon were called by Anna Manahan to her room, where Colm was in a state of delirium. They sent for an ambulance, and all three travelled with him to the hospital, where they were relieved to find four Irish sisters to whom they were able to explain the nature of his rapid decline. When they had taken Anna back to the hotel, Charles Roberts went to visit Colm, who said, 'My ribs are crushing my lungs'. Poliomyelitis, which has an incubation period of a mere two to five days, was diagnosed. Colm O'Kelly died that night.

Now the whole company was in a turmoil. First, Anna had to be comforted. The women took it in turns to stay with her. Priests arrived, and the mass and funeral were arranged for the following day. But what of tonight? It was *Dorian Gray*, in which Anna had two parts – Caroline, Marchioness of Narborough, and Ivy, a cake-walk dancer. Milo O'Shea immediately offered to play Colm's part, which Micheál MacLíammóir cut down there and then to make it learnable in an afternoon. Hilton Edwards said they would not make an announcement, because 'it is not the actors' job to expose their emotions.' Then Anna, in the best traditions of the profession, declared that she would go on that night. 'It was a miracle,' MacLíammóir later wrote. 'She never played with greater absorption, with more truth, with slyer or wickeder humour. Not once did she falter. When it was over and the curtain down she walked to the side of the stage and stood there for a moment smiling at us, her eyes dazzled as it seemed, by the light as though she had stepped out of a dark room. Maureen and the other girls helped her to change and dress and got her home somehow . . . '

Colm O'Kelly was buried on Wednesday 11 April 1956, in the Latin Cemetery of Alexandria, with the whole Gate Theatre company present, as well as a large number of Irish residents who had read about his death. There was no Irish legation in the city, but the British consul and his wife attended. Later, Eithne Dunne approached Hilton Edwards and said that Anna must not be talked into staying on for the Maltese trip, and it was agreed that she should return to Dublin at the end of the Alexandria week. When she was tidying up her wardrobe, Micheál took the black ribbon off one of her wigs – it had been restyled from the one he had worn in *Berkeley Square* – and gave it to her. She kept it ever since, saying she shared with him a fondness for inanimate objects which reminded her of people.

The audiences in Alexandria were very small, for it transpired that there had been very little advance publicity. The numbers grew each night, but there was a real worry that the loss might eat into whatever profit had been made in Cairo. Pam Pyer accompanied Hilton Edwards on a round of meetings in Cairo during the week which followed, including a courtesy call on the Minister for Education, who appeared pleased with the result of the ticket scheme for students. The profit on the season turned out to be £1,496, which was greater than expected, and the day before she flew to Valetta, she made arrangements with the assistant manager of Barclay's Bank in Cairo for the money to be transferred to the National Bank in Dublin, knowing that it would be dispersed at once to sundry creditors.

THE ROYAL NAVY TO THE RESCUE

When negotiations with Valetta's Radio City Opera House had first opened, Hilton Edwards wrote to a friend in the Irish Naval Service, Commodore H.J. Jerome, asking if he could use his influence with his Royal Navy counterpart, in the matter of transporting the company's scenery. Now that the Malta engagement was suddenly secure after a long period of waiting, there was little time in which to make arrangements, even if the Royal Navy were to agree to what was in fact a most outlandish request. A Captain Henley R.N., deputising for Sir Guy Grantham, Commander-in-Chief, Mediterranean Station, Malta, contacted Pam Pyer to enquire what *exactly* the company had in mind, and she replied to say that, as far as dates were concerned, the frigate H.M.S. *Mediator*, leaving Port Said on 25 April, would be preferable to the destroyer which he had mentioned as sailing a few days later, as it might not reach Valetta in time for the opening of *The Merchant of Venice*. Captain Henley then conferred with Mr Baldacchino of Radio City, who wrote to Hilton Edwards stating that everything seemed to be agreed with the Royal Navy, but describing the *Mediator* as a 'tug'. In response to a further enquiry, Henley wrote to Hilton Edwards to say that '*Mediator* could carry eight men on an austerity basis as well as the scenery; they would be required to pay 7/- a day to cover messing, exclusive of wine and other personal expenses for which they would naturally be asked to pay individually . . . As the Commander-in-Chief stated in his letter to Commodore Jerome, he cannot guarantee dates, any of which can be changed for operational reasons at short notice.'

If the officer in charge of messing was hopeful of collecting his seven shillings a day from the eight actors who embarked from Port Said on 23 April, he must have been disappointed, for the Libyan Gulf quickly turned from ultramarine to grey and then to black, and though none of the actors was quite sure as to which was stem and which was stern, gales shook the frigate from one to the other, and when they weren't rolling out of their hammocks to be sick, they were falling out of them because of the swell. Leo Leyden felt that death would have been preferable. They were met at the naval dockyard in Senglea on 28 April by Eithne Dunne and Pat McLarnon (who had flown *via* Tripoli), and all of them looked 'in flitters'. So, it transpired, was the scenery, some pieces of which were unrecognisable; and MacLíammóir, with a number of helpful members of an amateur drama group, spent two days trying to disguise the worst blemishes with coats of paint, while he ran from one understudy rehearsal to another, and gave interviews on the history and objectives of the Dublin Gate

Theatre for Rediffusion. The efficient organisation backstage and front-of-house at the Radio City Opera House (which replaced the Valetta Opera House, destroyed by German bombs, and resembled any number of suburban cinemas from Tooting to Sidcup) impressed everybody: here was a small Mediterranean island with a definitely North African look to its architecture and streetscapes, yet a firmly British sense of order and decorum. Distinctly *passé* English slang terms were also in use, and these seemed oddly endearing, coming as they did out of the mouths of small dark-skinned people with rather Italian-sounding accents, when they addressed each other as 'old chap'; and everything was either 'jolly dee' or 'scrummy' or 'awful rot'.

Drastic editing of scripts, and frantic redoubling and trebling of parts, covered the loss from the cast of Colm O'Kelly and Anna Manahan. Micheál MacLíammóir, who in Alexandria had taken on O'Kelly's Salerio (who is essential to the plot) and cut out his own Aragon (who is not) in *The Merchant of Venice*, found a way of restoring Aragon by giving Salerio's lines at a later stage in the play to Salarino (a character originally omitted from this production), Salarino now taken on by Reginald Jarman. The most crucial change was that Pam Pyer, who had never appeared on any stage in her life and had no wish to do so, was press-ganged into taking over Anna Manahan's comic rôle of Mademoiselle Capulat in *Ring Round the Moon*. 'When everybody's around you, you have to agree!', she said. She learned the lines without any difficulty, but could not be heard in rehearsal. After her débût, however, MacLíammóir described her as 'audible as a quavering but crystal-clear Last Trumpet', and when congratulated by the whole – and much relieved – company, she declared that acting was 'a mug's game, and I wouldn't be an actress for all the money in the world!'

True to form, Edwards and MacLíammóir went for a luxurious Sicilian holiday with Patrick Bedford at the Hotel Bel Soggiorno in Taormina, before returning to Dublin, where, as expected, writs and creditors awaited them. Among the piles of unwelcome mail was one touching letter from Kevin and Catherine O'Kelly of 3, St Mobhi Drive, Glasnevin, parents of Colm O'Kelly, to whom the partners had telegraphed their condolences from Alexandria. Mrs O'Kelly mentioned 'Miss Dunne and Mr McLarnon who were such good friends to him in his hour of most need,' and ended by saying, 'It is with great pride that we read that you thought so much of Colm's work, realising, indeed, as we do, that it is from you he learned his craft.'

There were immediate matters of business to be addressed. Terence de Vere White must be consulted. The manager of the National Bank in College Green had to be interviewed. Where was all this money which was supposed to have come from Egypt? The account was incomprehensibly overdrawn. Then a communication arrived from Barclay's Bank in Cairo stating that, due to legislation recently introduced by the government, no moneys could be exported from the Egyptian Republic.

Chapter 14
The End of the Rainbow

'As I hear you are back with lots of money from Egypt, I thought it would be no harm to ask if Micheál and you are still in any way interested in this old place,' Edward Longford wrote with unveiled sarcasm to Hilton Edwards on 13 June 1956. 'My reason for asking is that we are all going to be tried for our lives on 6th July, unless the hearing has been postponed again, as has already happened twice.' The hearing was Longford's attempt to quash an order from the fire officer requiring additional exits, fire escapes, rewiring and other drastic alterations to the Gate Theatre. Longford had appealed, but it was likely that a court decision in favour of the order would be made in the interests of public safety. On the advice of Terence de Vere White, Edwards wrote a friendly but non-committal reply. He then wrote to Orson Welles to acquaint him of the company's and his own position, and to ask if there were any developments in a number of projects which they had discussed.

'We are now so deep in that we will have to shut down. I see no hope of ever earning enough in this country to meet our liabilities. This has not yet been officially announced, though in Dublin, as you can imagine, it's no secret. We are endeavouring to keep on our house, though we may not be permitted to do so. I think it necessary to do this, firstly because we've got to have some bolt-hole, and secondly because of Micheál: this I am sure you will understand. We will, therefore, have to free-lance and try to make enough to keep ourselves and pay off our personal debts, which are not great. So that's the end of the bloody old Gate as far as I'm concerned . . . I am producing a revue for Elliman at the Gaiety in which Micheál is to appear, and there's quite a lot of tatty work going over here if I want it. When the revue is on I'm going to chance my arm in London, but don't look forward to what I've dreaded for years: up the agents' staircases.'

In the midst of preparing the revue for the Gaiety and of ceaseless representations to the Egyptian authorities, Edwards wrote thanking the numerous individuals and public bodies which had helped with the Mediterranean tour. In a letter to the long-suffering Holts he outlined the causes of their current financial embarrassments, from Limerick to Alexandria. He blamed the poor houses in Alexandria on 'dear Raphael, who as a person I really quite liked; not being able to distinguish between advertising and publicity . . . he omitted to put adverts in the papers on the day we opened. The latter – publicity – was non-existent. For instance, the Greeks were allowed to assume that because the programme was in English that it was an English Company and as a result a good many of them clutched Cyprus to their bosoms and stayed at home.' As the engagement of Raphael the Roumanian had sprung from a suggestion passed on by the Holts, they were not amused. Adrian Holt replied curtly: 'We were most interested to hear of your experiences in Cairo. Sorry the subvention did not come up to your expectations, but it took us ten months of daily blood and sweat to raise that £4,000 for you, and we are considerably out of pocket over it. I should be glad if you would let Helen have the £250/300 agreed upon.'

Before *Gateway to Gaiety* opened on 6 August the partners issued a declaration to personal and company creditors, through their accountant: 'It is with great regret that we have to inform you that Dublin Gate Theatre Productions Ltd is not in a position to meets its obligations . . . It is, therefore, reluctantly compelled to suspend operations. It is significant to realise that by far the greatest creditor is Micheál MacLíammóir, and to a lesser extent Hilton Edwards, who have over a considerable period poured into the company their personal resources gained from activities outside the country . . . ' It was with profound regret, the document continued, that they were forced to discontinue 'the enterprise which for over a quarter of a century has been the source of much employment, the passage of a considerable amount of money among the tradesmen of the city, and which has given pleasure and intellectual stimulus and, we may say without hesitation, no ill reputation to the city of Dublin'. The secret, which Edwards had told Welles could not be kept a secret in Dublin, was now official. The local gossip was that The Boys were now 'starving in Jammet's', Dublin's most exclusive restaurant. They were, indeed, often seen there, but more often than not as the guests of Yvonne Jammet, who remained one of their most loyal supporters. (She dined every fortnight in Harcourt Terrace, where the *cuisine* was not always so reliable.)

Terence de Vere White continued to canvas support at the highest social level, and did not cease in his efforts to keep the Arts Council in touch with the dire situation. During the summer he submitted a carefully worded paper to the secretary, followed by a six-page statement of accounts. 'They cannot even afford to go through the process of liquidation,' he concluded. 'I think there are two considerations, (1) the national loss, and (2) the national debt to these artists who gave disinterested service to this country.' On 10 August, de Vere White received private notification that the Taoiseach had sanctioned the payment of £2,000 to the Arts Council from a fund in his control, to be passed specifically to Edwards-MacLíammóir Productions, and that the Council itself proposed to match this with a further £2,000. The grant would not be paid, the secretary of the Arts Council later wrote, if Dublin Gate Theatre Productions Ltd went into liquidation. The Council – which had been in consultation with Louis Elliman – further required that Dublin Gate Theatre Productions Ltd present three months' of drama at the Gaiety Theatre during the following year, and that Mr Elliman should undertake the business management of Dublin Gate Theatre Productions Ltd during those three months. In addition, the Council required that all moneys received from Egypt should be applied towards the payment of liabilities – and a list of headings was attached. Certified accounts were also requested. The communication was addressed to Terence de Vere White at his chambers, and he was asked to provide written confirmation that the conditions outlined were acceptable to the partners.

The court case regarding the theatre as a fire hazard was postponed until September, when the judge himself made an inspection of the building, and later pronounced that the theatre would have to meet the Corporation's safety requirements, or close as a place of public entertainment. Lord Longford's financial advisers believed he had spent far too much of his personal estate on the theatre – he had even cashed his life insurance policy – and it is likely that they pressed him to abandon his connection altogether; but he doggedly repeated that the Gate must remain in operation, and this inspired the slogan for the fund-raising campaign which he set in motion, 'Keep the Gate open!' He and Christine, and many of the members of Longford Productions, collected money in the foyer and in the streets. He also sent out an appeal to everyone he knew who might subscribe even a pound or two, but he knew there was no point in asking Edwards and MacLíammóir, for it looked as if they would never appear in the Gate again. He, like them, applied to the Arts Council for help, and in due course was sent £1,000. He found this insulting, and returned the cheque; the Council had second thoughts, and doubled it.

*

While Pam Pyer and Terence de Vere White and his staff continued working on the backlog of debts, Edwards and MacLíammóir involved themselves in as much free-lance work as they were able to find. Edwards did go to London to tread 'up the agents' staircases', but he was fortunate in rediscovering Joan Reddin, daughter of Tony Reddin who, in 1927, had been the first theatre manager in Dublin to employ him. She had acted with the Gate as a very young woman in the 1940s, and since then had been round the world in cabaret. In 1954 she set herself up as an agent, quickly becoming a most influential one. Edwards asked her for advice, and she said he should go back into acting; while he was in her office, she telephoned Michael Barry, Head of Drama at BBC Television, who was producing a new serial of *David Copperfield*, and said, 'I have Mr Micawber standing here before me!' Within an unusually short space of time he found himself cast in the part. Joan Reddin also gave a party to introduce Edwards to casting directors. He was to appear in six out of thirteen episodes, in a complicated schedule of rehearsals and recordings, which took him from 1 October until Christmas, and immediately the inherent difficulty of the free-lance life made its appearance: the clash of dates.

Gateway to Gaiety, which as far as the general public was concerned, had the double attraction of Micheál MacLíammóir and Jimmy O'Dea heading the bill, was retained for a week, which meant that the opening of Paul Vincent Carroll's new comedy, *The Wayward Saint*, which Edwards had agreed to direct in the same theatre (with MacLíammóir sharing the billing with Liam Redmond and Noel Purcell) was postponed, making Edwards' availability for the first days of television rehearsal in London extremely unlikely; then Louis Elliman, pleased with the outcome of the revue, invited him to direct the Christmas pantomime, suggesting that MacLíammóir and O'Dea should be paired as the ugly sisters. A correspondence ensued between Edwards, Michael Barry, Joan Reddin and Louis Elliman – they all seemed unaware of the invention of the telephone; airline timetables were consulted, and the result was that Edwards saw *The Wayward Saint* through its opening night, arrived only a day late for *David Copperfield*, and throughout the rest of the autumn worked on the pantomime script from London, rehearsed it in Dublin whenever he could, and finally had only three working days to attend to its staging before opening night on 26 December. He had exchanged the pressures of running a company for the pressures of the theatrical market-place. Passing by Christine Longford's table in Jammet's, he stopped to dilate in great discontent about the overlapping of engagements. She looked at him for a moment, and then said in her quizzical drawl, 'Aren't you lucky to be working?'

In London, Edwards met Meriel Moore, ironically enough through her second husband, William Devlin, who was playing Mr Murdstone in the third episode of the Dickens serial. She had heard that the Gaiety revue was 'very good – and do you know, even my illiterate relations noticed how well lit it was.' There was 'talk' in Dublin that Edwards and MacLíammóir should not be involving themselves in such lighthearted fare, that it was 'beneath them', and that they were 'wasting their talents'. This was simply bourgeois disdain for the popular, an attitude which could not comprehend the fact that the same resources of talent and technique were called upon, whether one was playing a part in a comedy sketch of one's own authorship, or in a scene by Sheridan or Anouilh. One of MacLíammóir's solo turns was entitled *Six Characters in Search of a Porter*, in which he gave himself scope for portraying a series of persons with varying national and social traits; this may have given him the idea, which he put to Louis Elliman, for a musical which would feature Jimmy O'Dea as a Dublin man 'from very bottom drawer' who had won a large sum of money and was taking his daughter – to be played by Maureen Potter – on an international tour, where they would meet 'Myself, in various guises as fortune-teller, guide, madame, dragoman, purveyor of postcards, fortune-hunter, etc; lovely opportunity for Alice [Dalgarno] in Eastern, Norwegian and Spanish numbers.' There are echoes of *Home for Christmas*, and such a scenario should have had box-office potential, but Mr Louis does not seem to have responded to it.

The Gaiety production of *The Wayward Saint* transferred to the BBC television studios in Shepherd's Bush, to be shot in settings which were not much more than enlargements of those used on the Dublin stage. While at the Sandringham Hotel in Lancaster Gate, MacLíammóir had time to talk to Edwards (now deeply engrossed in Dickens) about Mr Louis' panto, in which he and Milo O'Shea – not Jimmy O'Dea, who preferred to play Buttons – were to be the ugly sisters (this time without Pirandellan overtones) and for which he had been commissioned to write some lyrics, to give spice to the conventional Howard & Wyndham book. On 3 November, he wrote to Elliman to say that 'the television has eaten into every minute of my time here, but I have squeezed out a lyric for the sisters . . . I am hoping you may be able to pay me a little more than for the revue. I hope, too, that I will be frightfully funny as a sister, and, like Queen Victoria, have resolved to be Good – O I Will Be Good.'

Back in Dublin, he wrote to Pam Pyer, who had returned to her home in London but was helping with occasional typing – one of her correspondents was President Nasser, to whom Edwards had decided to appeal – to say that the pantomime rehearsals were 'a shambles. Scenery pretty provincial commonplace and I am writing hard at my own numbers and scenes and ignoring the rest.' There was undoubtedly an uneasy feeling of 'two cultures' insensitively thrown together, once Louis Elliman had made the decision that Edwards-MacLíammóir and O'D Productions should meet on the same stage. Rumours in the two camps were rife. Vernon Hayden, O'Dea's straight man and company manager, believed that Edwards-MacLíammóir took 50% of the gross box-office income, where in fact both were on salary (at £60 per week plus 1%) and MacLíammóir had an additional royalty of £12.10.0d per week for his writing. There was now less worry about the possible (or inevitable) loss of money on theatre productions, for Louis Elliman was the unopposed impresario; if he did not approve the choice of play, or the size of the cast, or the scale of the settings, changes had to be made. His production company, which appeared in publicity under the banner 'T.R. Royle Presents', was now responsible for any Gate collaboration, as well as for revues and pantomimes.

The choice for the spring season, which followed immediately upon the closing of the pantomime, was *Julius Caesar*, Donagh MacDonagh's second Gate play, *Step-in-the-Hollow*, and Marcel Maurette's speculative drama about the fate of the only surviving child of Tsar Nicholas II, *Anastasia*. Hilton Edwards, aware that the notion of dressing Shakespeare in the habiliments of times other than his own, in order to indulge the outlandish whims of costume designers, had become something of a visual platitude, wrote a very strongly-worded programme note in support of the (none too original) idea that the play represented the 'timeless struggle between the forces of tyranny and those who resist them, and the plight of a people swayed and torn by the conflict of their leaders.' The play was advertised as *Julius Caesar 1957*; and though the thought did not strike any of the critics, it looked far more like 'Julius Caesar 1939', for the uniforms, the banners, the podium bristling with microphones, the exaggerated salutes, the goose-step marching, produced a feeling of the Rome of Mussolini, rather than that of some imaginary post-war state. Christopher Casson played Caesar as a weak-spirited autocrat, Anew McMaster was a stern unemotional Brutus, Liam Gaffney a watchful Cassius, and Micheál MacLíammóir a thickset, middle-aged Mark Antony, very much the practical military man, rather than the romantic hero-worshipper which he had projected in 1934, and which was still expected of him. He was the antithesis of the Ugly Sister of the previous two months, and those who did not know him would not have believed it was the same actor. Marjorie McMaster did not approve of this messing-about with history; she preferred togas any day, and said that Mac and Micheál 'looked like two out-of-work bus conductors'.

Coralie Carmichael played Portia. It is a small part, with one very intense scene for which she summoned all her energy, so much so that no one in the audience could have known that she was dying. Those around her believed that it was her determination and nothing else which kept her going. She could not have sustained the part of the Dowager Empress in *Anastasia*, for which Ria Mooney was cast. It was many years since Ria had played with the Gate, and she had latterly been resident producer at the Abbey Theatre, a post which had tired her greatly. She had the command, but not the regality, for the part, and she did not manage to project the feeling that there were centuries of privilege behind her. There was also a physical difficulty, very obvious on the stage: small of stature, she was cast opposite Blanaid Irvine, who had previously played Anastasia in Belfast to much acclaim; though not overly tall, Blanaid Irvine made Ria Mooney look almost comically dumpy.

It was not a brilliant season; it was not even a particularly good one. The theatrical event of the year, however, was to come in June, and the very fact that it took place at all surprised the participants as much as it did the observers of Gate politics and personalities. Brendan Smith, director of the Theatre Festival, believed there was much to be gained by a co-operative venture between Edwards-MacLíammóir and Longford Productions; such a thing, naturally, had never occurred – and it is unlikely that anyone else would have contemplated anything so abstruse. The Gate Theatre, which Lord Longford was keeping open until all the estimates for repairs had been accepted and the contractors ready to start work, was very much in the public eye, due to his much-publicised street collections. It was unlikely that any artistic or idealistically promoted scheme would bring the two companies together, but Brendan Smith had the advantage of a budget, and was prepared to subvent such an enterprise from the festival funds. He brought the parties together with the help of their mutual friends Michael Scott and Lord Killanin, and a preliminary agreement was made to the effect that Hilton Edwards would direct whichever one of two plays was chosen; if it was to be *Dr Faustus* – which Longford favoured – Aiden Grennell, now a leading player with his company, would play the title rôle opposite

MacLíammóir's Mephistopheles; if it was to be *The Old Lady Says 'No!'*, Iris Lawler, Longford's leading lady, would play Sarah Curran, and MacLíammóir his celebrated part of the Speaker.

The Old Lady Says 'No!' was chosen because MacLíammóir wanted another chance to play his most famous part. The festival guaranteed £1,000 – a very large sum – and Denis Johnston wrote from America giving permission to 'the boys'. Supporting parts were to be played by members of Longford Productions; MacLíammóir was apprehensive of working with Iris Lawler, who had been represented to him as somewhat formidable, but their collaboration was the start of an enduring friendship. He wrote to Denis and Betty Johnston, 'She should really be called *die Lawler* rather than *la*, there is positively something Baltic about her . . . and she, good pliable soul, is open to any suggestion and more than willing to co-operate. She really and truly is very *nice*, and has worked with a sort of fluttering concentration that has nearly killed us all.'

The resident designer for Longford Productions, Alpho O'Reilly, was assigned to sets and costumes. He used the cyclorama to create a swirling cobweb pattern in shades of grey, in which vague silhouettes of old Dublin buildings were suspended, to exemplify the confusion in the mind of the chief character. MacLíammóir had designed all the previous productions, using cut-out pieces, and retaining a feeling that the action was taking place partially backstage in a theatre. O'Reilly was apprehensive of what MacLíammóir might think of his new concept, but when he first walked on to the set, without having seen it from the front, he stopped, performed a kind of twirl, and said into the darkness of the auditorium, where the technicians were sitting, 'Alpho O'Reilly: this is a triumph!'

*

The play, and the mystique surrounding its first performances, had become legendary. A new public came out to see it, and MacLíammóir was able to tell Johnston that, 'as I suppose you've heard, the *Old Lady* has had almost its biggest success here. Why, I can't imagine. Hilton has done one or two things that I think you'd both approve, and I have endeavoured to get back the remoteness that you, Mr Johnston, found lacking in my Bad Middle Period, and I like it – the part, I mean, not me in it – better than ever.' He went on to describe a 'ghastly accident', the cause for which he humorously ascribed to a stage-hand, Mick Lambert, who had polished the floor too energetically, causing him to slip 'arse-over-tip into the audience, on the appropriate line "my bed was the ground". I am now in plaster of Paris up to my left (luckily) elbow and in great misery. It has, however, taught me a lesson of renewed admiration for poor Coralie, whose right arm is permanently crippled, as you know. This makes us a pretty pair indeed.'

There is a scene in *The Old Lady Says 'No!'* where the 'actor' who plays Robert Emmet is knocked out, and the stage manager comes on to ask 'is there a doctor in the house?' A 'planted' doctor then comes on the stage. When it was found that Micheál MacLíammóir was seriously injured, Hilton Edwards went out during the interval and asked again if there was a doctor in the house, to be greeted with derisive laughter. 'No!', he cried, 'Mr MacLíammóir is genuinely hurt!' A young doctor rose sheepishly, expecting to be made a fool of, but on examining the patient backstage he said he must go at once to the accident department in Jervis Street Hospital. This was the theatre, however, not real life in any of its forms, and Robert Emmet promised to go to the hospital when the performance was over. There was a short delay, and then part two began, the chief character appearing with his arm in a sling.

Robert Emmet was twenty-five at the time of his execution in 1803, but the actor does not have to be of that age, for the part is more a figure than a character, and that is how MacLíammóir was able to continue playing it without the usual snide twitter in the dress circle bar about his sagging chin. It was undoubtedly his greatest creation – Hamlet, Oedipus, Trigorin, Oswald, Enrico IV, are the property of dozens of leading actors, and Diarmuid, Billy Quinlan, Dan Dempsey, Lee in *Ill Met by Moonlight* and Martin in *Where Stars Walk* are not parts of such stature. His mellifluous speaking of the final lines – which have been anthologised in collections of verse as well as prose – provide a supreme example of the synthesis of performer with performed. Kay Casson, passing through the darkened auditorium one evening when MacLíammóir was rehearsing quietly to himself on the stage, said it was the most moving thing she had ever heard . . .

> Strumpet city in the sunset
> Sucking the bastard brats of Scot, of Englishry, of Huguenot
> Brave sons breaking from the womb, wild sons fleeing from their Mother.
> Wilful city of savage dreamers,
> So old, so sick with memories!
> Old Mother
> Some say you are damned,
> But you, I know, will walk the streets of Paradise
> Head high, and unashamed.
> There now. Let my epitaph be written.

*

The Gate Theatre closed for extensive renovations on 29 May 1957, after the last performance of *The Old Lady Says 'No!'*, which was to be the final performance of the play given on that stage. Lord Longford wrote a letter to The Times contradicting a report that the building was to be demolished, and soliciting subscriptions towards its repair. There was sporadic correspondence between Longford and his solicitors on the one hand, and Edwards and MacLíammóir and their solicitors on the other, but it was obvious that Longford did not expect Edwards-MacLíammóir Productions to appear there under their own management again, and equally obvious that the partners did not expect to appear there again at all. Seven years later, however, they did so – but that was after an extraordinary turn in their fortunes.

PATIENCE AND PERSEVERANCE

Hilton Edwards sought ways of financing a new company. He wrote to Sir Laurence Olivier, John Clements, Julian Braunsweg and several others, enquiring about the possibilities of co-productions, and transfers of Dublin productions to London, receiving courteous replies, most of them stating that they would be interested if a specific proposal were made. The money paid by the Cairo Opera House was at last released, and this allowed de Vere White to deal with the list of creditors, of which there were ninety-seven, ranging from an estimate for arrears of income tax (which was disputed, and in time reduced) at £2,000, to the Court and Mirror Laundry at £2.7.2d. Lord Longford was sent £352.3.4d for electricity consumed by the company in the theatre, and Maura Laverty £190.2.2 for unpaid royalties. H.M. Naval Dockyard in Malta was paid, as were Major and Mrs Holt, and all those who had subscribed privately before the Mediterranean tour so as to ensure that it would take place – among them the Jammets, Lady Headfort, Lord Killanin, Frank Benner the Belfast fruit importer (who had been the most munificent at £500), Marjorie Hawtrey and the McMasters. Pam Pyer remarked that it was 'quite a thrill to be sending money instead of excuses'. MacLíammóir wrote to de Vere White on 20 November 1957, to say that 'all your goodness to us amounts to my largest debt, which I can never hope to pay.'

INSCRIPTIONS AND MEMORIALS

Between 1957 and 1960 there was little pattern to the partners' lives. The productions in which they took part in Dublin – though some of them were nominally promoted with the Gate logogram – were all produced by other managements. Certainly there was little which could be described as 'new' or 'interesting', save perhaps Edwards' work on *The Informer* at the Olympia in 1958 and *Mother Courage* at the Gaiety in 1959. The plays in which they appeared for Louis Elliman were revivals of earlier successes, such as *The Man Who Came to Dinner* and *Arsenic and Old Lace*. There was a considerable amount of work from recording companies for MacLíammóir – *The Canterbury Tales*, *The Faerie Queene*, *The Rubaiyat of Omar Khayyam*, and poems of Yeats and Poë in separate programmes, which MacLíammóir recorded for the BBC. Edwards directed a series of Shakespearian productions on disc for release in the United States. He also appeared in several episodes of a Granada television show, *The Verdict is Yours* – Micheál MacLíammóir and Finola O'Shannon joined him for one of them – but when invited to accept a long-term contract in the same series wrote to Denis Forman regretting that he could not do so because 'I have got myself into a position that involves others more irrevocably than I realised'. The only engagements which he had in view at the time were to direct *Mother Courage* at the Gaiety and restage *St Joan*, and all parties could probably have 'worked around' the dates to suit Granada; the real reason was a curious and telling one – he found the life of the television performer unacceptably lonely in Manchester, and dreaded the social evenings with his fellow actors in the hotels where they stayed in Fallowfield and Levenshulme.

Glen Byam Shaw, the director of the Shakespeare Memorial Theatre, who had seen MacLíammóir in *Hedda Gabler* in London, invited him to play at Stratford-upon-Avon for the full season from February to November, 1958. The parts were Claudius, Gower, Don Pedro and – presumably in a novel, mature, interpretation – Mercutio, at £50 per week. It was a very interesting offer, and MacLíammóir understood from their discussions that Edwards was to be approached for something similar. When he later wrote to enquire the position, it seemed, reading between the lines of the reply, that Shaw had forgotten there were strings attached, or had decided to cut loose from them. He replied that there were certain 'cameo' rôles in which Edwards could make an 'important contribution', and these were the second gravedigger in *Hamlet*, Antonio in *Twelfth Night*, Antiochus in *Pericles*, and the Friar in *Much Ado About Nothing* – definitely parts of much lesser *réclame*. There is a saying in the theatre that 'there are no small parts, only small actors', and the partners were well aware of it, as the vagaries of their careers had shown, yet severe umbrage was taken at this apparent slight, and the outcome was that both withdrew. It is hardly worth speculating how matters would have turned out if they had accepted; what is significant is that, despite their uncertain financial state, they retained their sense of professional and personal pride.

Micheál MacLíammóir went to Edinburgh in the fall of 1957, as a featured player in the festival production of *The Hidden King* by Jonathan Griffin. There was a cast of over fifty, among them several old friends including Robert Bernal, Ernest Thesiger, Robert Speaight and Robert Eddison. Described as 'an adventure story in a renaissance setting', the action swirled over the large thrust stage of the Assembly Hall, somewhat in the manner of Tyrone Guthrie, who had introduced a pageant-like style of presentation in the same venue some years before. As is always the case during the Edinburgh Festival, the afternoons were packed with press conferences and public discussions, and at these Micheál MacLíammóir astonished his colleagues by answering foreign journalists amusingly in French, Spanish and German. He quickly became a 'festival personality', speaking on radio and television in programmes which had little to do with the work in which he was appearing. He spent much of whatever free time he had with the Irish writer Ulick O'Connor, who was reviewing the festival for the Irish Times. O'Connor remarked on how well-known he was in Britain, and he replied, 'I'm not known outside Ireland, except for Judge Brack in *Hedda*.' O'Connor was not sure that this was entirely so. Yet MacLíammóir clearly needed a vehicle in which to convey all his peculiar talents together; his own plays had caught the attention of an appreciative public, wherever they had been performed, at home or abroad, but not to the extent which he would have liked; and he was never likely to be in competition with the Richardsons and the Gielguds as an actor. He was certainly in demand as a *raconteur*, but he had no wish to devote the rest of his life to chat shows and lectures to womens' clubs from Boston to Seattle, though he had often been asked. The work he had just finished, in organising a commemorative plaque to Oscar Wilde in Dublin, might have given him a clue as to the direction his career could take him as an internationally acclaimed author and performer, but for the moment there was no revealing light.

In 1954, the centenary year of Wilde's birth, MacLíammóir wrote to the press suggesting that members of the public might subscribe to the placing of a suitable tablet on the façade of the house in which Wilde had been born at 21, Westland Row, Dublin. There was no local-authority scheme at that time to pay for the erection of such memorials, and he soon found himself secretary and honorary treasurer of a self-appointed committee. A Dr O'Carroll, the owner of the house, was glad to co-operate, and a Mr Sawyer, a monumental sculptor on Aston's Quay, wrote stating that he had 'had the honour to design and execute the Bernard Shaw plaque at 33 Synge Street to the approval of Mr Shaw. If you would permit, I would have pleasure in estimating costs for the Wilde plaque on your design.' The cost was only £62.12.6d, but the subscriptions, even at £1, were slow to come in. Bórd Fáilte, the Irish Tourist Board, refused to be associated with the project, as did leading commercial organisations – it was believed that there was still a slur over Wilde's name, although half a century had passed since his trial and imprisonment in London. The Minister for Education, Donagh O'Malley, in a note accompanying his personal donation, exclaimed, 'You amaze me! I understood that Bórd Fáilte has funds at its disposal for the very work you envisage! . . . Many of the people who consider themselves as leaders of the arts would not know a Whistler from his dog!'

The Authors' Guild of Ireland subscribed, as did the Irish Academy of Letters, O'D Productions, and Methuen & Company; the list of individuals demonstrates how small and circumscribed was Irish literary and artistic society at the time. It would have been easy to guess correctly what names would be present – the Jammets, the Killanins, the Longfords, the Glenavys, the Ganlys, the Solomons, the de Vere Whites, the radio producer Micheál O hAodha, the architectural historian Maurice Craig, the poet Austin Clarke and the Gate Theatre patron Carmel Leahy. The plaque was unveiled by the playwright, Lennox Robinson, who received a tomato on his shirt-front for his pains. Much copy was made from this in the press, though it was thought that the missile had been thrown as a prank by one of a group of students who were wearing green carnations and drinking more champagne than might have been good for them, rather than one of a number of outraged citizens who had written feelingly to the Evening Mail about the impropriety of such a commemoration, to which the editor had responded with a leading article, advising that the campaigners should be given 'the cold shoulder'.

It was Carmel Leahy, a member of the publishing firm of Browne & Nolan, and her sister Sheila, who suggested to Lord Longford that a commemorative plaque should in turn be erected to Micheál MacLíammóir and Hilton Edwards in the Gate, to coincide with the reopening of the theatre in January 1958. Longford wrote to Edwards on 4 November 1957 to enquire if he approved, and Edwards facetiously replied 'I would be quite delighted to have a plaque marking the spot where I fell.' There was no suggestion that the Longfords should be commemorated, or if there was, they turned it down. There was some discussion about placing a memorial to Colm O'Kelly, whose premature death was very much in everyone's mind, but it was concluded that if this were done, there should be plaques to other deceased members of both companies; the Leahys' gesture was towards the founders, rather than all those who had subsequently worked there. A modest ceremony was arranged to take place in the upper foyer on 17 February 1958, shortly after Longford Productions re-opened the theatre with *The Tempest*, in a building defaced by exceptionally ugly concrete fire-escapes, which were fortunately on the garden rather than on the Cavendish Row side. The whole refurbishment had cost in the neigh-bourhood of £30,000, much of it from the Longfords' private purse. Coralie Carmichael was present, as well as the other founders of the Gate, Toto Cogley and Gearóid O Lochlainn. Only the names of Edwards and MacLíammóir app-eared on the plaque, a rectangular bas-relief with their heads carved in profile.

*

The only new production given by Edwards-MacLíammóir in 1958 was an adaptation of Liam O'Flaherty's novel of the civil war, *The Informer*. It was part of the agreement made with the Arts Council that the partners should produce three months of drama with Louis Elliman, but as Elliman's Gaiety Theatre was so heavily booked with other attractions, he took the Olympia, in association with its lessees, Stanley Illsley and Leo McCabe, leading to a highly confusing list of promoters' names – of little interest to the ticket-buying public – on the posters. *The Informer* had been made into a Hollywood movie – one of the earliest films directed by John Ford – with Victor McLaglen as Gypo Nolan, the violent bucolic who betrays his friend for a police reward. MacLíammóir wrote to O'Flaherty, who was living in the United States, that 'it might be very wonderful on the stage – possibly with a looser and more expansive treatment than in the film: a great space with no literal or localised scenery so that the audience is present at whatever place the actors tell them about, in the Chinese or Elizabethan way.' This is a curious suggestion coming from a designer whose mode was decorative – sometimes to excess; but its inspiration is not hard to find, for it is really Edwards speaking through MacLíammóir, almost in the words he used in his book of collected essays and radio talks, *The Mantle of*

Harlequin, which had just been published by Progress House. Edwards had been seeking a simplified style of presentation for certain kinds of play which might be described for convenience as 'epic', and had made use of his own ideas in this regard most tellingly in *Liffey Lane* and *St Joan*. He had read Brecht, but did not see the Berliner Ensemble until 1956 (in London), when his excitement was something akin to that of Keats looking into Chapman's *Homer*. He did not make the mistake of so many directors of the time, who snatched upon what they believed to be Brecht's theory of alienation, applying it improvidently to texts which simply could not stand the strain; he rather sought to adapt it where and when appropriate, as in Sam Thompson's *The Evangelist* in 1963. When he directed *Mother Courage* in 1959 and *St Joan of the Stockyards* in 1961, he made a more deliberate attempt to follow Brecht's *diktat*.

A cast of thirty was assembled for *The Informer*. Seven leading actors were approached for the part of Gypo Nolan, all in turn, according to Hilton Edwards, greatly regretting that they were 'in a film at Ardmore', 'unreleasable from the Abbey', 'doing a television play in London'; as the first date of rehearsal approached, there still was no leading man, and MacLíammóir reluctantly allowed himself to be cajoled into taking on the part, which was so much against his type – 'physical qualities to meet the demands of height and weight, and enough imaginative ability to grapple with the aspects of bull, tree, stone and soap-box orator' – that his friends, and the Gate *aficionados*, blenched at the thought of what he might do with it. (There is of course the possibility that he had dramatised the book with himself in mind, and that Edwards had merely gone through the motions of contacting other actors whom he knew would be unavailable.) As it turned out, he surprised everybody, especially Seamus Kelly of the Irish Times, who wrote that he was the 'cunning, scheming, stupid peasant dolt that O'Flaherty drew, in every line, every leer, every twitch and touch'. Brian Phelan, who was in the cast, confirmed thirty years later that 'Micheál had the huge lumbering presence of Gypo Nolan'.

The script was praised rather less than the chief performance. The consensus was that it was much too long, and that MacLíammóir as writer had allowed himself to be carried away in supplying richly comic scenes for Laurie Morton, May Ollis, Marie Conmee, and Maureen Potter, who, Seamus Kelly noted, 'has the part of a lifetime as Katie Fox'. Patrick Bedford as Frankie McPhillip, the man on the run, was warmly praised; he was now very much the company's young male lead, 'a fine actor, as bright and darkly shining as a black diamond,' as Micheál later described him in a magnanimous moment, for Bedford was Hilton's particular friend; and Micheál also had to accept that Patrick, because of his youth, was now much better suited to the parts he himself had created, in the plays which they were now reviving.

'A wonderful evening! – a triumph of acting!' wrote Terence de Vere White to Micheál MacLíammóir the following day. 'But!', he continued, giving the conjunction a line to itself, 'S.Kelly is not far wrong. The end seems to drag because there is too much *before it* . . . You have been too generous. Cut the I.R.A. severely, and do something to Act II, and you have a world success.' The script was pruned after the opening night, and it had an immense Dublin success; but the interest shown by British, Dutch and American impresarios evaporated when they saw the size of the cast.

*

Coralie Carmichael died during the run of *The Informer*. She had been received into the Roman Catholic church the previous year by the Franciscan priest, Fr Cormac O'Daly, and her funeral mass took place in his church on Merchants Quay. The list of those attending reads like a Who's Who of the Irish theatre. Micheál wrote an appreciation for the Irish Times, which was published a few days later. 'She has been with us through all our history at the Gate Theatre,' he said; 'a fine actress, an inspiring comrade, a really wonderful friend. I think in all those years no cloud ever came between us, no moment of doubt, no bitterness, no shadow of resentment. She was loyal, brave, witty and generous . . . ' Louis Elliman gave the use of the Gaiety Theatre without charge for a memorial concert on 28 February 1958, the proceeds of which went to pay the expenses of her funeral.

The Informer did not travel, as had been hoped, after its late autumn run in the Olympia, but MacLíammóir went to London to take up what was really an open invitation from the impresario, Julian Braunsweg, to join the cast of *Where the Rainbow Ends*, which he produced for Anton Dolin. Dolin had bought the rights of this old-fashioned children's fantasy-play, which had music by Roger Quilter, in 1950, and performed it with the Festival Ballet every Christmas; Alicia Markova danced the Spirit of the Lake. 'I persuaded Micheál MacLíammóir to come from Dublin to play the Dragon King,' Dolin wrote in his autobiography, *Last Words*. 'And what a Dragon King! Red lights seemed to flash from his eyes, and all over his body, which was covered in a garment of shiny beads. But for me the greatest sight of all was to see, after every performance, this magnificent artist sitting patiently in a tiny dressing-room, spectacles on the end of his nose, sewing on beads which might fall off . . . ' (MacLíammóir had designed his own costume, which Eileen Long made up in Dublin, and he wore it again when he returned to *Where the Rainbow Ends* a year later.) The backstage atmosphere was very much what it must have been for *Peter Pan* almost half a century before – magical effects, fairies, grotesque villains and children who were the epitome of goodness, bravery and innocence. MacLíammóir gave Dolin an idea for a short ballet which he felt could be devised from Yeats' early poem *The Song of Wandering Aengus*, and Dolin decided to commission it. When the Festival Ballet presented it at the Theatre Royal in Dublin the following September, it was very well received, though the Delius score was generally thought unsuitable for such an obviously Celtic Twilight piece.

Micheál MacLíammóir was not present at the opening of his ballet, for he had accepted an invitation to play Don Pedro in John Gielgud's production of *Much Ado About Nothing*, with Gielgud as Benedick and Margaret Leighton as Beatrice, at the Cambridge Festival in Massachusetts. The American actor, Hurd Hatfield, who had appeared as Dorian Gray in the film of the Wilde novel, and who later settled in county Cork, was cast as Don John. One evening Hatfield was late for an entrance, but instead of a silence in which the actors invented bits of business while anxiously peering into the wings, MacLíammóir astonished everybody with a totally impromptu speech in blank verse, which he was later asked to transcribe for the sake of posterity, though when it came to it he could only remember the first two lines –

My brother tarries, as it is his wont
To walk the crowded streets, now filled with flies –

'In a way,' wrote the Boston columnist Elliot Norton, 'it is too bad Hurd Hatfield didn't loiter longer. The likelihood is that MacLíammóir might have invented a whole soliloquy.'

In Boston MacLíammóir was able to visit Mary Manning, now Mary Manning Howe, and Denis and Betty Johnston. When *Much Ado* transferred to the Lunt-Fontanne Theatre on Broadway, he saw a great deal of Brendan and Marie Burke – Brendan had composed the music for *Not for Children* at the Gate, and Marie was the daughter of the actor F.J. McCormick – both of whom found his performance most impressive – 'Oh, darlings, I'm just one of those Shakespeare *drears*,' he cried, when they came round to his dressing-room; but he was described by the New York Times as 'outstanding, in an outstanding cast'. He told a journalist that he found the New York audiences receptive, but – perhaps recalling the sparse houses for his own plays in 1948 – that they depended too much on the critics: 'In Dublin, they go to a play because they want to go. In New York too many go because some paper said it was a great hit, and everybody else was going.' Towards the end of the run, Denis Johnston arranged for him to speak at a commemoration of the Fenian writer, John Boyle O'Reilly, in Boston. 'We finish (indeed I will not be anguish-torn) on the 7th of November,' MacLíammóir replied from the Lunt-Fontanne; he would have to do a little reading on John Boyle O'Reilly, 'of whose life, I need hardly say, I know almost nothing – but it seems he died in Boston, and really I don't wonder.'

THE WELLES VORTEX

While Micheál MacLíammóir was in the United States during the fall of 1959, Hilton Edwards directed a revival of Denis Johnston's *The Dreaming Dust* at the Gaiety. He was, once again, in discussion with Orson Welles on a number of projects, each one seeming to vanish in a cloud of vapour as the next arose, like the apparitions in *Macbeth*. Jan de Blieck was interested in any Dublin productions of the calibre of *St Joan* which Edwards might propose for continental venues. The combination of Welles' anarchic enthusiasm and de Blieck's precise attention to administrative detail might, in other circumstances, have resulted in a truly productive enterprise, but it emerges from the correspondence that their respective *modus operandi* were irreconcilable. Edwards, in his efforts to create interesting work for himself and for those around him who still considered themselves to be part of the Gate *ménage*, often found himself plodding through sloughs of misunderstanding, which stemmed from personalities as much as from difficulties of organisation and finance. The arbiter was Louis Elliman – cool and clearsighted, and having the ultimate advantage of owning the theatre where these undertakings might originate.

For some time Orson Welles had been talking of making up a dramatic evening for himself as Falstaff, in excerpts from Shakespeare's *Henry* plays and *The Merry Wives of Windsor*. The idea developed into a study of the relationship between Falstaff and Prince Hal – Welles had a lifelong absorption, which almost amounted to a fixation, on the relationship of mentor to pupil; the Hollywood director, Richard Fleischer, became startlingly aware of this at a meeting in Paris, where Welles, in his forties, became a schoolboy in the presence of Hilton Edwards. The plan expanded from a one-person to a two-person performance, and then, less interestingly, to a series of fully cast scenes hacked out of the plays and strung together in chronological sequence, under the title *Chimes at Midnight*. As early as June 1959 Welles and Edwards discussed the business implications with Louis Elliman, who 'pencilled in' a date at the Gaiety for the following spring.

Edwards then approached Molly McEwen to design sets and costumes, but she was not free, and Welles proposed that he should look after this aspect himself – a road leading to disaster, which Edwards should have barricaded immediately. In July, Welles came forward with an idea for producing *The Merchant of Venice* with the same cast on alternate nights, and this interested Jan de Blieck for a possible season in Paris. In the meantime, de Blieck offered Edwards an engagement in The Hague, directing *A Winter's Tale* at a very attractive fee, which Edwards accepted and then cancelled because the dates conflicted with preparation for *Chimes* in Dublin. De Blieck was most disappointed and wrote saying so, implying in the letter that Edwards was disorganised – to which Edwards replied, 'It is very much against my nature to be indefinite.' In early December, de Blieck wrote to say that Welles was agreeable to playing *The Merchant* at the Théâtre Sarah Bernhardt in April, but only for a short season, 'so as not to become the slave of success'! This rapidly evolved into a two-production tour of Paris and the Benelux countries. Then George Lodge of the Grand Opera House in Belfast read of these plans and offered his theatre, provided Welles was playing. Edwards thought it would be a useful gesture to audiences there to cast a Belfast actor, and approached Harold Goldblatt for the part of Tubal – 'above all, I do want an authentic Jewish note, or the scenes become "stage-Jewish"'. Next, de Blieck had second thoughts about *The Merchant*, because he hoped to add Germany to the itinerary, and an 'anti-Semitic' play would be tactless; he talked to Welles about an alternative, and it appeared that Welles was greatly taken by the thought of playing Malvolio in *Twelfth Night*. Edwards was now going frantic, for no casting had been done, and those actors whom he had approached tentatively had to be put off. It was not entirely clear either if Welles wanted him to direct the plays or simply to produce the season; he suspected the latter.

Micheál MacLíammóir returned from America into the midst of what he described as 'the Welles vortex', which spun between Dublin, Amsterdam and Paris. In early January, he wrote to Welles to say that Hilton had had a fall, was in bed with a temperature of 104, and was fussed about dates and casting. A few days later, he wrote again saying, 'I have a suggestion which will probably make you open the sprinkler stop-valves on me and leave me on the apron singing "Abide with Me". (However I will risk it.) . . . Would you ever concentrate for the moment on one show, *Chimes*, which is the readiest; spending an all-out effort on it; devoting yourself selflessly to your acting of Falstaff, so that without dissipating energies we could deliver one slap-up production instead of two shaky ones? It is quite enough to hold Belfast for one week and the Gaiety for three weeks.' Welles must have accepted this advice, for *Chimes* was in fact rehearsed singly in London to open in Belfast and move to Dublin, where *Twelfth Night* supposedly would go into rehearsal.

Hilton Edwards must have gone to London to make arrangements for *Chimes*, for when MacLíammóir telephoned Terence de Vere White very late one night there was no one else at Harcourt Terrace. MacLíammóir said that something 'terrifying' had happened, and begged him to come round at once. He and his wife decided that they should both go. They found Micheál in bed, in a distraught condition. He said he had just received a call from Orson on the subject of casting, and discovered that he was expected to play Henry IV rather than what he had assumed all along – Henry V, or Prince Hal as he would be known in this version. He was completely astounded by Orson's 'insensitivity', and also because the 'world' would 'expect' him to appear as Prince Hal. (The world would certainly not have expected anything of the kind: Prince Hal was a teenager.) To compound the insult, Orson had then offered him a choice between Henry IV and the Chorus. The de Vere Whites reasoned with him as gently as they could – Henry IV was a very good part, he would make a fine figure in it, there were excellent speeches for the Chorus too; but MacLíammóir felt betrayed, and was inconsolable.

Rehearsals opened in London in early February – but without MacLíammóir as either of the Henrys, or the Chorus. The rising English star, Keith Baxter, was cast as Prince Hal, and, as he had done so often in crises at the Gate, Reginald Jarman 'took over' – this time as Henry IV. Hilton Edwards was not billed as director, though he undertook everything a director would normally do: 'The play staged by Hilton Edwards' was equivocally printed in the programme.

Many of the members of the cast were young, untried English players, to whom Welles had taken a liking at audition; fearing a weak cast, and feeling that Baxter and Jarman were the only ones he could rely on at the outset, Edwards insisted that Patrick Bedford be engaged from Dublin for Poins. The highly experienced stage director, Alastair Davidson, later said he had never worked in so disorganised a group; he believed Welles to be a genius, and continued to believe it, but found him lazy and capricious as well. Davidson and Edwards attempted to keep the rehearsals going, for Welles did not always make an appearance. A number of people had been engaged to design and build the sets and costumes, but when Welles found that the results did not appeal to him, he designed alternatives himself, as he had threatened to do six months before. Davidson recalled that Welles' designs were 'marvellous – once he had got them down on paper'; but they were late, and in the ensuing rush were skimped in execution.

The company moved to Belfast on Sunday, 21 February 1960, for an opening on Tuesday 24. The whole of Monday morning and afternoon was taken up with technical rehearsal, and the dress rehearsal lasted for twelve hours, with Welles on the stage constantly suggesting brilliant changes to Edwards, who was shouting and spluttering from the stalls. MacLíammóir arrived from Dublin and crept into a dark corner of the dress circle, occasionally emerging to mutter comments into Edwards' ear. He refused to speak to Welles, and remained in the background, dressed in black, throughout the run of the play.

On the opening night, Orson Welles was not sure of all his lines, but the company rose to him and helped him out, in the way that even the most misused actors invariably do at such times, and he created a forceful impression through sheer power of personality. A local correspondent for The Times said he was 'a wonderful Falstaff, not only physically but temperamentally'; Keith Baxter as Prince Hal was 'a gay-spirited, carefree young man until he donned the crown and then showed how suited he was to wear it'; and Reginald Jarman 'brought pathos and nobility to the old king'. Others were less impressed. One thought that Welles, in his padded suit, looked like 'the Michelin man'. In Dublin, press and public were even cooler, for the concept seemed to be too much of a hotch-potch. Rehearsals then began for *Twelfth Night*, but members of the company felt this was more to show Louis Elliman that the contract was being adhered to than from any real desire on Welles' part to continue with the venture.

After two weeks, Orson Welles decided to withdraw some performances of *Chimes at Midnight*, and on alternate nights he gave a one-man show of his own, with excerpts from *Moby Dick* (which he had presented in London the previous year) and readings from Shakespeare, Synge and others. The members of the company were not told about the change of programme, and had to rely on the daily papers for information as to what they were expected to perform each night. When it was confirmed that an initially interested West End management had decided not to transfer the production, Welles cancelled all further plans with Elliman and de Blieck, and left for London, whence he had received an invitation to direct Sir Laurence Olivier in *Rhinoceros*. He gave his reason for the failure of *Chimes at Midnight* in Dublin to inadvertent remarks of his wife's about 'the dirty Irish', made within earshot of a journalist, who had printed the story. Hilton Edwards had arranged for the Welles' to stay at Sir Basil Goulding's Dargle Cottage in County Wicklow; when they arrived, she alleged that she had found the chamber-pots had not been emptied, and so they fled to a hotel. As a result of his wife's reported description of this embarrassing incident, Welles stated, the population of Dublin had decided to stay away from his show!

Less than a year after their falling-out, Welles approached MacLíammóir about appearing with him in *The Duchess of Malfi* – the production never in fact took place – but MacLíammóir wrote, declining. 'Please don't be cross with me, Orson, about my refusal. The fact that Hilton and I are so proud to associate your name with ours should prove to you, if you need proof, that I am as anxious as you for the play to be a success . . . ' He could not forbear to advert to *Chimes at Midnight*; he had, it appears, been gravely disappointed that on refusing to play Henry IV, Welles had not pressed him to change his mind. 'If *you* believed my playing the King would have helped, you'd have got me to do it from the start . . . No, don't be cross with me. It will only necessitate a reconciliation scene in about ten years' time, and then I shall be far too feeble to play it.'

The reconciliation scene did not take place in ten years' time; probably it never did, though they met again in the 1970s, when Welles was making a documentary about the shooting of *Othello*. Ten years later precisely, MacLíammóir stated in a letter to Peter Bogdanovich that the fact that he and Orson were not on speaking terms was, 'alas, no Renoir illusion, but, as I said in my last letter, I still love him and hope that one day maybe, tra-la, tra-la, tra-la . . . ' In ten years' time Welles was a fading film star, and MacLíammóir was acclaimed as one of the greatest stage figures of the day. His sudden rise to real international fame came so soon after the *Chimes at Midnight* disappointment that it looked as if the gods had decided to take pity on the emotional and professional tribulations of both MacLíammóir and Edwards, and allow them a fruitful period of respite and recognition. This being the case, the gods sent, as they invariably do, a divine intermediary; and the intermediary took the form of the ample shade of Oscar Fingal O'Flaherty Wills Wilde.

Chapter 15

The Importance of Being Hilton and Micheál

After the Orson Welles season of 1960 at the Gaiety Theatre, a coolness developed between Edwards-MacLíammóir Productions and Louis Elliman. Elliman may have felt that Hilton Edwards should have warned him when the arrangements were not going well, for a play with such a star ought to have been highly popular. Edwards may have felt guilty at not having kept Elliman in the picture. When the autumn season to coincide with the Dublin Theatre Festival came up for discussion, Elliman delegated the matter to his house manager, who confirmed dates which were not those which Edwards recalled having agreed. Edwards wrote intemperately to Elliman on 30 August, complaining of being 'let down'; this was followed immediately by a letter from MacLíammóir, enquiring 'what compensation you would be prepared to offer us for what appears to me to be [our] breath-taking elasticity and willingness to be pulled and pushed hither and thither?'

Edwards-MacLíammóir had proposed *God's Gentry* and *The Informer*, hoping to get two weeks out of the one and three out of the other, and they also spoke of an untitled new play which could be rehearsed in time to fill the fifth week, should it be decided that two weeks each was enough for the revivals; but Elliman was now prepared to back a four-week season only, and *The Informer* was out of the question because of the cost. The mysterious new play was not mentioned again, and may not even have existed. Thus the partners were left with a space to fill, and they seemed bereft of ideas. Furthermore, the festival committee was far from enthusiastic about the inclusion of any revivals in its programme.

'That *lunatic* wants to do that boring old play *Berkeley Square*!', Edwards complained to Patrick McLarnon one afternoon at Harcourt Terrace. The lunatic was not Elliman, but MacLíammóir, who was casting his eyes up to heaven with a martyred look. The latest foreign play guides were examined – nobody seemed to be writing anything interesting. Whatever they chose, it must have a small cast; a one-person show would be ideal, McLarnon suggested, knowing that MacLíammóir was an admirer of Ruth Draper; but it was so much easier for a woman, MacLíammóir said, to transform herself from character to character with the help of a shawl or a lace veil or a quick pinning up or letting down of the hair; changes of moustaches and beards took time, and there was something ludicrous about a series of bowler hats, toppers and trilbys; in any case, *Six Characters in Search of a Porter*, short as it was, had seemed too long for some observers in *Gateway to Gaiety*. Emlyn Williams as Charles Dickens had proved immensely popular all over the world; when he was performing at the Olympia Theatre, Edwards and MacLíammóir had sat in on the dress rehearsal of his new Dylan Thomas programme, and had been much impressed. Perhaps something on the same lines could be devised. But what?

McLarnon and MacLíammóir went out into the garden, and sat below the window of the room in which Edwards was working. The subject should be Irish, of course. McLarnon suggested Yeats: wasn't it obvious? Too obvious. Shaw? Lacking in charisma and mystery. Wilde? That seemed more likely. As a child, MacLíammóir had instinctively recognised a sympathetic voice in *The Happy Prince and Other Tales*; he had been given an edition illustrated by Arthur Rackham, while on tour in *Peter Pan*, and had pored over it in countless railway-carriages and hotel rooms; he had even shed tears when the swallow had plucked out the sapphires which were the prince's eyes so that the poor people might have bread. The fusion of quasi-religious introspection with sharply ironic comment had appealed at once. Later, when he came to follow its development into the covertly erotic, over-cultivated half-world of *Dorian Gray*, he was in a position to transform a sensual work of prose fiction into an equally sensual and highly entertaining stage piece. *Salomé*, significantly, had been one of the five plays chosen for the Gate Theatre Studio's inaugural season in 1928 – and they had produced all of Wilde's society comedies (except *A Woman of No Importance*, which MacLíammóir thought was no better than *East Lynne* with a handful of epigrams from *The Picture of Dorian Gray* thrown in). And once, at the age of thirteen, when taken out to lunch by friends during the run of *Joseph and his Brethren* and introduced to some people at another table, one of whom was Lord Alfred Douglas, Alfred Willmore had innocently enquired, 'You knew Oscar Wilde, didn't you?' – causing a startled silence followed by eager and animated conversation on every other topic imaginable.

'Patti-Pans', Micheál called up to Hilton's study window, using McLarnon's nickname, 'Patti-Pans has had a brilliant idea for a show on Oscar Wilde!'

'Fine!', shouted Hilton. 'Then fucking well get on with it!'

*

In 1945 Hilton Edwards had suggested the adaptation of *Dorian Gray*, and had helped to put it into a dramatic structure. He had also been a very stern critic of all MacLíammóir's original plays in English, flashing the editorial blue-pencil when literature threatened to overpower theatre. 'One of these days you'll die of a surfeit of words,' he said, 'and from that point of view Wilde's the worst person you could be working on. Oscar is at his weakest when he uses too many, and at his best when a line comes out like a pistol-shot.' MacLíammóir remembered that Peter Ashmore, the director of *Hedda Gabler*, had said to him across a lunch-table in Amsterdam that he ought to think about impersonating Wilde in his three phases – the aesthete with the sunflower, the successful playwright in white tie and tails, wearing a green carnation, and the convict in the arrowed suit; and when the import of that informal chat came back to him, he mentioned it to Edwards.

Edwards did not take to it at all. He thought there should be no attempt at portraying Wilde in the way Emlyn Williams had portrayed Dickens, by disguising himself in facsimile costume and makeup. It should be Micheál MacLíammóir talking *about* Wilde, not *being* Wilde; recreating the personality, the creative artist, and the era (which Wilde was said to have invented) by means of a judicious blend of description and quotation. The highly dramatised storytelling of the Irish *seanchaí* might serve as model: not exactly acting, but certainly a performance.

MacLíammóir read all the works of Wilde and all the contemporary memoirs. A script emerged, in two parts, not three. The trial, its barbed *ripostes* and *bon mots* already pillaged by dozens of writers of screen and stage biographies, was deftly placed during the interval, referred to before and after, but not directly quoted. By a curious coincidence, a few weeks before he was due to start rehearsal on his own script, MacLíammóir was cast as Wilde in an ITV reconstruction of the trial, with André Morell as the prosecuting counsel, Lord Carson. The Daily Telegraph said that he was 'physically much nearer the part than Robert Morley or Peter Finch in the film versions', and that he 'gave a very convincing performance'; but this did not cause him, or Edwards, to alter their position on the theatrical undesirability of impersonation.

Patrick McLarnon was present all the time as uncredited artistic adviser. He thought it essential that there should be very little furniture, only three pieces, in fact – a *chaise longue* covered in sulphur-yellow, a table, and a chair; in the background a pedestal with a huge urn full of waxen lilies, which became autumnal leaves for the second half of the programme. Molly MacEwen designed an elaborate octagonal stage cloth in violet and gold. (Later, a carpet to the same design was woven in Donegal.) All agreed that there should be no suggestion of a room; Edwards later described the setting as 'a moonlit space surrounding the gold lamplight; a setting utterly simple and at the same time sybaritic but which commits the action to no definite locality.' He felt that something more was necessary than for the actor, 'just because he was alone, to stand or sit upon the stage or to wander as the spirit moved him. A plan of movement must be designed that would have a purpose and significance, that would defeat monotony, and be both pleasing and effective.' The techniques of the modern stage supported the notion of the storyteller stepping in and out of the picture as occasion demanded, and gave whatever emphasis was needed to point the notion that this was to be a theatrical manifestation, not an illustrated lecture.

As the time for production approached, Louis Elliman consented to a revival of *God's Gentry*, in spite of the large cast, setting it against the comparatively low budget needed for *The Green Carnation* – if that was what this new one-man show was to be called. It would run for one week, and *God's Gentry* would follow for three, with Patrick Bedford in MacLíammóir's former part, and a strengthening of the cast, achieved by the replacement of some of the original players by Maureen Potter, Danny Cummins, Christopher Casson and Milo O'Shea. On 9 September, in very different vein from his previous letter in which he had almost accused Elliman of duplicity, Edwards wrote, 'A nice letter this time – first, thank you for your generous attitude. Micheál and I accept the arrangement you have suggested, with many thanks – Micheál to play Gaiety Mon. Oct. 3rd to Sat. 8th at 50%. We to supply all seen and heard, with exception of black and gold curtains and stage cloth . . . ' The dates for music rehearsals for *God's Gentry* were then given, followed by dates for full cast rehearsals, and confirmation of Edwards' direction fee of £200 plus one and a half per cent. (His fee for the Wilde production is not mentioned, but presumably was the same.)

Edwards also wrote to the London producers, Oscar Lewenstein and Hugh Beaumont, inviting them to see *God's Gentry*, with a view to a possible transfer. He did not mention the Wilde evening, which was not the priority of the moment; neither he nor MacLíammóir had any great hopes for it, though both felt it would fill the week in the Gaiety quite adequately. Thought was given to a title. *From Merrion Square to Reading Gaol* was abandoned at an early stage; *Rise and Fall of an Aesthete* seemed singularly uninviting; *The Green Carnation* was most acceptable to the Gaiety, until MacLíammóir started making permutations of titles which included one of Wilde's favourite words, importance; *The Importance of Being Wilde* was then selected, though Edwards said there was something wrong with the rhythm. It should end with a spondee: it should be Oscar.

Very little of Wilde's Dublin background was used in the text. The first part of the programme, which was called *The Happy Prince and the Green Carnation*, dealt largely with the London years, the American tour, and the theatrical productions; the principal excerpts were from fugitive early poems, *The Picture of Dorian Gray*, *An Ideal Husband* and *The Importance of Being Earnest*. The second part was entitled *De Profundis*. This posed difficulties. There was a danger of sentimentality, even morbidity. MacLíammóir's linking script, sparkling with extrovert wit and packed with ironic asides, would, it was hoped, lighten the load of self-pity which was bound to give a sombre colour to the selections from letters, and to the centrepiece of the hour, *The Ballad of Reading Gaol*. Throughout the three weeks of rehearsal in late September and early October, the second part was the anxiety which would remain until the presence of an audience banished it, or otherwise. With that in mind,

MacLíammóir, who confessed to being close to panic, decided that he would have to try out the performance somewhere else, far from Dublin, and in a place from which no word of the result would reach the press.

A convent was suggested – quite seriously, for anyone who had toured with the McMaster company knew what an appreciative audience was to be found at special matinées in convent boarding-schools; but perhaps such an audience would be over-appreciative. Jack Dunne, MacLíammóir's lawyer friend in Kildare, suggested the nearby army headquarters at the Curragh, where there was a lively amateur theatre group which might organise an evening. He contacted its producer, Captain Pádraig O Cearbhail – who turned out to be the same Pádraig O Cearbhail who had played the part of Diarmuid when MacLíammóir had directed *Diarmuid agus Gráinne* at the Taibhdheardhc seven years before. Contrary to what MacLíammóir expected, the army personnel, their wives, and residents of the neighbourhood besieged Captain O Cearbhail for tickets, once the word spread. MacLíammóir later described the evening as 'a real *première*'; the dreaded second half of the programme had gone as well as the predictably easy first, and many members of the audience at the reception in MacDonagh Barracks – named after the father of the author of *God's Gentry* – told him how much it had moved them. Yet he knew that the professional first night could be quite a different matter. Edwards was now rehearsing *God's Gentry* simultaneously with *The Importance of Being Oscar*, and it was not going well. This was ascribed to difficulties of integration between the styles of 'legit' and 'variety' performers, but he knew it was not that; the play was proving too intimate in scale to transfer from the Gate to the Gaiety, even when dressed up with choreographic and electronic effects. *Oscar* rehearsals were now not much more than repetitions. Brian Tobin, an airline employee who had earlier confessed much admiration for MacLíammóir when selling him a ticket to London, was recruited to hear his lines.

The Importance of Being Oscar opened on Monday, 3 October, to a very warm response. All the reviews next day were more than favourable. The booking was not good for the second night, but it improved so much on the third that Louis Elliman, in response to a heartfelt plea from Hilton Edwards – who said that *God's Gentry* could open the following Monday but would be a mess if it did – agreed to add an extra two nights of Wilde, and postpone MacDonagh until the Wednesday. It was announced that 'the enormous success of Micheál MacLíammóir's one-man show' was responsible for this change in dates. It was promotional hyperbole – but *The Importance of Being Oscar* was already a much greater success than anyone had anticipated.

Ulick O'Connor attended the opening as reviewer for The Times. Fourteen minutes after the curtain came down he telephoned his copy to London from a pay-phone in the Royal College of Surgeons (where his father was a professor) round the corner from the Gaiety; it was just in time for Tuesday's city edition, and it was read by Rachel Kempson and her husband Michael Redgrave. On

Wednesday MacLíammóir lunched with O'Connor, and was able to tell him that Redgrave had telephoned from London and had read out the review; so impressed did he seem, that he was going to fly over and see the performance, with a view to bringing it to the West End in partnership with his friend, the impresario Fred Sadoff. O'Connor was able to chide MacLíammóir on what he had said in Edinburgh about not being known outside Ireland: if he was not, he soon would be.

THEY ARE CHEERING STILL

God's Gentry played out its three weeks (less the two nights extracted for *Oscar*); the box-office fell from £929.19.0d in the first to £383.10.0d in the third. It had been an expensive show, and there was much sighing of the if-only-we'd-known variety, when it became obvious that *Oscar* could have played for the whole month. All thoughts of trying to find a home for it elsewhere were dropped, and attention given to this bouncing newcomer. Hilton Edwards was not present for the closing night of *God's Gentry*, for he was in London preparing for Monday's opening at the Apollo Theatre on Shaftesbury Avenue; in the astonishingly short space of three weeks, Redgrave and Sadoff had organised a full-scale West End première. Brendan Neilan, an insurance official with a taste for theatre and music, who had given much of his time helping at the Harcourt Terrace office during the post-Egyptian financial crisis, was among the Dublin *entourage* of well-wishers who travelled to London that weekend. He gave a pre-opening party for several of Micheál MacLíammóir's closest friends in a restaurant in St James' Street on the Sunday night – Sally Travers, Marjorie Hawtrey, Patrick Bedford, Hilton Edwards – and Brian Tobin, who resigned his position with Aer Lingus to manage the English tour and whatever (if anything) came after it. MacLíammóir said during the dinner that the house in which *The Importance of Being Earnest* had been written was only five doors from where they were sitting – a *pied à terre* where the dramatist was known to receive dubious visitors, one of them the pimp, Jack Taylor, during the afternoons. Was this a good or a bad omen? they all wondered.

'It is a success!', MacLíammóir wrote from the Curzon Hotel to Molly MacEwen in Edinburgh the following Saturday. 'Better, God knows, than a flop, which I more than half expected. The only advantage being that in the latter one is left a little peace. Any measure at all of success in this sweet old-world Tudor village on the Thames means telephone ringing *without any pause ever*, unknown yapping voices screaming 'Marvellous!' Invitations to every known and unknown form of asphyxiating boudoir ever invented by human society, roughly one appearance per day at Shepherd's Bush to say, smile and simper something at TV or on radio; dressing-room nightly crowded with from anything between 16 and 60 people all loudly shrieking so that by the time you *do* emerge every restaurant in this World Capital is shut up. Now don't think I'm ungrateful, dear, of course it's all Absolute Heaven!'

The Irish Ambassador, Mr Hugh McCann, attended the opening at the Apollo; so did the Redgraves, Noël Coward (who said he liked 'the prose bits', meaning MacLíammóir's commentary), Shelah Richards, Margaret Leighton, Anna Neagle, Herbert Wilcox, and Oscar Wilde's son, Vyvyan Holland, who was seventy-four and came back-stage to say that he had been 'deeply moved'. The whole battery of West End critics was there too. MacLíammóir had been warned about the 'withering satire' of Bernard Levin, then writing for the Daily Express, but Levin was not in satiric mood that evening. 'Across the years,' he wrote next day, 'MacLíammóir has joined hands with his great countryman and laid a beautiful flower on his tragic grave. As I left they were just starting to cheer. I dare say they are cheering still.'

Usually, any run-of-the-mill production will provoke at least one maverick rave review, which can be quoted in letters six feet tall on the billboards, just as a theatrical triumph invariably inspires one single critic to denounce it as the worst thing ever seen – the law of averages compensates for both of these extremes. With *The Importance of Being Oscar* in London, however, there was not a single unwelcoming paragraph. 'The lion of the Dublin theatre once again asserted his supremacy,' said Charles Marowitz a trifle ambiguously (who was the lion?) in The Observer; 'Using his mellifluous voice like a startled organ, MacLíammóir carries us soaring through the rarified heights and the soul-searching depths of Wilde's career,' Milton Schulman declared in the Evening Standard; 'To try and catch Ireland's best actor in a few hundred words is as impossible as painting him head and shoulders on the back of a postage stamp,' wrote Harold Hobson in the Sunday Times. (A reader subsequently sent MacLíammóir a passable likeness on the back of an Irish stamp.)

The Apollo season was billed 'for two weeks only', and, seizing the opportunity arising from so much favourable press coverage, Redgrave and Sadoff booked a short tour to whatever first-run theatres could offer a week each before Christmas. Emlyn Williams came to see the performance before it closed in London, and offered some suggestions for cuts in the text, which, as probably the most seasoned one-man-show artist in Britain, he had every reason to believe would be needed outside London. English provincial audiences had the reputation, he said, for waxing uneasy about anything which might, in their view, be described as 'long-haired'. MacLíammóir, urged by Edwards, accepted these cuts with a good grace, and had reason to be glad of them. (How different, he thought, from the provincial audiences in Ireland, where the longest-haired literary effusions, lasting late into the night, held everybody spellbound.) Having recorded a programme as 'Guest of the Week' on BBC Woman's Hour, he, Brian Tobin, and the company manager, Hugh Metcalf, set off for Southsea, Glasgow, Brighton and Oxford.

In Oxford, MacLíammóir found the audiences as acute and responsive as those in Dublin and London – and far more responsive, in the course of time, than in dozens of other much larger cities from New Zealand to New Mexico.

He was taken to visit Oscar Wilde's rooms at Magdalen, and saw the little drawings which Wilde had engraved with a diamond on the window-panes, at the age of nineteen. Enid Starkie, the intellectual sister of the Dublin author, Walter Starkie, gave a post-performance party. She had written her memoirs, much to the displeasure of her Dublin relatives, and had championed the election of W.H. Auden to the Oxford professorship of Poetry. The dons to whom MacLíammóir was introduced – and who, an hour before, had watched him moving gracefully among the arum lilies and bronze foliage on the Playhouse stage – found that he was as capable of scholarly analytical dissertation over the port and nuts, as he was of presenting a remarkably vivid theatrical image.

*

There was a pantomime at the Gaiety Theatre that Christmas, but MacLíammóir was not available to play in it, and Edwards was not invited to direct. This time, Jimmy O'Dea and Maureen Potter were spared the artificially inspired transplantation from a different culture into their own well-tried and better-understood medium. It was Christmas again with the McMasters, now living in a trim early-Victorian stucco house on the seafront at Sandymount, where the tide came in over the strand at the spot where Stephen Dedalus had watched Gertie McDowell and the fireworks exploding over the Star of the Sea church, and where Mac could take his year-round daily swim. The last nights of 1960 were spent in Limerick, where the indefatigable Mary Hanley, wife of a well-known pharmacist, who still lived 'over the shop' in a handsome eighteenth-century house in O'Connell Street, organised three performances of *The Importance of Being Oscar* at Amharchlann na Féile, the old Coliseum cinema now reconverted to theatrical use.

Mary Hanley was also the guiding force behind the acquisition and restoration of the tower at Ballylee, in which the poet Yeats had spent his summers in the 1920s. She drove MacLíammóir into county Galway to see it, and he regaled her with the recitation of poems from *The Tower* and *The Winding Stair*, which he knew by heart, as they travelled through the country of 'cold Clare rock/And Galway rock and thorn'. He found the Limerick audiences as stimulating as those in Oxford (had he forgotten that rain-sodden season four years previously, *en route* for Cairo, when the people of Limerick simply did not want to know that the Gate Theatre was in town?) and thought it incredible, remembering the differences in history and traditions of the two places, that the 'battle-worn, impoverished grey city on the Shannon' should respond to the sophistries of Oscar Wilde with such understanding and amusement. There was much to be said for success abroad – and Limerick was the first place in Ireland, outside Dublin, to respond to that success.

Redgrave and Sadoff decided that London could take a great deal more of this mixture of *fin-de-siècle* decadence and hedonism, as seen from the indulgent viewpoint of an articulate mid twentieth-century apologist, and accordingly made an arrangement with the English Stage Company at the Royal Court Theatre, for four weeks from 23 January 1961, to follow a new play by Shelagh Delaney, *The Lion in Love*. (Curiously enough, Micheál MacLíammóir had written admiringly of her first play, *A Taste of Honey*, in The Observer – and also of the author, whom he described as 'the psychic daughter of Maxim Gorki and Daisy Ashford'.) The English Stage Company under George Devine (a colleague from the *Hedda Gabler* cast) had been largely responsible for encouraging the shift in social emphasis among English playwrights from that of the established classes to the milieu of the more socially deprived or disregarded. The 1956 production of John Osborne's *Look Back in Anger* (in which the Gate's Helena Hughes played Helena Charles, and Kenneth Haigh, who had been a member of McMaster's company, was cast as Jimmy Porter, the prototype 'angry young man') had been staged here. Hilton Edwards was dubious about the Royal Court being the right venue for Oscar Wilde, but the apparent incongruity disturbed nobody. Indeed, MacLíammóir shortly received an invitation from Tony Richardson to play the part of the 'indolent, cultured, intelligent, extremely restless' Pope Leo X in Osborne's latest play, *Luther*, with Albert Finney, which, had he been able to accept, would have placed him very much in the same position as Laurence Olivier, who had just appeared as Archie Rice in Osborne's *The Entertainer*.

He was not, however, in a position to accept, for the American impresario Sol Hurok came to the Royal Court, and agreed with Redgrave and Sadoff that New York should be allowed the opportunity of seeing *Oscar*, if possible as soon as March. MacLíammóir wrote to Denis and Betty Johnston in Mount Holyoke, Massachusetts: 'I am supposed to be coming to New York in the spring, but the date is still uncertain as everybody quarrels incessantly about money. I don't mean H. and I – we, as you know, have other sources for such diversion. . . . My movements are so unsettled as to be unsatisfactory to the point of making H. urge me to change my agents, who are MCA, and the company that is presenting me is Michael Redgrave and his friend Fred Sadoff, known to the world as F.E.S. Plays Ltd. It seems I have signed some sort of optional thing with them for two years, and I am supposed to be doing (a) a month in London . . . , (b) a short season in New York . . . , (c) a cosy trip to South Africa . . . , (d) Brussels, Paris and possibly Berlin on my return to Europe, then a horrifying rumour that I have to go to Australia for part of the summer, and finally, if the New York tryout is proved a success, a coast-to-coast season for That Divine Fall . . . '

While this was being planned, some further dates were organised for the south of England. Brian Tobin had the dual function of overseeing what happened both backstage and front-of-house in each unfamiliar theatre, a task which MacLíammóir felt was quite impossible for one person, for there were certain times in the evening when local dignitaries had to be welcomed or plied with refreshments, and these naturally coincided with the most critical moments in dressing-room or wings; nor could anyone without the appropriate technical training be expected to explain Edwards' lighting-plot to the resident electrician. This was not an issue in most of the English theatres, but it was to become a matter of contention in many concert-halls, where the idea of lighting changes, let alone a special lighting rig, was met with expressions of disbelief.

The need for Tobin's all-embracing managerial duties, which extended from the box-office to the prompt-corner, was explained as salary-saving, and was accepted, for the time being, as such. What was not so easily accepted by touring managements anywhere was MacLíammóir's insistence on a travelling dresser. How could such a person be needed, he would be asked, when all he, the artist, wore was a dinner-jacket with the usual accoutrements? Actually (he had to explain) he had six evening suits, for he wore two each night, while two were generally out being pressed and cleaned and two kept in readiness for emergency. There were two shirts every night to be laundered. There was the packing and transporting of these, as well as the suits the artist wore for afternoon or evening receptions in town halls and mayors' parlours. There was also the need for a person who would keep the well-wishers at bay while the artist changed and showered after the show – and the need for someone to collect and sort the stage-door messages and mail. Where had these modern managements been brought up, MacLíammóir found it necessary to ask. Had they never been out on tour? Did they not know what it was like to be on the road with a thousand people waiting to be entertained for two and a half hours each night, with matinées on Wednesdays and Saturdays? How would they feel, if it was found on arrival at Leamington Spa that six pairs of trousers had been left behind in Tunbridge Wells?

He was granted his dresser, but the same monologue had to be repeated many times during the next dozen years, and almost in as many languages. For the moment, all was well. Edwards returned to Dublin, intent on making plans for further play productions – for neither he nor MacLíammóir was convinced that the success of *The Importance of Being Oscar* was anything more than temporary, and the thought of other one-person shows had not occurred to them; they would probably soon be back to the routine of the past decade in 'pulling the devil by the tail' to keep their professional careers on the move. Louis Elliman was talking of Brecht's *St Joan of the Stockyards*, and there was also strong talk of Radio Eireann inaugurating a television service, for which, presumably, dramatic material would be needed.

He had been home for only a few days when an event occurred which threw the partners, and the whole Dublin theatre community, into disarray. On the evening of 2 February 1961, Christine Longford was expecting Edward to return for dinner from a church meeting in County Kildare. Glancing out of the window, she noticed the car turning in the gate of Grosvenor Park, and then taking an erratic course across a flowerbed on to the lawn, where it stopped. She rushed out and found Edward fainting at the wheel. Helped by the cook, she dragged him into the house – a remarkable feat: he weighed sixteen stone – and called the doctor. He was immediately taken to Portobello Nursing Home, where, in a stately high-ceilinged room, looking out over the Grand Canal toward the Dublin Mountains, he died two days later of a massive stroke. Many people wondered how, with his gargantuan build and style of living, he had been spared for fifty-eight years. Micheál MacLíammóir, who flew from London to attend the funeral at Mount Jermone, said to Ulick O'Connor, 'The death of an enemy seems more distressing than the death of a friend.'

Anew McMaster, who opened at the Gate the following week, in his own production of the inappropriately-titled *When We Dead Awaken*, paid tribute to the Earl of Longford from the stage, praising his perserverance in touring to the small towns. Christine quickly made it known that she would continue to pay the salaries of the members of Longford Productions; but most of the players, among them Iris Lawler and Aiden Grennell, knowing that the money would come from her own meagre purse, felt they could not accept. The critic, Seamus Kelly, always one of the Gate's foremost supporters, wrote in The Irish Times that perhaps the nation – meaning the government – might think fit to make the Gate its memorial to a good Irishman. The nation, however, had no such frivolous intention, and it would take almost a decade of memoranda and deputations before the theatre was finally given that full recognition for which both the Longford and the Edwards-MacLíammóir companies had pressed, and which their audiences clearly believed was their due. For the present, there was a dismal rumour that the Gate might close forever.

Hilton Edwards wrote for advice to Terence de Vere White, two days after Edward Longford's funeral. He said that the press had been enquiring about the future of the theatre. He wondered if the majority of the shares in the holding company, of which Lord Longford had been chairman, would go to his brother Frank, and if Frank – the seventh Earl – would pass them and the house and lands at Tullynally to his son Thomas. He was anxious about the street collection which the Longfords had organised: where was it? and how much was it? Journalists were speculating about a figure of £4,000. Who would be the new chairman? Was there, indeed, a future for the Gate? 'Please, dear Terence, with your wisdom guide us.'

Hilton was in a state of frenzy. He had just completed a deal with Louis Elliman for a two-week revival of *The Importance of Being Oscar* at the Gaiety and he wanted to be on hand to supervise the production and set the lighting. Then he had to go to Limerick for a fortnight to adjudicate at the amateur drama festival at Amharchlann na Féile. After this, there would probably be only two days before leaving for New York, where *Oscar* was definitely due to have its first American showing on 14 March. Then there was the business about the new national television service, and an approach which had been made to him about the possibility of his becoming its first Head of Drama.

Had Hilton Edwards been provided with the gifts of the seer, he would have understood that, even if there were no future for the Gate, his own future had never been more secure financially. There would be regular royalty payments from *Oscar* over the next fifteen years. He would be offered and would accept an executive position in broadcasting. Other stage productions of an international significance now undreamt of would come his way. But, as MacLíammóir said, his middle name was Cassandra; and as Brian Tobin remarked more colloquially, Hilton was 'fit to be tied'. In Limerick, he was distracted by the noise: the whole hotel seemed to be in the process of being rebuilt around him. His hosts arranged for him to move to a quiet inn in the village of Adare, where he was unlikely to be disturbed, and where he was also unable to disturb them.

Terence de Vere White had no legal authority to enquire into the terms of Lord Longford's will, but as a friend of the theatre and a friend of Christine, he called on her at Grosvenor Park. He found her, as he wrote to Micheál, 'in a kind and good frame of mind'. She was quite determined that the Gate should continue and could not agree that there might be no future for Edwards-MacLíammóir Productions there. She told him that her brother-in-law Frank had already spoken to the Taoiseach, Seán Lemass, about a subsidy – Frank favoured Fíanna Fáil as the more dynamic party in Irish politics, where Edward had always supported Fine Gael, and Fíanna Fáil was now in power. She also mentioned that her husband had been exempted from surtax and income tax because of his theatrical losses, a fact which was not generally known – 'so his enterprise was not as philanthropic as all that'. Edward, she confirmed, had left his interest in the theatre to her, and she wished to put it to what she saw as its best use, which was to attempt to return to the precepts of the early 1930s. De Vere White advised that she would welcome the opportunity of joining the board, and that it would be in the interests of everybody if she were also asked to become chairman.

As usual, Terence de Vere White was acting as mediator. To him, more than to anyone else, was due the credit for healing the wounds caused by the Longford split. When the board met on 2 March, a month after Lord Longford's death, Hilton Edwards and Madame Bannard Cogley signed a declaration appointing Christine, Countess of Longford, a Life Director of the Company. She was then invited to take her place on the board, and having assented, was asked to take the chair. Hilton Edwards paid tribute to Lord Longford's work, and a vote of sympathy was passed. He then invited her to become a Director of Dublin Gate Theatre Productions (Edwards-MacLíammóir) Ltd, to which she agreed 'with pleasure'. The last motion was of an unprecedented nature, for it formally terminated the animosities of the past quarter-century. A press-release was issued stating that the Gate would remain open, and that Christine Longford would become its manager, as well as its chairman.

Hilton Edwards hurried back to Limerick, from where he was constantly on the telephone to Hurok in New York, MacLíammóir (now back in Dublin),

Redgrave and Sadoff in London (for they had agreed to act as associate producers of *Oscar*) and to Edward J. Roth, the new Director General of Radio Eireann, which was about to be designated Radio Eireann-Telefís Eireann. Then he and MacLíammóir flew to New York together, where on March 14 *The Importance of Being Oscar* opened to good reviews but, it appeared, a disappointing advance sale. He returned to Dublin, remarking that the New York audiences were 'slower', but that Micheál had been cheered as he entered Sardi's after the Lyceum opening, for several excellent reviews had come out a few minutes before their arrival. Then he started on detailed discussions with Ed Roth.

THE IMPORTANCE OF BEING HILTON

The Irish broadcasting service had been in operation since 1926. It was established directly under the control of the Department for Posts and Telegraphs, a situation which resulted in bureaucratic procedures and a cautious attitude towards news and current affairs. Many of its entertainment programmes were sponsored by firms which had almost complete control of content, the standard of which was often very low indeed. During the term of office of the Fíanna Fáil minister, Erskine Childers, earlier Broadcasting Acts were reviewed, and in 1960 an independent Authority was appointed under the Chairmanship of Eamonn Andrews, an Irish broadcaster of considerable international experience, who was very much in tune with the Ireland which was emerging under the more outward-looking leadership of Seán Lemass. Andrews also had commercial interests in radio, and film studios in Dublin. The Broadcasting Authority was given the task of inaugurating a television service, for those who owned television sets could watch only the two British channels. Irish television would have to compete with the high quality programming which was entering more and more homes, as transmitters in Wales and Northern Ireland came into operation. The Authority had, therefore, to recruit most of its technical and production staff from abroad, and to train young Irish people to replace them when they had set the new station on the air.

Many valuable components were inherited from the old Radio Eireann. There were the Symphony and the Light orchestras, the Singers under their matchless director, Hans Waldemar Rosen, several producers of imagination and talent – among them the playwright and novelist, James Plunkett – and a large number of highly experienced sound operators. There was also the Radio Eireann Players, known as 'the Rep', a body of two dozen actors, many of whom had worked at the Gate and Abbey. It was generally agreed that Radio Eireann had 'an excellent reputation for sport and drama', so much so that visiting television advisers were led to believe that these were the two chief preoccupations of the Irish people. Certainly the theatrical tradition was well maintained in radio, and the Rep had gained several international awards. Anew McMaster, Hilton Edwards and Micheál MacLíammóir had appeared as guests in several of its productions.

If the chairman, Eamonn Andrews, inspired recruitment from British television, it was equally true that the newly appointed Director General, Ed Roth, looked to his own country, the United States, for senior staff. A curious situation arose when it was found that two Heads of Design, two Heads of Lighting and two Senior Cameramen had been engaged by separate talent-spotters in those countries. No such mistake was to be made in the selection of Head of Drama. Andrews suggested that Roth talk to Hilton Edwards, who was not only the most gifted director working in Ireland, but also as an Englishman of longtime residence in the island, he possessed a no-nonsense perception of Irish institutions, the Irish people, and of course the Irish theatre. Roth, over a series of lunches, propounded the idea of making drama one of the staples of programming. Edwards found his reservations about tying himself to a large state-owned organisation slowly evaporating, as they discussed writers and actors, and the possibility of selling dramatisations of Irish novels and short stories to the television channels abroad. Roth thought the station should transmit one locally produced hour-long and one half-hour play a week, at least during the winter months, and perhaps a drama serial as well. Edwards grew more enthusiastic, and said he would need a large staff to carry out such plans. Roth asked him to prepare a document for inclusion in his report to the Authority, which Edwards in due course did. There seems to have been little discussion on the matter of budget, and none on the availability of studio space.

The Harcourt Terrace circle was agog with excitement over these negotiations. Hilton expressed his anxieties and was told not to be foolish. Besides, there was the matter of salary: it was rumoured that people were being offered a thousand pounds a year for quite ordinary positions! – and of course he should have it written into his contract that he could continue to direct in the theatre, when duties permitted. The profession in Dublin was already preparing itself for television, the expectation being that there would be a great deal more work for actors.

If, as Edwards had said, the audiences in New York were 'slow' for *The Importance of Being Oscar*, he was referring to their comprehension of the material, something which the partners had noted in the past, and which MacLíammóir had on occasion undiplomatically commented upon. But why should American audiences be expected to show instantaneous *rapport* with the life and work of a long-dead Irish author and aesthete, no matter how famous, any more than they should have appreciated MacLíammóir's whimsical comedies on Irish cultural themes? MacLíammóir did feel, on occasion, when reciting Wilde's admonition to Lord Alfred Douglas about undergraduate poetry, 'I reply to you with a letter of fantastical literary conceits. I compare you to Hylas, to Hyacinth, to Jonquil, to Narcissus . . . ', that the audience might be wondering if he were referring to Woolworth's catalogues of spring bulbs. But the audiences, if 'slow', were generous with their applause; and if the houses were not large – they would comfortably have filled the Gate twice over each night, but this, as was pointed out, was the Lyceum – the press reaction gave the impression that the show was a hit; and on the strength of this, Sol Hurok offered a three-month tour for the fall.

The six-week season was short enough for MacLíammóir not to get bored, or enervated by the constant social commitments. He had time to talk to past Gate actors who had made their homes in America. Brendan and Marie Burke were his guests at Sardi's on the opening night; he met Liam Gannon, and Norman Barrs; and Treasa Curley, who had played *Gráinne* in Galway, with her husband Michael Davison; MacLíammóir uged them to 'make lots of money and come back to act in Dublin' – but Michael was soon to die tragically in an airline accident, and so he never came back. In the fullness of time Treasa and her children did; and she became a much admired producer in radio.

MacLíammóir arrived home from New York in the middle of April and a few days later Edwards informed Roth that he would accept the position of Head of Drama, under certain conditions. A fifteen-point contract was prepared. He was to be responsible for the overall day-to-day administration and operation of the television drama group, and would have responsibility with the Programme Controller for the selection and purchase of all scripts: these were the two chief requirements. He wrote to Roth on 1 May agreeing, and added that though the situation 'was hardly likely to arise, but not knowing who the Programme Controller will be, and bearing in mind that just as RE Television would have to bear the brunt of any midjudgements on the part of the Head of Drama it would seem unfair that he (the Controller) would have to accept such responsibility in matters of which he did not entirely approve'. An extra clause was then inserted stating that 'the Head of Drama shall be subject to the rulings of the Programme Controller on all matters of policy, but the TV Drama Department will not be asked to implement programmes or details thereof, of which the Head of Drama has expressed disapproval on artistic grounds'.

It was an important addition, resembling a codicil to a will, a deviously Irish one, and probably suggested by one of his friends. The appointment of Programme Controller was announced a few weeks later. The choice fell upon Michael Barry, former Head of Drama at the BBC, whom Edwards had met while working on *David Copperfield*. Having obtained Michael Barry's permission to absent himself from his new duties for a production of *St Joan of the Stockyards* at the Gaiety in September, he took up the position on 22 May at a salary of £3,000 per annum for two years, 'subject to the terms of the Broadcasting Act 1960'.

Because building was still in progress at the Montrose site, the Authority rented an office block in Clarendon Street, and this became the hub for programme planning in all departments. Clarendon Street is situated a few paces from Neary's Bar (which has a back entrance opposite the Gaiety stage door) and Bewley's Coffee House, the two best known meeting places for theatre folk in town. Neary's and Bewley's quickly became more and more popular as members of the television staff popped out to meet their friends and dilate upon that morning's issue of confidential memoranda, or to describe the arrival of the latest producer from London or New York. Clarendon Street is only ten minutes walk from Harcourt Terrace, and Hilton Edwards used to stroll across St Stephen's Green wearing a neat executive's suit, waving a cigar in greeting to his new colleagues as he entered his office on the second floor each morning at ten o'clock. It was said that he dressed for the part, and the props were supplied with the costume.

He immediately set to work engaging departmental staff. An early recruit was Carolyn Swift, who had worked in the Gate years before and had subsequently made a reputation as the writer of satirical revues at the Pike Theatre, which she had founded with her husband, Alan Simpson. Then there was Pan Collins, who had played small parts at the Gate in the early thirties and had just resigned from her job in the Sunday Press. She met Carolyn Swift to discuss her prospects over a drink, and when she heard there might be reading work in the Drama Department, she immediately telephoned Hilton Edwards who offered her a week, which then developed into two months. After this she moved to what were then called Women's Programmes, and thence to the prodigiously influential Late Late Show. She was to arrange Micheál MacLíammóir's 'surprise' seventieth birthday party on that show eight years later.

There was also Eóin Neeson, a young journalist who had published novels and poetry and was the son of Hilton and Micheál's old friends Seán and Geraldine Neeson of Cork. Hilton next engaged Brendan Neilan, who had so efficiently dealt with the Gate's financial problems from time to time, as Casting Secretary – explaining that he did not approve of the term Casting Director because he felt it undermined the position of the director of the play. Neilan was not at all sure that he was the right person for the job, and went to Micheál MacLíammóir for guidance. 'I wouldn't have let Hilton ask you if I thought you couldn't do it', was his reply. Neilan retained the post for twenty-seven years, and when he retired in 1988, it was universally agreed that he was 'irreplaceable'. Next, Brian Tobin was engaged as Script Organiser – he was to solicit plays from writers, acknowledge and catalogue them, and circulate them among the readers. He had expected to manage the forthcoming *Oscar* tours, but MacLíammóir had become tired of his company, at the same time harbouring a sense of guilt at having 'lured him away' from his secure position in Aer Lingus; and considering, no doubt, that he had a family to support. It quickly became plain to the theatre fraternity that a thoroughly Gate-orientated unit was being built up – but, had he been asked, Edwards would have declared with perfect justification that these were the best people available. There was one key figure in the Drama Department, however, who was not associated with the theatre, and that was Philip Rooney, author of the novel *Captain Boycott*. He was seconded from radio, where he had adapted dozens of works for broadcasting, and given the title Chief Script Editor. His knowledge of writing, particularly Irish writing, was prodigious. This appointment would have mollified the Personnel Department, which was accustomed to filling positions by conventional means, and was quite unused to people being hired on contract with no more than a personal recommendation.

Hilton Edwards boasted in a humorous self-deprecating way that he knew 'nothing about television'. In spite of his avowed ignorance, or more likely to prove that he really was not so ignorant at all, he wrote and spoke a great deal of eloquent nonsense, spiced with a few acute observations, when called upon to do so in the months leading up to the first transmissions. He wrote in the new broadcasting journal, the RTV Guide, that whereas in 1928 he came to Ireland confident of what he had to offer and how to offer it,

> ... I now enter a fascinating and quite terrifying new medium, fraught with technical complications. I have plenty of theories, of course, but not the practical knowledge that sustained me in my early days in the theatre in Dublin. Of course a nose as long as mine cannot keep from poking into this and that, and I have already started a quest to isolate the television germ and discover the qualities that make it essentially itself, and other than cinema and theatre . . . The ace up television's sleeve is its capacity to penetrate the sacred circle of the family hearth. Another of its strong cards is to concentrate on and to highlight details in a manner denied to the theatre and discarded by the cinema since the adoption of the wide screen. Another trump is that of catching people, as it were, on the wrong foot, letting us glimpse how they are, not how they wish us to believe them.

In this last comment he was dealing with actuality television rather than the make-believe of his own discipline, anticipating the real change which the medium would affect in the Irish Republic within a very short period. Politicians and other leaders of society had been used to broadcasting their views on radio by means of prepared statements and 'talks', or having their pronouncements simply 'reported'. The television news interview changed that very rapidly, and went a considerable distance towards banishing the obscurantism and quackery which had been a feature of public life. The disclosure by television of a number of social abuses during the ensuing decade was to topple several images of clay.

Hilton Edwards then turned to Irish television drama:

> Initially we shall have to rely on existing works of the Irish and, I hope, international theatre, until such time as Irish writers have familiarised themselves with the television medium. I am therefore searching for those plays which the alchemy of television can transmute into a different quality, and therefore give them a renewed life. It is encouraging that we are beginning to find original Irish television writers – Brian Friel, who has given us a series called *Michael Mannion – Proprietor*, of which more in good time, and Brian and Veronica Cleeve who have lately won honours in English television . . . But I am still in search of plays that are unique to television and owe nothing to stage or film.

There was a vague feeling that television was radio with pictures. It soon occurred to Edwards that he should have at least one person who had worked in the TV backroom, and he mentioned this in passing to his agents, MCA of London. A member of the MCA staff suggested one of their former employees, Adrian Vale, at that time working at Westward TV in Plymouth; and Vale was invited to Dublin for an interview. He found Hilton Edwards sitting behind a huge desk, 'looking like a City Gent or a superior Travel Agent', and was surprised when he was immediately offered the post of TV Script Editor and handed a play to read on the plane back to Plymouth. When he moved to Dublin a month later with his wife, the actress Angela Vale, and their children, and had time to assess his new surroundings, he formed the impression that Edwards was 'not in an enormous rush to find new writers, but trying to see how many past successes from the Gate could be adapted. He was struggling intelligently to transform his huge experience of the theatre into television terms, but this really amounted to placing the camera in front of a cut-down existing play'.

Hilton Edwards also made it known that he required a secretary who was not just a typist and receptionist but was familiar with the twisty paths through the cultural thickets of Dublin. He found that person in Sheila Carden. She was much impressed by his enthusiasm as he dictated a flow of internal memos suggesting programmes for other areas as well as his own, and letters to people whom she only knew as Famous Names throughout the world – Orson Welles, James Mason, Anton Dolin and Michael Redgrave among them – soliciting material for Irish TV Drama. She understood that the Director General had given him *carte blanche*, and certainly the open-handed way in which he ordered equipment for the Drama Office and entertained celebrities to luncheons contrasted markedly with the parsimony which she observed in News, Public Affairs, Sport, Music and Religion. He invited Donald Wolfit to come from London to discuss a programme idea and arranged for him and his wife to stay at the Russell Hotel, then the most expensive in the city; when the bill reached Accounts there was loud tut-tutting, though not yet loud enough to set off the alarm-bells.

A RARE MONSTER

During the summer of 1961 the activity in Clarendon Street increased perceptibly and daily. Brendan Neilan was preparing 'a dossier' on all Irish actors, singers and other entertainers at home and abroad, the first time such an inventory had been made. Reports from the script readers were studied the minute they came to hand. There were planning meetings with the heads of the other departments. Hilton Edwards announced to the press in July that 'even the longest-haired may be confident that the output of the Drama Department will be on a slightly higher plane than the bang-bang horse-opera', and that he was aiming at 'those elusive if hackneyed words, "quality" and "prestige"'. There was a flying visit to Paris to light *The Importance of Being Oscar* at the Vieux

Colombier, but he was unable to leave Telefís Eireann to do the same in Amsterdam, Brussels and Vevay. Paris-Presse declared delightedly, 'Pour parler d'Oscar Wilde, MacLíammóir a trouvé l'exacte ton *fin-de-siècle*', describing Wilde as 'un monstre Irlandais,' and concluding that 'les monstres sont merveilleux quand ils savent rester rares'.

Television was also a rare monster, Hilton Edwards must have been thinking, as he tried to assemble a schedule of twenty-six hour-long and twenty-six half-hour plays for the initial season: a play-consuming monster. Then the new Programme Controller arrived, and the monster suddenly grew a hundred heads, for Michael Barry surveyed the programme plans throughout the organisation, visited the training studio in the assembly-hall of the Marian College in Ballsbridge, looked at the pilot productions which were being made there, and appeared distinctly unimpressed. A statuette of a harlequin holding two masks had been commissioned from a sculptor to be the logogram for Drama Department presentations; it was to be filmed on a revolving base, but fell apart once it started to move. A technician fitted it together again as best he could, but the incident carried with it a certain symbolism. When Michael Barry was shown the screened result, he said to Hilton Edwards, 'I have to tell you I think it's terribly chi-chi.'

Hilton spluttered. 'If it's chi-chi, then chi-chi is what Micheál MacLíammóir and I have thrived on at the Gate for years!'

A London colleague privately voiced Barry's own feelings about the quality of the programmes being planned: 'This is appalling! You can't go on air!' But the station *had* to go on air on the last day of the year, only five months away. Barry immediately engaged experienced British directors to take charge of the technically complicated programmes, drama among them, while the Irish drama directors, all of whom had come from the theatre, were ignominiously assigned to news, chat shows and quizzes. When production began in the Bourke-Strand Electric Studios in November – for the studios at Donnybrook were still under scaffolding – the accents of Balham and Scunthorpe were more frequently heard in the control-room than those of Killiney and Ballycotton. Thus it was that Hilton Edwards' earliest play productions were directed by Michael Hayes, Peter Collinson and Chloe Gibson, and it was chiefly due to their English expertise that the Drama Department's offerings impressed the avid Irish viewing public so much.

One Irish theatre director, however, was selected to contribute to the initial drama schedule. Hilton Edwards, ever studious in recommending former colleagues to the Director General, suggested that Shelah Richards should be invited to attend the television course 'with a view to expanding her theatre skills'. On 8 August Ed Roth wrote to her saying 'I'm delighted to learn from Hilton Edwards that you will be joining us as a Producer' – and so, in the phrase current in theatre circles that autumn, 'Shelah was in'. She was vague, not to say confused, when it came to calling the shots; but her stage reputation was so high and she exuded such a sense of fun and adventure in these totally alien surroundings, that everyone from the most elevated vision-mixer to the youngest trainee boom-operator saw to it that Shelah got through each recording with distinction.

Here was Shelah Richards – who had scandalised both the German and French ministers with her playing of Maupassant at the Gate, who had directed Chesterton's *Magic* there, who had made such an impression in her (then) husband Denis Johnston's play *A Bride for the Unicorn* at the time of the Longford split, who had acted on Broadway with Gladys Cooper and had run her own company at the Olympia, during the most dispiriting years of the Emergency, here she was learning about cross-cutting and the grey-tone-scale and the peculiar capabilities of the Mole Richardson crane – and here she was, leafing through scripts in Clarendon Street, wondering if she should do Flann O'Brien's *Thirst* or O'Casey's *The Moon Shines on Kylenamoe* for her television directing début at the age of – what was it? – almost sixty. And here was Geraldine Fitzgerald's son, Michael Lindsay-Hogg, taking to the mysteries of studio floor-management as if he had been born on a movie set, which he quite possibly had. And here was Alpho O'Reilly, who had just relinquished a much higher scale of fees from the Bernstein brothers of Granada and Sidney Newman of ABC, to return to design plays in his own country; not to speak of Charles Roberts, who had taken up a post in floor-management; and Joan O'Rourke from Longford Productions, who was to be in charge of the television wardrobe.

These people appeared through the autumn mist and the mud of the building site, setting up their drawing boards and costume racks in half-finished rooms with plasterless concrete walls, picking their way through pools of wet cement to the temporary canteen in Montrose House, the Victorian mansion in the grounds of which the studios were being built. Studio 3 was going to be ready on time for News and Public Affairs, Studio 2 *might* be ready for Light Entertainment and Music before opening night, but Studio 1 certainly would not house a drama, or *any* large-scale production for that matter, until well into the new year; so Bourke-Strand Electric in Abbey Street, a part of the empire of Eamonn Andrews and his wife's family, the Bourkes, was going to be needed every minute of the day and night: how fortunate they were to have it. – But how much drama could you produce in these circumstances?

Very little, was the opinion of Michael Barry. It should have been clear, he felt, that there simply would not be floor space on which to mount two drama productions per week, allowing three days for the major play and two for the shorter, with overnight setting, rigging and striking. Nor could drama be allowed a studio monopoly to the exclusion of productions from the other Departments. – 'I was given to understand . . . ', was Hilton Edwards' reply to a number of Barry's strictures: but they were no more than the physical facts. Furthermore, where was the Drama Department going to find fifty scripts a year, Barry wanted to know. In Britain, where there was a population of forty million, it was difficult enough for the five drama-producing stations to feed the insatiable monster, but in the Irish Republic, with barely three-and-a-half million, how could enough competent writers be found, granted the much-vaunted playwrighting tradition? This was a question which Hilton Edwards had indeed been asking himself over the past three months, and there seemed to be no answer other than to depend upon adaptations of existing work. Radical decisions would have to be taken – but not for the moment by the Head of Drama, who was taking leave-of-absence for three weeks to direct *St Joan of the Stockyards* with Siobhán McKenna.

He was especially interested in tackling this play and building on his experience with *Mother Courage*. A cast of forty-three was assembled, most of them armed with placards and placed in all parts of the auditorium as an alienating crowd. Edwards had hoped that Godfrey Quigley would be given the lead, but Siobhán McKenna insisted on a Broadway star, William Matthews. 'What can you do with an actor whose face looks as if it had been run over by a *pram*?' he expostulated after being introduced to Matthews over lunch in the Hibernian; but Matthews rose to the part, and was described by Kenneth Tynan, making one of his rare visits to Dublin on behalf of The Observer, as 'a craggy, movingly bovine Mauler'. Of Siobhán McKenna Tynan said that 'she would be our best emotional actress if only she could manage to stop being emotional once in a while'. His praise for the production was probably the reason for Oscar Lewenstein's interest in transferring it to the Apollo in London – there had been few major productions of Brecht in Britain and here was a chance to present one – but the cost of carrying such a large cast ultimately put an end to the proposal.

Louis Elliman then co-produced the third Dublin showing of *The Importance of Being Oscar*, during a space in Micheál MacLíammóir's touring schedule. Micheál was finding that television was beginning to take over Hilton's life, just as Hilton was finding that he could not be present at dress rehearsals, to say nothing of openings, in foreign cities. 'I see you in my mind's eye as not really happy', Micheál had written from some distant address; and he wrote to Molly MacEwen, 'Hard to have a success, which makes it difficult for the partnership, which is all I really care about.'

Chapter 16
Roscius Hibernicus

While Micheál MacLíammóir was playing at the Lyceum in New York, there came a telephone call to Harcourt Terrace from the British Council. A polite voice enquired if Mr MacLíammóir would consider a tour of South America, and, if so, could he possibly be free in June and July? The speaker seemed unaware that the Council had organised tours for the Gate Theatre before the war; he was even unaware that there was such a thing as the Gate Theatre! Members of the Council had seen *The Importance of Being Oscar* at the Royal Court, and had been been talking to Sir Michael Redgrave. MacLíammóir, through the now highly complex web of managements, pronounced that he would: on condition that there was a Travelling Dresser. The British Council was delighted to allow for such a person to travel from Ireland, as it would be so much less expensive than engaging a series of dressers in South America. (How this economic feat could possibly be attained was inexplicable, but it seemed the Council was sincere.) Ronald Davenport, therefore, was released by the Olympia Theatre, where he worked, and where MacLíammóir had found him to be 'for the most part calm and level-headed, with needles and safety-pins in his lapels, and, in emergencies, he was level-headed to no mean degree.' He was known as 'Brains'. The manager for this tour was a British Council nominee, who spoke perfect standard-southern-English and called everyone 'old boy', yet had the puzzling name of Hank, only partially explained by the fact that he was half Dutch. So the entourage consisted of Brains and Hank, and how could any cultural tour fail, friends in Dublin remarked, when organised by officials with such reassuringly respectable appellations?

In Rio de Janeiro there was little time between receptions and performances in which to view the breathtaking surroundings of the city; if MacLíammóir was taken to the top of Pao de Açucar, or to look out over the panorama of conical mountains from Corcovado, or whether Brains got the glimpse of 'Copeycabanna' for which he had said he was 'bursting', he did not describe them. (When he published *An Oscar of No Importance* in 1968, he said that he was not keeping a diary at the time, or if he had, he had lost it.) He did describe meeting a most distinguished Brazilian lady, with whom he conversed volubly at a lunch and then at a cocktail party in the British Embassy, and subsequently at a party which she gave in her own home, and he was convinced that two super souls had been brought together; but on the plane to Sao Paulo the Brazilian representative of the British Council disclosed that she was the most important critic in Rio, and MacLíammóir had not been told in case it made him 'self-conscious'. They then opened the newspaper for which this lady wrote, and although MacLíammóir could not speak Portuguese, he knew enough of the other Latin languages to understand that she had not liked what she had seen or heard, and probably did not like him either.

In Buenos Aires, MacLíammóir discovered a 'vivid comprehension' of his subject, and of Ireland, which he had not expected. Argentina is the only country in South America in which Ireland maintains a diplomatic mission at ambassadorial level, established by Eamon de Valéra in the 1930s in deference to the importance and material wealth of the country at that time, but probably also because of family connections going back to the late nineteenth century when there was much emigration of professional people – doctors and lawyers and engineers – thus forming a wealthy and influential emigré society quite different from the Irish of North America. Although *The Importance of Being Oscar* was promoted by the British Council, there was strong support from Irish embassy officials, and from people of Irish descent. It was not the usual case of having to explain (in press and television interviews) the predicament of the Irish writer of the past, categorised in literary histories as 'English' yet preoccupied with quite different problems, and writing in quite a different mode of the English language. (If MacLíammóir had had the opportunity of meeting Jorge Luiz Borges, and it is thought that he did, though no guest-lists survive, he would have found a ready advocate, if one were needed.)

The irony of this Gaelic-speaking Irishman's programme on the subject of a fellow-countryman who had fallen foul of Britain's laws, being presented by the British government's official cultural agency abroad, while Irish diplomats sat in the audience as guests, was one which discerning Argentinians, and there seemed to be many of them, must have found quaintly amusing; the added irony, that MacLíammóir was himself 'mere English', springing from that lower-middle-class North London suburbia which he so greatly despised, was something which neither the British Council nor the Irish embassy personnel would have been able to comprehend, for it was beyond belief.

The tour proceeded to Montevideo, Santiago and Lima. At Lima, while reciting the lines from *Dorian Gray* about 'the earthen jars of the Peruvians that have the shrill cries of birds', and 'the sonorous green jaspers that are found near Cuzco and give forth a note of singular sweetness', MacLíammóir made a mental note to himself that of course that was *here*; he asked if he could go to the ancient capital of the Incas, and was told he could not, because his programme was too full. He bewailed the fact that modern travel enabled one 'to arrive at any place in the world at a moment's notice, and see nothing at all'. The only views he glimpsed of the Andes or the Amazon were from the

portholes of a number of aeroplanes; whereas, in spite of an equally tough programme of work, he had been able to see whatever he wished in the Mediterranean countries and the Balkans, where 'travel' meant more than 'transport', and
had been by ship and train.

In Panama, he was the guest of the British ambassador and Lady Vaughan,
but he saw little more than the interiors of their cool green and white residence,
and the dusty Baroque theatre. In Bogotá, there was an amusing contraption in
the dressing-room which was explained as an oxygen-dispenser, because
European artists, unused to the altitude, often needed revival following an
emotional scene – and MacLíammóir found he was very glad of a few gasps
from it in the interval, sustained by the story that Eleonora Duse had regularly
made use of it. In Venezuela, he was able to see some of the country surrounding Caracas because an explosion the previous night in the *piazza* on which his
hotel was situated necessitated a change of accommodation – for which the
young local representative of the British Council apologised so agonisingly that
it seemed the explosion had almost been his fault. This official conveyed him
to a hotel on a nearby mountainside, which was offered with further heartfelt
apologies for the inconvenience.

The inconvenience was precisely what an over-worked touring artist required, for it meant peace – peace from the well-meaning reception-committees,
from impromptu coffee-mornings and cocktail-hours, even from those who
wished to arrange television interviews. MacLíammóir wrote in *An Oscar of No
Importance*, 'I have forgotten the name of that hotel in the hills above Caracas. I
have forgotten how long I was there . . . Only the memory remains, and will
remain for ever, of a place entirely dedicated to magic; a timeless, enchanted
place, a place where one seemed to have dropped back into a dream of childhood. And this mood for me was not shadowed but illuminated by being told
one day . . . that to drive more than ten miles beyond the mountain peaks that
rose above the valley and its crowning jungles would be dangerous, for there,
among unexplored ravines of mystery and terror, the Indians live, defiant to this
day of the laws that had been brought long ago from Spain, riding naked on
their lean horses, with bows and arrows in their hands . . . '

*

The coast-to-coast tour of the United States, genially announced by Sol Hurok
the previous spring as something to pencil vaguely into the distant months of the
diary, was now about to become a reality. During the few weeks' interim, there
was what was beginning to look like a 'regulation' fortnight's revival of *Oscar*
at the Gaiety, when all Dublin seemed to be trying to get seats, and a performance in Cork organised by the Cork Orchestral Society, the first MacLíammóir
had given in what almost everyone still believed to be the city of his birth.
Hilton Edwards was in his television office in Clarendon Street, wreathed in
cigar smoke, discussing which of the immigré British directors should be given

what play by which famous Irish author, to be recorded at the Burke Strand-Electric Studios so as to have 'something in the can' for the opening of the service in January. Brian Tobin was now established in an office on the same floor, surrounded by sheaves of paper, but other members of the staff could not fathom what he was supposed to be doing.

*

On this American tour the necessary dresser was to be supplied by the management. Fortunately both dresser and manager were congenial, for most of the journeys were to be accomplished by automobile, and Gary Petersen and Maury Tuckerman were also to share the driving. On arrival at the Park Chambers Hotel in New York on 21 September, MacLíammóir wrote to Edwards that his vaccination certificate had not been found in his passport, and the immigration officials had been 'very unpleasant'. He described Gary as a 'bonny blonde young man' who 'unpacked so beautifully I suspect him of being Valet by Profession – everything immaculately and sensibly laid out – so that side of life I hope will be comfortable. Am in room I had during Gielgud year, exactly the same, so I feel quite at home, and don't worry about me. Tomorrow we go to Princeton where we stay in a MOTEL if you please – it seems we'll do a lot of that in the university places. M.T. assures me we are going to have a Ball, which always makes me feel slightly Ominous. I love you so much – Mícheál.'

A month later he wrote from the Kellogg Center in Michigan State University, 'I'm tired of it already and long to be home, but what's the use of complaining?' It was certainly enervating, giving the performance, then driving part of the way to the next date, stopping at a motel, when the drivers felt they could go on no longer, and continuing the next day. Molly MacEwen's Donegal carpet was rolled up in the back of the huge limousine, with the pedestal, the lilies and the autumn leaves; the furniture made a 'miraculous' appearance on the stage in time for the curtain each evening. This timetable of one-night-stands was broken in November by a visit to Betty and Denis Johnston at a lakeside resort in Massachusetts, and it prompted MacLíammóir to write in *An Oscar of No Importance*, 'It was wonderful to be with them again, so woven they are into Hilton's and my life. Sad, too, to think of us all: I wondered, looking at Denis as we had supper to which many friends were invited, what had decided him to become, deliberately as it almost seemed, a man of talent instead of the genius he was going to be in the 'twenties and 'thirties: the greatest Irish playwright of his time we all believed, and we were right. Indeed, he probably still is that . . . '

In Cleveland, Ohio, a columnist described Micheál MacLíammóir as 'actor and racketeer', having misheard, or not knowing, the word *raconteur*. MacLíammóir, not deigning to correct him, took up the cue and continued the interview by stating that he had 'spent so much of his life endeavouring to be a racketeer, and that having conspicuously failed in this, I do my best to console myself by the discovery that I am described as "a man of law-abiding reputation"'. In Philadelpia, The Plain Dealer quoted him as saying that 'America is an emotional experience, while a country like France is an intellectual one'; and he must have given way to feelings of irritation when he complained sweepingly that Americans were 'indifferent to noise. I can't get away from the drumming of a radio, television or jukebox unless I hide in my room.' In answer to a question about Orson Welles from the same reporter, he replied, 'No, I didn't "discover" him. He sort of revealed himself to me.'

At the Library of Congress Theatre in Washington D.C., a performance of *The Importance of Being Oscar* was attended by the President's wife, Mrs Jacqueline Kennedy. The columnist of the Washington Post was more interested in what was happening in the audience than on the stage, and gushed: 'Mrs Kennedy looked ravishing in a raspberry red Shantung dinner-suit. She removed her jacket during the first half of the program, and revealed the short-skirted evening gown made camisole-type over blouse with wide straps. She wore a necklace of black jet beads. During the intermission she and her party sat together talking and looking at the audience. She had not been expected to stay to the end, but she did.' When introduced to MacLíammóir, who had presumably been warned by Gary Peterson of her impending visit to his dressing-room, she remarked that when at school she had written an essay saying that the three men she would most like to meet were Diaghilev, Baudelaire and Wilde; the essay had won her a prize in Vogue magazine. Here was a woman with whom MacLíammóir could have spent several hours in conversation, and quite possibly he was a man whose company she, too, might have relished, but Mrs Kennedy had other engagements that evening, and so she took her leave, accompanied (according to the Post columnist) by Mr L. Quincey Mumford, Librarian of Congress.

The tour progressed to unheard-of cities with romantic names, such as Cedar Falls, Iowa, and Ann Arbor, Michigan – all university centres; in such places MacLíammóir was fond of quoting Wilde's epigram 'The youth of America is their oldest tradition'. There were also theatres of the kind he was more used to, like the Civic Theatre in Chicago; and there were 'celebrity' evenings at prestigious venues, such as the one arranged at Hancock Hall in Boston, where the Johnstons and Mary Manning Howe were patrons. When he reached home in early December, he learned that he had been elected to the Royal Hibernian Academy of Arts; and he found Hilton engaged, day and night, at planning meetings, readings, rehearsals, and the viewings of the first ever Irish-produced television programmes, which were now being recorded.

ON THE AIR

Space had been found among the panel-discussions and household-magazines in the Bourke-Strand Electric studios for the first seven television plays – a drastically reduced output to cover the period of transmissions from January through March 1962. Hilton Edwards decided that Michael Hayes would direct

Moby Dick Rehearsed from the script by Orson Welles, as well as the morality, *Everyman*, in its original English text but set in the present day, and also Synge's *The Well of the Saints*. At least here was one work from the Abbey Theatre repertoire, chosen because it was of television length, and less hackneyed than Synge's other plays, as far as the public was concerned. Chloe Gibson would direct Saroyan's *Hello Out There*, and the only play genuinely set in present day Ireland, *Come Back*, by Brian and Veronica Cleeve.

In addition, there would be a five-part serial on the life of St Francis, adapted by Carolyn Swift from Housman. Hilton had supposed that they would use André Ghéon's dramatisation of the same story, which had been so well received at the Gate in 1935, but Carolyn Swift felt the Ghéon would require a more elaborate treatment than the facilities at Bourke-Strand Electric – and the budget – could bear. Hilton found the Housman version 'too Protestant', but Carolyn pressed her point about its simplicity, and he gave in. Peter Collinson, who had come from ITV as a floor manager to train the Irish floor managers and was constantly asking Hilton Edwards if he might direct a play, was given the script. A meeting was called in Clarendon Street, to discuss design. Edwards, harking back to the early Renaissance, kept mentioning Giotto. Exasperated, Collinson enquired, 'What's a jotto?'

It was decided that Shelah Richards would direct Frank D'Arcy's *Oliver of Ireland*, a play about the martyred seventeenth-century bishop, Oliver Plunkett, and the comedy *Thirst*, first performed at the Gate twenty years previously – and, it seemed, totally forgotten, for the press made much of the discovery of an 'unknown' work by the now celebrated Flann O'Brien. *Thirst*, indeed, would be the first play to be transmitted on Irish television; as a consequence, the calibre of the Drama Department would be judged on its showing: so a great deal of effort was put into *Thirst*. It is a simple piece to present on the stage and has only one set – a bar – and to Shelah Richards it offered no challenge other than the technical. Rehearsals took place in Four Provinces House, a ballroom and entertainment centre in the Bourke chain a few hundred yards from Harcourt Terrace. Everything was in order by studio day, 9 December. Hilton sat in a makeshift viewing-room watching the proceedings on a screen which suffered from acute bouts of frame-roll, causing him to cry out from time to time – when the lighting director would run in and make a simple adjustment. By midnight the play was recorded, and safely in the can.

There was justifiable cause for celebration. It was pointed out to Hilton that he need not be in the slightest bit demoralised by what he believed to be the 'downgrading ' of the Drama Department, for few television services in the world, other than those in England, had started with any drama at all in their first year, and he was producing seven plays – not to speak of the serialised scenes in the life of St Francis of Assisi, which were eagerly anticipated.

Hilton Edwards suggested to Michael Barry that Micheál MacLíammóir and Siobhán McKenna should record a recital of poetry for the opening night of television on 31 December 1961. Micheál returned from America for Christmas, and he and Siobhán chose poems by Pearse and Yeats. Their readings clearly represented Culture in the first evening's schedule. The transmissions began at 7 p.m., with the national anthem played by the Radio Eireann Symphony Orchestra to filmed shots of a dozen aspects of Irish life, finishing with a Boeing 707 taking off into the clouds – many viewers supposed that this was visual shorthand for Emigration. The State was represented by President de Valéra, seated at his desk in Aras an Uachtaráin, warning of the potential dangers which the new medium would expose to the people of Ireland – who, of course, would be sensible enough to withstand them. Then the Church made its statement in the form of Benediction of the Blessed Sacrament with the Roman Catholic Archbishop of Dublin, Dr John Charles McQuaid, who, years before, had described the Gate Theatre as 'brilliant but dangerous'. He was surrounded by altarboys, and a great deal of incense which the cameras had difficulty in penetrating, and was attended by the Taoiseach, Seán Lemass, uncomfortably placed on a kneeler foreground-left. This was advertised as coming direct from 'the Oratory at Montrose', a name given to Studio 3 for the duration of the twelve-minute ceremony. The highly un-dangerous poetry-reading followed, and the remainder of the night was dedicated to lighter fare. A live transmission of a variety programme from the Gresham Hotel, where the Head of Drama was to be observed as a member of the audience, led to the count-down into the New Year conducted by his erstwhile stage director, Charles Roberts, now, like himself, part of the paraphernalia of state broadcasting, and Telefís Eireann was one day old.

And what of *Thirst*, due for transmission on the evening of 3 January? It was discovered that an inexperienced technician had inadvertently wiped the video-tape, of which there were no copies. Hastily Shelah Richards, the cast and crew were summoned, the set put together again, and all other programmes banished for a day and a night from Bourke-Strand Electric. The play was re-recorded – but inevitably those concerned admitted that the spark of the original had not been re-ignited. It was well received by viewers, though no comprehensive critique appeared in the papers. As the members of the Drama Department were shortly to discover, the effort which went into the production of a television play, involving far more people and a great deal more money than a stage production, would rarely be noticed in the press other than as a passing sentence in a weekly review devoted to general programming. *The Well of the Saints*, with Harry Brogan and Eileen Crowe specially released by the Abbey Theatre and transmitted four nights later, was given slightly more press coverage, as behove its position as a classic from the period of the Literary Revival of half-a-century before.

Hilton Edwards' suggestion that Orson Welles should come from Hollywood to play the Governor, *alias* Captain Ahab, in his own version of *Moby Dick*, was welcomed by the Programme Controller, but after much altering of dates to suit his schedule, Welles at length found that he could not be available. It is likely that Hilton Edwards expected this outcome, for he allowed Michael Hayes to talk him into playing the part himself. The bureaucracy was such that he had to obtain written permission from the Controller and declare that, as he was on salary, he would take no performance fee. He and Hayes threw themselves wholeheartedly into the work, which was designed to emphasise the studio space and make no pretence of pictorial illusion, in a sense discarding the very qualities for which television was best suited. Edwards thought that they would create a televisual simplicity 'which could be compared to the simplicity of the Elizabethan stage' – a curious conceit.

The experiment certainly did not work in so far as it lost most of its viewers during the slow introductory half-hour. The studio looked like a studio; and it was only when the principal actors Norman Rodway, Jim Norton and Hilton Edwards were seen in close-up – television's greatest asset in any kind of production – that anything very telling came across. The minority who stayed with it were captivated by Edwards' delivery of the sermon, and by the strongly impressionistic sequence when the Pequod is finally sunk by the great white whale. Admiration was expressed by those critics who took the trouble to write about it – but it was admiration for the Drama Department's willingness to try something unusual at such an early stage in its history. 'This was highly imaginative TV', said G.A. Olden in the Irish Times, 'but it was not, on balance, a success'. Hilton Edwards blithely wrote to Orson Welles stating that as Welles owed him money from the past, he was keeping Welles' royalty fee for *Moby Dick*.

Michael Hayes' brooding, Bergmanesque production of *Everyman* was more generally appreciated; Sally Travers, now married and living in London, returned for this production, in which Norman Rodway played the lead. During Lent, Housman's *The Little Father* was transmitted week by week, and in spite of – or perhaps even because of – Ray McAnally's unusually self-indulgent and lachrymose performance, and Peter Collinson's busy camerawork, it drew sighs of approval, particularly, one must suppose, from among the faithful. The pity was – those connected with the production agreed – that Alpho O'Reilly's glowing little sets, based on the Assisi frescos now known in the Design Department as 'the jottos', could not be reproduced in colour.

WILY OLD MAN OF MONTROSE

One of Hilton Edwards' suggestions for a series of non-dramatic programmes was accepted partly because the idea of inviting distinguished writers and artists to talk about themselves, without the promptings of an interviewer, was thought to be one which would appeal to the new viewing public, and partly because of its low cost. The series was called *Self Portrait*, and it immediately made its mark. Frank O'Connor, Padraic Colum, Donald Wolfit and Anew McMaster were among the first to accept invitations to appear. (Years later, Edwards said in an interview in Aquarius Magazine that *Self Portrait* was 'the only decent contribution I made to television'; he was distressed that in spite of their archival value, the tapes had been destroyed.) McMaster sat in a huge carved chair and discoursed upon his favourite topics – Sarah Bernhardt, Mrs Patrick Campbell, and touring in the Australian and Irish outback.

After the recording, he talked to Hilton about a 'farewell' performance of *Othello* – not a Final Farewell Performance, he hastened to add, but simply a farewell to his greatest part, and would Hilton be interested in directing it? Hilton said he was now 'manacled' to his desk in Montrose – the Clarendon Street offices had been abandoned, and gradually the administrative staff were moving into tiny rooms with shiny black floors, separated from each other by wooden sheeting, in the studio block. Hilton said he could hardly ask for leave-of-absence during the first year of production. McMaster thought he should simply take holidays – everyone had to take holidays – and they should raise the topic with Brendan Smith. Micheál MacLíammóir might even be persuaded to play Iago, if he ever came back from his *Oscar* touring.

It certainly was an attractive proposition – an 'old-fashioned' production to emphasise the tradition which McMaster had maintained, with elaborate pictorial representations of Venice and Cyprus. Plans proceeded behind the scenes at Montrose, Brian Tobin carrying messages to and from Harcourt Terrace, while Hilton sat at his black formica-topped desk discussing television productions of Shaw's *The Shewing Up of Blanco Posnet* and Ibsen's *Public Enemy* – adapted to an Irish setting by Eóin Neeson, who then moved from the Drama Department to Public Affairs – and new plays gratefully received from James Douglas and Eugene McCabe. In the meantime, McMaster went into *The Desert Song* with Joyce Blackham at the Gaiety, and wrote to Mary Rose that he was 'the oldest juvenile in comic opera in the history of the stage'.

Prospective authors took up a great deal of Hilton Edwards' time. In his enthusiasm, he had given several to understand that their plays would shortly be produced, and he subsequently had to withdraw the offers because of the much smaller output of drama allowed, or because he had misjudged the suitability of the works for television. He bought plays by Micheál MacLíammóir which no television director would take on, because of their essential theatricality – though Micheál's adaptation of Jules Romain's *Dr Knock* reached the screen, severely pruned, with Aiden Grennell as a sinister doctor, and *The Liar* was well received, with Patrick Bedford in the lead. A limerick was circulated in the staff canteen:

> There was an old man of Montrose,
> With small eyes, and a very big nose;
>   He did plays by the score
>   By MacLíammóir,
> That wily old man of Montrose.

Maura Laverty submitted a number of ideas at Hilton's request. He was greatly taken by one of these and wrote saying they were going to produce it and that there would be 'a cheque in the post'. A few days later he wrote again to say that he was 'at this stage, much dependent upon the views of my Editors, who have more television wisdom than myself. ' His editors had pointed out a number of very telling reasons why Mrs Laverty's story would not be suitable for television. Had Maura been made of sterner stuff she might have asked her solicitor to write a sharp letter to the Director General about the cheque which was definitely *not* in the post; but she was a gentle person and knew Hilton's form from the protracted difficulties over *Liffey Lane* and *Tolka Row*. Besides, she was an old friend, so she simply replied,

Dear Hilton, If your Script Editors know so much more about television than you do, why are you employed as Head of Television drama?

Brian Friel's *Michael Mannion – Proprietor* was another casualty of the same order, but its disappearance from the schedule did not effect a highly fruitful collaboration two years later. Significantly, however, this would not be in television.

SOUTH AFRICA

Micheál MacLíammóir was not present to witness the results of his partner's efforts in what the press in Ireland still referred to as 'the new medium', for *Oscar* was presented by Redgrave and Sadoff, in association with Jan de Blieck, in Holland, Switzerland, Italy and Greece; and then, again under the auspices of the British Council, in South Africa. He was welcomed, in a dazed condition after a long flight which was delayed at Brazzaville, at Johannesburg airport, by one of the greatest personalities of the South African stage, Mrs Taubie Kushlick, and by a band of Irish pipers dressed in saffron kilts. At the unexpected press conference which took place in a VIP lounge, he was suddenly asked what was his attitude to male homosexuality – a question which, as he later admitted, he found somewhat startling, for journalistic ethics normally dictate that such topics are only discussed at private interviews and with the acquiescence of the interviewee – certainly not at public functions. He need not have been thrown, for Mrs Kushlik pounced on the reporter and told her that she need not trouble to join her colleagues at the lunch to which they had all been invited.

He found an agreeable manager in Robert Langford and spent pleasant hours in the company of the Irish consul, Reginald Scott Hayward, son of Richard Hayward, the Ulster humorist and author. Hayward briefed MacLíammóir on the realities of apartheid, which shocked him very much, so much so that he later said it was 'the only patch of sadness in a tour that otherwise was radiant'. One day in Cape Town, taking a taxi from the theatre to the Mount Nelson hotel, he sat beside the driver, who was black and who implored him to move to the back seat. MacLíammóir was merely doing what many naïve foreigners do in such a situation, demonstrating his disgust at prevailing laws and solidarity with the oppressed. The driver said that if the authorities noticed, both of them would be in for trouble; and sure enough, before they had travelled a quarter of a mile, they were stopped by a policeman, who asked MacLíammóir why he was not sitting in the back. MacLíammóir replied, 'Because I am sitting in the front!', and followed this with further facetious rejoinders, while the driver trembled beside him. Eventually, when it became plain that nastiness was developing in the direction of violence, he admitted to having had a black grandfather – which surely entitled him to sit beside the black driver. The policeman then examined his hands and said he did not believe it; but when MacLíammóir – his actor's skill all that was now concealing his own terror – blithely invited the policeman to the Mount Nelson, where, he said, all particulars of his ancestry were noted on his passport for the world to see, the policeman told them to get on the move and so they did. Whether the driver was later made scapegoat in some other trumped up offence, was something MacLíammóir often regretfully pondered.

He wrote to Hilton Edwards on 17 June 1962, 'How I love this place, and how I dread leaving it for some other wilderness of improved concrete like Johannesburg – the beauty of these towering mountains, the scarlet flowers, the hedgerows of deep orange-coloured buds and blossoms, the floating pink clouds across the unearthly God-filled blue of the sky – if only you were here with me! I think of you all the time. (Though I think it very queer of Brian, said Miss Mapp in sub-acid tones, to go on a holiday without a word to me.) Audiences are as stupid as the place is marvellous, and I don't care a Damn!'

He also played in Port Elizabeth, Durban and Pretoria and then a return visit to Johannesburg 'by public demand'; but in spite of the climate and the hospitality of the many friends which he made, he was often unwell, due, it was assumed, to strain – he was sixty-one and sometimes giving as many as eight performances a week. He was assailed by giddiness and something amounting to stage-fright during the first run in Johannesburg; 'high blood-pressure' was diagnosed, and medication prescribed. In Pretoria, he was admitted to hospital, suffering from inflammation of the larynx, but was taken by taxi each night to give his performance. It was suggested that rather than returning to Dublin by air, he should travel by sea; so, after a quiet three days in the gardens of Cape Town he embarked on a liner which took him to Southampton via Saint Helena, where he was so haunted by the presence of Napoleon that he wrote a poem which was printed in his Irish language collection, *Blaith agus Taibhse* (*Blossom and Ghost*), in 1964.

Breathnaíonn an ghrían féin go truamar síos uaithi
ar an muir ghaireata is ar na carraigeacha luaidhe
síos uaithi ar chnoca féaracha is ar bhóithre casta
mar a bnuill an lil bhán ag fás i measc na ngas trom cnáibe,

mar a bhfuil an lil bhan ag fás i measc na ngas trom cnáibe
is tóin aitinn is cactais ag blathú taobh le taobh . . .

BELOVED BROTHER-IN-LAW

It was evidently agreed by the Programme Controller at Telefís Eireann that the Head of Drama could take his annual leave in September, for it was announced in July that he would be directing *Othello* for the Dublin Theatre Festival, with Anew McMaster as Othello and Micheál MacLíammóir as Iago, and that the production would be followed by a continental tour under the management of Jan de Blieck. Immediately this was known, actors began writing for parts. Brenda Fricker, who had had a small part in *St Joan of the Stockyards*, hoped there might be a walk-on – but there was not, for the budget did not allow for even one waiting-maid for Desdemona. Michael Gambon wrote from London to say he was twenty-two and Irish, but had been trained in England; he was eventually engaged to double in minor rôles. Notes on casting were carried by Brian Tobin from the drama office in Montrose to the festival office in the Brendan Smith Academy of Acting. McMaster and MacLíammóir were to be paid £100 per week, after which there was a drop to £40 for Eithne Dunne, and it was hoped to find 'a real star' for Desdemona. 'If we do not get a Star', Edwards wrote, 'I should get a good Actress for about £35 to £50'.

McMaster heard that Margaret Anketell, who had been his Oliver Twist in Australia in 1949, was in England. She had become a very beautiful young woman, and was making a name for herself in the theatre and television. He telephoned her in London. 'Is that little Oliver? Would you like to come over to Dublin to play Desdemona, dear?' She came over, drove out to Sandymount, and thought that Marjorie looked like Wendy caring for an overgrown Peter Pan. She found that 'Mac had not changed at all. His physique was still magnificent. His gimlet eyes as bright as ever and the voice strong and resonant. We sat on a magnificent chaise longue with gold tassels. "Now dear, I must warn you, the part is not yet yours. You have to audition for Micheál and Hilton, and they must not know that you are a *protégée* of mine. You see, dear Micheál and I are great friends, and deadly rivals!"'

They worked on the murder scene until midnight. Next morning Margaret went to see Hilton Edwards at the Montrose studios, which appeared to be an annexe of the Gate Theatre, where she read for him. He seemed satisfied, but told her she would have to read again for his partner. The following afternoon she was invited for tea at Harcourt Terrace, where she found MacLíammóir's appearance distinctly alarming, but his charm quite captivating. She did not have to read, and she had the part.

On 19 August, McMaster appeared in a concert at the Gaiety in aid of the Equity Benevolent Fund. He gathered some of the actors from his most recent tour around him and played the final scene from *The Bells*. Afterwards he complained of feeling unusually tired. On 21 August, Edwards wrote to Brendan

Smith to say that on the European tour McMaster would not be able to play matinées on the same day as evening performances, and Jan de Blieck should be made to understand that 'he is no longer in the first blush of youth'. He pointed out that 'a vocal crack-up would be financially fatal'.

A few days later, after returning from a swim in the bay below his house, McMaster complained of feeling unwell. Dr Hazel Morris was called, and a blood clot was diagnosed in the upper arm. She ordered him to bed and wrote a note saying that 'Mr McMaster is suffering from overwork and will be unfit to resume work for at least three months'. On August 24, MacLíammóir went to see him, bearing a copy of Blanch Patch's book on Bernard Shaw. '*Poorly* is what you might call my condition,' Mac said, 'and those people at the hospital looked Askance, you might say, at the x-rays. I have to stay in me bed for three weeks like Sarah in *La Dame aux Camélias*. Three weeks! Oh, and I won't be able to play Othello with you and Hilton after all. We've never done Othello and Iago together, you and I'. MacLíammóir and Edwards went to see Brendan Smith about finding a replacement, for too many players had been engaged and too many theatres booked to make cancellation of *Othello* thinkable.

The same evening, while Mac and Marjorie were debating whether coffee would keep them awake, or whether coffee would be good for him at all, the telephone rang. Marjorie went downstairs to answer it. Her sister Peg was on the line, enquiring after the patient. He was fine – just needed rest, Marjorie told her. When she came back into the bedroom he was dead. The copy of Blanche Patch's book was on the floor. She telephoned her brother immediately: there had been no warning struggle, she said, no sound. Nothing like Coriolanus' cry.

The funeral took place on 27 August 1962, to Dean's Grange Cemetery after ten o'clock mass. It did not seem to occur to anyone that McMaster was a Presbyterian and, though he admired the Roman Catholic liturgy and had found it advantageous to be seen attending mass in country towns on Sunday mornings when on tour, theologically speaking a priest should not have officiated. Yet it seemed perfectly natural that his remains should be borne to the Star of the Sea church round the corner in Sandymount, and that mass should be offered there for the repose of his soul the following morning. The chief mourners were Marjorie, Christopher and his wife Gill who came over from Manchester, Mary Rose and her husband Jack Aronson from San Francisco, and Micheál MacLíammóir. The President was represented by his *aide-de-camp*. The huge number of cars with provincial registrations was noted: there were hundreds of unknown tear-stained faces. Who were all these people? They were McMaster's audience.

I HATE THE MOOR

The African-American actor, William Marshall, was engaged to replace Anew McMaster as Othello. Exceptionally tall and handsome, with a splendid voice, he seemed the obvious answer, although the convention of 'blacking-up' was still quite acceptable, even among younger actors. He had appeared in the Hollywood films, *Demetrius and the Gladiators* and *Something of Value*, and had just finished a run of *Toys in the Attic* in the West End. It was the BBC producer from Belfast, John Gibson, who recommended him to Hilton Edwards, on account of the fine performance he had given in *The Emperor Jones* on radio, for Edwards was much concerned about the vocal quality of the performer for this special rôle. Lona Moran was engaged to design the sets, though they could not be as elaborate as had been hoped due to the transportation logistics of the tour. Eithne Dunne was Emelia, Maureen Toal Bianca, Christopher Casson Brabantio, Reginald Jarman Montano, Patrick McLarnon the Duke of Venice and Derek Young Cassio – a 'strong' cast. The expectancy of early rehearsals was tinged with disappointment, as days passed without the arrival of William Marshall as the Moor.

'Sorry I'm late! I kinda got held up in Paris,' was his disarming apology when he arrived during the coffee-break at the Molesworth Hall, when MacLíammóir was measuring the cast for his Carpaccio-inspired costumes (shapeless gowns in heavy brocade for the women, tights with very short tunics for the men). The tape was gleefully run over Marshall's magnificent torso and his measurements read out to Kay Casson, who henceforth referred to this cast as 'Snow White and the Seven Dwarfs', occasionally altering her Disneyesque description of Marshall to 'Mighty Mouse'. (Later, one of the Cypriot soldiers dressed in the traditional kilt became 'The Goat Girl', and a Bedouin extra was 'Florence of Arabia'.)

At the dress rehearsal in the Gaiety, Hilton Edwards shouted at Micheál, 'You can't wear those ridiculous tights!'

MacLíammóir roared back, 'I have the best legs in Dublin!'

'It isn't your legs I'm referring to – it's your *derrière*!'

A row developed, spurred by the knowledge that there was a select invited audience in the Dress Circle.

William Marshall had no time for this, and became disdainful. The jealousy theme of the play was subtly counterpointed by backstage jealousy, especially when the reviews came out and Othello's were much more favourable than Iago's. Iago took to turning the notable *derrière* on the audience during Othello's lengthy speech before the Venetian Senate, muttering words, which certainly were not 'rhubarb', to the other members of the court: 'Christopher Casson looks like his mother opening a bazaar!', he whispered, in a voice which may not have projected to the stalls, but was certainly heard by the Moor of Venice. It did not bode well for a happy tour, especially as Hilton Edwards was not to travel with the company, duty calling him back to his desk at Montrose.

Brendan Smith had discovered that it would be cheaper to fly the company to Paris and take an overnight train to Geneva, than to fly the whole way. During the five-hour stopover, members of the company went sightseeing. The Stage

Manager, who had also been given the impossible task of doubling as Company Manager, found on arrival at the Gare Austerlitz that he had mislaid the train tickets, and several calls had to be made to Dublin to try and convince the SNCF officials that these people now attempting to board the *wagon-lits* were, in fact, bona-fide *comédiens* of the Dublin Gate Theatre. William Marshall arrived on the platform with two ladies whom he had met at a café *rendezvous* and announced that they would be accompanying him – indeed, they would be sharing his compartment! As the whistle blew, the Company Manager pulled out a handkerchief with which to mop his brow, a shower of tickets rained upon the ground, and the *comédiens* clambered aboard with shouts of merriment. At an early hour next morning the train suddenly came to a halt. The Company Manager woke with a start, pulled on his clothes, and shouting 'Geneva! Geneva!' along the corridor, jumped out. It was not Geneva, but a chasm in the Alps, and the train immediately pursued its journey without him. When the actors descended at Genève Centrale, there was no one to tell them which hotels they should go to, so they sat in the cold dawn disconsolately reading the London Sunday newspapers, which their own train, with a remarkable understanding of irony, had just delivered, and in which they read the uncomplimentary reviews of their production in Dublin the previous week.

Attendances were good in Geneva and Lausanne, but the press was not so kind. One review had to be kept from MacLíammóir, for it described his Iago as 'ce vieux pédéraste'. (It was felt that he might not object to the noun, but the adjective could cause an unseemly outburst.) The company travelled on an early train to Basel, MacLíammóir following a little later with his dresser, who promptly abandoned him at the hotel where, to his aggravation, all the best rooms had been taken by the first arrivals. He asked for his room to be changed three times, and then telephoned from the third to complain that it was unsatisfactory as well. The reception clerk went up to calm this eccentric guest – using the stairs, for the elevator appeared to be stuck. He was admitted by MacLíammóir, wearing a pair of red shorts, and shouting that he had been scalded by the shower. When the clerk returned to his desk some ten minutes later, he found that the safe had been rifled.

The police naturally deduced that the little diversion concerning the shower had been expertly devised to enable one member of the gang to de-activate the elevator, while another made off with the money. Who was in the hotel at the time? Actors! And Irish! Two well-known categories of questionable probity. All members of the company were ordered to assemble in the foyer. These were not the befuddled gendarmes of humorous Gallic fiction, but leather-booted black-helmeted officers of a more Teutonic strain. Nonetheless, the absurdity of the situation caused several members of the company to snigger, and when asked solemnly, 'Fhere vere you born?' they replied – disrespectfully, if truthfully – 'Mullingar' or 'Inchicore', causing further mirth. Eventually, overcome by sheer numbers, and clearly believing that they had met the inhabitants of a travelling asylum, the police stamped out of the hotel; but two were seen to be loitering at the Stadtspielhaus that night.

It had been noted that William Marshall had not attended this gathering. MacLíammóir, who was now suffering from influenza, allowed himself to be irked by Marshall's 'unprofessional' behaviour. Marshall did not appear for the half-hour call in the theatre that night, and there was pandemonium backstage. The splendid gilded auditorium was crowded. Three minutes after the curtain was due to rise, and at the moment when the Assistant Stage Manager, Mai McFall, was being urged by the Stage Director to go on and read Othello from the script, Marshall arrived, with a breezy 'Hi-ya!' to everybody. Kay Casson threw the long Venetian robe over his head seconds before his entrance, but an inch of jeans could be seen. MacLíammóir muttered to himself throughout the evening, both on and off stage.

The tour proceeded to Luxembourg, Antwerp and Brussels, finishing with a gruelling series of one-night-stands in enormous post-war theatres at Utrecht, Eindhoven, Rotterdam, Nijmegen, Heerlen and Deventer, punctuated after Rotterdam by the charming eighteenth century Royal Theatre in The Hague which had mercifully escaped the bombs of both Luftwaffe and RAF.

MacLíammóir wrote to Edwards from the Rijn Hotel in Rotterdam:

> . . . I have been so unwell. Spent a fortune on specialists and clinics and remedies. I am lucky to have found a pal in Matthews' [*one of the supporting actors*] 'who has bandaged my throat with anti-phlogestine, given me inhalations of this and that and the other under Turkish towels, and done everything he could . . . I forget what it is like to have anything unpacked or to wear a shirt that is not nylon and washed by myself at the sink. William Marshall took it into his head 3 nights ago to attack me for reacting in Senate scene (mind you, it is possible I overdo reaction stuff – John Gielgud said I worked too hard and got busy!) – he (W. Marshall) attacked me however in quite the wrong spirit and started, while I was changing cloak for arrival in Cyprus scene, *to shake me about and scream* like a Baritone Bat at Twilight. You can guess the effect of this: I did a lot of "How DARE you?" etc. & I fear SNEERED at him (I felt like it) & we haven't spoken since. However, this most pleasing as I find him most embarrassingly boring when we are on speaking terms. We mutually pretend the other isn't there except when on the stage (I dread the Jealousy Scenes every night) . . .
>
> The ONE person you ought to give a prize to is Lona Moran . . . She travels on the lorry, she doesn't eat, sleep or sit down. She is at every fit-up and get-out, and there has been hardly a hitch – but honestly, Hilton, that this idiotic tour has gone up, or on, or through at all, is entirely due to L. Moran . . .

There was also the perennial problem of the dresser. The managements of the individual theatres did not provide them, indeed had never heard of such a thing, and he was forced to hire his own man at £30 per week – a Dutch airman who was looking for a job while on leave, but who showed far more interest in the ladies of the company than in MacLíammóir's wardrobe and wig. Everything was a dreadful strain, and to make matters worse the autograph hunters waiting at the stage door each night were only interested in William Marshall.

During a matinée in The Hague, MacLíammóir was disgusted to see that Marshall had not bothered to change from his Venice to his Cyprus costume. Why bother to design them if they weren't worn? 'Look at him!' he whispered loudly in the wings, 'Bloody amateur!' The bloody amateur heard, left the stage, and knocked MacLíammóir over the prop-table, scattering scrolls, goblets, swords and crockery with an exceedingly loud crash. Then he returned to the stage and continued where he had left off. What the audience made of this noisy exit and re-entrance was hardly the question: was MacLíammóir badly injured? Only shaken, it appeared. 'Poor Micheál!' – the ladies of the company ran for aspirins and coffee and brandy, surrounding him with remedies and affection. There were telephone calls to Hilton Edwards and Brendan Smith in Dublin, and to Jan de Blieck in Amsterdam, but all three had far more pressing matters to attend to, and besides, there were only three more nights to play before the end of the tour. Then William Marshall announced that he was not going to play that night. The cast deputed Patrick McLarnon to ask him to change his mind in the interests of the reputation of the Dublin Gate Theatre. 'I'll go on, on condition that that bloody bastard apologises!' He went on, and a conciliatory meeting (it was hoped) was arranged to take place in Nijmegen next day.

In Nijmegen, Marshall made a speech of apology to the cast. He said that playing Othello was a great strain. He was exhausted, and had got carried away. There was a long silence. Now it was MacLíammóir's turn. He raised his hands, gave three slow claps and left the room. A cloud of despondency enveloped the company for the final nights. In Deventer, after the final performance, a member of the company met MacLíammóir wandering along a desolate hotel corridor in the early hours of the morning. 'Will someone please help me? My dresser has deserted me and I cannot get out of this corset by myself!'

On returning to Dublin, Dr Brian Mayne issued a letter, to be shown, if necessary, to managements pressing for performances of *The Importance of Being Oscar*: 'Mr MacLíammóir has been seriously overworking, and has been forbidden to undertake fresh work, or any involving any serious mental strain, during the next few months.' He certainly had been overworking – for several years – but he probably did not take the doctor's advice very literally, for he was preparing his poems for the publisher Sáirséal and Dill, and an edition of *The Importance of Being Oscar* for the Dolmen Press, in association with the Oxford University Press, and he was probably making notes for a new one-person show – but at least he was keeping off the stage. Hilton Edwards was completely immersed in supervising television productions of Rattigan's *Heart to Heart*,

Maurette's *Enquiry at Lisieux*, Johnston's *The Glass Murder* (an adaptation of his radio play), and the work of two young Irish writers, James Douglas (*The Bomb* – which earned the 'television actress of the year' award for Ria Mooney) and Eugene McCabe (*A Matter of Conscience*). It was an eclectic programme – or a programme without any discernible policy, whichever way one wished to look at it.

There was also the curious case of *Our Representative Will Call*, a television version of Orson Welles' famous radio broadcast of 1938, *The War of the Worlds*, when America was paralysed by fear of what listeners believed to be a real invasion from Mars, resulting in national fame, and a number of law-suits, for Welles. The Telefís Eireann imitation took nobody in, and the only complaints were from viewers who felt the national station was wasting licence-payers' money.

Directors' royalties had been coming in since the first performance of *The Importance of Being Oscar*. This now amounted to what Edwards described as 'a sizeable income', when he was being expansive with brandy and cigar in the Restaurant Bernardo, where once a month some of those concerned with tele-vision drama used to meet for dinner; when in more flippant humour he would say he was living on 'immoral earnings'. Assuming that he and MacLíammóir could devise further lucrative one-man productions, his immoral earnings need never diminish. He was finding the supervision of television plays frustrating, for he sat, during camera rehearsal, in a glass-panelled viewing chamber, and, because of his professed lack of technical expertise, rarely interfered, even when he felt he knew better than the director, which was probably quite often. In spite of the fact that he was working in an organisation where 2,000 persons were employed, he was feeling isolated; the fact that his audience was numbered in millions instead of a few hundred a night did not lessen the sense of being out of touch. Furthermore, the political affairs of Montrose studios had little attraction for him, he was hating the eternal memo-writing and planning-meetings – at which he had a tendency to make frivolous remarks, or, on occasion, to go to sleep. It was unreal: and as those who had followed him into television from the theatre began to understand, reality for him meant, paradoxically, the stage. James Plunkett told Denis Johnston that Hilton was 'suffering from Coronary Montrositis'.

VIR VARIUS ET MULTIPLEX

He went to Belfast in December to light *The Importance of Being Oscar*, for MacLíammóir was feeling up to performing again, and said that the lighting had been dire in every venue on four continents. Kenneth Jamison – later to become Director of the Arts Council of Northern Ireland – was the organiser of the season for the Council for the Encouragement of Music and the Arts, and attended a number of parties in MacLíammóir's honour. One was given by an Irish-speaking organisation, at which MacLíammóir spoke wittily. It quickly became obvious who was fluent in the language and who was not, by observing those who laughed spontaneously, and those who laughed when they laughed. Kenneth Jamison was also present at a party in the home of the architect, Henry Lynch Robinson, at which, as the night progressed and MacLíammóir collected a devoted crowd around the fire, 'I marvelled at his capacity as a raconteur and at his incredible sense of timing, and repertoire of anecdotes. I did not know it at the time, of course, but it became clear a year later when he returned to Belfast, that he was preparing his next one-man show *I Must be Talking to My Friends*, for I saw him tell the same stories, this time to a packed and spellbound audience. I had been present at a gathering where, without revealing his purpose, he was trying out his new material.'

MacLíammóir had tried out some material at a concert in the Gaiety Theatre shortly before Anew McMaster's death, in which he, Peter Ustinov, and McMaster, had each given a short recital in aid of a charity; but his 'impromptu' recital in the Belfast drawing-room was not taken from the works of Shaw and Johnston, but from his own experiences, and these were to form the backbone of the new show. He wrote to Pat Turner, the actress who had become secretary at Harcourt Terrace and was later to be the Gate press officer, 'All going well here though I find everybody terribly lackadaisical about getting anything done: the publicity is NIL, the papers never send critics, and how I have done so well I don't know. Wednesday night capacity, 100 turned away, so apparently it doesn't matter how they all slack as long as I kill myself!'

On Thursday 6 December, he might well have been seen as attempting to kill himself, for he travelled to Dublin and back in the morning and afternoon, arriving at the Grand Opera House with only an hour to spare before the show. The occasion was the conferring of an honorary Doctorate in Laws at Dublin University, the fourth and most important honour bestowed on him by a public body after the Douglas Hyde Award, the Gregory Medal and election to the Royal Hibernian Academy of Arts. He was robed in his scarlet gown and hood, with pink lining, in the Provost's House in Trinity College, and then walked in procession through Parliament Square to the Public Theatre, where the Orator, Professor D.A.E. Wormell, read the citation. '*Intra theatrum novum in pulpitum ingreditur scaenae Hibernicae decus, vir varius et multiplex, scriptor pictorque egregrius, doctor sermones utriusque linguae, partium actor primarum, Micheál MacLíammóir.*' ['On the stage of our Irish theatre, Micheál MacLíammóir makes his entrance, a man of many parts, author, a superbly endowed artist, linguist, but above all the greatest Irish actor of the day.']

The orator continued with a list of his achievements, enquiring midway, '*Nonne nuper alumnum nostrum illustrem Oscarum Wilde tanta arte repraesentavit . . . ?* ['Who can forget his superb portrayal of one of the most illustrious sons of this college, Oscar Wilde . . . ?'] In conclusion, he announced, '*Praesento vobis Roscium Hibernicum, histrionem omnibus numeris absolutum. Vos alacri clamore hunc excipere soliti, nunc universitati nostrae ascriptum vel alacriore honorate plausu.*' ['I present to you the Irish Roscius, the glory of our stage. You who have so often greeted him with applause in the past, pay a fitting tribute to him now.']

The organ played a victorious fanfare, and the whole assembly in the stately eighteenth century hall rose to acclaim the Irish Roscius. The Irish Roscius himself, acknowledging the applause with the dignity which came of so many years as (in the words which he had just heard in the oration) 'king or slave, rich or poor, occidental or oriental, Moor or Dane', may well have been thinking to himself that a doctorate from the University of Dublin was not a bad accolade for a little Cockney boy from Kensal Green.

Chapter 17
Wilde and Friel

The gossip following the conferring of the doctorate on Micheál MacLíammóir centred round the accepted view in the profession that without Hilton Edwards there could have been no Micheál MacLíammóir, certainly not the MacLíammóir who had written a substantial body of plays, or who had celebrated, in so grandiloquent a way, the life and work of the illustrious Trinity graduate referred to, for Edwards' contribution to the structure and cohesion of these works was well known to everyone engaged in the theatre. There should, it was felt, have been a *joint* ceremony, recognising the contribution which both partners had made to the theatre in Ireland, for one could not function creatively without the other. It was obvious that the academics who had chosen MacLíammóir for this honour had no conception of the essentially collaborative art of the theatre, or of the collaborative nature of this partnership. It was assumed that MacLíammóir had been chosen because he was the more ostentatious personality, and because he was Irish – for doubts upon the latter issue were confined to a very few persons.

If Edwards felt slighted, he laughed such feelings away. When someone telephoned, looking for 'Dr MacLíammóir?', he replied, 'No, this is Nurse Edwards!' Nurse Edwards, in the early months of 1963, was preparing to assist at the *accouchement* of another literary-theatrical child, while at the same time continuing to work in the aseptic environment of Montrose, where even the air-conditioning was getting on his nerves – 'in a climate like this, where there's no day so cold it can't be answered by ordinary central heating, and none so hot that you can't solve the problem by taking off a waistcoat'; but his real quarrel with the air-conditioning was that it had cost so much to install – money which he believed should have been spent on better programmes.

Ed Roth, Telefís Eireann's first Director General, moved to ATV in London. Edwards spoke to his successor, Kevin McCourt, about his wish to set up a new theatre company with Louis Elliman, and McCourt made arrangements for him to be released from his contract, while remaining for a year on a consultancy basis. On 18 February 1963, Edwards wrote to McCourt 'accepting with gratitude', and then wrote to Roth, 'From April Fool's Day next . . . I am to be retained in an Advisory Capacity at £1,000 p.a. (tho' as they don't take my advice now, I don't see why they should then, and you know that Oscar Wilde said "to give advice is bad, but to give good advice is absolutely fatal"). I am a little apprehensive as to how they propose to continue running the Drama Department . . . Things appear to be settling down to that level of mediocrity as I feared.' Edwards relinquished his shiny black desk on 1 April. Adrian Vale, the senior script editor, remarked that he left after two years, knowing nothing more about television than when he had entered.

Brian Tobin's contract with Telefís Eireann was due for review in June, and the Controller invited him to remain for a further three months 'to allow me to evaluate the overall situation in the Programme Division', but in September Tobin was informed that 'in the reorganised Programme Division there will no longer be a post of the precise nature for which you were recruited'. Micheál MacLíammóir, in *An Oscar of No Importance*, recalled that Brian Tobin left Telefís Eireann with Hilton Edwards, but this was not the case. He wrote , 'It was suddenly decided – I can never remember precisely how or when – that Brian should become Hilton's and my manager'. MacLíammóir, for all his often very rudely expressed comments on Brian Tobin's efficiency at work and unpredictability as a companion, did feel morally obliged to look after his material interests, for it was he who had encouraged him to leave his safe post in the airline office. Thus, like it or not, Tobin was to be present in one capacity or another for the rest of MacLíammóir's life. When visiting Boston on another *Oscar* tour, Mary Manning Howe thought Tobin was the ideal manager and confidant – 'Micheál relied on him enormously – he was the calming influence Micheál needed so much.' Brian Friel noticed how MacLíammóir used to make fun of Tobin, and then, in remorse, consult him on some erudite subject, to which Tobin always had a highly considered opinion.

The plan for a 'new company' with Louis Elliman was not much more than a reconstitution of the unwritten arrangement which had existed in the 1940s and, less regularly, in the 1950s. Elliman was much impressed by the international success of *The Importance of Being Oscar*, and now that the partners' two-year contract with Redgrave and Sadoff was due to expire, it is likely that he foresaw a financially advantageous association arising through further co-operation with this resilient couple. He presented MacLíammóir's new one-man show *I Must Be Talking to My Friends* at the Gaiety on 15 April, and Sam Thompson's *The Evangelist* on 16 June. Other new Gate plays given at the Gaiety before the end of the year were *The Last P.M.* by Conor Farrington and *The Roses Are Real* by Patrick Paterson; but in 1965 Elliman decided to sell the theatre to a consortium headed by Eamonn Andrews. Two further Edwards-MacLíammóir productions, Brian Friel's *Philadelphia, Here I Come!* and Fay and Michael Kanin's *Rashomon*, took place before the change of management; but with one exception – Brian Friel's *Crystal and Fox* in 1968 – there were to be no more new Edwards-MacLíammóir productions at the Gaiety. Louis Elliman died shortly after he handed over the theatre to Eamonn Andrews; the theatre staff believed that he died 'of a broken heart' because, of all the dominions that made up his empire, the Gaiety was the one he loved the most.

I Must Be Talking to My Friends opened under Mr Louis' benign surveillance on 15 April 1963. It turned out to be a selection of Irish literature from early anonymous writers to those of the present day with whom MacLíammóir felt a special affinity; but they were authors whose work had to fit into the storytelling mode which he had devised. The focus, in this case – since he was not celebrating a single figure like Oscar Wilde – had to be himself; and the linking script had to provide as much interest as the literary excerpts, otherwise the evening would have become a recital of 'My Favourite Poems and Stories'. The connection between the poems and stories was MacLíammóir's own discovery of them at different moments in his life, whether coming across Yeats when he was an art student in London, or meeting Gaelic writers of the past through the garrulous talk of his landlady while he was working at the Taibhdheardhc in Galway; and also MacLíammóir's own reminiscences of private encounters with writers not long dead, such as Augusta Gregory. The script itself was highly allusive – Tom Moore's Ireland was 'a passionately virginal Madame Récamier in an emerald gown', and there was Joyce's 'unmercifully brilliant dinginess'. Hilton Edwards devised a series of moves and static positions which subtly gave the feeling that there was no staging at all, in a setting suggestive of some remote and timeless Irish dwelling, created mainly from a few pieces of traditional furniture and an irradiation of changing light.

'There is no room for doubt,' Seamus Kelly wrote in The Irish Times, 'that every single critic will be able to list at least ten mortal sins of omission from this anthology;' but he continued, 'no mortal man could encapsulate Ireland and what made it into three hours' staging if he were to force in any more voices: no mortal man that I know of could have done a better job of it.' All the Dublin critics were highly appreciative, save one, Seán Page of the Evening Press, who divined immediately that the piece had been made for export. 'His linking script makes the assumption that the audience is composed of children or foreigners, who need to have all the references spelled out for them, and all the tags translated . . . Insofar as the audience is considered "local" the show makes the assumption that we Irish, let them say what they like about us, really are a loveable lot, all our virtues heroic and all our vices endearing.' *I Must Be Talking to My Friends* presented a highly subjective image of Ireland, which Seán Page immediately recognised: it was uncontentious and comfortable. Certainly it would do well in other countries; but it also did well in Ireland, for it had consistency as a stage piece, and it reappeared over the next decade almost as often as *The Importance of Being Oscar*.

The President of Ireland, Eamon de Valéra, whose visits to the theatre were extremely rare, attended the opening of *I Must Be Talking to My Friends*, placing the official seal of approval on performer and performance. Three weeks later MacLíammóir was appearing in Peter Daubeny's World Theatre Season at the Aldwych in London – a tribute to Daubeny's faith in a new show which he had not seen when planning his programme. A few critics had difficulty with the rural accents which MacLíammóir introduced in the excerpts from Boucicault and Synge, and there were the inevitable carps about who and what had been left out (no O'Casey? no Goldsmith?), yet the consensus proclaimed another hit, so much so that the theatrical entrepreneuse, Kitty Black, decided to present both *Friends* and *Oscar* in London again – though, due to MacLíammóir's multiplying engagements, and also to increasing problems of health, this would not be for another eighteen months – at the Queen's and the St Martin's theatres.

MacLíammóir's sight was beginning to fail. He still attributed this to the glare of the lamps on the *Othello* set – but hundreds of film actors manage to work without eye strain, and there is the suspicion that he illogically blamed anything untoward on that particular period of association with Orson Welles. Caroline Fitzgerald, niece of Geraldine Fitzgerald and a frequent visitor to Harcourt Terrace, said it was 'pathetic to see Micheál feeling his way round the dressing-room at the Aldwych, when he had given such a marvellously steady performance on the stage'. In early August, he had an eye operation, but was back in hospital two weeks later for two more; he cancelled a visit to Edinburgh, where he was to speak on 'Nationalism and the Theatre'; and then withdrew from the cast of Conor Farrington's *The Last P.M.*, which was the Edwards-MacLíammóir contribution to the 1963 Dublin Theatre Festival. It was providential that Brian Tobin would now be accompanying him on his overseas tours, some of his friends thought, even if the two were bickering, and indulging in dreadful silences: it was asking a bit much to expect unknown theatre personnel to take a completely sympathetic interest in the physical welfare of the solo artist.

There were many short engagements of *Oscar* and *Friends* in Ireland and Britain, among them some wintry weeks in cities of the north of England at the close of 1965, when Kitty Black's car had to be dug out of the snow, and costumes and properties, consigned to public transport, failed to keep to schedule. There was a one-night-stand in Whitby on a Sunday, when no dress-hire shop was open, and MacLíammóir positively was not going to interpret the moods of Oscar Wilde dressed in travel-creased grey trousers, beige jacket and red shirt. *Peter Pan* was playing in the same theatre the following week; he supposed that, in the Barrie tradition, the actor who portrayed Captain Hook would be doubling as Mr Darling, and so he entered the men's dressing-room and, sure enough, there among the costumes for pirates and Indians and crocodiles was a Victorian evening suit. Brian Tobin was horrified that he should requisition it without permission, but what was he to do? The audience which turned up during a blizzard was small, and MacLíammóir said he should have retitled the show *I Must Be Talking to Myself*.

They went to Australia for the spring of 1964, staying for two months in an apartment at Pott's Point overlooking the harbour, in the King's Cross neighbourhood of Sydney, described by MacLíammóir as 'a kind of paperback

English translation of Montparnasse'. The management of the Phillip Theatre was wary of *I Must Be Talking to My Friends*, and did not try it out until the last week of the season, which was regretted by everyone because it was an instantaneous success. Yet MacLíammóir admitted to being 'violently miserable', and was often on the telephone to Dublin – a habit he had not previously indulged – and when asked what was wrong, he replied that the weather was lovely and the people the soul of kindness and the business excellent, and therefore he could not explain. (On one occasion Hilton asked him had he discovered that Sydney was Clapham Junction in a heatwave, and he replied that it was not.)

The answer must have been loneliness: it was how Hilton had felt in Manchester. On 17 May, he wrote to Pat Turner from the Windsor Hotel in Melbourne, '''Tis Autumn! Leaves fall all around. Winds blow, all is yellow and tawny brown – and it is May! I can't bear it! Still, I like Melbourne better than that Sydney; *that* Sydney, in spite of COMFEY FLAT with GORGEOUS VIEW, plus BRIGHT SUNSHINE, was all that to me is most loathsome. *I will not speak of Sydney.*' Pat thought that Micheál might have been finding Brian's presence oppressive, and wondered if perhaps Brian had a lady-companion in Sydney which was causing him to neglect Micheál socially, or if Micheál merely suspected he had a lady companion; she sensed something of the kind, but felt it prudent not to enquire. In *An Oscar of No Importance*, MacLíammóir outlined a theory that great friendships can grow and prosper from mutually shared labour, but that friendships which spring from shared pleasures, 'like talking and dining and walking', fail when transported into the workplace.

They went to Brisbane and Adelaide and Canberra, and then the tour was extended to New Zealand. In Auckland audiences were sparse; this was attributed to a prolonged visit from the Beatles, which suggested that, unlike anywhere else, people of all ages, professions and tastes in New Zealand were Beatles' fans, to the exclusion of everything else. Then they went back to Sydney, where MacLíammóir was engaged to read the commentary for a four-sided longplaying record on the History of the Vatican, which caused him much amusement; and they returned to Dublin with breaks in Cairo, Athens and Rome, where he felt more at home; at least people spoke their own languages, and culture was not of a debased Anglo-Saxon variety.

SAM

Hilton Edwards' visit to Belfast, to light *The Importance of Being Oscar* (at the time of the conferring of Micheál MacLíammóir's doctorate) afforded him an opportunity of meeting Sam Thompson, a shipyard worker and devoted tradesunionist, who also wrote a radical newspaper column and had had one play, *Over the Bridge*, produced. The Ulster Group Theatre was to have presented it, but the theatre's board felt it was too outspoken politically, and one of the Group players, James Ellis, decided to direct it for a splinter company at another theatre. It was rapturously received by a public starved of strong social comment on the stage; none of the predicted acts of violence occurred; Thompson and Ellis became local heroes; and the long established Group Theatre died an ignominious death. Thompson had hoped that his new play, *The Evangelist*, which dealt with religious hypocrisy, would be produced by the same company, but it had a very large cast and financial backing could not be found in Belfast.

Hilton Edwards received the script from Louis Elliman while he was Head of Drama in Telefís Eireann. Carolyn Swift, whose opinion he sought, saw that the *The Evangelist*, if produced on the stage, would be taken as courageous, whereas if produced on television before a less sophisticated public it might be taken as an attack on Protestantism (rather than on a dubious evangelical cult and its leader, a religious confidence-trickster). In the Irish Republic, the state broadcasting organisation had to be seen as pristinely impartial; but in any case *The Evangelist* was very much a theatre piece, requiring broad statement rather than the minute realistic detail which was television's *forte*. Carolyn Swift wrote to Edwards, 'Louis Elliman has undoubtedly picked wisely in asking you to direct it. It demands the handling of large numbers on the stage and gives plenty of opportunity for mass grouping. It would attract considerable publicity and audiences, as controversial plays of this nature are bound to do, particularly in view of the success and controversy attached to Sam's last play.'

It was with some trepidation that Edwards went to meet Thompson for lunch, for he feared his guest might find his accent and manner patronising, Thompson having the reputation as being very much a man of the people. 'I was absolutely wrong,' he told a BBC reporter some years later. 'I found him warm, generous, co-operative, exceedingly friendly – everything one could desire in an author.' He was much taken by Thompson's attitude to the theatre – 'the only place where you get democracy – where people can object.' The writing was careless, Edwards thought, as if set down hurriedly, 'with racing pulses and warm blood'. During their period of collaboration, Thompson accepted Edwards' suggestions in the manner of a tried professional, rather than as the author of a single success. Edwards liked his use of Gospel hymns, and thought the theatre might be converted to look like the interior of a mission-hall; this proved impractical in the rococo Gaiety, so he had a ramp built out over the orchestra pit, to make the audience feel that they were part of the crowd in the hall. Ray McAnally, who played Pastor Earb, found this difficult at first, for he had to leave what, as an actor, he knew as the safety of the stage 'cut off', as he said, 'from the support of fellow actors. When I marched out on the ramp I was setting myself up as a Hot Gospeller. Some people in the audience got up and joined in the "Hallelujahs", and I realised I was *there*.'

The Evangelist opened at the Grand Opera House in Belfast on 16 June 1963, and proceeded to the Gaiety in Dublin, just as *Chimes at Midnight* had done, but to a completely different reaction. It had a strong cast – Ray McAnally, T.P. McKenna, Gerry Alexander, Derek Young, Geoffrey Golden, Dermot Tuohy, Catherine Gibson, Barbara Adair, and many experienced players from the sadly defunct Ulster Group Theatre. Betty Lowry of the Belfast Telegraph praised Hilton Edwards' 'tremendous regard for atmosphere', but felt that ultimately Thompson's script failed to reach 'the heights – or depths – of tragedy'. John Jay in The Irish Times saw it as a 'beautifully constructed theatrical spectacle, an object-lesson in how this sort of thing should be done', and agreed that once two or three characters were left on the stage 'banality blinks through'. Nevertheless, it was clear that Thompson was not just a promising playwright, but one from whom more and greater could be expected. There were pious remarks in the Dublin press about his heralding a new era in Ulster playwriting, for there had been few good new northern plays since the heyday of Shiels, Ervine and Tomelty, and Edwards-MacLíammóir Productions were complimented for bringing such a renaissance to the attention of the southern public.

Thompson kept in touch with Edwards. He stood unsuccessfully as a Labour candidate for South Down in 1964, the year in which his next play, *Cemented with Love*, was recorded by the BBC, but not transmitted, because the corporation was dithering about its theme of personation at elections being too sensitive for viewers in Northern Ireland. Thompson sent the script to Edwards, with the suggestion that he might adapt it for the stage, but he died suddenly at the Labour Party headquarters in Belfast on 15 February 1965, before a decision had been reached. Edwards felt a real personal loss on the death of his new colleague, with whom he had hoped to continue a harmonious working relationship. (The BBC thought better of its attitude to *Cemented with Love*, and the play was transmitted *post mortem*.)

MEMORABLY BIZARRE

The Evangelist was followed at the Gaiety by Conor Farrington's *The Last PM* and Michael Redgrave's dramatisation of Henry James' story, *The Aspern Papers*. Micheál MacLíammóir had not been well enough to appear in either, but he was determined to recover in time to take the part of Adolf Hitler in *The Roses Are Real*, a play by an English author, Patrick Paterson, on 28 October 1963. Two leading West End players, Mary Kerridge and Thorley Walters, were engaged because Louis Elliman foresaw a transfer, eliciting a warning from Dermot K. Doolan, the watchful General Secretary of Irish Actors Equity, about the balance of Irish and overseas actors. Mary Kerridge recalled the play as a 'splendid bit of melodrama in which Micheál gave a great frightening performance. Jack Hylton, a hard-headed entrepreneur, was so impressed that he put it on at the Vaudeville Theatre in London.'

Hilton Edwards stipulated that if the play were to transfer, the Dublin stage management, Ruth O'Meara and Caroline Fitzgerald, were essential and must travel with it. They did so, and remained in London throughout January and February of 1964, which was rather longer than most of the London critics thought the play deserved. 'Another play about Hitler,' complained Bernard Levin in the Daily Express, 'and this one is a schtinker. It is set in a lunatic asylum, as well it might be . . . Mr Micheál MacLíammóir is reported in yesterday's Daily Mail (which means it must be true) to have said of his part as Hitler: "I don't think I can play him." I am perfectly certain he can't.' An unsigned review in The Times declared that 'the main point of interest in this import from Dublin is that it gives connoisseurs of curiosities a chance – perhaps all too transient – of seeing Micheál MacLíammóir in the role of Hitler. We hear a good deal nowadays about the advantages of casting actors outside their usual range, but the practice is seldom carried to lengths as extreme as this. The sight of Mr MacLíammóir struggling to confine his expansive life-affirming presence into a posture of rigid fanaticism is memorably bizarre. Lank forelock carefully in position, Mr MacLíammóir pounds the table and stabs the air with a raised finger, but geniality consistently breaks through the mask, just as his honeyed brogue filters disconcertingly through his gutteral bark. It is, in fact, one of Mr MacLíammóir's demon king performances, and makes us look forward to a time when Hitler gains a foothold in Christmas pantomime . . . '

THE EXPANSIVE WORLD OF BALLYBEG

The two most substantial new plays which Dublin managements were considering for the 1964 Dublin Theatre Festival were Eugene McCabe's *The King of the Castle* and Brian Friel's *Philadelphia, Here I Come!* McCabe had not written for the stage before, but Hilton Edwards produced his first television play, *A Matter of Conscience*, with Shelah Richards directing, for Telefís Eireann. McCabe then sent him *King of the Castle*, an exceptionally powerful drama of the new rural, but rootless, rich, in tone somewhat reminiscent of the middle phase of O'Neill, and greatly to Edwards' liking. Its setting suggested an 'Abbey play' – but its theme, the eternal myth of the disappointed successful man who has no offspring and must go to extremes to produce an heir, would have been considered altogether too libidinous by Ernest Blythe, the Abbey's managing director. Edwards received the script of *Philadelphia, Here I Come!* from the festival director, Brendan Smith, because another management, Gemini Productions, was having difficulty casting it. *Philadelphia*'s setting and *dramatis personae* also suggested the 'Abbey' category; but far from being the stock-in-trade Abbey play of youth *versus* reactionary age in dear-old-Donegal, its implication was much wider, and its technical innovation of two actors playing the interior and exterior facets of the central character might have proved too taxing a departure for Ernest Blythe's somewhat restricted understanding. The point was, neither play reached the National Theatre, but both reached the exiled Gate at the Gaiety; and the further point, which the passage of time made plain, was that these two plays became twin milestones in the development of the Irish drama.

It was agreed between the managements and the festival that Gemini would produce *King of the Castle*, and Edwards-MacLíammóir *Philadelphia Here I Come!* Brian Friel had had three plays staged elsewhere, as well as several performed on radio. He had spent some months with Tyrone Guthrie at the theatre in Minneapolis and had found the experience liberating; he told the editor of *Aquarius* that he returned with a 'perspective' on Ireland and on playwriting. (Guthrie thought *Philadelphia* 'very subtle'; why Friel did not ask him to direct it remains a mystery, but may be explained by Friel's modesty about his own work.) Edwards wrote to Friel to congratulate him on the play and to confirm a production at the Gaiety 'for the second week of the Dublin Theatre Festival, and let it run there after the Festival, according to public demand. I understand, of course, that Mr Oscar Lewenstein has an arrangement with you about this play and I am sure that, if he decides to transfer it to London, he will make an equitable arrangement with us.'

A correspondence ensued between Edwards in Dublin and Friel in Kincasslagh, County Donegal. Edwards made a number of suggestions about the structure of the work. He felt that a bar scene should be disposed of and the dialogue brought into the O'Donnell home, giving a unity of place, and that two companions should be enough for young Gar O'Donnell rather than three; Friel disposed of the bar and cut the character Joe – 'his murder is fresh on my hands and I feel guilty about this'; Edwards then replied to say that if Friel had an intuition about a character he should stick to it, to which Friel replied 'I just *feel* that three boys are needed – for which I can offer no formal argument'. Joe was therefore disinterred. 'At this stage,' Friel wrote on 10 August, 'I prefer not to think of your other suggestion – that we cut the play during rehearsal by 15 mins. I know this is going to be a Chinese Death By 1,000 Cuts for me, and I resolutely refuse to allow the prospect to undermine my fight against the weather here. I'll face this damnation when the time arises (although I *know* now that every word of the play is vital!).'

The play deals with the moment when Gar O'Donnell's boyhood ends and his young-manhood begins, the parting of past with future, and the love between father and son which cannot be expressed. The setting is Ballybeg, where there is a tradition of emigration; the characters are every bit what one would expect to find in that small community, yet they night be living in Turgenev's Orel, or Wilder's Grover's Corners. Their Donegal speech gives them a particularity, but they belong to the wider world of human will and human fate. Much of the comedy derives from the 'unheard' remarks of Gar Private, which contradict the conventional and predictable words of Gar Public, but the comedy stemming from deeply-drawn character is equally strong, and gives volume to the waters of regret and sadness which flow never far below the surface.

Edwards approached Alpho O'Reilly for set and costumes. O'Reilly was Head of Design in RTE and was already taking his holidays to design *Laurette* with Siobhán McKenna at the Olympia, and *You Never Can Tell* at the Gate, and he said there was not the remotest possibility of his taking on another play. Edwards pleaded with him to read the script, which O'Reilly took along one lunch-hour to Sandymount Strand, quite determined to look it over and repeat his refusal; but after a few pages he found himself captivated, told Edwards he'd do some quick sketches for him to show to the author next day in Derry, and spent most of the night at his drawing board. The play was in several scenes representing the shop and the adjoining rooms of the O'Donnell dwelling, but O'Reilly felt the whole should be seen together, rather in the mode of Arthur Miller; so he cut the house in half and revealed its internal ramification, upstairs and down. Edwards knew at once that this would help to keep the action moving, and he later reported that Friel had found it 'fascinating'. When the design had progressed further, O'Reilly suggested that at the end of the play an upper window should remain lighted, to give the notion that S.B. O'Donnell is unable to rest after his son's departure for the new world.

It is curious that Hilton Edwards did not take the Donegal accent – an essential in several subsequent productions of *Philadelphia* in Ireland – into consideration when casting, to give 'a local habitation'; perhaps he felt that the 'universality' of the work required something unspecifically rural in the manner of the Abbey's much-lampooned 'Kiltartan'. Both Eamon Kelly (S.B. O'Donnell) and Máirín O'Sullivan (the housekeeper, Madge) were from Kerry, and the overall tone was taken from them. The three American characters – Aunt Lizzie, her husband and her gentleman companion – certainly did not appear to come from a single *milieu* in the United States (the actors were from London, Belfast and Dublin, which may have had a bearing); Patrick Bedford and Donal Donnelly (Gar and his alter-ego) used safe middle-class non-accents; but all this remained unnoticed by the critics, so strong were the leading performances, the direction, and above all the play. Eamon Kelly said that much of the success of the production was due to Friel's presence at rehearsal, and Edwards acknowledged this in a gracious little speech to the cast after the opening night – which was on the Monday immediately after the final Saturday of *King of the Castle*. (The era of extended dress rehearsals followed by previews had not begun in Dublin.)

During the first run of *Philadelphia, Here I Come!*, Hilton Edwards went into a nursing-home suffering from bronchitis and 'dizzyness', emerging to correspond with Friel and Lewenstein about transfers to London and New York. Lewenstein told Friel that he favoured New York: he believed that in London there would be a *succès d'éstime* and a box-office flop. Dates and theatres in both were investigated, but a major difficulty was Donal Donnelly's other engagements, and all felt that the production would be unthinkable without the restrained glee of his performance. Edwards enquired of Friel if the rumours that he was writing a new play were true, and Friel replied in December that there was 'the tiniest wee grain of truth in them, but that's about all. I am working on a new play; I have written millions of notes on it; I have completed the first act five times . . . If I could content myself with a conventional three-act play in the straightforward style, all would be well . . . I would like to talk over the technical difficulties with you some time – they are legion.'

In a postscript to the same letter, Friel asked, 'Do you like the title "The Loves of Cass McGuire"? Cass McGuire is not Lolita but a a 68-year-old Irish-American (Aunt Lizzie, only much worse) who comes back to live with her married brother, accountant, solidly middle-class etc etc and who ends up in a genteel Old People's Home where the play is set.' In April he gave Edwards the script, and, unusually for Edwards on reading a new play for the first time, he immediately started suggesting actresses for the leading part – among them Marie Kean and Hermione Baddeley. The problem of who should play Cass McGuire was to vex them for a full year, when a decision was made – and the decision continued to vex them thereafter. The cast for a Dublin revival of *Philadelphia* was also discussed at this time; Friel was dubious about re-engaging some of the players from the first production, and found that Edwards was in agreement with him. Eleven months had passed since the initial performance, nothing was fixed for Broadway or the West End, but at least Dublin would see the play again, and this time at the Gate – the first time Hilton Edwards had directed there under the Edwards-MacLíammóir slogan in seven years. It was an auspicious return, with so lively and stimulating a work.

*

While the changing plans and delays on the American production of *Philadelphia* and *Cass McGuire* were occupying Hilton Edwards sporadically, he directed a recording of *The Importance of Being Oscar* for CBS, and was present when both *Oscar* and *Friends* were recorded for Telefís Eireann (for which MacLíammóir won the Jacobs' award for best television performance of the year). He also played the title rôle in a BBC television play, *The Old Man of Chelsea Reach*. He went to Spain in January 1964 for a proposed part in the film version of *Chimes at Midnight*, but had to withdraw due to illness. Mícheál, who thought Hilton was too unwell even to consider travelling, wrote from the Queen's Theatre in London to Pat Turner, 'I am so upset with H. going to Spain I don't know what to think. Spain is pride, pleasure and *doom* to me. *Remember I said that*. It will kill H. or me in the end.' Patrick Bedford, who played Nym in the film, stayed on for five weeks during a spell of very bad weather and confessed to being miserable. When Hilton Edwards came out of the nursing home in Dublin, he took up the neglected *Philadelphia* correspondence with Louis Elliman. 'Fortunately, but quite genuinely, I got one of my really bad bronchial attacks in the freezing cold of sunny Spain, which let me out very nicely, thank you. Orson has since added to his liver complaint a stone in the kidneys (this should be quite a collectors' piece). He is now quite monstrous in every way and although my relations with him are friendly, the old Orson has disappeared in what I can only suspect is a growing uncertainty . . . '

In June, Micheál MacLíammóir gave a new recital, *Talking about Yeats*, at the Shelbourne Rooms in Dublin. It was 'produced' by Hilton Edwards, but not provided with a theatrical ambience, for it was in the nature of an illustrated lecture. He repeated it many times in Ireland, Britain and the United States, and it led to collaboration with the poet Eavan Boland on a book, *W.B. Yeats and his World*, which was published in 1977. After the August revival of *Philadelphia* at the Gate, MacLíammóir went to Sweden and Finland with his two one-man shows, and Edwards went to Amsterdam to direct *De Ploeg en de Sterren* by Sean O'Casey. MacLíammóir and Tobin passed through Amsterdam twice while Edwards was there – the first occasions when their paths were to cross on their separate missions, and this was to happen regularly during the next two years, mainly in America, during the runs of Brian Friel's plays. MacLíammóir thought that 'the subtle nostalgic quality' of *Philadelphia* 'suited Hilton's later style of direction beautifully . . . For me there was a sad note about it all, which oddly echoed the nostalgia that floats over the work itself, and this was that, because of my eternal running about with *Oscar*, I had no share in the production at all . . . and the sight of Alpho O'Reilly's lovely *décor* stirred not only my admiration but a sense of jealousy.'

Suddenly, after much proposing and retracting of plans, *Philadelphia, Here I Come!* was announced for the Helen Hayes Theatre in New York for February 1966, preceded by a week – appropriately enough – in Philadelphia, and two weeks in Boston. Patrick Bedford, Donal Donnelly, Eamon Kelly and Maírín O'Sullivan were considered essential, and were allowed working visas. (It was questioned why Kelly should be needed, for he had 'so few lines' – there being no management comprehension of the value of an actor's silent presence in a scene – or of what should have been very obvious from a reading of the script, that the things which S.B. O'Donnell leaves unsaid are of such significance.)

The remainder of the cast had to be recruited in New York. When Hilton Edwards returned to Dublin after a short visit, he wrote to all the members of the Gate cast to explain that he was entirely in the hands of American Equity and the David Merrick management. 'I very much regret this, not only for personal reasons, but because – and I hope this is of some minor consolation to you – having auditioned some 240 actors during my brief stay in New York, I have not yet found a cast which I believe to equal the one we had at the Gate.' Neither Alpho O'Reilly nor his set travelled either. Merrick cabled with an offer to buy the Gate set for a very low figure, but O'Reilly said 'No' – not because of the fee, but because he knew the set was not suitable for a large Broadway theatre. He asked that he be brought to New York to make an appropriate design, but Merrick refused, and engaged an established American. When Edwards was shown the plan and elevations, he had to have them changed, explaining that in Ireland, for reasons of climate as well as architectural tradition, rooms are separated by doors.

For the Irish players, the glamour of Broadway was first made manifest by means of rehearsals in a dark theatre and the dimly lighted lobby of a vast hotel, and its operational efficiency by the hiring and firing of actors who were hardly given a chance to show their capabilities. They all found this unnerving.

Edwards said that dozens of the actors he had auditioned were 'highly trained and highly untalented', but he was prepared to 'teach' them; it was the New York management that fired them. In desperation he got both Merrick and Equity to agree to bringing Eamonn Morrissey from Dublin for the part of Joe, which brightened matters. The Irish players also found some of the Americans extremely slow in their stage responses. There was a discrepancy of styles; but, as far as John McCarten of the New Yorker was concerned, 'under Hilton Edwards' direction, all seem at home in Ballybeg.'

The New York opening, on 16 February 1966, followed several previews during which a running battle between the impresario, David Merrick, and the critic of the New York Times, Stanley Kaufman, came into the open. Kaufman liked to attend previews (and rehearsals, if possible) in order to give himself time to consider the work, rather than scribble a hasty review before deadline. The Dramatists' Guild complained, as did the League of New York Theaters and the Society of Stage Directors and Choreographers: they did not wish to have their work criticised until they were sure it was ready. Kaufman requested two tickets to the last preview of *Philadelphia*, and Merrick sent them to him, with a note saying, 'At your peril'. Kaufman duly arrived at the Helen Hayes, and was told the performance had been cancelled. 'There is a rat in the generator', a spokesman for Mr Merrick told him. Eleven hundred disappointed patrons were given their money back. The members of the cast were stunned by the experience, and despondently forgathered with director and author at the Algonquin Hotel, where Brian Friel's agent, Audrey Wood, and her husband William Leibling were waiting for news. 'You've got a million dollars worth of publicity,' said Mr Leibling. 'That's what Merrick wanted!'

Kaufman's review, following the official opening, was not favourable, but he was in a minority. The cast forgathered again, this time at Sardi's, as the good news came in. Brian Friel, arriving with Eamon Kelly, was surprised by the applause of the diners, and, wondering what it was all about, looked back to see if some very famous personage was entering behind him. The truth dawned. 'It's us!' he whispered, adding an appropriate Donegal expletive. When Edwards and MacLíammóir came to New York in May, the players hosted a party 'to honour the founders of the Dublin Gate Theatre', at which the Irish members of the cast nobly gave a scene from the play they had been performing the same evening, and MacLíammóir, not to be outdone, gave this select public a preview of *I Must Be Talking to My Friends*, which opened its American tour two nights later at John Hancock Hall in Boston, as part of an Irish arts festival, upon which Mary Manning Howe had an important influence.

By this time, plans for *The Loves of Cass McGuire* were taking shape. Brian Friel favoured a Gate transfer from Dublin (rather than an American production) and thought that Ruth Gordon, the noted American actress whose name had been put forward, might agree to rehearse and play in Dublin before coming to New York; Tyrone Guthrie had spoken very highly of her. On 3 April Friel wrote to Edwards with several casting suggestions for the supporting parts, all of them Irish. 'I have no doubt at all that Merrick's office can line up 647 actors and actresses who will read for you. But what about their calibre? I know that your reply for this is that in this play we are not looking for a peasant quality. But what we are looking for is perhaps something more subtle. This play is about the *new Irish*, the Harrys who have made money and drive big cars and golf at the Hermitage and who have forgotten that their fathers were tatty-hokers in Scotland. And Cass, who still has the shanty, tatty-hoker mentality, comes back to this strange land that is half-American and half-slick and has totally forgotten the Troubles . . . and all the things Cass remembers.'

Brian Friel continued pressing for a Dublin opening: 'We had, during the pre-Broadway trials [of *Philadelphia*] the assurance and achievement of Dublin behind us. How often were we able to say: This worked in Dublin; it damned well must work here too.' Friel was rewriting scenes during July and August, and sending them to Harcourt Terrace – 'I am always *terrible* at rewriting at this stage: I can't part with a comma without sweating blood.' David Merrick, however, decided on an American production. Ruth Gordon was agreeable, would be a draw, and the play would open in Boston at the end of August and transfer to New York in early October.

From the start of rehearsals, Hilton Edwards had difficulty in communicating with the star, both on a professional and personal level, so much so that Brian Friel often had to 'translate' for them. The atmosphere was not improved by Edwards speaking of her to other actors as 'Lady Crocodile'. After the initial weeks, both Edwards and Friel had doubts about her suitability for the part. When the play opened, some of the critics found her performance excessively coarse, and attributed this to the text. Desmond Rushe of the Irish Independent, who went to New York specially for the opening, wrote home that it was 'an incredibly disastrous piece of casting'.

Philadelphia, Here I Come! moved to the Plymouth Theatre in order to accommodate *The Loves of Cass McGuire* at the Helen Hayes. Though *Cass* was not generally considered the equal of *Philadelphia*, Brian Friel had two plays running simultaneously on Broadway, and Edwards-MacLíammóir had four productions running in the two most important theatrical capitals of the English-speaking world, for *The Importance of Being Oscar* and *I Must Be Talking to My Friends* were now playing on alternate nights at the Haymarket Theatre in London. *Philadelphia* was judged joint-runner-up (after the *Marat-Sade*) by the New York Drama Critics Circle as best play of the year; and Patrick Bedford, Donal Donnelly, Eamon Kelly and Maírín O'Sullivan were all nominated for Tony Awards. The play ran on Broadway for eleven months, after which there was a national tour lasting from November 1966 to April 1967.

Towards the end of the year Hilton Edwards wrote to Brian Friel about stomach complaints, apathy, and overwork on the film, *Half a Sixpence*, in which he had a supporting part. He referred to *The Loves of Cass McGuire*: 'Nothing will blot out the wrongness of the Gordon, but I see here a great danger, that we might hold her responsible for too much.' There is an undercurrent of *mea culpa* in the letter. Friel replied on 13 December, 'You are more than generous in accepting "blame" for what happened in America. I don't think either of us should assume any great responsibility. Miss Gordon was never right. Merrick broke my heart. You worked yourself to the bone . . . But the play as it stands is the play as I want it done.'

STRIVING FOR THE CROWN

The Abbey Theatre produced *The Loves of Cass McGuire* in the spring of 1967. Brian Friel, writing from his new home in 'merry Muff', County Donegal, told Hilton Edwards that he was pleased with Siobhán McKenna's interpretation – 'very strong, very vital, very physical'. Edwards was now studying Friel's latest play, *Lovers All* or *Lovers' Meeting* or, finally, *Lovers*. Now that Louis Elliman was dead, there was little chance of finding backing for a play at the Gaiety unless another management were involved, so he was hoping to produce it at the Gate, which Christine Longford was now running as a receiving house for companies willing to pay a weekly rental. He also felt that the intimacy of *Lovers* would suit the Gate space.

The script is in two parts – in the first, the death of two lively, imaginative and engaging school-leavers, Mag and Joe, is prefigured scene by scene by a chillingly detached chorus; in the second, the middle-aged and unprepossessing Andy and Hanna have to conduct their courtship while loudly reciting Gray's *Elegy in a Country Churchyard* – so that Hanna's pietistic mother, an invalid in the upper room, will be unaware of the nature of the proceedings. Tyrone Guthrie had read the play and thought Friel should not have ridiculed the two middle-aged characters; Friel did not believe he had done so, and wrote to Edwards for reassurance, which Edwards provided. In casting the four main parts, both were sure that Fionnuala Flanagan, who had played in the Gate revival of Philadelphia, was ideal for Mag; they thought Eamonn Morrissey, still on tour in *Philadelphia* in the United States, was also ideal for Joe, but there was the question as to whether he might appear too old for a lad of seventeen. A message was sent to Baltimore asking him to send a recent photograph; he wrote back saying 'I really feel I can look and behave young enough . . . I think five minutes of reading the part would mean more than half-a-dozen photos.'

When the play opened on 27 July 1967 at the Gate, Fionnuala Flanagan and Eamonn Morrissey captivated press and public with the joyous innocence of their playing of the doomed young couple. Anna Manahan and Niall Toibín drew every hilarious nuance out of Andy and Hanna, without neglecting to underscore the sadness and frustration of their circumstances. 'A delicate, sensitive and lovely comedy,' said The Irish Times; 'Brian Friel continues to write brilliantly, poetically and funnily,' echoed the Irish Independent. For Anna

Manahan, this production was 'the happiest time'; she felt she had reached a kind of maturity since her early appearances with the Gate; she found that she was now able to talk back to Hilton in a way which he enjoyed, and she was also able to step back and observe the care which he took with the younger players – 'A pause is not a vacuum: it must be filled with thoughts and with feeling' – 'The whole craft of the actor is to make it *look* well: in the theatre you have to make it bigger'. When talking to her in introspective mood about his present international success, he remarked, 'You strive for the crown all your life – and when you eventually get it you don't care.'

With *Lovers*, it was not so much a question as to whether the play would be seen elsewhere, as when; but the next move in the complicated chess-game was the opening of *Philadelphia, Here I Come!* on 20 September at the Lyric Theatre in London – with the original quartet of leading players and some changes in the supporting cast – where Irving Wardle of The Times wrote that it was 'fully deserving of its reputation'. Joan Reddin said she was 'in floods of tears' at the end of the performance, to which Hilton rejoined that 'it *must* have been good to make an agent cry.' Eamon Kelly felt that American audiences had a greater understanding of the play, for 'no American is many generations distant from the hard fact of emigration, and most English have been rooted in one spot for centuries.'

When, ten months later, *Lovers* opened at the Vivian Beaumont Theater, New York, it was without the original quartet of players, for the Broadway producers required an American star, and insisted that that star be Art Carney, a comedian known to millions through his television series with Jackie Gleeson, *The Honeymooners*. Hilton Edwards did everything possible to retain his other leading players; initially he was told he could only have two; then Anna Manahan obtained a visa as a 'distinguished foreign artist', and Fionnuala Flanagan and Eamonn Morrissey were granted the two visas allocated to the production. The Dublin cast, stung by the absence of Niall Toibín and wondering what kind of an actor they would get in his place, were none the less charmed by Art Carney as a fellow-worker; he had not appeared in a stage play for some years, but his return in *Lovers* was triumphant; one critic wrote, 'Until you have heard Mr Carney deliver Gray's "Elegy" as he is frolicking on the couch with the ample Anna Manahan, there will be something missing in your life,' and the producers were thanked 'for bringing over Anna Manahan, a solid figure of a lass, and as droll a comedienne as you could wish for. Hilton Edwards has done a bang-up job with *Lovers*.'

Micheál MacLíammóir, *en route* for a Canadian tour of *Oscar* and *Friends*, arrived just in time for the New York opening, and was espied by David Nowlan of The Irish Times as the lights dimmed, semaphoring a good-luck message across the auditorium to Hilton Edwards. Eamonn Morrissey's fiancée, Ann O'Connor, was also in the audience. After *Lovers* had been running for a month, the producer, Morton Gottlieb, wrote to Brian Friel, asking him if he would 'come over to New York to bathe in the glory of a smash hit'. He had made arrangements for the play to transfer to the Music Box ('the best theatre for a play in New York'), and Art Carney had made himself available for another two months, after which, if it was still a 'giant success', they could think about replacing him with another actor. (Milo O'Shea was invited, but was going into the musical, *Dear World*, with Angela Lansbury.) In the same letter Gottlieb referred to correspondence with Hilton Edwards regarding Friel's newest play, the mordant and bitter tragi-comedy of life in a disintegrating fit-up company, *Crystal and Fox*, which he thought was Friel's best to date; he was hoping to have Richard Burton in the leading part. In November, the stage manager of *Lovers*, Warren Crane, wrote to Edwards to say that Carney 'hated leaving the show, but is looking forward to coming back in February . . . Peter Lind Hayes is now playing "Andy" with that splendid group at the Music Box Theatre'; he reported that Peter had to learn the part in ten days, and 'good old Anna' was very helpful about jumping in with a cue in rehearsal when it was needed. Crane thanked Edwards for notes which he had sent for the younger players – 'You never cease to amaze me the way you can put your finger right on the problem of the moment. I guess that is the difference between a good director and a great one . . . Mr Gottlieb asked for more cuts in the first play [*Winners*] and I sat down with both Fion and Eamonn and we worked some out. They are very minor, but it made Mort feel that we were making the effort. The kids are very good about it, both helping find the places and taking the places I found . . . ' He concluded, 'I hope we get to do *Crystal & Fox* as I loved it when I read it.'

Business slowed down after Art Carney left *Lovers*, but he returned for the national tour, which was another smash hit. Anna Manahan thought it remarkable that the play worked so well in very large theatres, including the O'Keefe Centre in Toronto, which had over two thousand seats more than the Gate. When the tour ended, the Irish members of the company had been playing in *Lovers* for a year.

Morton Gottlieb did not find the star he was seeking for *Crystal and Fox*, but it was produced at the Gaiety Theatre in Dublin by Edwards-MacLíammóir and Eamonn Andrews Productions as a commercial venture. Brian Friel had initially sent the script to Hilton Edwards, hoping that he would like it and want to direct it – 'if for any reason you do not wish to take it on, don't have the least hesitation or feel the least embarrassment in sending it back to me. Of course I would be disappointed: but you know as well as I that it is only on fundamentals we disagree! There is one ideal Fox Mellarkey, and he is Cyril Cusack. (I'm afraid I have strong and stubborn ideas – as usual.) . . . '

Hilton Edwards sent copies of the script to Cyril Cusack and Siobhán McKenna. Siobhán replied that the part of Fox 'is one of the deepest studies of mankind I've come across, and starts one thinking strange things about God – but I had better not go into that' – for she was not free on the dates proposed. Cyril wrote that he liked the play and would like to be in it, but 'I am not the best picker of parts for myself and should probably only play as cast'; later he expressed himself as delighted when he heard that Maureen Toal also liked it, and was going to play Crystal. Micheál MacLíammóir thought Crystal 'a wonderful creation: we could have more of her.' He felt that the texture of the conversation of the touring artistes in 'the Fox Mellarkey Variety Show now playing in Ballybeg' needed to be 'more comic, more desperate'. This was the first Brian Friel play for which MacLíammóir designed the set – the interior of a vast marquee with a stage-within-the-stage, and a front cloth suggesting the harsh countryside in which it was pitched; at the end, the tent vanished and all that was left was a signpost in the middle of nowhere. The production and performances came in for greater praise in Dublin than the play; but business was good enough to justify a move to the Gate when the Gaiety run ended, and, once inside the smaller theatre, the play itself seemed to grow, and there it prospered.

The production did not prosper greatly at the Mark Taper Forum in Los Angeles, where Morton Gottlieb presented *Crystal and Fox* the following year. Hilton Edwards experienced the same kind of difficulty he had had in New York with Ruth Gordon – but on this occasion with the whole cast. For the first time in the United States he was confronted with a company none of whose members he knew; he did not seem to be able to understand any of them, and they, brought up in another tradition, understood neither his methods nor his language. It had been different at the Old Vic for *The Clandestine Marriage*, where, though there was only one familiar face, the system was familiar; in Amsterdam, too, he had worked with strangers in *De Ploeg en de Sterren*, but, as Brian Tobin commented, 'the rules tallied with those on the home pitch, and he was able to make the running'. Here he seemed at a loss. He did not speak of what he considered to have been his failure – and perhaps he had not failed as greatly as he thought – except to Pat Turner in the Harcourt Terrace office, who always listened sympathetically to both of the partners, and in whom they both confided. For Hilton, it was a dispiriting conclusion to the 'Friel years', which took their place in the historical scheme in the manner of the 'Gaiety years' and the 'Laverty years'; but the world, in its eastern theatrical hemisphere at any rate, was not aware of his disappointment. The world only knew that Edwards-MacLíammóir Productions, far from failing in later middle-age to attend to the sounds produced by the rising generation, had hearkened to the most eloquent and articulate new voice on the Irish stage, and had helped to amplify and direct that voice to a large and receptive audience.

Philadelphia, Here I Come! was a Gate play; so were *Lovers* and *Crystal and Fox*, and so, by an arguable extension, was *The Loves of Cass McGuire*. The Gate had marked Ballybeg on the chart of the world's drama.

Chapter 18
The Gate Renaissance

'I don't understand the contemporary theatre,' Micheál MacLíammóir told Kevin Kelly of the Boston Globe during one of his tours of North America. 'There is Brian Friel in Dublin, simple, direct. I understand him. But the rest, Beckett, Pinter, Ionesco. I weary. I'm aware that your interest lags after you've reached 50, unless you're Shaw and go about in short pants. My extension goes to Stravinski, Picasso, Cocteau, then I stop. It's my lack, I suppose, but I just don't get the new boys. I watch their work, say Yes in my head, but my heart yawns.'

He was almost seventy when he made this admission. In future, with a few notable exceptions, he and Hilton would be promoting the past, if not living in it. *I Must Be Talking To My Friends*, which was itself a celebration of the past, brought MacLíammóir back to America many times, often to rather slow academic audiences, in deference to whom he felt himself adding an explanatory tone to his voice. He felt lonely on the tours when Brian Tobin did not accompany him because of work which had to be accomplished in Dublin, but quarrelled with him when he was present. He liked to visit Brendan and Marie Burke and go for walks in Central Park – except for the squirrels, which he said were 'rats in drag'. He liked to meet Liam Gannon – 'a spoiled Proust' – who had settled in New York after his separation from Helena Hughes, which Micheál found a sad decision, for he had written the village lovers in *The Mountains Look Different* for them. Liam recalled how on these later occasions Micheál counselled him against moods of sadness and discouragement – 'I think we both consoled each other'. Geraldine Fitzgerald gave a party in New York after a performance of *The Importance of Being Oscar*, to which Micheál arrived amazingly early – it appeared that the backstage area had gone on fire during the interval and the theatre was evacuated. The reason, Micheál explained, was that on coming off the set at the end of the first half he had been confronted by his dresser wearing a voluminous crinoline and feathered bonnet: 'What price Scarlett O'Hara!' the young man exclaimed, backing into an electric heater, which immediately caught his velvet frills. 'I thought it would cheer you up!' he sobbed, as the stage manager sprayed him with an extinguisher, and a *posse* from the New York fire brigade burst into the building.

While *Crystal and Fox* was running at the Gate, Micheál received a surprising invitation from Alan Simpson, the new artistic director at the Abbey Theatre. The surprise was not so much that in his seventieth year he was being offered a very large rôle – the name part – in a new play by one of the 'new boys', Eugene McCabe, but that the director was to be Tyrone Guthrie. Guthrie's view of Gaelic Ireland and its appurtenances was well known: he despised it, and said so with pithy sarcasm in broadcasts and in print: it was out of date, and so was its National Theatre, which, he said, 'basks in past glories'. He wrote in a magazine article that 'Micheál MacLíammóir is widely acknowledged as our greatest contemporary player. Out of pure loyalty he stayed in Dublin, but he stayed too long.' (Had he known that MacLíammóir was not Gaelic at all, but was acting a part, he would probably have felt the same way.) Here was one of the leading directors in the English-speaking theatre accepting an engagement at the Abbey, and with a leading actor for whom he was known to have no great respect.

In 1967, Guthrie was in search of a play about Jonathan Swift for the tercentenary of the writer's birth. Eugene McCabe, whose *King of the Castle* he admired, provided a script. A reading, with a cast drawn from the National Theatres of Ireland and Great Britain, was given at the Belfast Festival, with Colin Blakely as Swift. In 1969, Alan Simpson decided the Abbey would produce it; Guthrie was keen to direct, if a suitable Swift could be found (Blakely was unavailable). Hilton Edwards was suggested, for he had given two interpretations of Swift in the plays by Longford and Johnston, but Guthrie would not hear of it – probably because he did not relish the thought of directing a director. Travelling by car from Monaghan to Dublin with McCabe one day, McCabe tentatively suggested MacLíammóir. Guthrie suddenly burst into song – 'Wagnerian and frightening', McCabe recalled. Then he said: 'I think we'll give the old lady a chance.'

The old lady, never one to sit idle when invitations to try something new arrived in the mail – that was, perhaps, the major problem of his career: an inability to pause and select – accepted the part, in spite of its length, and in spite of his eye condition, for he was now almost blind. Mary Rose McMaster, who was home from the United States to visit her ailing mother, and Brian Tobin's daughter, Valerie, taught him the part, speech by speech. (Eugene McCabe said he never really got the lines, but gave his own approximation of them.) He sat very quietly at rehearsal, much embarrassed by Guthrie's incessant, and unavailing, attempts to instil a discipline into some members of the Abbey cast – 'It was the *ancien régime*,' McCabe said, 'the landlord dressing-down the peasant.' Guthrie and MacLíammóir got on reasonably well; Guthrie was at that time promoting a fruit-preserving co-operative in County Monaghan – there is an apocryphal story of Micheál, dissatisfied with a stage direction, exclaiming 'And I don't like your jam either!' Such observations tend to take on too much significance when repeated outside the context of workplace irony.

Swift was not the production the script deserved. Guthrie said that with the blind and ageing leading actor the rehearsals were 'like pushing a train up hill.' The Irish Times, nonetheless, felt that MacLíammóir had captured 'the misanthropy and the wit, the passion and the dotage, the paradox of Swift's charitable malice'. The Northern Standard wrote of 'Monaghanmen's Abbey Theatre Success', in terms suggesting that neither Guthrie nor McCabe had enjoyed any previous renown. Guthrie, after five weeks of close professional contact with 'the old lady', altered his view somewhat, for he wrote to Brian Friel that the play was 'not helped by poor old M.MacLíammóir being so blind. His perf. of the 1st night was gallant in the extreme (he's a *very* nice, good person under all the disguises) but only a pale paraphraze [sic] of the text.'

*

Gay Byrne, producer and presenter of the longest-running and most popular programme on what was now called Radio Telefís Eireann, the *Late Late Show*, devoted his whole evening to Micheál MacLíammóir's seventieth birthday on 26 October 1969. The research was undertaken by Pan Collins, who bullied the programme executive into letting her spend £300 on a copy of *The Importance of Being Earnest*, signed by Oscar Wilde, which her daughter had found at Blackwell's in Oxford. Sir Michael Redgrave, Siobhán McKenna, Maureen Potter, Christopher Casson, and many past members of the now largely-non-existent though soon-to-be revitalised Gate company, were present. Clips from telerecordings of *The Importance of Being Oscar* and *I Must Be Talking to My Friends* were shown, there were tributes from Eartha Kitt, Sybil Thorndike, Donal Donnelly and others; a cake, which almost caught fire due to a draught from the air-conditioning, was cut, and slices handed round the audience. Micheál himself paid numerous tributes, especially to Anna Manahan for her bravery at the time her husband Colm had died in Alexandria. After the programme, when thanking Pan Collins, he told her that she had succeeded in bringing Denis Johnston, Betty Chancellor and Shelah Richards together for the first time in over thirty years. The theatre correspondent of the Waterford News and Star reported the following week that MacLíammóir 'was looking more like fifty than seventy'.

He went into Monkstown Hospital at the end of the year for an eye operation. The question of health had always been a concern, but during the last decade of the partners' lives it became a major one. Both attended a number of doctors at the same time, and kept accounts with several chemists. Hilton carried a case full of remedies, particularly for stomach complaints, which travelled with him wherever he went, and from which he made daily selections; this case was as crucial to his existence as Micheál's make-up box. One general practitioner was often telephoned at the oddest hours, when one or other thought himself to be under unusual stress, either from work or from private pressures. He would be asked to write a note for Hilton to show to Micheál, saying how ill he was, and *vice versa*: 'When one went to see Micheál one went to see Hilton. One morning my secretary received a call from a member of the staff at Harcourt Terrace asking me to go there immediately. When I arrived, Micheál was on the telephone, and he whispered "You've just come in time – Hilton's upstairs – not well – being very difficult", and when I went upstairs Hilton said, 'It's Micheál – he's downstairs – being so difficult.' When *The Importance of Being Oscar* was recorded on videotape by Radio Telefís Eireann, there was a private viewing, which both partners attended. Afterwards, Hilton sent for a doctor, who went to the house immediately. 'Micheál is *so* insensitive! We went to this viewing, and in the darkness I took out my teeth and put them on the table. Micheál thought they were an ashtray, and stubbed out his cigarettes on them!'

Hilton's false teeth were an endless topic for serious and protracted discussion. He had several pairs made, each one more unsatisfactory than the last. When working on *The Loves of Cass Maguire* in New York he was fortunate enough to be introduced to a Dr A.S. Pomerance who had a surgery on East 55th Street, and who appears to have provided a satisfactory service for some time. 'Dear Dr Pomerance,' Hilton wrote from Harcourt Terrace, 'Your dentures – or, I suppose, they are mine – anyway, *our* dentures, are the best I have ever had, for which I am grateful. I am still inclined to gag when I get tired towards evening and I have not yet cured my habit of dispossessing myself of them unconsciously. But I really think I am getting better, and I have high hopes of conquering them altogether . . . I will write you again in a couple of months.'

Domestic tensions were not ameliorated by approaching old age. Since his success in *Philadelphia, Here I Come!*, Patrick Bedford was very much in demand as an actor on Broadway. Hilton missed his presence in Dublin, but was concerned at the same time for the furtherance of his career, writing a series of anxious and exhortative letters. Patrick returned to Dublin many times during the 1970s – notably to appear in *Rozencrantz and Guildenstern are Dead*, *The Real Charlotte*, *Noone*, revivals of *The Taming of the Shrew* and *Ring Round the Moon*, and subsequently to direct *Equus*, but he seemed to be generally suspended in mid-Atlantic. It was widely assumed that he would step into Hilton's position at the Gate, and clear that Hilton hoped he would, but his predilection was for performance, not administration. Recollecting his lifelong relationship with Hilton and Micheál, Patrick Bedford wrote in a magazine article, 'I was so bedazzled by the two Gate leaders, they became my surrogate fathers and began to fill the gaps in my sketchy education. In return, I became cook, chauffeur, nurse and *confidant*.' (He might have added, 'and a first rate actor.')

As time went on, and their desire to keep working outreached their capacity to achieve the best results, the frustrations sometimes became unbearable, and there were stormy outbursts, which saddened friends who in the past might have been amused by tempests which had all the appearance of being fugitive. Both partners were given to leaving angry notes to each other on the most trivial issues – displaying a deeply rooted disillusionment: 'For God's sake (and I mean it literally) do stop fighting with me,' Micheál wrote in one of these; 'I do mean well, and try in every way I can think of to make you happier. If you would only trust the good will and intention of which my heart is full and not be so violently impatient with my smallest mistake – right, so I had misunderstood the meaning of Mother Hubbard, so, really, what? – it would be easier. It is so horribly sad to see friendship and love with this blight of irritable manners and harsh fault-finding creeping over it like lichen. Please, please believe that from the moment I entered the room your tone was not that of a friend but of a displeased sergeant-major to a very stupid and deeply unwanted recruit. I have tried: I am trying: I will go on. Will you meet me, if not half, then a tiny bit of the way? We haven't so much more time left. Your loving Micheál.'

Marjorie McMaster died in March 1970. A few months before, she had told the journalist, Mary Gaffney, that nothing interested her any longer. 'With Mac gone,' she said, 'what future is there?' Micheál visited her frequently at the seaside house in Sandymount, which she had divided after Mac's death so as to have a regular income from the garden-level apartment; Micheál contributed to her expenses when she moved to the Portobello Nursing Home. He wrote an identical letter to Mary Rose and Sally before her death to reassure them that everything possible was being done. 'I never believed until a couple of years ago that it would be possible to pray day and night for the death of someone I love so much. Every single day since I can remember anything at all, she, my mother, and other three sisters are my earliest and most enduring images . . . As for Mana herself we have sat silently side by side through the greatest performances of Nijinsky, Pavlova, Karsavina, Bernhardt, Caruso and many others as well as sitting side by side over lesson books which through her hands and mind formed by far the greatest part of any conventional education I have received . . . ' Mary Rose, who was rehearsing *Dylan* with her husband Jack Aronson in the United States was unable to attend the funeral; she knew her mother would 'understand', but she regretted it ever after. Christine Longford wrote to Micheál, 'You must be proud that you made her so happy: be thankful for that for ever.'

*

Terence de Vere White had relinquished his legal practice on being appointed literary editor of The Irish Times, but he continued to help the partners with their administrative affairs, though both had become financially secure – Mac-Líammóir due chiefly to his one-man shows, and Edwards from the royalties he earned as their director, and for his work in directing other productions – chiefly Brian Friel's plays, which brought in substantial percentages from 1964 to 1970. The Gate Theatre remained a sadness, for they could afford to play there only occasionally, Christine Longford letting it out to whatever other companies wished to pay a rental. When she felt she could no longer continue as manager, the post passed in a kind of natural succession to Brian Tobin. De Vere White kept pressing for a subsidy through his contacts in the government. In May 1969, the Edwards/MacLíammóir Playhouse Society was launched by a group of well-wishers inspired by Mary Manning, who had returned from the United States following the death of her second husband, and was living in an old house in Blackrock, surrounded by a large garden, and visited by her old friends – Con Leventhal, Betty and Denis Johnston, Shelah Richards, Norah McGuinness and the Boys. A very influential patrons' list was announced, including Mrs Sybil le Brocquy, Dr Andrew Ganly, Professor Roger McHugh, Mr Cearbhall O Dálaigh (the Chief Justice, soon to be President of Ireland), Lord Moyne and Dr C.S. Andrews. Their immediate priority was to collect funds for the refurbishment of the theatre. Among the subscribers were Mrs Josephine McNeill, now Ambassador to the Netherlands, who had attended the first performance of *Diarmuid agus Gráinne* at the Taibhdheardhc in 1928, Samuel Beckett – who recalled seeing *Julius Caesar* six times (when James Mason was Brutus) – Peter Luke and Brian Friel; Oscar Lewenstein declined, saying he was 'not quite as well disposed towards the venture as I might have been had Hilton not made separate arrangements with Brian Friel for his third play'.

The Society also hoped to raise the temperature of official awareness by means of their personal contacts with people in government. Sybil le Brocquy called on a prominent member of the opposition, C.J. Haughey, whom she knew to be interested in the arts. Within a few months there was a general election; the government changed and C.J.Haughey became Minister for Finance. Terence de Vere White was on friendly terms with the new Taoiseach, Jack Lynch, who recommended a meeting with Haughey. Both Edwards and MacLíammóir said they were 'far too busy with rehearsals!' – MacLíammóir's comedy, *The Liar*, was going on at the Gate as a curtain-raiser to Conor Cruise O'Brien's *King Herod Explains*, which was virtually a solo rôle for Edwards. Exasperated at their lack of response to this crucial discussion, de Vere White used all his wiles, and they at last reluctantly agreed to come with him to the Department of Finance, where Haughey and his advisers received them cordially. On 10 September, the Department announced that the Minister had decided 'to make grants towards the renovation of the Gate Theatre, and towards its running costs.' The condition was that the theatre must also be made available to other companies, 'competent in the opinion of the Board of Directors to stage productions of high quality'. Effectively, this meant that the arrangement with Longford Productions in 1936, for Edwards-MacLíammóir Dublin Gate Theatre Productions to occupy the stage for six months of the year, was reinstated, except that this time there would be a subsidy for productions; just how much the subsidy would be was the question nearest to the partners' hearts. At an official celebratory dinner, Micheál found the person sitting beside him very heavy going, and was too blind to recognise the face; he enquired in a loud stage whisper, 'Who arranged the seating?' and received a kick from Hilton: it was the Minister for Finance.

They had to wait for a grant assessment. In the meantime, the Gate was closed for renovations for the second time in its forty-year history – but this time there was no need for an Edward Longford to perambulate O'Connell Street shaking a collecting-box, for the £68,000 required was provided by the government, and this was followed by further sums when dry rot was discovered and the building declared unsafe – the roof and floor had to be removed and replaced. The fundraising work of the Playhouse Society was thus rendered unnecessary. Hilton Edwards applied for the money already raised, but the committee decided that it should purchase four enormous Waterford glass chandeliers, and these were ceremoniously presented to the theatre when it reopened on 15 March 1971, with a new programme of plays produced by the original Gate founders.

It was as if they had never been away. The annual subsidy, when agreed, was £30,000 – an extraordinarily high figure, considering that up to then there had been no subsidy at all, save rescue sums of £4,000 and less, in the 1950s. 'It is the answer to an ageing maiden's prayer,' MacLíammóir told the Evening Herald. He remembered to write to the Taoiseach, Jack Lynch, to thank him for his part in the proceedings, and the Taoiseach found time to reply by hand thanking MacLíammóir in turn, and enquiring in a concerned way about his health. The Gate Theatre was now officially 'recognised'; the irony was that its founders were elderly and, by their own admission, out of touch with recent trends in the international theatre. They did, however, set to with a will to create a series of annual six-month programmes, through which the work of at least three important younger playwrights was to emerge; but, as expected, most of the productions were revivals, and this provoked a sour attitude from the press.

What the press forgot was that there is always a new audience for the oldest plays; and while there may have been critical groans about the proliferation of Shaws, Wildes and Shakespeares, these three playwrights drew much larger crowds, and sustained much longer runs, than they had ever done in the past – and what was more, they introduced new and younger faces to the Gate stage. Jeananne Crowley, Susan Fitzgerald, Kate Flynn, Pat Leavy, Maria Mac-Dermottroe, Claire Mullan, Máire O'Neill, Ann Rowan, Gerry Alexander, David Byrne, Derek Chapman, Conor Evans, Laurence Foster, Scott Fredericks, Bill Golding, Desmond Keogh, Gerard McSorley, Derry Power and others found themselves playing leading parts in a company which heretofore had a poor reputation for encouraging players from outside a certain *demi-mondain* circle. Betty Chancellor saw *Heartbreak House* shortly after she returned from the United States, while she was moving into the house Denis Johnston had bought at Sorrento Terrace in Dalkey; she wrote to him that it was 'exactly the same Gate show' as she had been in in 1933, and she liked Finola O'Shannon in the part she used to play.

Romeo and Juliet introduced Frank Grimes and Sorcha Cusack to the Gate. *The Importance of Being Earnest* brought back Noëlle Middleton, who did not think she could possibly manage Gwendolen, but Hilton told her that the passing years should be the least of her worries – 'It was probably the only time in history,' she said, 'that Lady Bracknell was younger than her daughter!' Mary Manning, who by now had returned to the reviewing scene, wrote in *Hibernia* that 'Miss Middleton had a deft way with parasols and gloves, and had clearly seen more than one London season.' *The Importance of Being Earnest*, with Patrick McLarnon and Desmond Keogh as the new Jack and Algy, was so successful in 1971, that *An Ideal Husband* was revived in 1972 and *Lady Windermere's Fan* in 1973. Claire Mullan joined the company to play the ideal husband's ideal wife, Lady Chiltern; one night the theatre shook, and she noticed small pieces of plaster landing on her dress – there had been an explosion caused by a bomb supposedly planted by the Ulster Volunteer Force half a mile away, in which a number of people were killed. The audience was told it could leave – but nobody did. *An Ideal Husband* ran from October until March, the longest ever Gate run; the cast of the next production, *A Servant of Two Masters*, was standing by all the time – on salary, which demonstrated the effectiveness of the new financial dispensation. When repeatedly asked when the next play would be coming on, Hilton replied equivocally, 'I have a cabbage in the oven' – meaning presumably that this curious dish would be served when the first course had been consumed.

The period which the actor David Byrne called the 'Gate renaissance', from the re-opening of the theatre in March 1971 until Patrick Bedford's production of *Equus* in 1977-78, had an inauspicious start. The first play in the new programme, *It's Later Than You Think*, was one of Anouilh's lesser works and provided a leading part which did not suit MacLíammóir; besides, he was unwell, and it was thought preferable to abandon the play after two weeks when he had to go into hospital with bronchial pneumonia, rather than rehearse an understudy. He was well enough to give a week of *The Importance of Being Oscar* in mid-May, and, while *Romeo and Juliet* was running, to rehearse a work which partially restored the Gate's image as an innovative theatre. This was *The Signalman's Apprentice* by Brian Phelan, who had acted several times with the company and was making a name for himself as a writer. *The Signalman's Apprentice* had already been produced by the Oxford Playhouse Company; Donal Donnelly had read it, and he sent the script to Micheál, who immediately wrote to Brian to say 'I came down to breakfast and asked Hilton if he'd heard anything from Brian Phelan lately, and Hilton said No, Why? and I said I'd dreamt I was touring with him in Chekhov on the Russian Steppes! I opened my mail and there was the script of your play! . . . We *must* do it. It was *meant*.' The play is set in a signal-box at Fulham, occupied by two elderly railway employees and a vicious apprentice; both partners wanted to play in it, with Eamonn Morrissey as the younger man; they invited Chloe Gibson, who was now the Head of Drama at RTE, to direct. Brian became aware of an absence of rapport at the first reading. Micheál commented, 'It's very boring the way these working-class characters repeat themselves!' Chloe Gibson chain-smoked and appeared to be making notes on another part of the text. Micheál was very slow on the lines – but Hilton had no difficulty at all, and at the very shaky opening performance helped his colleague many times. When in difficulties, Micheál would interject 'Lumme!' and 'Gor blimey!' and 'Lor love-a-duck!', in a very convincing accent. One of the critics took the unfortunate author severely to task for using so much out-dated Cockney slang.

This was another case of a play not receiving the treatment it deserved. There were fifteen subsequent productions in Germany, and it ran for a year and a half in Paris; the Gate production had the potential, but not the *finesse*, for another tour of the English-speaking world, but circumstances were against it. Hilton glibly told Brian the reason they had chosen the play was because the two main characters mirrored his and Micheál's relationship. Brian, depressed by the muted reaction in the press, replied 'It's a bloody shame you didn't play it like that!', which surprised and hurt Hilton, and Brian was immediately sorry – but he knew the ingredients had been present for a real success. There was much public interest, for the partners had not been seen together on the stage since *The Roses Are Real* in London, eight years before. As it turned out, they never appeared together again.

*

If Micheál's energy was flagging, Hilton's definitely was not. He impressed many of the players who were new to the company – some of whom had not even seen his productions in Dublin, so sporadic had they been during the latter part of the 1960s – in the way he had at first impressed the staff at Telefís Eireann, when confronted with a new challenge there. Desmond Forristal, a priest who produced radio and television programmes at the Catholic Communications Centre found Hilton functioning 'one hundred per cent' when he directed Forristal's first play *The True Story of the Horrid Popish Plot*. The play deals with the trumped-up case instigated by Titus Oates which resulted in the execution of the Archbishop of Armagh, Oliver Plunkett, for allegedly plotting the murder of Charles II. MacLíammóir was much attracted to the part of the king, especially as it involved several changes of costume, but he had to withdraw because of an impending eye operation. Aiden Grennell, who had not appeared in an Edwards-MacLíammóir production for several years, found that the old sense of dedication to the visual elements still prevailed – 'it was beautifully costumed and lighted: the scenes looked like a series of old masters – Lely or Van Dyck.' The première was notable for the attendance of the new archbishop of Dublin, Dermot Ryan; his predecessor, John Charles McQuaid, had forbidden priests of the diocese to attend the theatre, with the result that the players often came across black-coated figures lurking furtively in the wings – drama-loving religious to whom the stage-doorman had accorded surreptitious entry.

Gerard McSorley was twenty-one when he first started at the Gate; he was suddenly called in to replace an actor in *The True Story of the Horrid Popish Plot* and astonished everyone by learning the part in an afternoon, even getting the right laughs. Thereafter he was in several of Hilton's productions and absorbed a great deal of the practicality of the Edwards' technique. 'Clarity! Be clear!,' Hilton would exclaim: 'There must be clarity of articulation *and* thought.' 'It is the function of the stage performer to act in a theatrical way – the emotions have got to be large – you have to feel it a hundred times larger to get it across to the audience.' David Byrne recalled the importance Edwards gave to the presence of the audience – 'You have to sweep the audience through the play'; the audience had to be the focus of the piece: they were there to be involved, Hilton said. He could not abide the school which treated the audience as something outside, looking in.

MacLíammóir did not appear in either of Desmond Forristal's next two plays, *Black Man's Country* and *The Seventh Sin*; there was no suitable part for him in the former, and he was not well enough when the latter was ready for production in 1976. *Black Man's Country* caused a commotion at the Nigerian Embassy – Hilton, 'as a courtesy', sent a script to the ambassador, for the setting was the Ibo country during the Biafran war, and at the conclusion of the play two Irish missionaries are expelled by the Nigerian authorities. The ambassador requested that the play be withdrawn, and, when it was not, lodged a complaint with the Minister for Foreign Affairs, Garrett Fitzgerald, who took no action. (It was a much less sensitive issue than that of *Roly Poly* in 1940, and politicians were also more sophisticated.) He then made representations to the Papal Nuncio, and Archbishop Ryan told Desmond Forristal that if the play went on, it was probable that no Irish missionaries would be allowed into Nigeria again; but the archbishop did not instruct the playwright in any way. An embassy official telephoned Hilton Edwards to say that students would be placing a picket on the theatre: Edwards replied, 'That's wonderful: I'll tell the press!' The affair immediately subsided. Desmond Forristal submitted *The Seventh Sin* under the title of *Celestine* – it concerned the fifth pope of that name – but Hilton said the title would not do, for 'Celestine' sounded like a milkmaid in a French comedy. His production had the appearance of a mediaeval religious pageant; Seamus Kelly of The Irish Times declared it to be one of his best in thirty years.

Two new plays were produced at the Gate in the Dublin Theatre Festival in the autumn of 1973. The first was Joe O'Donnell's *Noone*, and, to the surprise of both press and public, the second was a new work from Micheál Mac-Líammóir, who had not written a play since *A Slipper for the Moon* in 1954. Joe O'Donnell had worked both as actor and stage director for Hilton Edwards, and *Noone*, which had won the Irish Life award, was to be performed at the Gate by Phyllis Ryan's Gemini Productions. It was a work requiring much crowd and choral work, as well as magical illusions. Phyllis Ryan, who described it as the first Irish crisis-of-identity play, felt that Hilton was the *only* director who could cope with it; she gave him the script, and he immediately said he wanted to do it. He imported the magician's tricks from London, and the cast had tremendous fun playing with them. Patrick Bedford played the lead, which, as Phyllis Ryan said, 'took him from utter despair to triumph'. Joe O'Donnell found the partners 'hugely supportive', making him feel very much at home on his return to the Gate, this time as playwright.

THE PASS OF KAZBEK

As soon as *Noone* opened, rehearsals for the new MacLíammóir play, *Prelude in Kazbek Street*, began, with Christopher Cazenove in the lead as Serge, an Irish-born ballet dancer with a Russian name. Had it been produced thirty years before, and had MacLíammóir played the lead – which would have completed a circle of self-indulgence – it would have caused an uproar, for the focus of the work is on the relationship between a homosexual man and an older woman; however, one may be quite sure that had he written it in the 1940s, the Gate management, for all its reputation for sensationalism, would not have dared produce it, and the script would have been consigned to the bottom drawer; it could not have been produced in the United Kingdom either, because of the theatre censorship. Social attitudes change very rapidly, and the irony is that by 1973 the outlook of the general public had changed immeasurably; where both Edwards and MacLíammóir genuinely believed they were taking a risk, humorously casting their eyes heavenward and telling the actors that they'd all be put in jail, audiences were, if anything, surprised by the cautionary nature of the advance publicity, and there was a sense of anti-climax.

Thamar, Queen of Georgia is said to have inhabited a castle in the Kazbek Pass between Georgia and Russia, where her guards lay in wait for handsome young men who were passing, and carried them to their queen as playthings. Micheál MacLíammóir could have seen the Diaghilev ballet *Thamar* at Drury Lane in the summer of 1913, when he was rehearsing *Joseph and his Brethren*; it was Nijinsky's last season before he was expelled from the company. The background of mythology and ballet is hardly explained in the play; thus, the title *Prelude in Kazbek Street* is more than a little obscure – but it is that kind of poetic obscurity which can cause fascination for a potential theatre audience. Thamar was, in the words of Hilton Edwards, 'a man trap', but in MacLíammóir's play her part is subsumed by that of the modern Serge, who is also a kind of man trap, and who possesses certain characteristics of Nijinski. Serge lives in a luxurious Parisian apartment in the 1970s, and is an international star; he has everything which fame and fortune can bring save, as in the fairy-tales, happiness. His special problem is that he is unable to maintain a relationship. It would seem that while Thamar trapped men to have her wicked way with them, Serge seizes them out of fear of loneliness, destroying them and perpetuating his own condition of despair.

Prelude in Kazbek Street, though no more than moderately successful on the stage, is quite revelatory in regard to the professional and personal relationship of Hilton Edwards and Micheál MacLíammóir, especially so since it appeared during the last decade of their lives. The comments which Edwards made on what was probably an advanced draft of the script reveal how much he influenced MacLíammóir's work long before it went into the rehearsal process. Nine pages of carefully categorised notes confirm a precise and analytical mind. It was a commonplace for authors who had plays produced at the Gate to remark that while Hilton's verbal criticism of a technical or structural nature were exceedingly astute, he was less helpful when it came to matters of theme and characterisation. Perhaps had they asked for written reports they would have been better satisfied, for it is clear from his work on *Prelude in Kazbek Street*, and on a few plays by other writers where a *précis* survives, that, given the time to assemble and transcribe his thoughts, he could formulate a comprehensive overview of the subject in question. 'There is a tendency,' he wrote of *Prelude in Kazbek Street*, 'to fear the theme and to dance off into comedy, which is inclined to make the comedy – excellent in itself – obtrusive.' He found the theme 'tenderly expressed, with great reticence . . . Any statement of the physical is the only area [in] which the theme could be distasteful . . . [avoid] self-pity or putting a bigger demand upon life than the average will think it reasonable for Serge to make.' On its comic content he wrote that while it was accepted, particularly in Irish plays, that comedy can be intermingled effectively with serious themes, often strengthening the tragic impact, 'I think that the juxtaposition should not be too violent, nor in a play which contains a theme as serious as this one, should it ever react as farce. If it does, the gamut is too wide: goes too high in the treble and then reaches down too low in the bass: the whole should be played in the middle register.'

The typewritten report has marginal comments pencilled by Micheál, in very shaky handwriting. 'Superb advice!' and 'Yes!', and much underlining of passages which he must have felt were important. Hilton also added typed exclamations of a more personal nature here and there – 'Have confidence, Micheál! You have got a master touch. Don't blur it!' and 'Please Micheál, please forgive this scathing comment . . . It is well meant and a lot of it possibly wrong, but I do not think so.' The tone is affectionate, but there is always an undercurrent which suggests that he was afraid of causing altercation. When *Prelude in Kazbek Street* was produced, Micheál played the small part of Paco Gonzalez, which he described in the *dramatis personae* as a 'middle-aged Spanish impresario: distinguished, dignified, unconsciously funny'; it was what casting-directors would call a 'cameo rôle', and he made it quite consciously funny, ad-libbing lines which were often better than the script, when he could not remember exactly what he had written. There was also a traditionally rustic Irish manservant, of the same genus as those in *Where Stars Walk* and *Ill Met by Moonlight,* this time played by Patrick McLarnon.

There was a revival of *Ill Met by Moonlight* in 1969, which Micheál directed, with Patrick Bedford as the rustic Lee. When Bedford had to leave for an engagement in New York, Micheál took over this part himself. Máire ni Ghráinne, who had to play opposite him as the servant girl in the rôle created by Sally Travers, felt that the result might be ludicrous, but 'he played it as an older man with such charm that I thought, "Well, this little girl isn't getting such a bad deal for a husband after all: he'll be very good to her".' Micheál's sense of fun also appealed to her – during the Irish-language exchanges in the second act he put in sentences about the audience, because he was sure the audience could not understand what he was saying. He played Mr Lofty in *The Good-Natur'd Man* at Christmas 1974, continuing until the end of March, probably the longest run this lesser of Goldsmith's two comedies had enjoyed since the eighteenth century. He would turn on his final line – 'I have to tell you that I'm bent,' then pause, and continue 'on another course of action', which amused the cast on the opening night but palled somewhat thereafter. Máire O'Neill, who played all the female leads at the Gate during a year's leave-of-absence from the Abbey, recalled that 'on the nights when Micheál was feeling well he was absolutely brilliant.' On 14 March, he wrote to Mary Rose McMaster in San Francisco, 'I am prostrate with a vile and violent cold . . . I have to stay in bed all day and get up at night to play Mr Lofty . . . I did a rather cute thing last night, though; being overcome with a sudden attack of wheezing in a scene with Mrs Crocker I whipped out a Kleenex – hoping it looked like a lace handkerchief – and said, A thousand pardons, madam, I am plagued with a severe chill: me physicians are in despair about me delicate constitution,' and trumpeted away. I thought it sweet, but nobody else seemed to. Hilton is very good, but he is in league with our doctor and forces me to take antibiotics, which I think are fatal and leave me suicidally depressed.'

Mr Lofty in *The Good-Natur'd Man* is always cited as the last part Micheál MacLíammóir performed in a play – excluding his own one-man shows, which were still taking him to places as diverse as Valetta, Liverpool, Newry and Cologne, where he had no problem with the lines, for they seemed to be permanently etched on his brain. He did have difficulty finding his way onto the stage – once he was on he was alright, for the moves between the set pieces of furniture were second nature. There was, however, one further part after Mr Lofty – Titus Oates in a revival of *The True Story of the Horrid Popish Plot* in the summer of 1975; Frank Kelly, who had played it previously, being unavailable. The result, according to members of the cast, was 'woeful'. Micheál was 'quite lost on the stage'; he 'said other people's lines as well as his own', and there was chaos. Everyone covered up for him, and the press was understanding.

He was unwell after the run finished, and did not bother to read the dramatisation of the Somerville and Ross novel, *The Real Charlotte*, which had been made by Terence de Vere White and Adrian Vale. When *The Real*

Charlotte opened during the Dublin Theatre Festival in October, he did not care for it at all. He was said to have had a row with Hilton prior to the press reception when the plays which had opened during the week were discussed in public; Hilton excused himself on the pretext of nervous exhaustion, and Micheál went instead. When asked by a journalist what he thought of the adaptation, he replied that it was very difficult to make anything out of such unmalleable material. Terence was a novelist, he said, and Adrian a radio and television scriptwriter: they could hardly be expected to make the book come alive on the stage. He then said that he had dramatised five novels, and therefore understood the problems. Members of the company were astounded by this show of disloyalty. Terence de Vere White – largely responsible for Edwards-MacLíammóir Productions still being in existence – exclaimed 'You dirty rotter!' and fled the hall. Hilton, hearing of this from the actors, telephoned Terence in a ferment of apology and mortification, inviting him to lunch – which Terence graciously accepted. Hilton explained that 'Micheál's idea had been that if he ran down the play the critics would be unable to do so.' Later, forgetting he had made this excuse, he said that Micheál was 'so blind he did not see that there were reporters present'!

The Real Charlotte was followed by a revival of *The Importance of Being Oscar* at the Gate. It is probable that Micheál suffered a slight stroke during the second week, for he found it difficult to co-ordinate his movements, though his memory and speech were unaffected. Theatre and household staff tried to persuade him to cancel the last performances; Hilton was in a frenzy; but Micheál was obdurate – this was his own show and he was not going to disappoint the audience. He spent each evening reclining upon what in his Irish language notes in the margin of the script he called the 'seastán' – *chaise-longue*; those who had not seen the show before noticed nothing amiss. Word reached the President, Cearbhall O Dálaigh, that Ireland's leading actor was probably giving his final performance; he came to the Gate on the Saturday night, and when the curtains closed, he climbed unannounced on the side of the stage and told the audience that they had seen 'something wonderful'. Micheál, who had an aversion to the President's high-pitched voice, muttered satirically to himself as he was guided to his dressing-room.

Two days later he underwent brain surgery. When he was discharged from Mount Carmel hospital he was without his wig; nor did he trouble further with make-up. He was now seen as a distinguished white-haired elderly gentleman; friends could hardly believe how well he was looking, and said so. 'Oh, I look dreadful – you're only saying that to flatter me!', was his invariable reply. He continued to write. *Enter a Goldfish* came out from Thames and Hudson in July 1977. It received a very warm reception in the British press, though there is the inevitable tinge of the detached English patronising the wayward Irish: the fact that the author was actually English was not yet revealed. The question of the book's classification was addressed by most of the reviewers; Sheridan Morley in The Times wondered why it should be a 'novel' – 'Partly, perhaps, because some of its details have already been outlined in the rich if confused tapestry of MacLíammóir's other writing: more probably, I suspect, because it details one or two homosexual and other encounters which even at this late stage the author is not prepared to document more fully . . . The only problem is that the novel leaps from probable fact to possible fiction.' Dublin reviewers were less inclined to dote over the author's 'Irish charm' and 'mischievous flickering smile'; Denis Johnston in Hibernia was especially blunt about the form: 'This insistent vein of anonymity has the peculiar effect of encouraging a reader – and particularly a reviewer – into a deeper suspicion of the facts than of the fiction, if indeed there is any fiction at all. What is it all in aid of? – one asks oneself, because there is nothing disreputable or actionable against any of the facts as one knows them . . . and there is no reason for any circumlocutions and disguise.' What Johnston – curiously, for one so involved – either failed to appreciate or deliberately chose to remain mystified about – was that Micheál MacLíammóir's life was in itself a circumlocution and, as Tyrone Guthrie had observed, concealed by many disguises.

*

A great sadness for Micheál MacLíammóir was the enforced departure of Brian Tobin from the post of theatre manager. Tobin had attempted to run the administrative side as competently as possible, but business acumen was his weakest quality, and a number of unsolved problems came to the attention of the board. As a member, MacLíammóir had to agree that Tobin be asked to retire on pension; and in due course Tobin accepted. Hilton Edwards busied himself with the continuing scheme of productions, engaging others to direct for him from time to time – Christopher Casson undertook a succession of highly popular Shaw revivals, *The Doctor's Dilemma* with Scott Fredericks as Dubedat, *The Devil's Disciple* with Fredericks as Dick Dudgeon, and *Major Barbara* with Anita Reeves. Micheál MacLíammóir appeared at opening nights, a seventy-eight-year-old 'smiling public man', often guided gracefully through the throng by Desmond Rushe, the columnist and senior theatre critic of the Independent. He was always at costume parades, complaining that he could not see – but when something was not right, like the wrong type of buttons on a waistcoat, he was suddenly able to see well enough. He helped Bill Golding with the four foreign accents required in his own old part in *Home for Christmas*, a spectacularly successful revival, which kept Gate audiences laughing well into 1977. He was not greatly interested in Peter Shaffer's *Equus* – which Patrick Bedford directed, having appeared in the New York production. Derek Chapman, who came from the Abbey to play the boy, Alan Strang, found Bedford to be a most understanding director for actors, and 'his notes were superb'. As for the partners, he said 'you could still see the magic in both of them – you couldn't take your eyes off them, which, I suppose in a way, was bad!' After the dress rehearsal, Micheál offered Chapman a dozen unsolicited and helpful notes – such as 'Don't use the Irish double-you: the English say "Wen?" and "Were?" and "Wat?"'

DESIGNER, WRITER, LINGUIST, AND BOON COMPANION

Equus was the earliest play seen in Dublin which contained both male and female nudity; Derek Chapman was interested that Hilton should have rejected the 'glaring white light' prescribed by the author and substituted 'something more atmospheric', believing the glare would create an uncalled-for feeling of prurience. The play was revived at Christmas 1977 and continued into the new year, achieving its hundredth performance on 21 February 1978. Hilton sent a note to the theatre from Harcourt Terrace: 'Dear Patrick, Will you please read this note to the company and all concerned. Micheál, as you know, is in hospital and I am only just out today and forbidden by the doctors to come down to the theatre tonight, which distresses me very much, but I know I can rely on you to pass on to the company and to the staff both before and behind the curtain this message, and to accept it also for yourself: The congratulations and thanks of the Board to you all, on this 100th performance of EQUUS at the Gate. . . . Coming at a time when we have been assaulted by "unwellness", you have, between you, given us something more precious than mere lucre: time. We are proud to be associated with the production, and we send you our love, and thanks, and good wishes. Yours gratefully . . . ' The words 'Hilton and Micheál' are typed at the foot, preceded by two scrawled signatures, both of which look as if the writers were on their death-beds. The fact was, Micheál was enduring his final illness.

He was interviewed for radio by Donncha O Dulaing from his bed in the Meath Hospital a few weeks before he died. His breath was short, and he spoke between gasps. He said he believed in the theory of [re]incarnation: 'It's the same system as rehearsing a play. You go back and learn what you failed to learn the day before.' The person he would most like to meet, he said, was Chopin – 'to me he seems to talk in music of something I feel I understand – Beethoven is so damnably predictable!' When asked what made him feel happiest, he replied without a hesitation, 'Very little, except Hilton being well and happy. He's not well at present.' He often telephoned Geraldine Neeson in Cork. Mary Manning went to visit him at the Meath Hospital. 'He was like a ghost lying there. As I was leaving he raised himself up in bed and said, "Mary, would you put a question-mark after *Youth's the Season* – ? now?" I wiped away the tears. "No, Micheál. No."' She left the hospital knowing she would not see him again. While he was there his grand-nephew, Michael Travers, often called. Micheál wanted to come home, and would give Michael words to use with Hilton as if he had thought of them himself – reasons why he should not stay in hospital, where Hilton knew he was much better off. Fr Desmond Forristal asked him if he would like the last rites: 'Oh, yes', he said, perhaps wondering if, as a member of the Church of England, he was entitled to them. He seemed to make a slight recovery, was allowed home, and was put to bed in the room on the ground floor overlooking the garden with its pear tree.

On the evening of 5 March, Pat Turner was writing a press release in the theatre when Mary Cannon telephoned from Harcourt Terrace asking her to inform Patrick Bedford that Micheál was 'very low'. She was at home when Mary telephoned again to say, 'He's gone'. Pat went immediately to Harcourt Terrace, where she found Hilton 'dazed' but surrounded by friends. Patrick arrived from the theatre as soon as the performance of *Equus* was over. Pat Turner stayed till 2 a.m., answering the telephone. The tributes started appearing in the papers next morning, and continued throughout the week. The Irish Times devoted its first leader to him, opening with the words 'Nobody can assess the contribution to the Irish theatre that was made by Micheál MacLíammóir'; only Oscar Wilde, the editor concluded, could have supplied an adequate epitaph. Conor Cruise O'Brien wrote in The Observer about the Gate having been 'the main centre for intellectual freedom and excitement in Dublin'; he picked Micheál's Oswald in *Ghosts* opposite Sybil Thorndike as 'incomparably the finest [performance] I ever saw him give.' One of the most charming short tributes came from Sir John Gielgud in the Daily Telegraph: 'I only acted with him once, in America, when he played Don Pedro in *Much Ado About Nothing* with characteristic panache and imperturbable good nature . . . His Judge Brack in *Hedda* with Peggy Ashcroft was to my mind a definitive performance. My last meeting with him was three years ago, a Sunday spent in Oxford, where, though beset by illness and failing eyesight, he had troubled to fly from Dublin (though acting then in a play of his own) to appear for ten minutes in a benefit gala for the Playhouse. We adjourned to the Randolph Hotel in the intervals of a long rehearsal, where he regaled us with a typical stream of jokes and stories in his inimitable voice and style. Designer, writer, linguist and boon companion as well as actor, he was a uniquely talented and delightful creature.'

Pat Turner made out the order for Mass with Fr Seán Quigley, who said prayers with the members of the household before the removal of the remains. Hilton asked for the text of the lesson from *Corinthians*, so that he could rehearse it for the following morning, when Fr Dermod McCarthy and Fr Desmond Forristal concelebrated Mass round the corner from Harcourt Terrace, at the Catholic University Church – which inevitably brought memories of *The Comedy of Errors*, for it is decorated in the Byzantine style. The President of Ireland was there, as well as the Taoiseach and five government ministers, the leader of the opposition, the leaders of the Labour and Workers' parties, as well as other state, church and municipal dignitaries. 'He did not fear death,' Fr Forristal said in his address, 'he welcomed it. He had done everything he wanted to do, he had used all the talents God had given him, and he had used them to the full. His bags were packed, his passport was stamped, he saw no point in waiting any longer.' A huge crowd waited outside the church; Peter Luke, now resident in Ireland and a member of the Gate board, was impressed that traffic was stopped and policemen saluted as the *cortège* went on its way through the city to the Gate Theatre, where it paused as the stage director, Yvette Hally, placed a wreath on the coffin; then the procession continued to the cemetery at Sutton, where Hilton Edwards, who had earlier said to reporters 'I am unashamedly inconsolable', spoke the Dirge from *Cymbeline:*

> Fear no more the heat o' the sun,
> Nor the furious winter's rages;
> Thou thy worldly task has done,
> Home art gone, and ta'en thy wages;
> Golden lads and girls all must
> As chimney-sweepers, come to dust.

Across the road from the strand, and in the lee of Howth Head – beloved of Diarmuid and Gráinne, of Mary O'Keefe and Aunt Craven, and half a league from the cottage which was once the home of Anew and Marjorie McMaster – Alfred Willmore of Kensal Green was laid to rest: but not upon a foreign shore, for he had become a part of the land which he had seen in a vision through the writing of William Butler Yeats, half a century before.

Chapter 19
The Gift of Theatre

Bobby Edwards from East Finchley lived on in Regency refinement at Harcourt Terrace, and also as the revered Director of Productions at the Gate Theatre; but he told Michael Williams, who had been looking after the partners' legal interests since Terence de Vere White ceased to practice, that he'd learned and spoken words by the world's great authors and wits, but the only appropriate quotation for his present condition was from Jerome Kern's *Showboat* – 'tired of living, and feared of dying'. Claire and Conor Evans were frequent visitors to the house, even at times when they were not playing at the Gate; he kept repeating to them that death was his greatest desire. He crumpled under the weight of guilt, when he thought of the unnecessary rows which he had had with Micheál, and the thoughtless insults which had escaped his lips. His friends found it impossible to convince him that he was lacking a sense of proportion, and that in time he would see things in clearer perspective.

The surprising impact of the Gate renaissance from 1970 was probably the reason why the National University of Ireland decided to award a Doctorate in Laws to Hilton Edwards in 1974. The general feeling was that because he was a less flamboyant character than MacLíammóir he had, quite simply, been over-looked. He was considerably moved when the Chancellor of the University, Eamon de Valéra, handed him his scroll at a ceremony in Iveagh House, and the President of University College Dublin, Professor Thomas Murphy, reminded the throng that as an actor he was 'a master with an inspired and impeccable technique' and as a director 'courageous in his experiments, demanding on his performers'. He concluded with a reference from *All for Hecuba*: 'When Micheál wondered whether he should have chained this London elephant in our Dublin Zoo, Hilton replied that he would not have remained if he had not wanted to. He said that he considered the Irish public "as good as any other in the world". To this I would add that the Irish public found Hilton Edwards as good a man of the theatre as any other in the world. It is for this reason the National University of Ireland honours him today.' As a genuine *immigré* he must have been even more pleased when he and his partner had been jointly installed as Freemen of the City of Dublin, though he jokingly said that what meant most to him was the free transportation on the city buses.

The months immediately after Micheál's death coincided with the period in which the theatre was on lease to other companies, so Hilton had plenty of time in which to brood. The golden jubilee of the founding of the Dublin Gate Theatre Studio was about to be celebrated with a major exhibition at the Hugh Lane Municipal Gallery of Modern Art; the prospect seemed to depress him rather than the reverse. This event would coincide with the Dublin Theatre Festival, and it was supposed that he would present one of his now celebrated revivals of a former Gate triumph, with a new cast – *Where Stars Walk* and *Liffey Lane* were mentioned. No one could understand why he decided to open on 3 October 1978 with a play which, in the opinion of those who appeared in it, 'should never have been put on'. This was a dramatisation by Peter Luke of Benedict Kiely's short novel set in contemporary Northern Ireland, *Proxopera*. 'The novel must contain a great heart of compassionate anger in its tale of the Binchy family caught up in the random violence of someone else's "Ulster war"', David Nowlan wrote in The Irish Times on 4 October. 'Alas for Peter Luke's dramatic adaptation of the tale; it must be one of the major disappointments of the jubilee and the festival . . . on the stage *Proxopera* is subverted by its structure and undermined by its mechanics.' What is curious is that the staging was at variance with Edwards' own aesthetic: changes of location indicated by lighting and the commentary of a ballad-singer stood out awkwardly in a production where naturalistically painted buildings and a 'real' station-wagon patently made of cardboard were central to the action. What was worse, on the opening night the 'farmhouse' fell over, and had to be held up by one of the actors, while he was making a passionate plea against the IRA's use of violence. The stage director was unable to see what was happening and wondered why the players were improvising lines; suddenly Hilton appeared in the wings having dashed round from front-of-house and told her to bring in the curtain and send out the singer. The words of his ballad, *My God, what have they done?* brought an unwholesome roar of laughter.

At the end of the performance, champagne was served backstage to commemorate the first Gate Theatre Studio production of fifty years before, when Hilton Edwards had so distinguished himself at the age of twenty-five as Peer Gynt. Many of those in the audience who had been invited to the party went home, too embarrassed to attend. Gerard McSorley, who was in the play, never forgot the solitary image of Hilton: 'People were afraid to approach him, because there was nothing to say'. He and other members of the cast did their best. Mary Cannon told Desmond Forristal that normally if some mishap occurred, Hilton would arrive backstage roaring like a lion, but tonight he was like a wounded one. Never could anyone recall such a disastrous opening at the Gate, nor one that was less propitious.

The conscientious Pat Turner had to face the customary Theatre Festival press forum at the Shelbourne Hotel next morning. 'Having sat in a corner drinking coffee and reading the dreadful notices, I was terrified when the time came for Brendan Smith to call on me to speak on behalf of the Gate. I apologised for the absence of other Gate representatives, and made the excuse that they were preparing for the opening of the Jubilee Exhibition that afternoon. I mumbled something about technical difficulties, but everyone knew the score, and I wasn't asked to elaborate.' She then hastened to Charlemont House to help prepare the reception for the President, Dr Patrick Hillery, who formally opened the exhibition at four o'clock. Everyone thought Hilton looked miserable, but he spoke with his usual sturdiness and clarity. The exhibition, organised by Richard Pine, who also compiled a superbly illustrated catalogue, occupied the whole upper floor of the Municipal Gallery. It contained set and costume designs, drawings, photographs, manuscripts, posters and stage memorabilia, and demonstrated graphically the congruity of outlook and style of the Gate and its founders. Other theatres in the British Isles, where régimes were regularly convulsed by administrative change, where directors and designers were engaged for no more than a season or two, and where modes of presentation altered as frequently as the weather, could not be compared with the Dublin Gate Theatre for sheer consistency of creative endeavour and rationale; and in Europe, only the Cartel des Quatres – Gaston Baty, Charles Dullin, Louis Jouvet and Georges Pitoëff – in its component parts so influential on the work of Edwards and MacLíammóir, possessed anything like the continuing *panache*.

Almost a hundred individuals and institutions lent items for the exhibition. Much of the material came from the Special Collections Department of the Library of Northwestern University, Illinois, to which the partners had sold much of the content of their files. Erstwhile members of Longford Productions were annoyed that there was nothing representing that company, but Pat Turner had approached Christine, who told her she did not have anything; what Pat failed to realise was that Christine was suffering from one of the bouts of depression which were increasingly overtaking her. The press was cordial in its coverage of the exhibition, but there were murmurs about the direction in which the Gate was moving, or failing to move. David Nowlan, in his end-of-year summary of the theatre for The Irish Times, remarked on the bitter irony of MacLíammóir's death taking place in the year of the partnership's golden jubilee; 'While the deeply bereaved Hilton Edwards had been left to us to continue the work of the Dublin Gate Theatre, there was a hollow certainty that the succession in this seminal enterprise had not been secured.' Tomás MacAnna, who had directed what was by all accounts a most imaginative production of Micheál MacLíammóir's *The Mountains Look Different* in Irish as *Tá Cruth Nua ar na Sléibhte* at the Peacock Theatre, wrote to Denis Johnston on this topic:'

The Gate situation is an intriguing one – who will inherit? After all, Yeats, Gregory and co. made sure there would be a continuum at the Abbey. H and M I think assumed their immortality. Rumour has it that the mantle will fall on PB. Others talk of Peter Luke. It would be a great pity if the work of 50 years were to stop short and the Gate just became a 'hired-out' Theatre like the Eblana. Oh well – we must wait and see.

Hilton's mind was not moving on such mundane matters when he wrote to Denis Johnston on 24 October, in reply to a message of congratulation: 'It took Micheál and myself all our time to keep the Gate going by our joint efforts. How I will be able to manage without him I cannot foresee, but the Board are most considerate and helpful . . . I am fully aware of how much we owe to our friends, and those who have helped us in the past, and it is sad that Christine Longford is so unwell that she is again in hospital and I fear cannot be approached, as I dislike to invade her need for privacy.' Four days later he wrote again to thank Johnston for his article in the commemorative book *Enter Certain Players*, which Peter Luke had edited. 'I have a flop on at the moment at the Gate, for which I feel largely responsible in choosing a play which I knew from the first was really television material, but I have attempted the impossible sometimes before, and hoped to get away with the presentation of a stationary car, with sound effects, which was supposed to be moving. I realise now one can do this in comedy – *Dr Knock* or Thornton Wilder – but not in a play with tragic connotations . . . Again I thank you for your splendid article and for so much that we owe to you in the past, I remain (I should say barely remain) Your battered old friend, Hilton.'

The barriers were coming down, and past rages and misunderstandings consigned to oblivion. Christine Longford died on 14 May 1980, only three weeks after receiving an honorary Doctorate in Literature from the National University of Ireland. (The novelist John Broderick described her as 'a reluctant genius.') Hilton wrote a short tribute in the theatre programme the following week, in which he said that she had the scholarship and talent that would have conquered any subject to which she chose to devote herself, ending, 'Micheál MacLíammóir and I never ceased to admire, respect and to be fascinated by a personality unquestionably unique. Our gratitude to her and to Lord Longford is eternal.' These final words could not have been contemplated during the years following the Longford split, nor indeed until after Edward Longford's death.

During the years 1978 to 1982 Hilton Edwards directed only four productions. *Proxopera* was taken off after three weeks and replaced by an independent production of a new play by Hugh Carr with Patrick Bedford in the lead. While this was running, the promised revival of *Where Stars Walk* was rehearsed, often in Patrick's house, because it was warm and Hilton found all rehearsal halls draughty. Jonathan White played the reincarnation of Midhir and Biddy White-Lennon was the modern counterpart of Etáin; Molly MacEwen came from Edinburgh to design the set and costumes for what had, in the intervening years, become a 'period piece'. She was much amused, when visiting the exhibition at Charlemont House, to find herself walking on the carpet she had designed for *The Importance of Being Oscar*, laid down in a room devoted solely to that production. *Where Stars Walk* was welcomed by

David Nowlan as 'a gentle, charming, perceptive and witty evening of theatre', and Desmond Rushe noted that 'justice has been done to its brilliant creator.' In October 1979, Hilton directed *Captive Audience*, a new play by Desmond Forristal, dealing with malign de-programming or re-orientating of personality. There are two characters – played by Gerard McSorley and Liz Bono – and a third 'expected' character who does not appear, but whose name was given on the programme in order to involve – or mislead – the audience; Pat Turner wrote a highly plausible CV for the non-existent actor, stating that he had taken part in the Abbey production of *Borstal Boy* and in Noel Pearson's musical *Crock*.

Hilton Edwards' idea in producing Wilde's Socratic dialogue *The Critic as Artist* as part of a double bill, in June 1980, was that the actors should play as if they were Oscar Wilde and Lord Alfred Douglas – but there was no way in which this notion could be transmitted to the audience, and what came across was a lengthy conversation with no dramatic feeling and no stage business. Hilton was suffering from the aftermath of a prostate operation – he said he found it impossible to 'spend a penny' but 'could just manage to spend a farthing' – and the discomfort kept him from attending most of the rehearsals. In any case, neither Scott Fredericks not Brian de Salvo were convinced that his heart was in it. If there was any distinction to be gained for them it was the negative one that they had appeared in Hilton Edwards' last production.

OPENING WINDOWS

The Arts Council, which had taken over the function of subsidising the chief theatres from the Department of Finance, began, quite discreetly, to voice concern about Hilton Edwards' health. Micheál MacLíammóir had said in a television interview some years before that 'quite frankly we have our own tradition: I imagine it will die with us.' It is possible that Hilton still hoped that Patrick Bedford would take over the theatre in the fullness of time, but he was continuing to spend much of his working year in New York. For the moment, most of the plays produced under the Edwards-MacLíammóir banner were directed by two much younger men, Paul Brennan and Patrick Laffan. The Arts Council was also worried that the selection of plays was not adding up to a balanced annual programme. At the end of 1980, Mary Cannon assured the drama officer of the Council that an advertisement was being placed for 'an assistant artistic director or a resident director' answerable to Hilton Edwards, but time passed and no appointment was made. In March 1981, the chief item on the agenda for the Gate board was 'Dr Edwards' Health and Welfare', and this was followed by a special meeting, where Hilton Edwards discussed the theatre's future with the Chairman and Director of the Arts Council, with Michael Scott attending as a member of both bodies. Hilton agreed to accept an 'unconditional pension' – he was seventy-seven: most men would have retired at least a decade earlier. It was also agreed that separate arrangements should be made for Edwards-MacLíammóir Productions and the Gate Theatre. On 10 September Mary Cannon wrote to the Director of the Arts Council that 'Hilton Edwards will be most happy to accept a Co-Artistic Director (particularly one of the calibre of Patrick Laffan, who has in Hilton's opinion done a splendid job in "Amadeus").' Patrick Laffan was not appointed until 5 April 1982 and in fact directed only one play in his new capacity – the immensely successful satiric comedy, *Semi-Private*, by Mary Halpin – before Hilton Edwards' final illness. Ann Myler, the stage director, was constantly pinning messages from Hilton on the backstage board, wishing the company well for dress rehearsals or opening nights, and apologising for being under doctor's orders not to attend.

The playwright, Andrew Ganly, who spent part of his retirement lecturing on the history of the classical world, convinced Hilton that he should come on a luxury tour to Greece. He did, but stubbed his toe, not on a piece of antique sculpture as the story was related, but on the more prosaic porcelain plinth of a hotel shower, so that he had to be pushed for part of the trip in a wheel chair. He held forth on the acoustics of the ancient theatres, and at Epidauros was helped on to the *skene*, from where he astonished the party, and all the other tourists who were clambering over the masonry, by declaiming a passage from the Yeats version of *King Oedipus*. What astonished was not so much the clear acoustic of the theatre, but the splendid carrying voice of the protagonist.

During the run of the Gate's 1982 contribution to the Dublin Theatre Festival, *Semi-Private*, Hilton Edwards went into a nursing-home in Dalkey. He did not like it, and telephoned Mary Cannon to arrange for his discharge. Both she and his doctor thought such a move would be most unwise, but Mary agreed to get the house in order for his convalescence, which would mean engaging a full-time nurse. Hilton announced that he would install himself temporarily in the Shelbourne Hotel, but the doctor talked him out of that. Finally, he agreed that he should be transferred to another nursing home, which had been highly recommended to him, but it turned out to be a geriatric home and he felt entirely depressed among the halt and confused; before he had been there for a day he telephoned to Mary Cannon, 'Get me out of here!' His doctor ordered him to the Royal City of Dublin Hospital.

Gerry Alexander, who had played a memorable Shylock in 1977 with Hilton directing – it had been one of Hilton's favourite parts – thought he was being neglected in hospital; but he had arrived at one of the rare times when there were no other visitors. Patrick Bedford was in frequent attendance. Cyril Cusack was interested to note that when offered the sacrament by the chaplain on Sunday morning, Hilton replied with what seemed genuine humility, 'I am not worthy'. Charles Roberts visited, and Hilton said 'We've always loved you, Mickey and myself'. On the evening of 16 November, the matron told Mary Cannon that he had 'turned his face to the wall'. He died on Thursday 18, of 'diverticulitis'. Patrick Bedford and Mary Cannon arranged for his body to be brought back to Harcourt Terrace.

Caroline Walsh of The Irish Times wrote that 'he looked resplendent in his dress suit, a red carnation in his lapel, as close friends came to make their last farewell.' It seemed that Micheál's obsequies four years before had been a dress rehearsal for this final funeral, amid the variegated mosaic and eastern tiles of the Catholic University Church. The prayers of the faithful were read by Sally Travers, Christopher Casson, Michael Scott and Conor Evans.

Micheál MacLíammóir and Hilton Edwards had written mirror-image wills, each leaving his possessions to the survivor. On 12 February 1982, Hilton wrote a new will, in which he made a number of bequests to friends and professional colleagues. He left 'sufficient of my shares in Dublin Gate Theatre Productions Ltd to my friend Michael Scott absolutely which will vest in him a 51% of the Company carrying voting rights.' He left his piano and car to Patrick Bedford, his books on visual art to Molly MacEwen, a tapestry screen and a mirror which had belonged to her father to Mary Rose McMaster, his collection of gramophone records to Brendan Neilan, and 'to Patrick McLarnon my travelling dressing case in mahogany and silver.' This latter item proved, upon examination of the initials, not to have been his dressing case, but that of Alfred Willmore, Micheál MacLíammóir's father. The remainder of his property, including the house in Harcourt Terrace, was left to Sally Travers and Patrick Bedford, one half to each. When the will was proved and registered in the probate office, the gross value of the estate was shown as £101,192.11.

The Irish Times' leading article on the day of Hilton Edwards' funeral stated that he served Ireland memorably 'by presenting so many generations with the gift of theatre which nourished alike the mind and senses. At its best it is magic; at his best, Hilton Edwards was a magician.' 'Magic' was the word Patrick Bedford repeatedly used many years later, when recalling the Gate. Mary Rose McMaster used it too, adding, 'and the fun!' After the Requiem Mass, Máire O'Neill said that her year with the Gate had been the most exciting period of her life. Conor Evans declared that Hilton Edwards had 'opened windows'. 'My professional life,' said Anna Manahan, 'hangs on what Hilton gave me'; she knew she would never forget his admonition to 'dig your furrow deep at rehearsal'. 'The Gate,' wrote Denis Johnston in recognition of Hilton's work as teacher, 'never had an acting school. It was itself a school for Everybody and had provided an Apprenticeship for a series of Visitors who have gone on to stardom – Welles, Mason, Cusack, Herlihy, Fitzgerald . . . '

At noon in St Fintan's graveyard on Monday 22 November 1982, the boys from East Finchley and Kensal Green were reunited in the shadow of the Hill of Howth.

Select Bibliography

Arnold, Bruce, *Mainie Jellett and the Modern Movement in Ireland*. New Haven and London, 1991.

Baedeker, Karl, *Egypt*. London 1929.

Bakst, Léon, *Bakst*. London 1977.

Bannister, Winifred, *James Bridie and his Theatre*. London 1955.

Bonnici, Joseph, and Cassall, Michael, *The Royal Opera House, Malta*. Valetta 1990.

Boylan, Henry, *A Dictionary of Irish Biography*. Dublin, 1978.

Brady, Anne M., and Cleeve, Brian, *A Biographical Dictionary of Irish Writers*. Mullingar, 1985.

Bridges-Adams, W., *The Shakespeare Country*. London 1932.

Bridges-Adams, W., *The Irresistible Theatre*. London 1957.

Callow, Simon, *Being an Actor*. London 1988.

Cooper, Gladys, *Gladys Cooper*. London 1931.

Cowell, John, *No Profit But the Name*. Dublin 1988.

Carlson, Julia ed., *Banned in Ireland*. London 1990.

Cave, Richard, and Pine, Richard, *The Dublin Gate Theatre*. Cambridge, N.J., 1984.

Clarke, Brenna Katz, and Ferrar, Harold, *The Dublin Drama League*. Dublin 1979.

Cobb, Richard, *A Classical Education*. London 1985.

Collis, Robert, *To Be a Pilgrim*. London 1975.

Courtney, Marie Therèse, *Edward Martyn and the Irish Theatre*. New York 1952.

Craig, Maurice, *The Architecture of Ireland*. London 1982.

Cronin, Anthony, *No Laughing Matter: the Life and Times of Flann O'Brien*. London 1990.

Cuddon, J.A., *Yugoslavia*. London 1986.

Dantanus, Ulf, *Brian Friel*. London 1988.

Deale, Kenneth E.L., *Beyond Any Reasonable Doubt?* Dublin 1960.

de Blacam, Aodh, *Gaelic Literature Surveyed*. Dublin 1973.

de Breffny, Brian, *Ireland: a Cultural Encyclopaedia*. London, 1983.

Dolin, Anton, *Last Words*. London 1985.

Ellis, Ruth, *The Shakespeare Memorial Theatre*. London 1949.

Ellmann, Richard, *Oscar Wilde*. London 1987.

Ellmann, Richard, *Yeats: the Man and the Masks*. London, 1949.

Esslin, Martin (ed.), *Encyclopaedia of World Theatre*. London 1977.

Fisher, Clive, *Noël Coward*. London 1992.

Fitz-Simon, Christopher, *The Arts in Ireland*. Dublin 1982.

Fitz-Simon, Christopher, *The Irish Theatre*. London 1983.

Forsyth, James, *Tyrone Guthrie*. London 1976.

Foster, R.F.(ed.), *Illustrated History of Ireland*. Oxford 1989.

Garafola, Lynn, *Diaghilev's Ballets Russes*. Oxford 1989

Gielgud, John, *Early Stages*. London 1939

Gielgud, John, *Shakespeare: Hit or Miss?* London 1991

Gordon, Lois, *Harold Pinter: a Casebook*. London 1990.

Gorham, Maurice, *Forty Years of Irish Broadcasting*. Dublin 1967.

Grisewood, Harman, *One Thing at a Time*. London 1968.

Harwood, Ronald, *Donald Wolfit*. Oxford 1983.

Hepworth, Cecil M., *Came the Dawn*. London 1951.

Hickey, D.J., and Doherty, J.E., *A Dictionary of Irish History* 1900-1980. Dublin 1980.

Higham, Charles, *Orson Welles: the Rise and Fall of an American Genius*. Sevenoaks 1968.

Hobson, Bulmer, *The Gate Theatre Dublin*. Dublin 1934.

Hogan, Robert, *After the Irish Renaissance*. London 1968.

Holland, Vyvyan, *Oscar Wilde and his World*. London 1966.

Holroyd, Michael, *Bernard Shaw* (four vols.) London 1988-92.

Hunt, Hugh, *The Abbey, Ireland's National Theatre*. Dublin 1979.

Inglis, Brian, *Downstarts*. London 1991.

Kavanagh, Peter, *The Irish Theatre*. Tralee 1946.

Kennedy, Brian P., *Dreams and Responsibilities*. Dublin 1990.

Lancelyn Green, Robert, *Fifty Years of Peter Pan*. London 1954.

Lansdown, Charles, *Offstage*. London, 1973.

Leaming, Barbara, *Orson Welles*. New York 1983.

Lee, J.J., *Ireland 1912-1985*. Cambridge 1989.

Luke, Peter, ed., *Enter Certain Players*. Dublin 1978.

MacDonald, Nesta, *Diaghilev Observed*. New York 1975.

McIlroy, Brian, *World Cinema – Ireland*. Trowbridge 1989.

Mason, James, *Before I Forget*. London 1981.

Matlaw, Myron, *Modern World Drama*. London 1972.

Morley, Sheridan, *James Mason*. London 1989.

Moody, T.W., and Martin, F.X., *The Course of Irish History*. Dublin 1967.

Mooney, Ria, ed.Val Mulkerns, *Players and Painted Stage*. Newark 1978.

Murphy, Daniel J., (ed.), *Lady Gregory: the Journals*. Gerrards Cross 1987.

Naremore, James, *The Magical World of Orson Welles*. New York 1978.

Noble, Peter, *The Fabulous Orson Welles*. London 1956.

O'Brien, George, *Brian Friel*. Dublin 1989.

O'Connor, Ulick, *Biographers and the Art of Biography*. Dublin 1991.

O hAodha, Micheál, *Theatre in Ireland*. Oxford 1974.

O hAodha, Micheál, *The Importance of Being Micheál*. Dingle 1990.

O'Leary, Liam, ed., *Cinema Ireland 1895-1976*. Dublin 1976.

Ostwald, Peter, *Vaslav Nijinsky*. London 1991.

Payn, Graham, and Morley, Sheridan, *The Noël Coward Diaries*. London 1982.

Pearson, Hesketh, *Beerbohm Tree*. London 1956.

Pine, Richard, *All For Hecuba* (catalogue). Dublin 1978.

Pine, Richard, *Brian Friel and Ireland's Drama*. London 1990.

Pinter, Harold, *Mac*. Ipswich 1968.

Purdom, C.B., *A Guide to the Plays of Bernard Shaw*. London 1963.

Quayle, Anthony, *A Time to Speak*. London 1991.

Read, Jack, *Empires, Hippodromes and Palaces*. London 1985.

Robinson, Lennox, *The Irish Theatre*. London 1939.

Robinson, Lennox, *Ireland's Abbey Theatre*. London 1951.

Rosso, Diane de, *James Mason*. Luton 1982.

Ryan, Philip, *Jimmy O'Dea*. Dublin 1990.

Share, Bernard, *The Emergency*. Dublin 1978.

Sheehan, Helena, *Irish Television Drama*. Dublin 1987.

Simpson, Alan, *Beckett and Behan and a Theatre in Dublin*. London 1962.

Spencer, Charles, *Léon Bakst*. London 1973.

Swift, Carolyn, *Stage by Stage*. Dublin 1985.

Ronsley, Joseph, *Denis Johnston*. Gerrards Cross 1981.

Terry, Julia Neilson, *This for Remembrance*. London 1940.

Tynan, Kenneth, *Curtains*. London 1961.

Ward, Philip, *Bulgaria*. New York 1989.

Williams, Harcourt, *Old Vic Saga*. London 1950.

Wilson, Simon, *Beardsley*. London 1976.

Vier, Jacques, *Le Théâtre de Jean Anouilh*. Paris 1976.

Vinson, Janet, ed., *Contemporary Dramatists*. New York 1977.

Wood, Audrey, and Wilk, Max, *Represented by Audrey Wood*. New York 1981.

Newspapers and Periodicals

IRELAND

Armagh Gazette, Ballymena Observer, The Bell, Clare Champion, Comhar, Commentary, County Down Spectator, Cork Examiner, Cork Weekly Examiner, Belfast Newsletter, Belfast Telegraph, Connacht Sentinel, Connacht Tribune, Derry Journal, Donegal Democrat, Dublin Magazine, Dublin Opinion, Enniscorthy Echo, Evening Echo, Evening Herald, Evening Mail, Evening Press, Freeman's Journal, Hibernia, Impartial Reporter, Inniú,

Irish Independent, Irish News, Irish Press, The Irishman, Irish Tatler and Sketch, The Irish Times, The Leader, Limerick Leader, Motley, Northern Standard, Northern Whig, Radio Review, RTE Guide, Southern Star, The Statesman, Sunday Independent, Sunday Press, TCD, Times Pictorial,The Word.

GREAT BRITAIN

Birmingham Mail, The Bulletin, Coventry Telegraph, Daily Express, Daily Graphic, Daily Mail, Daily Mirror, Daily News, Daily Sketch, Daily Record, Daily Telegraph, The Era, Evening Citizen, Evening News, Financial Times, Glasgow Herald, The Globe, Gramophone, The Guardian, Harper's Bazaar, Illustrated London News, The Lady's Pictorial, The Listener, Liverpool Echo, Manchester Guardian, Modern Society, Morning Leader, Morning Post, New Statesman, News Chronicle, Nottingham Guardian Journal, The Scotsman, The Sphere, The Stage, The Observer, Pall Mall Gazette, Punch, Radio Times, Tatler and Sketch, The Sketch, South Yorkshire Advertiser, The Stage, The Star, Sunday Dispatch, Sunday Empire News, Sunday Express, Sunday Graphic, Sunday Telegraph, Sunday Times, The Times.

ASIA

The Times of India.

NORTH AMERICA

Boston Globe, Boston Herald, Chicago Daily News, Chicago Daily Times, Chicago Daily Tribune, Chicago Herald and Examiner, Chicago Sun Times, Christian Science Monitor, New York Daily News, New York Herald Tribune, New York Post, New York Times, New Yorker, Philadelphia Enquirer, Philadelphia Sunday Bulletin, New York Post, Saturday Review of Literature, Toronto Globe and Mail, Toronto Star.

SOUTH AMERICA

Buenos Aires Herald, El Clarin, Estado de Sao Paulo, Folha de Sao Paulo, O Globo, Journal do Brazil, El Païs, La Prensa, Southern Cross.

AUSTRALIA

Sydney Bulletin, Adelaide News, Canberra Times, Perth Record, The Sun, Sunday News, Sydney Bulletin, Triad.

WESTERN EUROPE

Afen Posten, Basler Zeitung, Berlingske Aftenavis, Berlingske Tidende, Bild am Sonntag, Dag Blade, Deutsches Allegemeines Sonntagsblatt, Le Figaro, France, France Soir, Ill Gazzettino, Il Giorno, Hamburger Abendblatt, Hamburger Morgenpost, Helsingborgs Posten, Helsingen Sanomat, Journal de Genève, Lordags Avisen, La Nazione, La Nova Venezia, Paris Press,

Het Parool, Social Demokraten, Sydvenska Dagbladet, Politiken, Le Soir,
Il Tasonomat, Die Tat, De Telegraaf, Tribune de Genève, Die Welt,
De Volkskrant, Die Zeit.

MEDITERRANEAN AND BALKAN

Bourse Egyptienne, Danea, Hrvatski Dnevik, Jutarnji List, Kathimerni, Kaipon,
Malta Chronicle, Messager d'Athènes, Obsor, Le Phare Egyptien, Slovenski
Dom, Slovenski Narod, Times of Malta, Egyptian Gazette, Egyptian Mail,
Gazette of Alexandria.

Index

Aiken, Frank, 179
Allgood, Sara, 85
Aldrich, Richard, 149, 152
Alexander, Gerry, 291, 308
All for Hecuba
  (MacLíammóir), 53, 55,
  72, 82-3, 88, 92, 110,
  116, 143-4, 303
An Philibín (J. H. Pollock),
  55-6
Andrews, Bobbie, 20, 29,
  39, 46
Andrews, C. S., 290
Andrews, Eamonn, 238, 268
Anketell, Margaret, 145, 258
Archer, J. Kane, 131
Arkell, Reginald and
  Elizabeth, 37
Aronson, Jack, 259
Asche, Oscar, 15
Ashcroft, Dame Peggy, 192,
  301
Ashmore, Peter, 192, 228
Atkins, Robert, 37, 47, 53
Atkinson, Brooks, 150

Bakst, Léon, 29, 51
Baldacchino, E., 203, 205
Ball, Edward, 90-1, 144
Barrs, Norman, 149, 152-3,
  240
Barry, Michael, 209-10, 240,
  244-6, 252
Baty, Gaston, 305
Baxter, Keith 223-4
Beardsley, Aubrey, 16
Beaumont, Hugh 192, 229
Beckett, Samuel, 53, 56, 63,
  78-80, 130, 137, 285,
  290
Bedford, Patrick, 32, 36, 49,
  163, 198, 206, 219, 224,
  229, 231, 255, 276-8,
  280, 288, 292, 295, 297,
  299-301, 306, 308-9

Beerbohm, Max, 16
Benois, Alexandre, 51
Benson, Sir Frank, 37
Benson, Hamlyn, 140
Bernal, Robert, 216
Bernhardt, Sarah, 29, 255,
  289
Betjeman, John, 130, 137
Bibesco, Prince, 169
Bibesco, Princess, 119
Biddle, Esmé, 16
Birkett, Viva, 26
Bissing, Toska, 104, 109-19,
  152
Black, Kitty, 193, 270
Blakely, Colin, 286
Bláth agus Taibhse
  (MacLíammóir), 257-8
Blythe, Ernest 65, 274
Bogdanovich, Peter 163-4,
  225
Boland, Eavan, 278
Bonham-Carter, Lady
  Violet, 99
Bono, Liz, 307
Bools, John, 195, 200
Boucicault, Dion (the
  younger), 26, 31
Brambell, Wilfred, 137
Brecht, Bertolt, 219, 246
Brennan, Denis, 132, 137,
  149, 174, 180, 183-4,
  198
Brennan, Paul, 307
Braunsweg, Julian, 215, 220
Bridges-Adams, W., 80, 100,
  104, 108, 187
Bridie, James, 148
Brock, Patrick, 86
Broderick, John, 306
Brogan, Harry, 253
Brown, Christy, 126
Brunnick, John, 179-80
Burke, Brendan and Marie,
  221, 240, 285

Byrne, David, 291-2, 294
Byrne, Gay, 287

Callow, Simon, 75, 191
Campbell, Hon. Gordon, 56,
  61, 66
Campbell, Mrs Patrick, 60,
  255
Cannon, Mary, 301, 304,
  307-8
Capek, Karel and Josef, 88
Carden, Sheila, 243
Carey, Brian, 111
Carey, Denis, 53, 178
Carey, May, 52, 56, 100-1,
  111, 119
Carey, Patrick, 111-13, 137
Carmichael, Coralie, 17, 52,
  56-8, 64, 72, 76, 78, 85,
  91-2, 108, 113-15, 121,
  137, 138, 166-7, 194-5,
  198, 202, 212, 218
Carney, Art 282-3
Carr, Hugh, 306
Carroll, Niall, 167, 170, 174
Casey, Dorothy, 167
Casson, Christopher, 104,
  113, 119, 124, 135-6,
  137-8, 143, 145, 198,
  212, 229, 260, 287, 299,
  309
Casson, Kay, (*née*
  O'Connell), 23, 104,
  137-8, 214, 260, 262
Casson, Sir Lewis, 104, 138
Cazenove, Christopher, 295
Chalmers, J. Kendall, 113,
  118-19
Chamberlain, Neville, 107,
  117
Chancellor, Betty, 56, 72,
  75-6, 78, 85, 87-8, 96-7,
  127, 137-41, 149-53,
  221, 234, 250, 287,
  290-1

Chapman, Derek, 291, 299-300
Chase, Pauline, 26, 28
Chiati, Abdel Rahmed, 196-7, 199
Childers, Erskine, 146, 238
Clark, Ann, 16, 98, 100-01
Clarke, Austin, 79, 217
Cleeve, Brian and Veronica, 242, 252
Clements, John, 215
Cloutier, Suzanne, 158-60
Cluskey, Frank, 13-14
Cocteau, Jean, 285
Cogley, Daisy Bannard ('Toto'), 52, 61, 66, 218, 237
Collier, Constance, 46
Collins, Pan, 241, 287
Collinson, Peter, 244, 252, 254
Collis, Robert, 124-7, 148, 171
Colum, Padraic, 254
Conmee, Marie, 219
Cooper, Gladys, 15, 245
Copeau, Jacques, 49, 92
Corkery, Daniel, 105
Costello, John A., 196
Court, Emmerton, 124
Coward, Noël, 21, 26-7, 39, 41, 152, 232
Cowell, John, 68, 72, 87, 122
Craig, Gordon, 43
Craig, Maurice, 217
Craig, May, 132
Crane, Warren, 283
Cross, Joan, 48
Crowe, Eileen, 132, 253
Crowley, Jeananne, 291
Cruise O'Brien, Conor, 290, 301
Cummins, Danny, 229
Cummins, Peggy, 100, 149
Curley, Treasa (*née* Davison), 187, 240
Curran, C.P., 53-4, 56, 62, 64, 79, 140
Cusack, Cyril, 42, 73, 94, 105, 127-8, 149, 164, 194, 283-4, 308
Cusack, Sinéad, 127
Cusack, Maureen (*née* Kiely), 127, 149
Cusack, Sorcha, 127, 291

Dalgarno, Alice, 144, 210
Dancing Shadow, The (MacLíammóir), 134, 164
Darlington, W.A., 147
Daubeny, Peter, 269
Davenport, Ronald, 247
Davidson, Alastair, 224
de Blieck, Jan, 221-3, 258-9
de Laforcade, 135
de Salvo, Brian, 307
deValéra, Eamon, 91, 121, 135, 178, 248, 253, 269, 303
deVereWhite, Terence, 176, 181-2, 195-6, 202, 206-9, 215, 217, 223, 236-7, 289-90, 298, 303
Delaney, Shelagh, 234
Delany, Maureen, 42, 132, 149
Devine, George, 192, 234
Devlin, William, 210
Diaghilev, Sergei, 28, 295
Diarmuid agus Gráinne (MacLíammóir), 49-51, 54-5, 57, 60-1, 186-7, 230, 290
Dickens, Charles, 227-8
Doherty, Bran, 149-50, 152-3
Dolin, Anton, 220, 243
Donnelly, Donal, 276, 278, 280, 287, 292
Doolan, Dermot K., 184, 273
Doran, Charles, 32, 37, 47, 108, 128, 177, 187
Douglas, James, 255
Douglas, Lord Alfred, 227, 239, 307
Draper, Ruth, 226-7
du Maurier, Gerald, 29
Dullin, Charles, 305
Duncombe, Hubert, 46, 61, 77
Dunne, Eithne, 137, 141, 180, 198, 202, 204-6, 258, 260
Dunne, Jack, 45-6, 71, 230
Dunsany, Lord, 40, 86
Duse, Eleonora, 249
Dyall, Valentine, 187
Dymoke, Lionel, 72, 101

Eddison, Robert, 216
Edwards, Emily (née Murphy), 33-6
Edwards, Hilton Robert Hugh ('Bobby'), *passim*

Edwards, Thomas George Cecil, 32-5
Elephant in Flight (Edwards), 17
Elliman, Louis, 128-9, 142, 144, 146, 166, 210-11, 218, 220, 222, 224-6, 229-30, 235, 267-68, 272-3, 277
Ellis, James, 271
Elliott, Maxine, 30
Ellington, Duke, 163
Enter a Goldfish (MacLíammóir), 21-2, 27, 38-40, 45, 298-9
Enter Certain Players (Luke), 306
Evans, Conor, 34, 291, 303, 309
Fallon, Gabriel, 140, 153
Field, Lila, 24-5
Finch, Peter, 228
Fine, Harry, 81, 86, 88-92, 94, 138, 144
Finegan, J. J., 33, 171
Fitzgerald, Alexis, 195
Fitzgerald, Barry, 105, 132
Fitzgerald, Caroline, 270, 273-4
Fitzgerald, Garrett, 294
Fitzgerald, Geraldine, 73-4, 85, 245, 270, 285, 309
Fitzgerald, Susan, 291
Flanagan, Fionnuala, 281-3
Flanagan, Pauline, 188-9
Fleischmann, Aloys, 110
Fleischmann, Georg, 166
Flynn, Kate 291
Flynn, Renée, 49, 144
Forbes, Dick, 144
Forbes-Robertson, Jean, 49, 97-8
Forbes-Robertson, Sir Johnston, 83
Ford, John, 218
Ford of the Hurdles, The (MacLíammóir), 60, 82
Forman, Denis, 215
Forristal, Desmond 293-4, 300-1, 304
Foster, Barry, 188
Fox, R.M. 174
Foster, Laurence, 291
Forster, E.M., 68
Frankau, Ronald, 48-9, 144
Fredericks, Scott, 291, 299, 307

Fricker, Brenda, 258
Friel, Brian, 34, 242-3, 256,
  274-5, 289, 290
Gaffney, Liam, 86, 198,
  200-1, 212
Gaffney, Mary, 289
Gambon, Michael, 258
Ganly, Andrew, 98, 217,
  290, 308
Gannon, Liam, 149, 150-1,
  285
Gibson, Chloe, 244, 252,
  292-3
Gibson, John, 260
Gielgud, Sir John, 37, 76,
  217, 220-1, 301
Gielgud, Val, 134
Gifford, Blake, 91
Gill, David Basil, 16, 25, 29
Goddard, Paulette, 149, 152
Godfrey, Peter, 50-1, 137
Goldblatt, Harold, 222
Golden, Edward, 149
Golding, Bill, 291, 299
Gottlieb, Morton, 282-4
Gordon, Ruth, 279-81
Gregory, Lady, 54-5, 57,
  105, 110, 265, 269
Grennell, Aiden, 137, 212,
  236, 255, 293
Grimes, Frank, 291
Grisewood, Harman, 40
Grossmith, George, 28
Guinness, Alec, 76
Guthrie, Sir Tyrone, 80, 177,
  275, 279, 286-7, 299

Hagan, George, 16, 18
Haigh, Kenneth, 188, 234
Hall, Anmer 84, 88, 93
Hally, Yvette, 302
Hamlet, Robert, 45
Hanley, Mary, 233
Hatfield, Hurd, 221
Haughey, C.J., 290
Hawthorne, Denys, 188
Hawtrey, Marjorie, 167, 198,
  215, 231
Hayden, Vernon, 211
Hayes, Michael, 244, 251,
  254
Hayward, Reginald Scott,
  256
Hayward, Richard, 256
Healy, Gerard, 115
Hempel, Herr, 135
Hennessy, Robert, 89, 178

Hepworth, Cecil, 31
Herbert, Brian, 149, 152
Herlihy, Daniel, 137, 309
Hitler, Adolf, 107, 112, 273-
  4
Hill, Roger, 80
Hillery, Patrick, 305
Holland, Vyvyan (né Wilde),
  232
Holloway, Joseph, 42, 107-8
Hobson, Harold 147, 232
Holt, Adrian, 196-7, 199,
  203, 207-8, 215
Holt, Helen, 196-7, 199,
  203, 207-8, 215
Home for Christmas
  (MacLíammóir), 165-6,
  172, 192, 210, 299
Hsiung, Shih, 85-6
Hughes, Helena, 132, 148-9,
  151, 153-4, 162-3, 166,
  191, 198, 234, 285
Hughes, Isa, 84, 89, 93
Humphries, Walter, 91
Hunt, Hugh, 97, 177
Hurok, Sol, 237
Hyde, Douglas, 130, 265
Hylton, Jack, 273

*I Must Be Talking To My
  Friends* (MacLíammóir),
  265, 268-71, 285, 287
Iliff, Noël, 134
Ill Met By Moonlight
  (MacLíammóir), 131,
  133-4, 144, 147-9, 155-6,
  164, 214, 297
Ilsley, Stanley, 218
*Importance of Being
  Micheál, The*
  (O hAodha), 70
*Importance of Being Oscar,
  The* (MacLíammóir), 45,
  191, 229-40, 243, 246-
  51, 255-66, 268-71, 277,
  280, 287-8, 292, 298,
  306
Ireland, Harry, 15, 38
Irish Theatre
  (MacLíammóir), 158
Irvine, Blanaid, 212
Irving, Roy, 64, 73, 86, 102,
  113, 136, 149, 152-3
Jamison, Kenneth, 264-5
Jammet, Louis, 69, 215, 217
Jammet, Yvonne, 69, 208,
  215, 217

Jarman, Reginald, 37, 70,
  149, 186, 198, 206, 223-
  4, 260
Jellett, Bay, 65, 91-2, 99,
  101-2, 112-15
Jellett, Mainie, 59, 65, 79,
  89, 130
Johnson, Fred, 94
Johnston, Denis ('E. W.
  Tocher'), 55-60, 63, 70,
  74-5, 84, 89-91, 93-6,
  127, 138-40, 150-3, 173,
  178, 213, 221, 234, 250,
  264, 286, 287, 290-1,
  299, 306, 309
Jouvet, Louis, 103, 159, 305

Kaiser, Georg, 88
Karsavina, Tamara, 289
Kaufman, Stanley, 279
Kavanagh, Patrick, 130
Kean, Marie, 277
Keating, Sean, 130
Kelly, Eamon, 276, 278-80,
  282
Kelly, Frank, 297
Kelly, Seamus ('K'), 145,
  167, 171, 174, 179, 219,
  236, 269
Kempson, Rachel (Lady
  Redgrave), 80, 192-4,
  230, 233
Kennedy, Rev. Brian, 124
Kennedy, Jacqueline, 251
Keogh, Desmond, 291-2
Kerridge, Mary, 273
Kettner, Frau, 202
Kiely, Benedict, 304
Killanin, Lord, 149, 212,
  215, 217
King, Cecil, 25
King Farouk of Egypt, 91
King George II of Greece,
  101-2
King George V of England,
  28
Kitt, Eartha, 163-4, 287
Koestler, Arthur, 176
Komisarjevski, Theodore, 80
Kushlick, Taubie, 256

Lá agus Oíche
  (MacLíammóir), 63
Laffan, Patrick, 307-8
Lancaster, Osbert, 130
Langford, Robert, 256
Lappin, Joan, 171

Laverty, Maura, 154, 169-76, 190, 256, 284
Lawler, Iris, 213, 236
Lawrence, Gertrude, 152
le Brocquy, Sybil, 290
Leahy, Carmel 217-18
Leahy, Sheila, 218
Leavy, Patricia, 291
Leibling, William, 279
Leighton, Margaret, 221, 232
Lemass, Seán, 237, 253
Lewenstein, Oscar, 229, 246, 275-6, 290
Leventhal, A. J., 53, 59, 131, 290
Lexy, Edward, 89
Leyden, Leo, 198, 201, 205
Liar, The (MacLíammóir), 255, 290
Lindsay-Hogg, Michael, 245
Lodge, George, 222
Longford, Christine (Countess of), 66, 68-70, 72, 79, 96, 122, 144, 210, 217, 235-7, 281, 289, 305-6
Longford, Edward (Henry Arthur Pakenham, VIth Earl of), 66, 68-70, 72-3, 78-9, 84, 87, 89, 91, 93-6, 100, 122, 136, 144, 147, 194-5, 207, 209, 212-14, 217-18, 235-7, 291, 306
Luke, Peter, 290, 304, 306
Lúlu (MacLíammóir), 52
Lynch, Jack, 290-1

McAnally, Ray, 254
MacAnna, Tomás, 305-6
McCabe, Eugene, 255, 274, 286-7
McCabe, Leo, 218
McCann, Hugh, 232
Macardle, Dorothy, 55, 76, 91
McCarten, John, 279
McCormick, F. J., 105, 132, 221
McCarthy, Fr Dermod, 301
McCarthy, Lillah, 29
MacConghail, Muiris, 130
McCourt, Kevin, 267
MacDermottroe, Maria, 291
MacDiarmada, Proinnsias, 51-2

MacDonagh, Donagh, 79, 173, 174, 176, 178-9
McEntee, Seán, 56, 65
MacEwen, Molly, 48, 97, 102-4, 128-30, 151, 194, 222, 228, 231, 246, 250, 306-7, 309
McFall, Mai, 262
McGowran, Jack, 137, 183
McGuinness, Norah, 56, 94, 130, 290
McHugh, Roger, 131, 194, 290
McKenna, Siobhán, 167, 182-6, 246, 252, 275, 281, 283-4, 287
McKenna, T. P., 32
McLarnon, Patrick, 137, 198, 204-5, 226-8, 260, 263, 292, 296, 309
MacLíammóir, Micheál (*né* Alfred Willmore), *passim*
McMaster, Andrew, 20
McMaster, Anew, 14-21, 25, 29, 37-46, 50, 60, 80, 88, 98-100, 113, 137, 144-5, 177, 188-90, 212, 215, 230, 233, 236, 254-5, 258-9, 265, 302
McMaster, Christopher, 23, 80, 145, 259
McMaster, Gill, 259
McMaster, Marjorie (*née* Willmore), 15-21, 23-4, 27, 29, 44, 46, 80, 145, 188, 212, 215, 233, 258-9, 289, 302
McMaster, Mary Rose, 23, 80, 145, 188, 259, 286, 289, 297, 309
McNeill, James, 51
McNeill, Josephine, 51, 290
McQuaid, Archbishop John Charles, 70, 253, 293
McSharry, Deirdre, 198
McSorley, Gerard, 291, 294, 304, 307
Maffey, Sir John, 130
Magee, Patrick, 188
Mageean, James, 134
Manahan, Anna, 198, 200, 203-4, 206, 281-3, 287, 309
Manning, Mary, 62-4, 74, 77-9, 90, 96, 221, 251, 268, 279, 290, 292, 300

Mantle of Harlequin, The (Edwards) 218-9
Markova, Alicia, 220
Marowitz, Charles, 232
Marshall, Peggy, 174, 188, 198
Martyn, Edward, 43
Marshall, William, 259-63
Mason, James, 73, 85-7, 144, 159, 243, 290, 309
Mason, Ronald, 187-8
Matthews, William, 246
Maxwell, Elsa, 152
Mayne, Rutherford (*né* Waddell), 40, 59
Meredith, Burgess, 149, 152
Merrick, David, 278-81
Metcalf, Hugh, 232
Middleton, Noëlle, 137, 166-7, 291-2
Miller, Arthur, 163, 167
Mistinguett, 103
Moiseiwitsch, Tanya, 97
Monson, Cecil, 90-1, 97, 124
Montague, John, 179
Mooney, Ria, 73, 85, 87, 212
Moore, Meriel, 56, 59, 76-9, 85, 92, 108, 116, 138, 149-50, 187, 210
Moran, Lona, 260, 262
Moran, Nuala, 109, 128
Morell, André, 228
Morley, Robert, 228
Morley, Sheridan, 86, 298-9
Morris, Dr Hazel, 259
Morrissey, Eamonn, 279, 281-3, 292
Morton, Laurie, 171, 198, 219
Mountains Look Different, The (MacLíammóir), 131-2, 153-4, 164, 285, 305
Mulkerns, Val, 187
Mullan, Claire, 291-2, 303
Mumford, T. R., 39
Murphy, Thomas, 303
Murray, Patrick, 166
Murray, T. C., 49
Myers, Richard, 149
Myler, Ann, 308
Mussolini, Benito, 101, 212

Nasser, Gamal Abdel, 211
Neeson, Eóin, 50, 241, 255
Neeson, Geraldine, 49-50, 241

Neeson, Seán, 49-50, 241
Neilan, Brendan, 231, 241, 243, 309
Neilson Terry, Phyllis, 29
ní Ghráinne, Máire, 297
ní Scolaidhe, Máire, 51-2, 61
ní Scolaidhe, Móna, 61
Nijinsky, Vaslav, 28, 289, 295
Norton, Elliot, 221
Norton, Jim, 254
Nolan, Pat, 149
Novello, Ivor, 15, 46
Novikoff, Vladimir, 28
Nowlan, David, 282, 304-7

O Bríain, Líam, 50, 73, 167
O'Brien, James, 15, 38
O'Brien, Flann (*né* Brian O'Nolan), 139-40
O'Brien, Maurice, 143, 198
O'Callaghan, Maurice, 188
O'Casey, Sean, 123, 171, 270
O Cearbhail, Padraig, 187, 230
O Conaire, Padraic, 43, 179
O'Connor, Ann, 282
O'Connor, Frank, 79, 105, 125, 130, 254
O'Connor, Ulick, 216, 230-1
O'Connor, Una, 42, 44
O Dálaigh, Cearbhall, 290, 298
O'Dea, Jimmy, 133, 182, 210-1, 233
O Dereain, Mairtín, 51
O'Doherty, Colm, 145
O'Donnell, Joe, 294-5
O'Donovan, Harry, 133
O Dualainn, Donnchada, 300
O'Faoláin, Sean, 79, 126, 130
O'Flaherty, Liam, 176, 179, 218-9
O'Herlihy, Michael, 167, 180
Oidhcheanna Sidhe (MacLíammóir), 43
O'Keefe, Mary ('Máire'), 17, 18, 39, 41-6, 68, 143, 191, 302
O'Keefe, Mrs. ('Aunt Craven'), 39, 41-6, 103, 191, 302
O'Kelly, Colm, 198, 200, 203-4, 206, 218, 287

O'Kelly, Seán T., 187
Olden, G. A., 254
O'Leary, Liam, 42
Olga, Princess of Yugoslavia, 115-6
Olivier, Sir Laurence, 85, 179, 215, 225, 234
O Lochlainn, Gearóid, 52, 218
O'Malley, Donagh, 217
O'Meara, Ruth, 273-4
O'Moore, Pat, 77
O'Neill, Eugene, 49, 107, 274
O'Neill, Máire (1), 164
O'Neill, Máire (2), 291, 297, 309
O'Reilly, Alpho, 213, 245, 254, 275-6
O'Rourke, Joan, 245
Oscar of No Importance, An (MacLíammóir), 247, 249, 268
O'Shannon, Finola, 198, 291
O'Shea, Milo, 137, 193, 198, 204, 211, 229, 283
O'Sullivan, Máirín, 276, 278, 280

Page, Seán, 269
Pageant of St. Patrick (MacLíammóir), 82, 189-90
Pakenham, Frank (VIIth Earl of Longford), 237
Papayanni, Zoë (Mrs. Andrew McMaster), 20
Pavlova, Anna, 28-9, 289
Paxinou, Katina, 101
Pearse, Padraic, 69, 253
Percy, Raymond (*né* Wood), 16, 108, 134, 149-51
Perrott, Patrick, 78, 130, 137
Petersen, Gary, 250-1
Phelan, Brian, 219, 292-3
Pine, Richard, 305
Pine, Tyrell, 101, 136, 144
Pinter, Harold, 188-9, 285
Pirandello, Luigi, 193, 176
Pitoëff, Georges and Ludmilla, 49, 137, 305
Playfair, Nigel, 29
Plunkett, James, 238, 264
Poë, Edgar Allen, 215
Potter, Maureen, 219, 229, 233, 287

Power, Derry, 291
Prelude in Kazbek Street (MacLíammóir), 296
Purcell, Noel, 210
Put Money in Thy Purse (MacLíammóir), 155, 176
Pyer, Pam, 193-4, 197-8, 200-1, 203-6, 211, 215

Quigley, Godfrey, 137, 185, 246
Quigley, Fr Seán, 301
Queen Mary, 28
Quirke, Senator William, 121

Rackham, Arthur, 16, 43, 227
'Raphael the Romanian', 199, 207-8
Rapp, Mr. and Mrs., 113, 115
Reddin, Joan, 134, 209-10, 282
Reddin, Norman, 42, 61, 66, 89, 95, 136
Reddin, Theresa, 42
Reddin, Tony, 42, 49, 134, 209
Redgrave, Sir Michael, 148-9, 150, 230-4, 238, 243, 247, 256, 268, 273, 287
Redmond, Joanna, 40
Redmond, Liam, 210
Reeves, Anita, 299
Relph, George, 30
Rendel, Sir George, 119
Return to Glenascaul (Edwards), 166
Rice, Elmer, 88
Richards, Shelah, 57, 72, 76, 78, 84-5, 94, 96, 106, 125-7, 134, 136, 138, 149, 166, 232, 244-5, 252, 274, 287, 290
Richardson, Sir Ralph, 125, 217
Richardson, Tony, 234
Ricketts, Charles, 16
Roberts, Charles, 200, 203-4, 245, 253, 308
Roberts, Hilda, 74
Robinson, Lennox, 57, 105-7, 125, 134-5, 217
Rodway, Norman, 254

Rogers, Cathleen, 62
Romains, Jules, 176
Rooke-Ley, Wilfred, 21, 29, 40-1, 143
Rooney, Philip 241-2
Roth, Edward J., 238-40, 244, 267
Rowan, Ann, 291
Rushe, Desmond, 32, 36, 307
Russell, Bertrand, 68, 191
Ryan, Archbishop Dermot, 293-4
Ryan, Phyllis, 294-5

Sadoff, Fred, 231, 233-4, 238, 256, 268
Schulman, Milton, 232
Scott, Leslie, 183
Scott, Michael, 60, 146, 159, 212, 309
Sedky, Pasha, 196-7
Shaw, George Bernard, 26, 86, 123, 176, 217, 227, 285, 299
Shaw, Glen Byam, 216
Sheehan, Dr. Patricia, 125
Sheehy-Skeffington, Owen, 80
Shields, Arthur, 42, 105
Simpson, Alan, 241, 286
Slipper for the Moon, A (MacLíammóir), 192-4, 294
Smith, Brendan, 184-6, 212, 255, 258-9, 260, 263, 274, 305
Smith, Gretta, 62
Song of Wandering Aengus, The (Yeats/Dolin/ MacLíammóir), 220
Speaight, Robert, 41, 125, 216
Starkie, Enid, 233
Swan, Jeremy, 186

Swete, E.Lyall, 41
Swift, Carolyn, 241, 252, 272
Synge, J. M., 49, 79, 105, 179, 224, 270

Talking about Yeats (MacLíammóir), 277
Tearle, Godfrey, 29
Tempest, Marie, 29
Terry, Fred, 20
Terry, Julia Neilson, 20
Thesiger, Ernest, 216
Thomas, Dylan, 227
Thompson, Sam, 271-3
Thorndike, Dame Sybil, 104, 138, 145, 287, 301
Thorndike, Russell, 37, 47
Tinney, Mary, 197
Toal, Maureen, 198, 200, 203-4, 260, 284
Tobin, Brian, 230-2, 234-5, 237, 241, 250, 255, 258, 268, 270-1, 285, 290, 299
Toibín, Niall, 281-2
Travers, Martin, 23
Travers, Michael, 23, 300
Travers, Sally, 23, 44, 80, 139, 231, 254, 289, 309
Tree, Sir Herbert Beerbohm, 24-6, 29-31, 37, 83
Tuckerman, Maury, 250
Tuohy, Dermot, 133
Tynan, Kenneth, 177, 246

Vale, Adrian, 243, 268
Vale, Angela, 243
Vanbrugh, Irene, 29
Vanbrugh, Violet, 25
Vernon, Diana, 98

Waddell, Ginette, 137
Wakeley, Phyllis, 45
Walsh, Caroline, 309

Walters, Thorley, 273
Waterlow, Sir Sydney, 101
Watkinson, Eve, 73, 75
Welles, Orson, 73-75, 80-4, 154-68, 172-6, 181, 186, 191, 195, 197, 221-6, 243, 251, 253-4, 264, 309
Where Stars Walk (MacLíammóir), 42, 129-31, 133, 141, 148-9, 151-3, 191, 214, 296, 304, 306-7
Wherry, Daniel, 141
White, Jonathan, 306
White-Lennon, Biddy, 306
Whittaker, Herbert, 150
Whitty, Dame May, 30
Wilcox, Herbert, 232
Wilde, Oscar, 16, 201, 217-8, 225, 227-36, 244, 265, 268-9, 287, 301, 307
Williams, Emlyn, 118, 227-8, 232
Williams, Michael, 303
Willmore, Alfred (Senior), 22-5, 309
Willmore, Alfred (Junior), real name of Micheál MacLíammóir, *passim*
Willmore, Christine, 23, 44
Willmore, Dorothy, 23
Willmore, Marjorie (see McMaster)
Willmore, Mary ('Sophie'), 23-5, 44
Wolfit, Sir Donald, 37, 76, 110, 176-7, 243, 254
Wood, Audrey, 279
Wormell, D.A.E., 265-6

Yeats, Jack B., 43, 57, 178-9
Yeats, W. B., 18, 39, 55, 57, 68, 97, 105-6, 110, 160, 215, 227, 233, 253, 278
Young, Derek, 260